Can Gun Control Work?

STUDIES IN CRIME AND PUBLIC POLICY
Michael Tonry and Norval Morris, General Editors

Police for the Future
David H. Bayley

Incapacitation: Penal Confinement and the Restraint of Crime
Franklin E. Zimring and Gordon Hawkins

The American Street Gang: Its Nature, Prevalence, and Control
Malcolm W. Klein

Sentencing Matters
Michael Tonry

The Habits of Legality: Criminal Justice and the Rule of Law
Francis A. Allen

Chinatown Gangs: Extortion, Enterprise, and Ethnicity
Ko-lin Chin

Responding to Troubled Youth
Cheryl L. Maxson and Malcolm W. Klein

Making Crime Pay: Law and Order in Contemporary American Politics
Katherine Beckett

Community Policing, Chicago Style
Wesley G. Skogan and Susan M. Hartnett

Crime Is Not the Problem: Lethal Violence in America
Franklin E. Zimring and Gordon Hawkins

Hate Crimes: Criminal Law and Identity Politics
James B. Jacobs and Kimberly Potter

Politics, Punishment, and Populism
Lord Windlesham

American Youth Violence
Franklin E. Zimring

Bad Kids: Race and the Transformation of the Juvenile Court
Barry C. Feld

Gun Violence: The Real Costs
Philip J. Cook and Jens Ludwig

Punishment, Communication, and Community
R. A. Duff

Punishment and Democracy: Three Strikes and You're Out in California
Franklin E. Zimring, Gordon Hawkins, and Sam Kamin

Restorative Justice and Responsive Regulation
John Braithwaite

Maconochie's Gentlemen: The Story of Norfolk Island and the Roots of Modern Prison Reform
Norval Morris

CAN GUN CONTROL WORK?

James B. Jacobs

OXFORD
UNIVERSITY PRESS

2002

OXFORD

Oxford University Press

Oxford   New York
Auckland   Bangkok   Buenos Aires   Cape Town   Chennai
Dar es Salaam   Delhi   Hong Kong   Istanbul   Karachi   Kolkata
Kuala Lumpur   Madrid   Melbourne   Mexico City   Mumbai   Nairobi
São Paulo   Shanghai   Singapore   Taipei   Tokyo   Toronto

and an associated company in Berlin

Published by Oxford University Press, Inc.
198 Madison Avenue, New York, New York 10016

www.oup.com

Oxford is a registered trademark of Oxford University Press

Library of Congress Cataloging-in-Publication Data
Jacobs, James B.
Can gun control work? / by James B. Jacobs.
     p. cm.—(Studies in crime and public policy)
Includes bibliographical references and index.
ISBN 0-19-514562-3
1. Gun control—United States.   I. Title.   II. Series.
HV7436. J3 2002
363.3'3'0973—dc21   2002020133

9 8 7 6 5 4 3 2 1

Printed in the United States of America
on acid-free paper

With heartfelt thanks I dedicate this book to Daisy Carrington, Frieder Duenkel, Kay Franks, Henner Hess, Emily Kuwahara, Jeffrey Lauren, Adam Menzel, and David Sorrell, friends who rushed to Berlin when Tom was hospitalized with a brain tumor. And to those new friends, living in Berlin, who supported us during that difficult time: Nick Capetillo, Elizabeth Pruesser, Carol and Joel Levy, Karen Kramer, Marie Biege, and Tom's student colleagues in the Stanford-in-Berlin Program. And thanks to those friends who supported Tom, Jan, Sophi, and me along the road to recovery.

Preface

To a large extent, gun control is something that people *believe in*. It is embraced in principle without attention to practicalities, implementation and enforcement problems, and costs. Many people assume that effective, cost-efficient gun controls are available for the taking, if only the opposition of the evil gun lobby could be overcome. There are no scholarly articles and few advocacy documents that provide the details of particular gun controls and grapple with questions of implementation and enforcement.

I approach gun control as a problem of regulation. In the pages that follow, I will examine the administrative challenges, enforcement dilemmas, and unintended consequences of the whole range of gun control options. The bad news is that this book is hard work. The good news is that the hard work will be repaid. It is no doubt far easier, and certainly more satisfying, to debate gun control *in principle,* to locate oneself on the moral high ground and to demonize those who take the opposite position, than to deal with the extraordinarily difficult problems of designing, implementing, and enforcing a regulatory regime that would successfully deny access to firearms to some or all civilians, or keep track of the whereabouts and ownership of every weapon. It cannot be overemphasized that when it comes to considering the future of U.S. firearms regulation, we are not writing on a blank slate. The question we must address is not whether an armed citizenry is a good or bad idea or what policies would make sense for a brand new country that has few, if any, guns. We must confront a much tougher question: What options are available to the United States at this point in its history?

Many readers are likely to wonder why the United States cannot just adopt the gun control policies that work in European countries, Japan, and elsewhere. The simplest answer is that none of those countries has had to implement a strict regulatory or prohibitory regime at a time when almost half its households own guns and in a society with a powerful tradition of private firearms ownership and a thriving contemporary gun culture.

A cross-cultural comparison is far beyond my ambitions in this book. Such a study, while much needed, would be a tremendous challenge. Even for Europe, for example, it would be a mistake to assume that there is a single attitude toward guns or uniform gun controls. France and Belgium, for example, allow much more gun ownership than the United Kingdom (New York State, Massachusetts, Washington, D.C., and certain other U.S. jurisdictions have stricter gun control laws than practically any European country). Gun possession and use is increasing in Europe; in many big European cities, guns are readily obtainable on the black market. As this book goes to press, a horrific school shooting stuns Germany and a political assassination shocks Holland. Even in the strictest prohibitory regime, that of the United Kingdom, gun crime continues to increase. Suffice it to say that there is much to be said about cross-cultural comparisons, but this is not the place to say it. It is more than enough for this book to ask, for the United States today, where can we go from here with respect to controlling guns, with what costs, and with what likelihood of success.

You might well ask whether, if I take everything as given, doesn't that foreclose the possibility of change? The answer is emphatically "no." Directed political and social change is possible. Shifts in public opinion and political power are possible; public policy can make a difference. But it will be hard work. The "givens" constrain what is possible politically and administratively, and what is enforceable. If considering policy options for reducing interpersonal violence is to be a serious exercise, we have to get beyond clashing platitudes and slogans. What policies are administratively possible? What kind of enforcement apparatus would be necessary? What will be the most likely costs and benefits?

Effectively regulating weaponry poses a monumental challenge, often ignored or minimized by gun control supporters. The brute reality is that private citizens in the year 2002 possess at least 250 million firearms (including 80-plus million handguns). A large portion of gun owners believe that they have a right to keep and bear arms; they are suspicious of, even hostile to, the gun control agenda. These facts impose serious constraints on policy making, at least in the short (several decades) term.

Interestingly, many gun control believers are atheists when it comes to government regulation of mood- and-mind altering drugs. They insist that drugs cannot be kept out of the hands of those who want to use them. They point out that after an investment of many billions of dollars, and the incarceration of hundreds of thousands of individuals, our three-decade-long drug war has achieved few, if any, positive results. Does the drug war not cast doubt on schemes for gun prohibition or stringent regulation?

As we shall see, the challenge of regulating firearms is much greater than the challenge of regulating marijuana, cocaine, heroin, and other mood- and mind-altering substances.[1] Since drugs are a consumable good, drug users must constantly resupply themselves, so past regulatory failures do not have decisive consequences for future policy. By contrast, guns are durable goods that may last 100 years if properly maintained. A gun owner may only need to make one purchase in a lifetime, while a heavy drug user needs to make constant purchases. Ammunition, like drugs, is a consumable that needs replenishment. But like drugs, bullets are easy to manufacture and, in the event they were prohibited, would surely generate a black market.

Guns present a tougher regulatory challenge than drugs because they are more widely used and are more politically and socially acceptable. Drugs, at least cocaine and heroin, are regularly used by less than 1% of the American population. By contrast, there are firearms in at least 40% of American households. Drug use is not supported by a powerful movement or a fervent ideology. Only a small number of libertarians believe that Americans have a right to ingest whatever drugs they want. Most critics of the drug war regard drugs as an unfortunate social and medical problem that ought to be rooted out by persuasion, education, and treatment.

Tens of millions of Americans, including senators, members of Congress, governors, business leaders, and other members of society's elite, are unabashed gun owners who believe that the U.S. Constitution guarantees law-abiding Americans the right to keep and bear arms. Tens of millions of Americans participate in hunting and shooting sports, read gun-oriented magazines, and vote for pro-gun political candidates. More than 3 million Americans are members of the National Rifle Association (NRA), the most powerful single-issue interest lobbying organization in the United States.

Granted, the analogy between regulating drugs and regulating guns is imperfect. The goal of drug regulation is the suppression of drug use. Some gun controllers also favor prohibition and disarmament; others favor making the regulatory regime that we now have more effective, that is, allowing law-abiding adult Americans free access to personal firearms (but not assault weapons or machine guns), while denying firearms to potentially dangerous people.

The dominant federal gun policy evolved over three-quarters of the twentieth century. It began with the Federal Firearms Act of 1938, was strengthened by the Gun Control Act of 1968, and was carried forward by the Handgun Violence Prevention Act of 1993, popularly known as the Brady Act or Brady Law, which required licensed gun dealers to give the government an opportunity to carry out a background check on a prospective firearms purchaser before finalizing the sale. The Brady Law left the sale of secondhand guns by nondealers completely unregulated.

The 1993 Brady Law is this generation's most important federal gun control law; it was certainly heralded as such by President Bill Clinton, members of Congress, the media, and advocacy groups on both sides of the seven-year battle over its passage. The Brady Law wended its way through Congress as the most politically contentious piece of gun control legislation in U.S. history. It was a hot button issue in two sets of presidential debates and in four congressional elections. The citizenry was repeatedly polled and repeatedly gave its support. Scores of newspapers and magazine editorials opined on the virtues or defects of the Brady Law. Its proponents predicted that it would significantly reduce gun violence and, at the moment of its passage, praised it as a major turning point in the politics of gun control and crime control.

Was the Brady Law a major step toward effective gun control so that all that remains, if anything, is just some refinement at the edges? Or was the Brady Law just a small step toward effective gun control? Might it even have been a false step? The Brady Law's legacy is still being contested.

While the Brady Law represents the core of American gun control, it is not our only species of gun control. This book considers a wide range of gun controls, including (1) prohibiting guns; (2) prohibiting or strictly regulating ammunition; (3) meting out sentence enhancements for crimes committed with a gun; (4) prohibiting individuals who have been convicted of felonies and certain misdemeanors from possessing firearms; (5) requiring that firearms be registered; (6) making it criminal to possess or carry a firearm without a license; (7) establishing "gun free" buildings, environs, and zones; (8) prohibiting the manufacture, sale, and possession of machine guns, assault rifles, and other especially "dangerous" firearms; (9) requiring guns to be sold with safety locks; (10) requiring guns to be transported and stored in a specified manner; and (11) holding manufacturers civilly liable for firearms injuries.

Part I closely examines the nature of the gun problem, the history of U.S. gun controls, and the impediments to more controls. Chapter 1 reviews the American gun problem. Chapter 2 traces the history of federal and state gun control from the 1920s to the present, emphasizing the continuity from the 1938 Federal Firearms Act (FFA) to the 1968 Gun Control

Act (GCA) to the 1993 Brady Law. Chapter 3 illuminates the cultural, political, administrative, and law enforcement obstacles to more effective gun controls. Together, these three chapters provide essential background for thinking about future policy options.

Part II zeroes in on the Brady Law, the first major federal gun control legislation in thirty years. Chapter 4 analyzes the politics that led to the passage of the Brady Law. Chapter 5 explains what the Brady Law provides for and how it is supposed to work. Chapter 6 exposes the holes and weaknesses in the law, and chapter 7 evaluates its impact on violent crime.

Part III analyzes options for the future. Chapter 8 considers the feasibility of perfecting the FFA–GCA–Brady Law regime by extending the background check and waiting period requirement to sales at gun shows and ultimately to all secondary sales. Chapter 9 critiques proposals for comprehensive licensing and registration. Chapter 10 examines the feasibility of handgun prohibition and disarmament. Chapter 11 focuses on a range of other gun control proposals, including mandatory trigger locks, safe storage laws, one-gun-per-month limitation on individual gun purchases, ammunition controls, ballistic fingerprinting, and holding gun manufacturers civilly liable for the consequences of gun violence. Chapter 12 assays the desirability and possibility of intensifying street enforcement of gun laws and enhancing punishments for illegal gun possession and for gun crimes.

Warning—this is not a "feel good" book with a happy ending. Interpersonal violence is a complex problem, and gun controls, at best, are an indirect, difficult to implement and enforce, and marginally productive remedy. I am certainly not ideologically opposed to gun controls. And I am certainly not arguing that there is no control that could save a single life or make us a little bit better off. There are some controls that seem quite sensible to me. But gun control is no panacea.

This book illuminates gun controls in practice, highlighting difficulties of design, implementation, administration, and enforcement. It tries to focus the debate on practical solutions to real problems. There may be readers who, on confronting the problems and dilemmas in all their complexity, will see solutions that I am unable to see. Other readers may be persuaded that our nation ought to invest in non–gun control strategies for reducing violent crime. At the very least, I believe that this book will stimulate serious crime controllers to do the heavy lifting that is necessary to move the formulation of firearms policy forward.

Acknowledgments

I became interested in gun control policy by osmosis, in the infancy of my criminological career, when I was a student research assistant of Norval Morris, one of the first criminologists to call for handgun prohibition. My other University of Chicago Law School mentor in the early 1970s was Franklin Zimring, who even then was the foremost empirical scholar of gun violence in the United States. I began working on gun control in a scholarly way in the late 1970s at the behest of Don Kates, the peripatetic anti–gun control activist and scholar, who invited me to participate in a Law and Contemporary Problems symposium at Duke University. In the article I contributed to that symposium, I puzzled over several different versions of handgun prohibition, querying whether their exemptions (permitting gun possession) fatally undermined the prohibition.

In the early 1990s, I began teaching a law school seminar on the regulation of weaponry in a democratic society. After teaching it twice on my own, my colleague Ron Noble joined me as co-teacher. Soon afterward, Ron was appointed under secretary (for enforcement) of the U.S. Department of Treasury, a job that includes supervision of the Bureau of Alcohol, Tobacco, and Firearms. For the next several years, to the benefit of our nation and our seminar, Ron was involved in firearms policy formulation and enforcement at the very highest level. I owe a debt of gratitude to Ron, who is now director general of Interpol. (I hasten to add that he certainly is not responsible for any of the ideas put forward in this book; we disagree about many issues while remaining the closest of friends.) I also want to sincerely thank the five classes of New York University law students who participated in those gun control seminars. I have benefited immensely from more than 100 hours of classroom discussion and from scores of term papers by some of the most interesting and intelligent young people in America.

Throughout this project, I have been aided by terrific research assistants. Larry Newman and Ryan Papir helped in the early phase. During the 1999–2000 academic year, Danny Heumann (under the auspices of a Leslie Glass Criminal Justice Fellowship) began working on some aspects of the project. Part of his labors resulted in a 2001 coauthored article on the possibility of regulating gun shows. Other students who provided research assistance over the 1999–2000 academic year included Rebecca Blemberg, Kyle Chorba, Alissa Gonzalez, Lauryn Gouldin, and Mohan Nadig. During the 2000–2001 academic year, I received excellent assistance from Elise Kohn, Stephanie Lary, Domingo Villaronga, and Jessica Woodhouse.

In the fall of 2000, we convened an all-day workshop on a first draft of the manuscript. I am enormously grateful to my NYU colleagues Oscar Chase, David Garland, and Jerry Skolnick and to my professional colleagues Doug Husak (Rutgers), John Kleinig (John Jay), John Monaghan (Virginia), Stephen Morse (Penn), and Dan Richman (Fordham) for the penetrating and constructive criticism they leveled at my work in progress.

During the summer of 2001, I benefited from the outstanding research assistance of Adam Dressner, Michael Firestone, Alex Shults, and Clay Whitehead. Stephanie Lary stepped back in with very valuable editing. I could not have finished the book without them. (Even with all their help, I almost didn't make it!)

During the course of my research, I often reached out to and received generous assistance from Richard Aborn (HCI), Phil Cook (Duke), Mike Farrell (NYPD), Don Kates (gun owners' rights litigator and scholar) and his muse, C. B. Kates, David Kopel (Independence Institute), Gary Wicks (NICS), and Frank Zimring (Berkeley). At the very end of the process, I received very useful input from John Braithwaite, Henner Hess, and Steve Schulhofer and from a University of Pennsylvania Law School faculty workshop.

My secretary, Elana Dietz-Weinstein, is simply outstanding in every respect; she makes the working day a joy. As always, Dean (now NYU president) John Sexton provided all the support (and then some) that a scholar could ask for. My editor at Oxford University Press, Dedi Felman, spent a great deal of time with the manuscript and guided me to many important improvements. Finally, I thank all my NYU law colleagues who have created and sustained a terrific collegial atmosphere.

Contents

I. ESSENTIAL BACKGROUND

    1   Dissecting the Gun Problem   3

    2   Existing Gun Controls   19

    3   Impediments to More Gun Controls   37

II. AMERICA'S DOMINANT GUN CONTROL PARADIGM

    4   The Politics of the Brady Law   61

    5   What the Brady Law Says   77

    6   Holes in the Brady Law   99

    7   Evaluating the Brady Law   111

III. POLICY OPTIONS FOR THE FUTURE

    8   Closing the Gun Show and Secondary Market Loophole   123

    9   Comprehensive Licensing and Registration   137

    10   Prohibition and Disarmament   153

    11   Other Gun Control Strategies   171

12   Creating Gun-Free Public Spaces   197

13   Conclusion: The "Problem" Reconsidered   213

Notes   227

Bibliography   263

Index   279

I

ESSENTIAL BACKGROUND

Part I provides background information that is essential for anyone who wants to think seriously about the gun problem and gun control. Chapter 1 offers a perspective on the magnitude and nature of the gun problem. Chapter 2 provides a brief historical tour of federal firearms regulation and some background on state and local gun controls. Chapter 3 identifies political, cultural, administrative, and law enforcement realities that pose enormous impediments to formulating, passing, implementing, and enforcing more gun controls.

1

Dissecting the Gun Problem

There is a gun crisis in the United States. Between 1933 and 1982, nearly one million Americans were killed by firearms in murders, suicides and accidents. Since 1960 alone, more than half a million have died as the result of gun injuries. In 1992, at least 35,000 died by gunfire. Today, among all consumer products, only cars outpace guns as a cause of fatal injury, and guns will likely pass them by 2002.
—Violence Policy Center, 1998

As to the species of exercises, I advise the gun. While this gives moderate exercise to the Body, it gives boldness, enterprise and independence to the mind. Games played with the ball, and others of that nature, are too violent for the body and stamp no character on the mind. Let your gun be the constant companion on your walks.
—Thomas Jefferson, *Letters*

A single consumer product holds our nation hostage: the handgun. We live our lives in the shadow of the unparalleled lethality of these easily concealable firearms. This permanent state of fear has become so accepted that we rarely acknowledge it.
—Josh Sugarman, *Every Handgun Is Aimed at You*

Many books and articles have been written about whether gun controls are desirable, moral, and constitutional. This book seeks to fill a void in

3

the scholarly literature by addressing a different question: Can gun control work? Consequently, *it assumes that firearms regulation is desirable and asks whether specific proposals that have been put forward could be successfully implemented and enforced and, if so, with any likelihood of reducing injuries inflicted by firearms.*

This chapter then is not strictly necessary to my argument. Nevertheless, it provides important context. In order to evaluate the potential benefits of the various gun controls analyzed in part III, we need to have a grounding in the nature and magnitude of the problem for which various gun controls are proposed as the solution. In what ways are guns a problem? Are guns a primary cause of violent crime? Do they contribute significantly to the suicide rate? Do guns in the hands of private citizens prevent crime through active self-defense and deterrence? This chapter opens a window on empirical questions that have generated a small mountain of conflicting studies and statistics.

Many writers, in order to emphasize and dramatize the magnitude of the gun problem, begin their articles or books with a statistic on the total number of Americans killed by firearms, or just handguns, in a given year. For example, a recent publication by the Legal Community against Violence states that "30,708 Americans died from firearm related injuries in 1998. . . . In fact more Americans were killed by guns during the 18-year period between 1979 and 1997 than in all wars since 1775."[1]

Wouldn't it be useful to know that this horrific number of *people killed* combines homicides, suicides, and accidents? And that the number of firearm suicides outnumbers firearms homicides and fatal accidents combined? (For example, in 1999, there were 17,400 firearms suicides and 9,000 firearms homicides.) Indeed, I believe it makes sense to understand "the gun problem" as three separate problems: fatal accidents, suicides, and homicides (see figure 1.1). Each occurs in different contexts, has different causes, and may be amenable or not amenable to different gun controls. In any event, the potential benefits of various gun controls depend in the first instance on the nature and magnitude of the problems they are aimed at remedying.

Accidents

Recently, much attention in the gun control debate has focused on mandatory trigger locks and safe storage. Gun controls like these are aimed at preventing firearms accidents rather than gun crime or suicide. Indeed, gun control proponents frequently emphasize that the household

Figure 1.1. U.S. Firearms Deaths by Cause

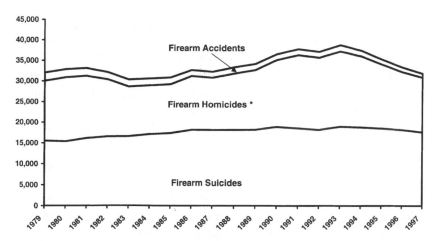

*Excluding law enforcement related, estimated at 270 in 1997.

Source: Data from CDC/National Center for Injury Control and Prevention.

firearm poses a risk to its occupants, especially children. Thus, many readers will be surprised to learn that in 1997, only 40 children under age 5 were killed in firearms accidents. That same year, 600 children under 5 died in drowning accidents and 1,100 died in motor vehicle accidents. Likewise, the numbers of fatal accidents involving children under 15 included 1,050 drownings, 3,100 motor vehicle deaths, and 220 firearms deaths.[2]

All accidental deaths and serious injuries are tragic, and we ought to strive to prevent as many as possible. Still, firearms accidents are not a leading cause of accidental deaths for Americans. Consider that in 1997 there were approximately 93,800 accidental deaths from all causes; of these, motor vehicle accidents accounted for 43,200, falls for 14,900, drownings for 4,000, and firearms for 1,500.[3] Moreover, the number of unintentional deaths inflicted by firearms has declined steadily for the past several decades, despite increases in the nation's population and in the number of firearms in private hands.*

*Gary Kleck points out that it is likely that several dozen firearms deaths coded as "accidental" each year are probably suicides or homicides. In addition, many accidental firearms deaths are the result of extremely reckless conduct. See Kleck, *Targeting Guns: Firearms and Their Control*, ch. 9.

Suicide

In 1979, there were 27,200 suicides; twenty years later there were 30,500. Approximately 57% of the suicides in both years were carried out by means of firearms. Does the fact that the percentage of suicides committed with firearms is much higher in the United States than in other countries mean that suicide, like homicide, ought to be thought of as a by-product of America's firearms policy? I think not. If there were a strong causal relationship between firearms and suicide, the United States would be a world leader in suicide as it is in homicide. But this is not the case. Unlike the U.S. homicide rate, the U.S. suicide rate is average for industrialized nations. The suicide rate for the United States in 1996 was 11.6 per 100,000. Comparable figures for some other countries are: United Kingdom 7.7; Canada 13.2; Germany 15.6; Japan 16.7; France 20.8; and Finland 27.2.[4] Many countries have much higher suicide rates than the United States; indeed, a number of countries have so much suicide that they have a higher *combined* suicide and homicide rate than the United States. While it is possible that some people commit suicide on impulse because a firearm is available, I think it more likely that Americans decide on suicide for the same reasons that people in other countries do. However, in deciding how to commit suicide, Americans frequently utilize firearms, a readily available and highly effective means.

Admittedly, Ronald Clarke's and Pat Mayhew's famous study of coal gas in the United Kingdom warns us not to dismiss the instrumentality hypothesis too quickly. They found that suicide dropped significantly when coal gas, a preferred method of suicide, was replaced by natural gas. Clarke and Mayhew conclude that the ready availability of an effective means of suicide led some people to commit suicide who otherwise would not.[5] But the data are subject to varying interpretations. In 2000, Gunnell et al. found that while there was indeed a 34% decrease in suicide by gas (for men), there was a 29% increase in suicide by drug overdose. Women experienced an 89% decrease in suicide by gas, but a 305% increase in suicide by drugs.[6]

It would be a mistake to see suicide as primarily or substantially a "gun problem."* It is hardly obvious that suicide would be substantially re-

---

*Perhaps it is perverse to ask whether guns might even be considered beneficial in providing people an effective means of committing suicide, but I ask the reader's indulgence in raising this point for the sake of completeness. After all, there is a contentious debate about the "right to die" and even about the right to receive and give assistance in terminating life that, because of physical pain and mental anguish, has become unbearable. Many Americans believe that providing terminally

duced, or reduced at all, if firearms were less available, as is the case in many countries with higher suicide rates. But, for purposes of this book, that question is beside the point. We will focus on whether there are any realistic strategies that could reduce access to firearms by persons at risk of suicide.

Multiple Killings and Rampage Killers

Multiple killings (more than two victims in a single episode) must be considered part of the gun problem. If guns didn't exist, we probably would not have suffered the December 7, 1993, massacre on the Long Island Railroad, the April 1999 Columbine school shooting, and other multiple homicides. Although firearms make mass killings possible, the 1993 World Trade Center bombing and the 1995 Oklahoma City bombing are two poignant reminders that guns are not the only way that madmen and terrorists can inflict mass destruction. (Just as I was putting the finishing touches to this chapter in September 2001, two incidents of mass murder in California and Iowa were perpetrated with knives.[7] Then on September 11, 2001, terrorists using knives seized four commercial airlines and crashed them into the World Trade Center, the Pentagon, and a field in Pennsylvania, killing 3,000 persons.) Fortunately, and perhaps surprisingly in light of the massive publicity they attract, multiple killings remain very rare in American society. Moreover, while the number of guns has been increasing steadily, the number of mass killings has remained fairly constant.[8]

Homicidal rampages at school naturally and justifiably attract enormous media attention, but it is important to examine these events realistically. Since 1992, when the U.S. Center for Disease Control (CDC) began tracking school violence, shooting deaths at school have declined every year. The 40 school shooting deaths in the 1997–1998 school year were within the midrange of the annual toll since 1992. According to the National School Safety Center, violent deaths in school settings (suicides and homicides) declined 27.3% between the 1992–1993 and the

---

ill people with assistance in ending their lives quickly and painlessly is a value, even a human and constitutional right. Gun suicides, like all suicides, are disproportionately concentrated among the elderly and those who have been suffering with health problems. There is no societal consensus that terminating this kind of human suffering should count as a social benefit, but neither should every intentionally self-inflicted firearms death be labeled part of "the gun problem."

1997–1998 school years.[9] In the 2000–2001 school year, the number of homicides and suicides in schools was 41% of its 1992–1993 level. Table 1.1 lists mass killings that the CDC has tracked in or near American schools since 1992.

Firearms are a necessary, but obviously insufficient, explanation for most mass killings. Obviously, the killer's mental condition is crucially important. In retrospect, many mass killers and the majority of recent school shooters gave indications or told others of an impending rampage.[10] True, *if* these unstable people could be prevented from obtaining firearms, they might not be able to carry out their demented plans (unless they used explosives), but this is a big *if*, given the very small number of events. (Moreover, federal law makes it a felony to knowingly sell or give a handgun to a person under 21 years old or a long gun to a person under 18.) Homicidal rampages should also direct attention to the school environment itself. Are our schools too large and anonymous? Is bullying allowed to go on unchallenged? Does depression and humiliation regularly go unrecognized and unaddressed? Concern about the availability of guns ought not to overwhelm questions like these.

Guns and Crime

What makes gun control such a compelling priority for many opinion leaders and a large segment of the population is the belief that violent crime is caused by the widespread availability of firearms and could be reduced by eliminating or limiting firearms availability.

There can be no denying that the United States has a serious *violent crime* problem. Frank Zimring and Gordon Hawkins have shown that U.S. property crime rates do not differ much from Britain's or Australia's, while the violent crime rate is vastly higher. In 1998, there were approximately 9,100 firearms homicides (and 14,088 total homicides) in the United States, while there were less than 50 firearms homicides (750 total) in Britain, which has ⅕ as great a population.* Ought we to infer that it is the availability of firearms (especially handguns) to private citizens that is responsible for America's immensely higher rate?

It would be a mistake to jump to that conclusion. The United States has much more violent crime, with and without firearms, than the other Western democracies. Our rape, robbery, and aggravated assault rates are much higher than those in other countries. But only a small fraction

---

*Nonfatal gun injuries are complicated to compute. Gary Kleck reasonably estimates the ratio of nonfatal gun wounds to gun fatalities at 3:1 during the 1990s. See Kleck, *Point Blank*, p. 24.

Table 1.1. U.S. "Student-Initiated Mass Killings" with Guns since 1992

Date	Location	Killed	Description
Dec. 14, 1992	Great Barrington, Mass.	2	Wayne Lo random shooting rampage; several others wounded.
Jan. 18, 1993	Grayson, Ky.	2	Teacher and custodian held hostage, then shot by senior Scott Pennington.
Sept. 25, 1993	Washington, D.C.	2	Gang-related shooting during Saturday pick-up game. Steven Chadwick and Anthony Dawkins charged.
Sept. 14, 1995	Olathe, Kans.	2	Student of Olathe High. Killed when shots fired from car on Sunday evening pick-up game. 22-caliber Jennings semiautomatic handgun. Alfred Williams, 17, from rival high school, suspected.
Oct. 12, 1995	Blackville, S.C.	2	Suspended student. Shot self with .32 after shooting math teachers Johnny Thompson and Phyllis Senn. Senn died.
Nov. 15, 1995	Lynnville, Tenn.	2	.22 rifle used to kill one student and one teacher.
Feb. 2, 1996	Moses Lake, Wash.	3	Barry Loukitas, 16, killed a teacher and two students with a rifle. Described as "nerd." Two days before incident, said he was going to "kill someone." Thought it would be "cool" to go on a killing spree like in movie *Natural Born Killers*.
Feb. 29, 1996	St. Louis, Mo.	2	Mother and unborn child die after young man enters bus with a .38. One other wounded.
Feb. 19, 1997	Bethal, Alaska	2	Principal and student shot. Two others wounded.
Dec. 1, 1997	West Paducah, Ky.	3	Michael Corneal, 14, kills three girls at informal prayer meeting before school. May have been teased by girls and football team. Used a .22.
Mar. 24, 1998	Jonesboro, Ark.	5	Mitchell Johnson, 13, and Andrew Golden, 11, ambushed and shot into crowd of students and teachers. Five killed, ten wounded. Golden was angry with a teacher.
Apr. 28, 1998	Pomona, Calif.	2	Rival gang violence kills two.
May 21, 1998	Springfield, Oreg.	2	Kipland Kinkle, 15, killed his parents, then two students and wounded twenty-one others.

(continued)

Table 1.1. (Continued)

Date	Location	Killed	Description
Apr. 20, 1999	Littleton, Colo.	15	Eric Harris and Dylan Klebold killed 15, including students and faculty, on a planned rampage in the school.
Mar. 5, 2001	Santee, Calif.	2	Charles "Andy" Williams shot two in a restroom, then fired randomly into a quad. Reloaded four times. Eleven wounded, two killed. Told people of his desire to shoot up the school. Friends patted him down.

Source: National School Safety Center's report on "School Associated Violent Deaths," 2001. A mass killing is defined as an event in which more than one person was killed, for reasons unrelated to an interpersonal dispute.

of those crimes are committed with guns (see figure 1.2); more than 90% of violent crimes are committed *without any weapon whatsoever.* Thus, we ought not to jump to the conclusion that America's violent crime problem is fully, essentially, or even substantially a consequence of the legal availability of firearms.

A close look at U.S. homicide data confirms that there must be more to the very high U.S. violent crime rate than just the large percentage of

Figure 1.2. Violent Crimes Committed with a Firearm, 1999

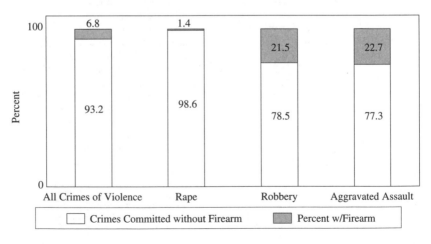

Source: Criminal Victimization in the U.S. Statistical Tables: Full Report (p. 77).

citizens who own firearms or the easy availability of firearms to private citizens. Homicides, much less robberies, do not occur randomly across all segments of the population. The majority of homicide perpetrators have criminal records as do the majority of the victims.[11] In other words, lethal violence occurs disproportionately within a criminal subculture, and in the last two decades especially among people involved in the drug trade.[12]

Undoubtedly, there are many factors that explain Americans' predilection for violence with and without guns: for example, the legacy of slavery and racial oppression, frontier tradition, vast income inequalities, a southern code of honor, terrible pockets of poverty, and weak community controls. There are huge literatures in history, psychology, sociology, and economics, attempting to account for violence in America.[13]

Figures 1.3 and 1.4 show that African-Americans are the victims of homicide six times more often than European-Americans, and that they are the perpetrators of homicide seven times more often than European-Americans.[14] Any satisfactory explanation of lethal violence would have to take account of the socioeconomic predicament and cultural norms of communities and neighborhoods with disproportionately high rates of violence.* Perhaps the emphasis on firearms availability (and drugs) provides a convenient distraction for those analysts who prefer to avoid addressing some very distressing questions about the nature of our society and ourselves.

Using international statistics, Gary Kleck has shown that the violent crime rate is not a function of gun availability; removing the United States from an analysis of international rates of gun ownership and homicide practically erases the correlation.[15] Some countries have high rates of firearms ownership (Switzerland and Israel) and low rates of violent crime. Likewise, some countries (e.g., Mexico) have low rates of private gun ownership (at least according to official data) and high rates of violent crime. Moreover, in the United States, there is no significant correlation between rates of firearm ownership and rates of firearm homicide at the state or city levels.[16] In other words, knowing the percentage of people in an American state or city who own firearms is of no help in predicting the firearm homicide rate in that state or city.[17]

---

*For example, researchers at the John F. Kennedy School of Government at Harvard found that youth homicide in Boston from 1990 to 1994 was confined almost entirely to Boston's poor, African-American neighborhoods and was committed primarily by 15–24-year-old African-American males. Office of Juvenile Justice and Delinquency Preventions, *Promising Strategies to Reduce Gun Violence*, p. 27. See also Elijah Anderson, *Code of the Street: Decency, Violence and the Moral Life of the Inner City*.

Figure 1.3. Rate of Homicide Victimization in the United States, 1976–1999, by Race

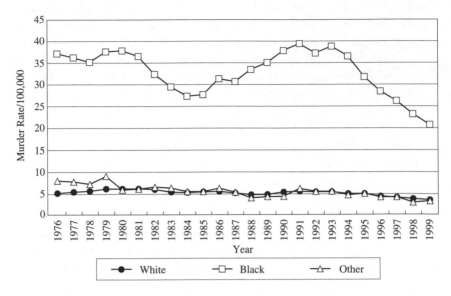

Source: "Homicide Trends in the U.S.," Bureau of Justice Statistics, 1999.

Figure 1.4. Rate of Homicide Perpetration in the United States, 1976–1999, by Race

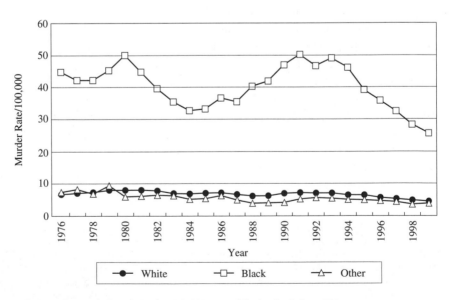

Source: "Homicide Trends in the U.S.," Bureau of Justice Statistics, 1999.

Figure 1.5. Increasing U.S. Gun Stock and Fluctuating Violent Crime

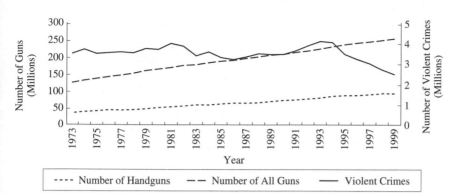

Source: Federal Bureau of Investigation, Uniform Crime Reports.

Perhaps adding to the puzzlement is the fact that while the stock of firearms in private hands has grown steadily during this century, the rate of violent crime has fluctuated (see figure 1.5). The United States experienced an extraordinary increase in violent crime in the 1960s and 1970s and a remarkable drop in violent crime in the 1990s. The number of firearms, especially handguns, in private hands increased by several million every year during this period. The relentless growth in the privately held stock of firearms cannot explain both the crime wave of the first period and the crime drop of the second period.

There is a good deal of research and scholarly debate on whether, even if guns don't cause crime, they cause greater likelihood of injury or death when they are used in crime.[18] This is also a complex issue to resolve empirically. Interestingly, although not surprisingly, robbers with guns less frequently cause any injury than robbers with knives; they get more victim compliance. But when bullets are fired and hit a human target, they do greater damage than knife wounds. Still, the differential damage might not be solely due to a gun effect; those who use guns may intend the most serious injuries. If so, even if they were somehow denied a gun, they might inflict grievous or deadly injury with a knife, tire iron, or their bare hands.[19]

All these issues about whether, and the extent to which, guns cause violent crime have generated an impressive and complex body of empirical research. To repeat, this book assumes that guns are a problem and asks what *policy* options are available to change the manner in which guns are produced, sold, purchased, possessed, and used in contemporary American society.

The Value of Firearms

We cannot properly assess the nature and magnitude of the gun problem without considering the offsetting benefits of guns. Many gun control proponents assert that guns, especially handguns, provide no benefits whatsoever, and that individuals who believe that guns make them safer are wrong, perhaps suffering from a species of false consciousness. Relying heavily on suicide statistics, they purport to show that owning a gun is more likely to lead to death or injury of the owner or someone in his family than to the death or injury of an intruder or attacker.[20] The following excerpt is typical:

> The home can be a dangerous place. We noted 43 suicides, criminal homicides, or accidental gunshot deaths involving a gun kept in the home for every case of homicide for self-protection. In the light of these findings, it may reasonably be asked whether keeping firearms in the home increases a family's protection or places it in greater danger.[21]

Gun rights advocates counter that the number of criminals killed or injured by citizens using their firearms in self-defense is not the right measure of the self-defensive value of firearms.* A homeowner can ward off an intruder, rapist, robber, or mugger without anybody being injured, indeed, without firing shots.[22] Using a survey, criminologist Gary Kleck found that Americans defend themselves 2.5 million times per year by warding off threats to their persons and property.[23] Phil Cook and Jens Ludwig put the number of defensive gun uses at 1.3 million per year.[24] Hemenway and Azrael's national survey, sponsored by the National Institute of Justice, found 1.5 million defensive gun uses per year.[25] All these surveys reveal a great deal of self-defensive use of firearms, in fact, more defensive gun uses than crimes committed with firearms.[26] (For 1999, the National Crime Victimization Survey estimated approximately 563,000 crimes committed with a gun; for 1997, the FBI's Uniform Crime Reports reported 425,000 firearm-related violent crimes.)

In addition to the number of defensive gun uses, gun owners maintain that guns provide a social benefit via the subjective sense of security that gun owners derive from having their guns available. This makes sense. We recognize life insurance as providing a social benefit, even if the policy

---

*Most firearm deaths in the home are suicides. Since some people obtain firearms *in order to commit suicide*, it is an error to conceptualize causation in the other direction, that is, that the presence of the firearm *caused* the firearms death or injury.

owner doesn't die; the value lies in the psychic protection it affords to the policyholder and his or her family. Likewise, automobile owners derive enormous psychic satisfaction from possessing and operating the automobile, even if it subjects them to risk of accident and death and is less efficient than public transportation. Gun ownership could be analogized to investments in door and window locks. Are such security devices valueless until they successfully prevent an intrusion? Clearly, security devices provide psychic security to the homeowner, even if never tested by an intruder.

In assessing the benefits and costs of firearms, it is senseless to lump all firearms together. Rifles and shotguns are infrequently used in crimes but widely used in hunting and competitive and recreational shooting. There would seem to be no basis for dismissing or discounting the individual and social benefits of hunting, target shooting, and gun collecting. People engage in many sports and activities that pose some risk to themselves, and, in some cases, to others. While rifles and shotguns can also provide self-defense, lightweight handguns are especially useful for this purpose. Handguns are not used as much in hunting, but there are some hunters who use them.[27] Some handguns are used in competitive shooting and recreationally. Most handguns are purchased for self-defense.[28] Most handguns owners claim to derive a feeling of security from being armed.

Guns and Deterrence

The private ownership of firearms provides a major social benefit if it deters crime. Even non gun owners benefit if potential criminals are dissuaded from committing crimes because they fear being shot by armed citizens. Perhaps would-be criminals in the United States think twice before commencing criminal activity because they know that private gun ownership is high? Maybe that explains why burglary rates are lower in the United States than in the United Kingdom?

Sociologists James Wright and Peter Rossi asked prison inmates in 10 states whether they took the defensive use of deadly force into account in deciding whether to commit crimes. Of these inmates, 43% reported that, at some point in their lives, they decided not to commit a crime because the victim possessed a weapon.* In addition, 42% reported that they had

---

*There are three main sources for figures on the defensive use of guns. First, a number of authors have used information from police records to estimate the number of justified defensive gunshot injuries (Kellerman and Reay, 1996; Kleck, 1997; Kellermann and Reay, 1986; Kellermann et al., 1993). Unfortunately, this type of survey excludes defensive gun use that does not harm the would-be criminal. Sec-

confronted an armed victim, and 38% said they had been scared off, shot at, wounded, or captured by an armed victim.[29]

Especially since the publication of John Lott's *More Guns, Less Crime* (1998), there has been a spirited debate among empirical criminologists about whether citizen gun possession actually *depresses* the amount of crime. Lott, an economist and research fellow at the University of Chicago Law School, examined the impact of state "shall issue" laws on violent crime. These laws permit "law-abiding citizens" (i.e., those without a disqualifying conviction or some other disability) to carry concealed weapons in public. Lott found that counties with shall issue laws experienced statistically significant decreases in violent crime, seeming to confirm the NRA's argument that an armed citizenry deters crime. Lott called shall issue laws the most cost effective method of reducing crime. He projected that, if shall issue laws prevailed in all counties, there would have been 1,400 fewer murders, 4,200 fewer rapes, 60,000 fewer aggravated assaults, and 12,000 fewer robberies.[30]

Lott's critics argue that his methodology is flawed because he did not control for numerous other factors that influence crime rates (such as poverty, drug use, gang activity, and crime control initiatives, including gun control laws).[31] They further argue that he did not adequately capture local time trends in crime rates,[32] did not adequately take into account regional and state demographics,[33] did not properly specify the deterrent mechanism in the model,[34] and did not measure frequency of citizen self-defense.[35] Some critics brand Lott's study illogical because his statistics show that shall issue laws reduced murders among people known to one another more than murders by strangers, while the opposite would make much more sense.[36] Other critics contend that shall issue laws encourage more criminal offenders to carry guns in order to overcome armed victims.[37] Most recently, Michael Maltz has persuasively argued that the Uniform Crime Reporting System (UCR) has too many holes and inaccuracies to support county-level statistical analysis.[38] The empirical issues have not been definitively resolved. Lott may well be proven wrong, but he has

---

ond, the National Crime Victimization Survey, underreports the number of defensive gun uses, since it does not provide the respondent an opportunity to respond directly to the question of whether he or she used a gun defensively; furthermore, it only allows the respondent to account for a subset of crimes. Finally, one-time telephone surveys tend to overstate the number of defensive gun usages because of a variety of measurement errors. See also Wright "The Ownership of Firearms for Reasons of Self-defense." Furthermore, Wright and Rossi conclude that there is likely an underreporting of "being scared off" and other numbers due to prisoners' desire to appear fearless (Wright and Rossi, 1994).

certainly established the deterrence benefit of private firearms ownership as a serious hypothesis worthy of continued research.

Conclusion

Many other researchers and writers have studied and written about whether, and if so, to what extent, widespread private ownership of guns constitutes a problem. This first chapter reminds us that the nature and magnitude of the American gun problem is controversial, both empirically and conceptually. As we examine in future chapters the administrative and enforcement problems that attend various gun control options, we will need to think again about the nature and magnitude of the gun problem.

It is not gun-inflicted suicides and accidents that generate demands for more gun controls. Suicide rarely ranks high on the U.S. social problems agenda: indeed, whether people should have a right to commit (and to be assisted in committing) suicide has attracted more attention in recent years than suicide itself. In any event, suicide is probably not best conceptualized as a gun problem. By contrast, injuries and deaths from firearms accidents are definitely a firearms problem, but the numbers are small and the cost of such accidents is born almost exclusively by gun-owning households which could be said to assume the risk. (Of course, there are child victims who have themselves not assumed the risk.) Violent crime is what makes guns a big social problem and animates the drive for gun controls.

Many people, especially Europeans, believe that America has more violent crime, certainly more gun crime, than other countries, because we have more guns in private hands. But that assumption has been rendered debatable by a mountain of empirical research. Simply consider that the rate of violent crime has fluctuated while the number of firearms has increased inexorably and that the states with the highest rates of gun ownership do not necessarily have the highest rates of violent crime. American violence is a very complicated subject; its causes are deeply embedded in our culture, history, demographics, race-relations, distribution of wealth, and national character.[39] The status of firearms are at least as much a consequence of these factors as a cause. Obviously, gun crime could not be committed without guns. But most violent crimes could be committed with other weapons, albeit with less risk of death to the victim. We must never be diverted from questioning why a higher proportion of Americans is willing to kill family members, friends, rivals, and crime victims than are citizens of other countries.

Having noted that violent crime and gun crime are complex phenomena, from this point on we put those doubts and complexities aside, and assuming that private possession of firearms is a major cause of America's violent crime problem, we ask what could be done about it. Can gun control work?

2

Existing Gun Controls

The federal government pays virtually no attention to the
design, manufacture, or marketing of guns. The two agencies
with potential jurisdiction over these matters, the BATF and the
Consumer Product Safety Commission (CPSC) currently lack the
authority to address them. This lack of federal supervision of
the gun industry allows several dangerous conditions to persist.
—Million Mom March Foundation, www.millionmommarch.org

With more than 20,000 laws on the books at the local, state
and federal levels, firearms are in fact one of the most
regulated products in America.
—National Rifle Association, Online Fact Sheet

The history of federal firearms regulation provides perspective on the
kinds of gun controls that are within the realm of the possible for the
United States. It is likely that future federal gun control legislation will
build upon the foundation that has been established over the past 75
years. Up until now the principal federal policy is that law-abiding
adults should be allowed to purchase and possess firearms, at least in
their homes, but that dangerous classes of people should be denied access to guns and should be punished for possessing them. Furthermore,
both federal and state criminal laws provide very serious punishment
for crimes committed with a firearm.

A Brief History of Federal Gun Control

The first federal gun control was a 1927 law prohibiting the sale of hand-guns to private individuals through the mail.[1] This was one of a series of federal laws dealing with vice by protecting the integrity of the U.S. mails. Admittedly, there was something sordid about the federal government's mail service being used to transport weapons to criminals. The law also represented an effort to prevent the gun controls of one state from being circumvented by residents of that state simply obtaining firearms by mail from a manufacturer, wholesaler, or retailer in another state. This ban on so-called mail-order murder had practically no significance since manu-facturers could still receive orders by mail and ship handguns to custom-ers via private carriers.[2]

During Franklin Roosevelt's presidency, there were two significant pieces of federal gun control legislation: the National Firearms Act of 1934 (NFA) and the Federal Firearms Act of 1938 (FFA). During this period both Houses of Congress, as well as the White House, were controlled by the Democrats. The NFA was a response to gangster violence during the 1920s and 1930s, the "tommy-gun era."[3] Competing organized crime groups en-gaged in spectacular assassinations and shootouts in public, sometimes in broad daylight. The media and the public demanded a government re-sponse. The federal government had neither jurisdiction nor organiza-tional capacity to combat these groups, but Congress finally sought to pre-vent civilian ownership of "gangster type firearms,"[4] defined as sawed-off shotguns (rifles and shotguns with barrels shorter then 18 inches), silenc-ers, machine (automatic fire) guns, and submachine guns.* Because law-makers doubted Congress's power to outlaw these gangster weapons out-right, the NFA imposed a heavy tax on manufacturers, importers, and dealers of these weapons.

The NFA required "every importer, manufacturer and dealer in fire-arms" to register its name, principal place of business, and other places of business with its local Internal Revenue Service collector and to pay an annual tax. Importers and manufacturers were taxed $500, dealers $200,

---

*A machine gun is an "automatic fire" weapon that fires many rounds of am-munition, fed via a belt or a clip, with a single pull of the trigger. By contrast, a semiautomatic weapon fires one bullet with every trigger pull, but each discharge automatically loads the next round into the firing chamber so that the weapon does not have to be "cocked." Firearms that are not semiautomatic include those that operate by bolt action, pump action, slide action, and lever action. Most modern firearms, including so-called assault rifles, are semiautomatics.

and pawnbrokers $300—very large sums at that time. There was an additional $200 tax on every transfer to an individual. Firearms that had been transferred before the passage of the act could not be transferred again, unless the tax was paid retroactively for prior transfers. The goal was, through taxation, to make these weapons too costly to produce or possess.* Owners had to register their gangster weapons within 60 days after the act became effective, and the law made it illegal to transport unregistered weapons covered by the act. Manufacturers and importers were required to affix an identification number on each firearm. The registration system, the National Firearms Registration and Transfer Record (NFRTR), exists to this day. In theory, it is a complete ownership record of all NFA weapons. In practice, as we shall see in chapter 9, there is reason to doubt its reliability.

Whether or not there was a significant law-abiding market for these NFA weapons, it was never expected that gangsters would go through the registration process. However, if they were found in possession of an unregistered weapon, the prosecutor could charge an easily provable crime with a 10-year maximum sentence. (The 1986 Firearms Owners' Protection Act outlawed the manufacture and transfer of new FFA weapons.) In hindsight, the NFA is important because it established an upper limit on weaponry suitable for civilian possession.

There has never been an evaluation of the NFA, even as to whether the NFRTR registration for machine guns is accurate and comprehensive.[5] But the use of tommy guns and machine guns by organized crime groups did go out of vogue. The organized crime groups of the 1950s and subsequent decades did not engage in the kind of open warfare that their predecessors did. Instead, they carried out their gangland "hits" with more subtlety. It seems doubtful that this change in organized crime's preferred instrument of assassination resulted from inability to get hold of submachine guns.†

---

*In *Sonzinsky v. U.S.*, 300 U.S. 506 (1937), the U.S. Supreme Court held that these heavy taxes on manufacturers, dealers, and owners of machine guns, sawed-off shotguns, and other gangster weapons were not unconstitutional.

†"The dangers of drawing a casual inference between federal regulation and the end of the 'Tommy-Gun Era' are, however, manifold. Available data on the use of gangster weapons before the NFA are not precise; thus a meaningful before-and-after study is difficult. Most important, it is hard to determine whether the use of these weapons was a phenomenon that had reached an unnatural peak just before the advent of federal regulation and would have abated in any event." Franklin Zimring, "Firearms and the Federal Law: The Gun Control Act of 1968," p. 133. See *Staples v. U.S.* 1793 (1994).

NFA
Firearms covered: "Gangster-type weapons," including silencers, sawed-off shotguns, rifles and shotguns with barrels shorter than 18 inches, concealable guns with silencers, and machine and submachine guns.   *Regulatory strategies*: High tax on manufacturers, dealers, and importers. Covered weapons had to be registered. Manufacturers had to affix ID numbers and maintain records. The Internal Revenue Service, subsequently the BATF, had to maintain the NFRTR.

Federal Firearms Act of 1938

The 1938 Federal Firearms Act established the dominant model of federal gun control for the rest of the twentieth century. The FFA sought to prevent the "criminal class" from using firearms and "to aid state and local efforts at tighter control."[6] The act made criminal interstate transfer of firearms to individuals who posed an unacceptably high risk of misusing a firearm, that is, those people under indictment, previously convicted of a crime of violence, or fugitives from justice. The law made it a crime knowingly to sell a firearm to an ineligible person and for an ineligible person to receive a firearm that had traveled interstate. It also outlawed trafficking in stolen firearms and in firearms with obliterated serial numbers.[7] It turned out to be difficult to convict violators of this law because the prosecutor had to prove that the defendant *knowingly* transferred a firearm to a felon or other ineligible person.

The FFA established the system of federally licensed dealers that has been the core of federal gun control ever since. A "dealer" was defined as "any person engaged in the business of selling firearms or ammunition or cartridge cases . . . at wholesale or retail, or any person engaged in the business of repairing such firearms or of manufacturing" virtually all types of firearms in any capacity. This was a *permissive* (as opposed to restrictive) *licensing system*. Dealers' licenses were not rationed or reserved for only the most responsible persons. The licensing system did not aim at weeding out irresponsible people but at raising money and generating a limited paper trail on retail sales. The annual fee for manufacturers and dealers was set at $25 and $1, respectively. While the Treasury Department did not maintain a firearms registry, dealers were required to keep records of their retail sales.[8] While it was criminal for a Federal Firearms Licensee (FFL) to knowingly sell a firearm to an ineligible person, the FFL did not have to verify the eligibility of the prospective purchaser or even check

---

FFA

Firearms covered: Virtually all.

Regulatory strategies: Established federal licensing system for manufacturers, dealers, and importers. Manufacturers and dealers could only ship interstate to other licensees or to individuals who were not required to have a license under state law. Made it a crime for anyone else to knowingly sell a firearm to a person under indictment, someone convicted of a crime of violence, or a fugitive from justice. Felons and fugitives prohibited from receiving firearms or ammunition that had been shipped or transported in interstate or foreign commerce; prohibited any person from shipping, transporting, or receiving in interstate commerce firearms with altered or obliterated serial numbers.

---

the purchaser's identification. So how would the dealer "know" the purchaser had a criminal record or was otherwise ineligible?

With the FFA, Congress provided another example of an inexpensive regulatory system that, in retrospect at least, seems mostly to have been for show.[9]

Gun Control Act of 1968

Gun control made its way on to the social problems agenda in the 1960s, when the crime rate soared. Still, the Gun Control Act (GCA) languished in Congress for five years, finally becoming law in the wake of the Martin Luther King, Jr. (Apr. 4, 1968), and Robert F. Kennedy (June 5, 1968) assassinations and dozens of urban riots around the country.*

The National Rifle Association successfully opposed the bill's licensing and registration provisions. Ultimately, the NRA and its allies were able to secure a preamble that stated that "it was not the intent of Congress to restrict unnecessarily the rights of American citizens to purchase and use firearms for lawful purposes, including personal protection." With both Houses of Congress and the White House held by the Demo-

---

*Congress actually passed two closely connected gun control statutes, the Omnibus Crime Control and Safe Streets Act of 1968 and the Gun Control Act of 1968. For simplicity's sake, both are treated together here. See Zimring, "Firearms and the Federal Law," p. 133; Vizzard, "The Gun Control Act of 1968," pp. 79–98.

crats and the country racked by race riots, the law passed by a comfortable margin.

The GCA had at least five objectives—prohibiting interstate firearms sales; prohibiting sales to an expanded list of dangerous categories of people; adding certain "destructive devices" to the NFA list of prohibited weapons; prohibiting importation of so-called Saturday Night Specials ("firearms not particularly suitable for or readily adaptable to sporting purposes"); and prohibiting importation of surplus military weapons.[10] The GCA placed responsibility for administering federal firearms laws in a new agency, the Bureau of Alcohol, Tobacco, and Firearms (BATF), located in the U.S. Treasury Department. The BATF was authorized to grant licenses to dealers and manufacturers and to enforce the GCA's other requirements.[11]

The GCA reinforced earlier law providing that firearms dealers needed to have a federal license. "No person shall engage in business as a firearms or ammunition importer, manufacturer, or dealer until he has filed an application with and received a license to do so from, the Secretary [of the Treasury]." The law defined dealer as any person, who on a full- or part-time basis, "devotes time, attention, and labor to dealing in firearms as a regular course of trade or business with the principal objective of livelihood and profit through the repetitive purchase and resale of firearms." Occasional sellers, buyers, personal collectors, and hobbyists, even those liquidating a large personal firearms collection, did not need a license.

From 1968 until 1993, it was a simple matter to obtain a federal firearms license. The fee was $10 for a three-year license that authorized its holder to ship, transport, and receive firearms in interstate commerce, as well as to engage in retail sales. The statute required BATF to issue a license within 45 days to anyone who was 21 years old, had premises from which he intended to conduct business, and who was not prohibited from possessing firearms. The GCA required that FFLs comply with any state or local firearms, zoning, or business laws. License applicants were suppose to notify the chief law enforcement officer in the applicant's jurisdiction of intent to enter the firearms business and to certify that they were in compliance with all state and local laws, but they often did not.

The GCA's sponsors meant to limit the discretion of BATF in denying licenses. In practice, large numbers of people who had no intention of becoming retail sellers obtained FFL licenses in order to purchase firearms directly from out-of-state manufacturers or wholesalers. Over time, the numbers of licensees began to swell; by 1992, there were 284,000 FFLs,[12] more licensed gun dealers than gas stations.

BATF regulations required that FFLs maintain "business premises," that is, "property on which the . . . dealing in firearms is or will be conducted. A private dwelling . . . shall not be recognized as coming within the meaning of the term."[13] But this law was not much enforced. The BATF was supposed to monitor and investigate FFLs, but its resources were always inadequate for that task.[14]

The GCA allowed law-abiding citizens to own and possess an unlimited number of long guns and handguns, but made it a federal crime for ex-felons and members of other dangerous social categories to own or possess any firearms. In addition to the categories of people the FFA defined as ineligible to purchase guns from an FFL, the GCA added minors (defined as those 18 years old and younger for rifles and shotguns, and as 21 years old and younger for handguns), unlawful users of illegal narcotics, and anyone "adjudicated as a mental defective" or previously committed to any mental institution.

The GCA required an FFL to confirm a prospective purchaser's age and in-state residency by examining a photo identification document and to obtain a signed statement of eligibility, but did not oblige the FFL to attempt to verify the accuracy of the purchaser's signed statement. Thus, if an ineligible person was willing to falsely swear that he was an eligible purchaser, he could easily buy a handgun from a licensed dealer, although he would be committing a crime in deceiving the dealer.[15] In effect, the act relied on an honor system.

The GCA included a section (now known as the felon-in-possession law) that made it a crime, punishable by up to a $10,000 fine and/or two years imprisonment, for a person who had ever been convicted of any state or federal felony (except a felony "related to business regulation") to possess a firearm.* This provision is now one of the most important pillars of federal gun controls; the maximum punishment has been increased to ten years.

For several years leading up to passage of the GCA, New England gun manufacturers had been seeking protection against foreign competition. The 1968 urban riots and the surge in violent crime led industry lobbyists to embrace a position held by some criminologists and police officials— the cheap guns favored by poor people in the inner city ought to be banned. The GCA prohibited the *importation* of surplus military weapons and other firearms not "generally recognized as particularly suitable for or readily adaptable to sporting purposes." BATF, left to flesh out this

---

*An earlier 1968 law imposed a five-year maximum sentence for felons who *received* firearms. In 1968, the two provisions were merged and the maximum sentence increased to 10 years. Title VII of Omnibus Crime Control and Safe Streets Act of 1968, 18 U.S.C. App. sec. 1202(a). See *Lewis v. U.S.*, 445 U.S. 55 (1979).

GCA
Firearms covered: All *Regulatory strategies*: Required license to manufacture or deal in firearms, even if business did not operate in interstate commerce; imposed higher licensing fees for manufacturers, dealers, and importers; made it illegal for dealers to sell to non-state residents or to sell at any place other than the licensee's place of business; added minors, unlawful users of illegal narcotics, and the mentally ill to the list of criteria disqualifying a person from purchasing firearms; required FFLs to see purchaser's proof of age and residency; imposed more recordkeeping requirements on FFLs; prohibited importation of cheap nonsporting handguns; prohibited manufacture of destructive devices; made it a felony for a person with a felony record to possess a firearm; made it a felony for a person to make material false statements to an FFL; created a separate felony for using or carrying a firearm in the commission of a federal felony.

subjective definition, came up with a system of "factoring criteria for weapons," which assigned points to each model based on safety features, size, weight, and frame construction. Certain cheap handgun models ("Saturday Night Specials") were banned from importation, but domestic manufacturers were free to continue manufacturing them, a policy that looked more like a trade protection for U.S. producers than a bona fide attempt at crime control. Moreover, because there was no ban on the importation of handgun *parts*, importers set up cottage industries, converting garages and churches into makeshift factories where imported gun components were assembled into serviceable handguns.[16] All in all, while gun control proponents heralded the GCA as a great victory, the law achieved little more than modestly advancing the regulatory system established by the 1938 FFA.

Armed Career Criminal Act of 1984

By the 1980s, law-and-order politics had become firmly entrenched. President Reagan, congressional Republicans, and the NRA argued that the country did not need more gun controls and certainly not more controls on "law-abiding" owners. They favored tougher punishment for individuals who commit gun crimes.

The Armed Career Criminal Act of 1984 imposed a mandatory minimum 15-year prison term on a convicted felon who had three previous convictions for robbery or burglary and who "possesses, receives, or transports a firearm in commerce."[17] This provision was amended in 1986 so that it would apply to those felons in possession who had three prior convictions for "a violent felony or serious drug offense."[18] The law also enhanced punishment "for whoever uses or carries a handgun loaded with armor piercing ammunition during or in relation to the commission of a crime of violence which can be prosecuted in federal court."

The Federal Sentencing Guidelines, passed in 1986, provided for sentence enhancement according to whether a firearm is possessed, brandished, or discharged in the course of committing the offense. The Anti-Drug Abuse Amendments Act of 1988 made it a separate crime to "knowingly transfer a firearm, knowing that such firearm will be used to commit a crime of violence or drug trafficking."[19] All these gun controls were directed at criminals rather than at "law-abiding" owners.

Firearms Owners' Protection (McClure-Volmer) Act of 1986 (FOPA)

In 1986, gun rights advocates partially succeeded in their two-decade-long campaign to cut back on the GCA. The NRA and its congressional supporters charged that BATF regularly violated the civil rights of law-abiding citizens in its zeal to enforce the GCA. The preamble to the new law stated:

CONGRESSIONAL FINDINGS—The Congress finds that—
(1) the rights of citizens—
    (A) to keep and bear arms under the second amendment to the United States Constitution;
    (B) to security against illegal and unreasonable searches and seizures under the Fourth Amendment;
    (C) against uncompensated taking of property, double jeopardy, and assurance of due process of law under the Fifth Amendment; and
    (D) against unconstitutional exercise of authority under the Ninth and Tenth amendments;
    require additional legislation to correct existing firearms statutes and enforcement policies; and

(2) additional legislation is required to reaffirm the intent of the Congress, as expressed in section 101 of the Gun Control Act of 1968, that "it is not the purpose of this title to place any undue or unnecessary Federal restrictions or burdens on law-abiding citizens with respect to the acquisition, possession, or use of firearms appropriate to the purpose of hunting, trapshooting, target shooting, personal protection, or any other lawful activity, and that this title is not intended to discourage or eliminate the private ownership or use of firearms by law-abiding citizens for lawful purposes."[20]

FOPA[21] (1) permitted sale of long guns to an out-of-state purchaser, as long as the sale complied with laws in both the purchaser's and FFL's states; (2) eliminated recordkeeping requirements for ammunition dealers; (3) reduced FFL recordkeeping violations from felony to misdemeanor status; (4) limited BATF to one unannounced inspection of an FFL per year; and (5) prohibited the federal government from centralizing the records of firearms dealers or maintaining "any system of registration of firearms, firearms owners, or firearms transactions."[22] The act also permitted FFLs to "conduct business temporarily at a location other than the location specified on the license if such temporary location is the location for a gun show or event sponsored by any national, state, or local organization, or any affiliate of any such organization devoted to the collection, competitive use, or other sporting use of firearms in the community, and such location is in the state which is specified on the license."[23] This provision led to a sharp increase in the number and popularity of gun shows.

There were also a few provisions favored by gun controllers, most notably, the ban on any further manufacture of machine guns, and no new automatic weapons could be registered through the NFRTR. The law also prohibited the importation of barrels for Saturday Night Specials.

FOPA
Prohibited prospective manufacture or transfers of machine guns by private individuals.
Prohibited any individual from knowingly transferring a firearm to an ineligible person.
Added to the list of ineligibles: illegal aliens, those dishonorably discharged from armed forces, and those who have renounced U.S. citizenship.
Gave the secretary of the treasury authority to relieve convicted felons of their ineligibility to possess a firearm.

Armor Piercing Bullets and Plastic Guns
(1986–1988)

Two laws favored by gun control proponents were passed in 1986 and 1988.[24] Perhaps they passed because they were directed at criminals using guns rather than at law-abiding gun owners. Therefore, they should have been acceptable to the NRA, but the organization had become radicalized in the late 1970s, and these laws, at least as first proposed, *could have* impinged on legitimate gun owners.

The 1986 law (Law Enforcement Officers Protection Act) banned the manufacture, importation, or sale of armor piercing "cop-killer" bullets. The NRA argued that there were no documented cases of bullets penetrating police body armor and that many kinds of bullets, including ordinary hunting ammunition for rifles, were capable of penetrating soft body armor at close distance. The original versions of the bill would, according to the NRA, have left shooters in the dark as to which bullets were legal and which were illegal. The final version, incorporating the NRA's concerns, defined the armor-piercing bullets in terms of their metallic content; bullets made of any of seven hard metals were banned.[25]

The battle over this law precipitated an important break between former allies, the police establishment and the NRA. Since the early decades of the twentieth century, the NRA had provided weapons training to the police and had supported the police on all law-and-order issues. The police establishment, however, was strongly in favor of banning armor-piercing bullets. Perhaps for the first time in American history, the Democrats were able to present themselves as pro-police and the Republicans as being unsympathetic to police safety. It was a strategy that Bill Clinton and the "new Democrats" would fully adopt and refine.

The Undetectable Firearms Act of 1988 banned the manufacture, sale, and possession of firearms not detectable by metal detectors and X-ray devices. The Democrats claimed victory because the NRA had opposed an early version of the law that would have banned a number of mostly plastic guns that were detectable by screening devices. No such guns existed.[26]

The Anti-Drug Abuse Amendment Act of 1988 created yet another federal crime related to firearms. It outlawed transfering a firearm, knowing that it will be used to commit a crime of violence or a drug trafficking crime.[27] Heaping punishment on those who supplied firearms to violent criminals and drug traffickers appealed to everyone.

Gun Free School Zones Act (1990)

In 1990, Congress passed the Gun Free School Zones Act, making it a federal crime to knowingly (or with reasonable cause to believe) possess a firearm in a school or school zone.[28] Since most states and localities already had laws proscribing such conduct, the practical value of the federal law was dubious. Neither Congress nor the public could have expected that the FBI or other federal agencies would be the primary enforcers of the law or that U.S. attorneys would routinely prosecute students or adults who violated it. In any event, the U.S. Supreme Court struck it down in 1995 (*U.S. v. Lopez*) on the ground that it unconstitutionally extended federal authority.[29] The Court held that Congress did not have authority under the commerce clause to prohibit carrying a gun in a school zone.* Chief Justice Rehnquist noted that if the commerce power could be stretched that far, it could be used to justify federal authority over all gun crime and perhaps all crime.[30] Congress re-passed the law in 1996, predicating federal jurisdiction on proof that the firearm, whose possession the defendant was being prosecuted for, had traveled in interstate commerce at some point since its manufacture.[31]

The Brady Law (1993)

In 1993, after a tortuous legislative history, Congress passed and President Clinton signed the most important gun control legislation in 25 years, the Handgun Control and Violence Prevention Act, commonly known as the Brady Law. Because the Brady Law is so important, marking the farthest advancement in the federal regulatory strategy of denying firearms to dangerous people, we will examine it closely in chapters 4 and 5. However, for purposes of our brief survey of the history of federal firearms laws, at this point, suffice it to say that the Brady Law required FFLs to delay gun sales by up to five working days in order that local law enforcement officials could conduct a background check on prospective gun purchasers. While the GCA permitted dealers to take the purchaser's word that he was an eligible firearms purchaser, the Brady Law provided for an independent government determination of eligibility. And it provided that after five

---

*Lopez, a twelfth-grade San Antonio high school student, arrived at school with a .38-caliber unloaded handgun and ammunition. Although Texas criminalized such conduct in 1974, Lopez was prosecuted federally. The maximum punishment was five years' imprisonment and a $5,000 fine.

years, this system would be replaced by an instant criminal background check system ("National Instant Check System" or NICS) that would require FFLs to phone the purchaser's name into a federal background checking system. The FFL would have to give NICS up to three days to block the sale in the event that the prospective gun purchaser is ineligible.

In 1995, two years after the Brady Law became effective, Congress expanded the class of ineligibles to include individuals subject to a restraining order for domestic violence, harassment, or stalking.[32] In 1997, Congress added misdemeanor domestic violence conviction to the list of disqualifying criteria.[33] In fact, the background check mostly amounts to a criminal records check in state and federal criminal records databases.

The Brady Law also raised the price of a three-year FFL license from $30 to $200. At the same time, the Clinton administration began cracking down on dealers without a business establishment and on FFLs who were not in compliance with local laws. The result was that by January 1997, the number of licensed dealers had been cut in half—to 124,286;[34] by the end of 1999, the number of FFLs had fallen to 80,600. Of course, no figures exist on the number of *unlicensed* dealers who rely solely on the secondary market for their inventory and sales, or on part-time casual sellers who do not want a license because they do not want to maintain records.

The Assault Weapons Ban (1994)

The Brady Law was enacted when the Democrats controlled both Houses of Congress and the White House. Just months later, the same forces that passed the Brady Law coalesced to pass the Assault Weapons Ban (Violent Crime Control and Law Enforcement Act), prohibiting importation, manufacture, sale, and possession of "assault weapons."[35]

Assault weapons are hard to define. Contrary to popular belief, they are not automatic fire or machine guns but semiautomatic rifles or quasi rifles that look like military or "action adventure film" (Rambo) weapons. While they work the same way as other semiautomatic weapons (which have existed from the early twentieth century), their unconventional design is frightening to many people. The 1994 federal law named 19 weapons as prohibited assault weapons and named several hundred firearms as not assault weapons. BATF was given authority to ban other models according to a point scoring system. Firearms that have any two of the following characteristics are banned: bayonet mounts, folding stocks, flash suppressors, protruding pistol grips, and threaded muzzles.

The Assault Weapons Ban illustrates the symbolic character of gun control politics. As we saw in chapter 1, most all gun crimes are committed with handguns, which are easily concealable. Assault weapons, assuming they could be clearly defined, are rarely used in crime. Moreover, they are functionally identical to all other semiautomatic long guns. From a technical standpoint, there is no reason to divide semiautomatic rifles into "good" and "bad" categories. The futuristic "assault weapons" and the more traditional-looking semiautomatics work the same way and do exactly the same thing.

The Assault Weapons Ban prohibited only post-1994 assault weapons. Not surprisingly, there was a huge increase in sales in the year before the ban became effective. Thus, hundreds of thousands of pre-1994 assault weapons continue to be lawfully bought, sold, and traded.

The same law also banned large capacity (more than 10-bullet) ammunition feeders, also known as "magazines" or "clips." These large capacity clips are hard to justify as necessary for any legitimate activity, but neither are they a big threat. Since an empty clip can be discarded from a firearm by pressing a release button and replaced with a new fully loaded clip in a second or two, a criminal or madman with two 10-bullet clips is essentially as dangerous as a criminal or madman with a single 20-bullet clip. Laws like this reflect and fan the flames of the symbolic conflict between gun owners and gun controllers, with little, if any, relevance to the crime problem.

State and Local Gun Control

The regulation of weaponry is not solely, or even primarily, a federal concern. There is a great deal of state and local gun regulation, although, not surprisingly, the states' firearms policies in our diverse nation differ widely.[36] Some states delegate gun control legislation to their municipalities.[37] Most states (e.g., California, Florida, and Maine) specifically preempt (prohibit) localities from enacting firearms regulations more restrictive than the state's law regulating firearms.[38] However, some states do permit municipalities to enact ordinances with more controls than those imposed by state law.[39] For example, while Arizona law authorizes citizens to carry unconcealed handguns, until 1994, Tombstone did not.[40] While Illinois provides for a gun licensing system, several Illinois municipalities, including Chicago, Evanston, Oak Park, Morton Grove, Winnetka, Wilmette, and Highland Park, prohibit handgun sales, purchases, and possession.[41]

Every state, like the federal system, provides for sentencing enhancements for use (and sometimes, just possession) of a firearm in the commission of crimes. All but nine states make it a crime for persons with criminal records to purchase or possess firearms.[42] Many states have laws prohibiting gun possession in a school zone.[43]

States differ widely on the ease with which law-abiding citizens can obtain licenses to possess and carry firearms and on registration. Thirty-three states (e.g., Arkansas, Georgia, Pennsylvania, Utah, and Vermont) do not require any kind of license or permit to possess a handgun.[44] Fifteen states require prospective purchasers to obtain a license (e.g., New York, New Jersey, and Massachusetts) in order to purchase a firearm or, in some cases (e.g., Connecticut), just handguns.[45]

States have various permutations of permissive and restrictive licensing to purchase and/or carry concealed firearms. Permissive licensing, which is much more common, allows everyone to have a license, unless they fall into a prohibited category. Restrictive licensing doesn't allow anyone to have a license, unless they can show good cause or special need. For example, New York State's famous Sullivan Law, passed in 1911, requires a prospective purchaser of a handgun (pistol or revolver) to obtain a license from the sheriff or police chief in the prospective purchaser's jurisdiction.[46] The applicant must persuade the relevant law enforcement officer that he or she has *good cause* to possess a firearm. Since good cause is not defined in the statute, the official has complete discretion in granting or denying the license, as long as the decision is not arbitrary and capricious.*

The NYS application procedure for obtaining a license *to carry a gun in public* is more rigorous. In New York City, for example, the applicant must provide the police department proof of citizenship, residence, business ownership, arrest information, and a "letter of necessity," explaining why the applicant's occupation requires being armed. The notarized documents must be accompanied by fingerprints and a $170 fee. The next step is an interview by a police department investigator, who reviews the documentation and writes a report to a police sergeant in the license division. The sergeant then recommends to a lieutenant that the carry license be granted or denied; the lieutenant makes the final determination. The applicant is notified by mail and has 30 days to appeal a denial.[47] Since this whole scheme is administered at the local level without statewide standards, rural and urban counties can have de facto different policies. Nevertheless, guns and gun carriers can migrate from weak control counties to strong control counties.

Some states have waiting periods running from the day that a firearms

---

*A denial must be in writing "specifically and concisely." The fee for a license is fixed separately by a board of supervisors in each county.

purchase is completed to the day that the purchaser may take possession of the weapon. For example, California imposes a 10-day waiting period, Connecticut 14 days, and Maryland 7 days. Maryland and Virginia limit an individual's firearm purchases to one gun per month.

Eleven states have firearms registration laws. Massachusetts, for example, requires that each time a handgun is transferred, the new owner must register the handgun with the secretary of state.[48] In theory, this should produce a comprehensive handgun registry, a paper trail documenting each transfer of every weapon, much like the automobile registration system. But, in practice, compliance has been low, administration weak and underfunded, and enforcement lax.[49] In North Carolina, all handgun sellers are legally prohibited from transferring a handgun to a person lacking a permit. However, the sheriffs' departments in Raleigh-Durham (and perhaps other municipalities) consider this statute to apply only to purchases of pistols from FFLs.[50] In other words, the regulatory system has been interpreted by local officials not to apply to secondary sales, that is, sales by nondealers.

Before 1985, only eight states granted the right to carry a concealed weapon to all applicants who met the statutory qualifications. However, in the 1990s, 31 states passed or reaffirmed "shall issue" laws that require the relevant government agency to issue a permit to carry a concealed weapon to any applicant who does not fall into one of the disqualifying categories.[51] These laws, as we shall see, have important implications for gun control policy options in the future.

States and localities have many other laws, for example, prohibiting discharging a gun in built-up areas and carrying a gun into a school, court, or other public building. The District of Columbia prohibits all manufacture, sale, and possession of firearms by private citizens. Chicago is almost as strict. A few states ban cheaply made guns, called "Saturday Night Specials," and a few states (e.g., New York) ban assault rifles.

Conclusion

Federal criminal and administrative firearms law has developed in a cumulative manner since the 1920s. The most important administrative law is the licensing system for manufacturers, wholesalers, importers, and retail dealers. There are far more dealers (FFLs) than manufacturers, wholesalers and importers. Anyone who is not ineligible on account of prior criminal record or other background factor can obtain an FFL license if he or she has a place of business and pays the licensing fee. Federal law regulates who may purchase a firearm. Convicted felons, domestic violence misdemeanants, drug users, fugitives from justice, illegal aliens, and certain others are prohibited from purchasing or possessing guns. The federal felon-in-possession law prohibits (punishable by a maximum 10-year prison term) any person who has ever been convicted of a federal or state felony from possessing a firearm. Federal and state laws provide significant sentence enhancements for crimes committed with guns. The Brady Law requires that dealers submit the names of would-be gun purchasers to a government background check. It is a felony to knowingly sell or otherwise transfer firearms to these ineligible persons.

Federal firearms laws often duplicate state and local laws, although the latter vary from state to state and even from municipality to municipality in the same state. The northeastern states, in general, have the most restrictive gun laws; the Rocky Mountain and southern states have the least restrictive. The laws of some U.S. jurisdictions (like the District of Columbia) are even stricter than almost any European state. However, the majority of U.S. states permit law-abiding citizens to possess and even carry firearms, albeit subject to time, place, and manner limitations.

3

Impediments to More Gun Controls

The fifth and last auxiliary right of the subject, that I shall at present mention, is that of having arms for their defense, suitable to their condition and degree, and such as are allowed by law . . . and is indeed a public allowance, under due restrictions, of the natural right of resistance and self-preservation, when the sanctions of society and laws are found insufficient to restrain the violence of oppression.
—William Blackstone, *Commentaries on the Laws of England*

Americans also have a right to defend their homes, and we need not challenge that. Nor does anyone seriously question that the Constitution protects the right of hunters to own and keep sporting guns for hunting game any more than anyone would challenge the right to own and keep fishing rods and other equipment for fishing—or to own automobiles. To "keep and bear arms" for hunting today is essentially a recreational activity and not an imperative of survival, as it was 200 years ago; "Saturday Night Specials" and machine guns are not recreational weapons and surely are as much in need of regulation as motor vehicles.
—Former U.S. Supreme Court chief justice
  Warren E. Burger, "The Right to Bear Arms"

That the Second Amendment poses no barrier to strong gun laws is perhaps the most well-settled proposition in American constitutional law.
—Former solicitor general and Harvard Law School dean
  Erwin Griswold, "Phantom Second Amendment Rights"

Let me state unequivocally . . . the Second Amendment clearly
protect(s) the right of individuals to keep and bear firearms.
—U.S. Attorney General John Ashcroft, letter to the NRA,
    May 2001

Policy making in the area of firearm regulation must take into account the
unique status of guns in American society. Examining what firearms mean
to Americans focuses attention on whose values and interests are threatened by proposals for more gun controls. This chapter examines five key
impediments to further gun regulation: (1) the entrenched position of firearms the United States; (2) the cultural significance of firearms; (3) American federalism and regional diversity of firearms traditions; (4) the active
opposition of the NRA; and (5) gun owners' beliefs about their right to
keep and bear arms.

The Entrenched Position of Firearms
in the United States

The greatest practical obstacle to implementing new gun controls is the
huge number of firearms already in private hands. No other democratic
country has ever been faced with the challenge of establishing a firearms
control system from the point where the United States is now. Consider
some of the facts. There are more than 250 million firearms in private
hands in the United States (see table 3.1), and the arsenal is growing
by about 4.5 million new firearms per year (see table 3.2).* Firearm

---

*Estimates of the number of firearms in private hands are produced by "survey-
based" and by "production-based" estimating techniques. Both techniques can be
used to estimate the number of *households* with guns and the number of *individuals*
owning guns.

The survey method suffers from two potentially serious problems, both producing estimates that are too small. First, a number of respondents will not admit to
interviewers or pollsters that they own a firearm—some estimates place this number
as high as 10%—or that there is a firearm in their household because (1) the possession is illegal (millions of Americans have a criminal record that makes it a
crime to possess a firearm), or (2) they fear that the poll will provide the government
information that will later be used to seize the weapon. In addition, some respondents may be unaware that a member of the household possesses a firearm.

The "production-based" technique adds gun manufacturers' annual figures plus
imports; subtracted from that total are annual exports and an estimated number of
guns annually lost through destruction. That net number is divided by the average

Table 3.1. Cumulated U.S. Gun Stock

	Handguns	Total
1993	80,913,433	228,660,966
1994	84,665,690	235,604,001
1995	86,864,690	240,516,001
1996	88,685,690	244,906,001
1997	90,458,690	249,148,001
1998	92,275,445	253,815,175
1999	94,157,425	258,804,085

Source: U.S. Census Manufactures; BATF statistics on imports and exports.

purchases surged in 1993 and 1994, the years that Congress debated and passed the Brady Bill and the Assault Weapons Ban and would surge again if and when passage of any major federal gun control measures seemed at all likely (see figure 3.1).

The 250-plus million firearms are distributed among 35% (lower estimate)[1] to 45% (upper estimate)[2] of all American households.[3] Estimates are that gun-owning households on average possess between 2.5 and 4.5 firearms.[4] Most gun-owning households own long-guns, or long guns and handguns; perhaps one in five has only handguns.

Long-guns (rifles and shotguns) outnumber handguns (revolvers and pistols) by 2 to 1; however, in the 1990s, sales for handguns nearly equaled those for long-guns. Tables 3.1 and 3.2 show how the national firearms stock has accumulated based on domestic production plus imports.*

Because gun ownership is so widespread, there is no single type of gun owner or reason for possessing a gun. To the contrary, gun owners are a diverse group, including, for instance, New Jersey collectors, Wyoming ranchers, Iowa farmers, Vermont professors, California sport-shooters, and big city criminals. According to survey data,† whites are more likely than

---

number of guns per household or per individual to produce the estimated number of gun-possessing individuals and households. The production-based technique also has limitations. First, police seizures and destruction of an unknown number of weapons are not counted. Second, unknown numbers of firearms are illegally imported and exported each year, including war trophies from World War II, Vietnam, and the Gulf War. Third, most firearms can last for at least 100 years if carefully maintained, but an unknown number are rendered inoperable due to improper care.

*Figures do not take account of exports or guns lost from the pool because they have become unusable or were destroyed.

†These surveys most likely underestimate gun possession by urban dwellers and minorities. Obviously, people whose gun possession is illegal will be less likely to admit to interviewers that they possess a gun. Cities have more gun restrictions and

Table 3.2. Net Additions to U.S. Gun Stock, 1993–1999

	Handguns	Long Guns	Total
1993	3,668,945	2,924,678	6,593,623
1994	3,752,257	3,190,778	6,943,035
1995	2,199,000	2,713,000	4,912,000
1996	1,821,000	2,569,000	4,390,000
1997	1,773,000	2,469,000	4,242,000
1998	1,816,755	2,850,419	4,667,174
1999	1,881,980	3,106,930	4,988,910

Source: U.S. Census Manufactures; BATF statistics on imports and exports.

blacks to own guns and blacks are more likely than Hispanics.[5] Residents of rural areas, both blacks and whites, are far more likely to own guns than urban dwellers.[6] Men far outnumber women as gun owners. Handgun owners almost always cite self-defense as their principal reason for owning a handgun.[7] Long-gun owners rank hunting and sport-shooting as more important than self defense.[8]

Firearms are common throughout the United States, but there is a higher percentage of gun-owning households in the South (60.6%) and West (49.8%) than in the Midwest (40%) and Northeast (28%).[9] Not surprisingly, residents of Idaho and New Mexico are more likely to possess firearms than residents of Massachusetts or New Jersey. There are also large differences in rates of gun ownership among different counties within the same state.

It is a core principle of regulation, as well as common sense, that it is easier to regulate a smaller number of persons or entities than a larger number. Thus, it would be easier to monitor and supervise 191 firearms manufacturers[10] than tens of millions of firearm owners or households.[11] Obtaining compliance for new gun controls from gun-owning individuals and households would be a tremendous challenge. How many agents and government officials would it take to implement, administer, investigate, and enforce a regulatory scheme covering so many people? Consider that despite there being a Department of Motor Vehicles office in every county of the United States, and hundreds of thousands of police officers regularly checking cars and drivers, there is still a great deal of noncompliance;

---

thus more illegal gun possession. African-Americans are much more likely to have been convicted of a felony, and thus gun possession by members of that group is more likely to be illegal. Finally, our big cities have a greater percentage of people who, because they have no fixed abode, are unlikely to be reached by the surveys.

Figure 3.1. U.S. Firearms Sales by First Sale Value* (in Millions of Current Dollars)

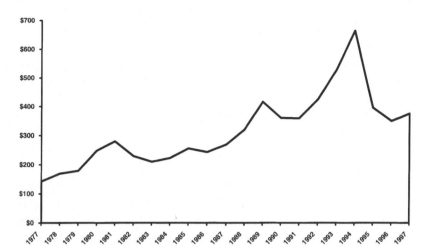

*First sale value typically reflects price to wholesaler.

Source: Data from www.amfire.com (National Association of Federally Licensed Firearms Dealers and the Professional Gun Retailers Association).

there are millions of traffic violations every year, and hundreds of thousands of licenses are revoked.

If a regulatory scheme is not enforced, it loses credibility and compliance declines further. If only 5% of firearms owners did not comply with a particular regulatory scheme, that would mean 4 million violators. Moreover, it is likely that noncompliance would be far greater than 5%; indeed, noncompliance with state laws requiring assault weapon registration amounted to a staggering 90%.[12] How would millions of violators be dealt with?

This observation does not mean that more regulation would not be worth the cost, but it does caution us that the implementation and enforcement costs of obtaining compliance from 50 million households would be very high, and that noncompliance might be so substantial that the regulatory regime itself would produce few benefits.

The Gun Culture

While Michael Bellesiles's recent and controversial book, *Arming America: The Origins of the National Gun Culture*,[13] calls into question the prevalence of privately held firearms in eighteenth- and early nineteenth-century America, there is no doubt that firearms are very deeply embedded in *contemporary* American society. That reality shapes what policy options will be possible for the next several decades and even beyond.

Like cars and alcohol, guns are an important part of Americans' imagination, fears, experience, and recreation. Guns are ever-present in American consciousness. There's probably no time, day or night, when a TV viewer would not see, on one or more channels, a gun displayed or brandished. All of us are influenced by the movies and TV images of guns, gunslingers, armed avengers, and armed law enforcement officers. Growing up on a diet of movies showing gun ownership as ubiquitous must have an impact on shaping expectations, attitudes, and conduct. Even Americans who do not own guns live in a gun culture just as people who do not own a television live in a TV culture. It is true, of course, that citizens in other societies watch U.S. movies and do not seek to arm themselves to the same extent. But they are watching shows about Americans, not about themselves.

One need not rely only on an amorphous concept like "culture" to demonstrate that firearms are deeply embedded in U.S. society. There are 191 firearms manufacturers, ranging from the largest, Smith and Wesson, to many very small firms.[14] All told, these manufacturers employ approximately 11,000[15] people and generate sales of $3.5 billion per year.[16] They advertise their products in dozens of magazines and provide work for wholesalers and retailers of firearms and associated products.

Hunting is one major strand of American gun culture. While hunting is slowly declining in popularity, it remains a major recreational activity that supports manufacturers, wholesalers, and retailers of clothing and all sorts of hunting paraphernalia. Hunting is most prevalent in the regions bordering the Mississippi River basin and the Rocky Mountains.[17] There are major organizations devoted to promoting hunting (e.g., Boone and Crockett Club, Buckmasters, Ducks Unlimited, Colorado Varmint Hunter, and Hunters for the Hungry), as well as an unknown, but certainly huge, number of local clubs. Consider that there are at least 33 print magazines devoted to hunting with a combined circulation of approximately 12 million (see table 3.3). (By comparison, auto magazines have a combined circulation of approximately 10.5 million.) These hunting magazines are loaded with advertisements and feature stories about firearms. In 1996, the total U.S. expenditure on hunting was $21 billion.[18] The 2001 National Survey of Fishing, Hunting & Wildlife found that there are 14 million hunters above age 16 in the United States.

In addition to hunters, 12.7 million Americans claim to participate in target shooting. (By comparison, 11.2 million Americans play tennis, 15.6 million Americans play softball, and 22.5 million jog for recreation.[19])

There are more than 9,000 outdoor shooting ranges in the United States.[20] The NRA sponsors approximately 1,500 shooting competitions annually. The following organizations are just a few of those that exist to promote shooting sports: the National Firearms Association, National Skeet Shooting and Sports Clays Association, National Association of Shooting Sports Athletes, and United States Practical Shooting Association.[21] Local pistol and rifle clubs across the United States provide a milieu where enthusiasts socialize around hunting and shooting.[22]

The magazines indicate the kinds of interests that gun owners have and the articles they read to reinforce their interests. There are specialty magazines for practically every one of the different types of shooting sports: airguns, indoor and outdoor handgun competitions, handgun silhouette tournaments, indoor and outdoor rifle shooting, skeet shooting, clay target shooting, cowboy action shooting, and others.

There are also numerous magazines devoted to firearms qua firearms, including *American Handgunner* (circulation 148,000), *American Rifleman* (1,365,000), *Guns & Ammo* (585,000), and *Handguns* (158,000).[23] We are not dealing here with some arcane activity for a few aficionados, but with a highly popular product which, like cars, millions of people enjoy using safely, and a small minority misuses with horrendous results.

Federalism

American federalism also presents an impediment to firearms regulation. It has and will continue to be very difficult to get a congressional majority to support far-reaching gun controls, especially in the U.S. Senate, where small states have the same voting power as large states. Gun ownership is very popular in the southern and western states. Even many Democratic senators and representatives in those states oppose strong gun controls. We must recognize that in much of the United States gun ownership is regarded as normal and desirable. In rural areas, children grow up familiar with shotguns, rifles, and even handguns. Their parents use guns to kill snakes and pests and to hunt. Their homes are far from police stations, and many (perhaps the majority) regard self-defense as a personal and familial responsibility.

Even if Congress could agree on gun control legislation, the Supreme Court has become less willing to permit Congress to exert authority over essentially noneconomic intrastate matters, like crime control. In the last few years, the Court has struck down the Gun Free School Zones Act, the Brady Law's requirement that state and local law enforcement officials carry out background checks on gun purchasers, and the Violence against

Table 3.3. Gun Magazines Organized by Category

Hunting	General	"Survivalist"	Military/Police	Trade	"Sport-Shooting"
American Hunter	American Handgunner	American Survival Guide**	Counter Terrorism & Security Magazine	American Firearms Industry Magazine	Accurate Rifle
Big Sky Journal	American Rifleman	The Eagle**	Firearms for Law Enforcement	Gun Tests Magazine	Black Powder Cartridge News
Black Powder Hunting	America's First Freedom	Gun-Ho**	Guns and Weapons for Law Enforcement	Shooting Industry	Gun Games
Buckmasters Whitetail	Combat Handguns	Survive**	Soldier of Fortune	Shooting Times	Gunlist
Deer & Deer Hunting	Complete Rifleman		SWAT	SHOT Business	Muzzle Blasts
Ducks Unlimited	Guns & Ammo		Weapons for Military and Police	Shotgun News	Precision Shooting
Fishing & Hunting News	Guns & Gear			Whitetail Business	Rifleshooter
Fur-Fish-Game	Gun Collector				Shoot!
Game & Fish	Guns				Shooting Sportsman
Gray's Sporting Journal	Guns of the Old West				Shooting Times
Gun Dog	Gun Week				Shotguns (Sport/hunting)
Hunting	Gun World**				Shotgun Sports
Michigan Hunt & Fish	Handgunning				Single Shot Rifle Journal

Midwest Outdoors
New York Sportsman
North American Hunter
North American Whitetail
Northwoods Group
Pennsylvania Sportsman
Peterson's Hunting
Sports Afield
Texas Fish & Game
Turkey & Turkey Hunting
Varmint Hunter
Vermont Outdoor
Western Outdoor Grouser
Point Almanac
Whitetail Hunting Strategies
Wildfowl
Wing & Shot
Wisconsin Outdoor Journal
Woods and Waters USA

Handguns
Handloader
Rifle
Rifle & Shotgun
Single Shot Exchange
Small Arms Review
Small Caliber News
Western Outdoors
Women & Guns

Skeet Shooting
Sporting Clays
Tactical Shooter
Trap & Field

**Magazine that is no longer published.
I am grateful to my research assistant, Domingo Villaronga, for compiling this list.

45

Women Act's provision allowing victims of domestic violence to sue their attackers in federal courts.[24] In all three cases, the Court held that Congress lacked authority to regulate what are essentially intrastate matters that our constitutional federalism leaves to the states.

The Supreme Court's 1995 5–4 decision in *Lopez v. U.S.* may pose a hurdle for some future federal firearms regulation. The Court struck down the federal Gun Free School Zones Act, which made it a federal crime for any person to carry a firearm within 1000 feet of a school. According to the justices, Congress could not criminalize intrastate gun carrying under its commerce clause authority merely on the ground that school violence affects learning which affects interstate commerce. Unlike the felon-in-possession law, the 1990 Gun Free School Zones Act did not require proof in each case that the firearm had moved in interstate commerce. Congress subsequently re-passed the law imposing just such a requirement. Nevertheless, the willingness of the Supreme Court to closely examine federal firearms regulation casts a shadow over future federal gun control initiatives.*

United States v. Printz, which is discussed in detail in chapter 5, held that Congress could not constitutionally force state and local law enforcement officers to carry out Brady-mandated background checks. Congress cannot commandeer state and local agencies to implement and administer federal programs. This decision would make it difficult, if not impossible, for Congress to establish comprehensive licensing and registration, unless it were to be a fully federally operated system.

Today there is no federal agency capable of administering and enforcing comprehensive gun controls. There is no federal police force with the authority or resources to carry out street-level policing necessary to en-

---

*The Court's *Morrison* decision, striking down part of the Violence against Women Act, reaffirms *Lopez* and bolsters the conclusion that, in the future, the Court will scrutinize federal crime control legislation. As the Court said, "Given these findings and petitioners' arguments, the concern that we expressed in *Lopez* that Congress might use the Commerce Clause to completely obliterate the Constitution's distinction between national and local authority seems well founded. The reasoning that petitioners advance seeks to follow the but-for causal chain from the initial occurrence of violent crime (the suppression of which has always been the prime object of the states' police power) to every attenuated effect upon interstate commerce. If accepted, petitioners' reasoning would allow Congress to regulate any crime as long as the nationwide, aggregated impact of that crime has substantial effects on employment, production, transit, or consumption. Indeed, if Congress may regulate gender-motivated violence, it would be able to regulate murder or any other type of violence since gender-motivated violence, as a subset of all violent crime, is certain to have lesser economic impacts than the larger class of which it is a part." *United States v. Morrison*, 120 S. Ct. 1740 (2000).

force gun laws against individuals. The BATF, of course, has experience in administering and enforcing certain gun laws. But that experience may be as much a liability as an asset. To say that the agency has never been popular would be an understatement.[25] Indeed, it has drawn constant criticism, deserved or undeserved, for violating the rights of law-abiding gun owners and for harassing licensed dealers. The 1993 assault on the Branch Davidian compound in Waco, Texas, was a fiasco that will take many years for the agency to overcome.[26] The scandal surrounding the "good old boys" round-up, the annual retreat at which some agents flaunted vulgar racist and sexist signs and behaved disgracefully, will make it very difficult for the agency to win greater authority and increased resources.[27]

Congress has micromanaged the BATF in ways that it would never consider for other enforcement agencies. For example, Congress restricted the kinds of records that the agency can maintain, has forbidden the agency to utilize electronic data processing, and has limited unannounced audits of FFLs by the BATF to one annually.[28] All this might change, but the agency's history is an obstacle to Congress's willingness to expand the agency's resources.

The problems standing in the way of comprehensive federal firearms regulation are so great that one feels compelled to reconsider whether national regulation is necessary. Crime rates differ from state to state and, more important, from locality to locality even within the same state. Most counties have very little crime. The most serious crime problems are found in the big cities, which is also where all sorts of social problems are concentrated: poverty, deteriorating neighborhoods, unemployment, weak social control, teenage pregnancy, poor schools, and so on. Support for gun controls also differs greatly from locality to locality. Why not leave firearms policies to states and cities, as, of course, is the current situation?

The conventional answer is that one state's firearms policy might undermine another's; if guns migrate from weak control states to strong control states, only national action will protect the strong control states. Why, gun controllers ask, should New York's gun control efforts be thwarted by South Carolina's or Wyoming's policies? But South Carolina and Wyoming citizens could ask why their preferences should be subordinated to the New Yorkers' interests. Furthermore, they are likely to charge that New Yorkers are conveniently blaming far away states for the big city's crime problem.* It is convenient, they may charge, for New Yorkers to avoid

---

*An exhaustive investigation of the source of Boston crime guns by a team of researchers from Harvard's Kennedy School of Government dispels the widely held belief that Boston youth gangs obtain the vast majority of their guns from southern

coming to grips with failed social policies, horrendous rates of violence in the minority communities, and inept political leaders by blaming inanimate guns and "rednecks." Is New York really doing everything possible to address the social problems of its citizens and to apprehend and punish violent criminals? How can we be sure that if South Carolinians and Wyoming citizens turn in all their guns, crime rates in the big midwestern and eastern cities would decline?

The National Rifle Association

Even if a large majority prefers a certain policy, a small, intense minority group which raises money, works for candidates, gets out the vote, and casts its ballots solely according to which candidate best supports its single issue can defeat that policy. In this case, gun owners have on their side one of the most powerful, if not THE most powerful, single-issue lobbying organization, the National Rifle Association.*

Historically, the NRA's[29] key assets have been the simplicity and clarity of its message, its ability to communicate with its members, the fervent commitment of its core membership, and money to spend on lobbying and elections. Political scientist Robert J. Spitzer observes: "The key to the NRA's effectiveness lies in its highly motivated mass membership and the organization's ability to bring pressure from that membership to bear at key moments and places."[30] The NRA has long been extremely efficient in exhorting members to make their voices heard. The NRA's core message

---

states with lax gun laws. Contrary to expectations, 34% of traceable guns were first sold in Massachusetts (which has extremely strict gun control laws) and an additional 15% were first sold in New England states. Office of Juvenile Justice Programs and Delinquency Prevention, *Promising Strategies to Reduce Gun Violence*, p. 28.

*The NRA is not the only organization that lobbies on behalf of gun owners' rights. The American Firearms Council, "an industry educational foundation," lobbies against gun controls and promotes firearms safety. The American Shooting Sports Council, the trade association of the firearms industry, campaigns against many proposed gun controls. Citizens Committee for the Right to Keep and Bear Arms claims a membership of 600,000, affiliates in all 50 states, and more than 100 members of Congress on its national advisory committee. Other gun owners' rights organizations include Democrats for the Second Amendment, Doctors for Integrity in Policy Research, Doctors for Responsible Gun Ownership, Firearms Owners against Crime, Gun Owners of America, Independence Institute, Jews for the Preservation of Firearms Ownership, Lawyers' Second Amendment Society, National Firearms Association, and the Second Amendment Foundation. For information on all these organizations, see Glenn H. Utter, *Encyclopedia of Gun Control and Gun Rights*.

is that: (1) gun control proposals are a smoke screen for confiscation, (2) the Second Amendment constitutes an absolute bar to gun controls, and (3) no gun control has ever, or will ever, work.

A small minority of NRA members are the kind of one-issue true believers that make politicians sit up and take notice. An academic commentator or policymaker who talks about gun control on a radio talk show can be sure that one of these hard core members will call in. No matter where a forum on gun control is held, the conveners can count on an NRA member being present, whether invited or not. At every town meeting where a politician appears, an NRA member will invariably demand to know the representative's position on gun controls.

The NRA has benefited enormously from its close working relationship with the Republican Party leadership. The NRA endorsed Ronald Reagan in the 1980 election, the first time the organization had ever supported a presidential candidate.[31] Perhaps to reciprocate, President Reagan addressed the organization's 1983 convention in Phoenix. He told the NRA members that "good organizations don't just happen. They take root in a body of shared beliefs. They flow from strong leadership with vision, initiative, and determination to reach great goals. May I just say we have great respect for your fine, effective leaders in Washington."[32] Basking in the glow of presidential support, the NRA set its sights on scaling back the 1968 Gun Control Act (GCA).

The NRA's attack on the GCA partially succeeded with passage of the Firearms Owners' Protection Act of 1986 (FOPA). Among other things, the law permitted some interstate rifle and shotgun sales,[33] eased dealers' recordkeeping responsibilities,[34] and limited BATF inspections of dealers to one per year.[35] However, even as the NRA was savoring its legislative success, its strength was ebbing due to power struggles, leadership instability, financial problems, estrangement from long-time law enforcement allies, and the ability of Handgun Control Inc. and other pro–gun control interests to define the NRA as extremist.[36]

The NRA suffered a major political defeat when, by opposing legislation to prohibit armor piercing ammunition (1986), it alienated the law enforcement establishment. After passage of the Brady Law (1993) and the Assault Weapons Ban (1994), some gun control proponents, as well as some scholars and observers, declared the NRA in decline. That prediction proved premature. The NRA changed leadership, reorganized, and rejuvenated.

In the 1994 federal election, the NRA campaigned across the country for pro-gun candidates and against congresspersons and senators who had voted for Brady and/or the Assault Weapons Ban. It contributed large sums to individual candidates' campaigns and, through its PAC, the Political

Victory Fund, spent an even larger sum attacking pro–gun control politicians. The Republicans won a huge victory, gaining control of both Houses of Congress for the first time in a generation. Tom Foley, Democratic Speaker of the House of Representatives, and Jack Brooks, chairman of the House Judiciary Committee, were both defeated; both attributed defeat to the anti–gun control forces. President Clinton blamed the election debacle for the Democrats on the NRA. He said that "the NRA is the reason the Republicans control the House,"[37] and that "the fight for the assault weapons ban cost 20 members their seats in Congress." Upon becoming the first Republican House Speaker in 50 years, Newt Gingrich announced that no gun control legislation would reach the House floor.

The 1994 election demonstrated that the NRA could mobilize its 3-million-plus members and gun owners generally.[38] This voting bloc, according to Harris and Gallup polls, ranges in size from 23 to 27 million voters.[39] Those who viewed the NRA favorably voted 72% to 28% in favor of the Republican candidates.

Charlton Heston, the movie star, was elected the NRA's vice president in 1997 and its president in 1998. In 1999, *Fortune* magazine ranked the NRA second on its "Power 25" lobbying list.[40] In 2000, the NRA replaced the American Association of Retired Persons (AARP) as the most influential lobbying organization in the nation (see table 3.4).[41] In the same year, the Institute for Legislative Action, the NRA's lobbying wing, raised an unprecedented $25 million, while its political action committee, the Political Victory Fund, also outpaced past years by raising $4 million.

Gun control was not a high-profile issue in the 2000 presidential debates or even in the campaigns, perhaps both candidates cautiously avoided antagonizing either of the competing sides. However, the NRA and the gun magazines expressed great anxiety about the gun controls that might accompany a Gore presidency. Consequently, the gun owners' rights groups worked hard for Bush's election. Voters with guns in their homes cast their votes for Bush 61% to Gore's 36%. This may well have been decisive in key states like Arkansas, Tennessee, and West Virginia, all of which went for Bush.

Looking back on the election, some Democratic leaders, including vice presidential candidate Senator Joe Lieberman (D-Conn.), opined that the Democrats' association with gun controls cost a Gore/Lieberman victory in crucial swing states. Lieberman noted, "We lost a number of voters who, on almost every other issue, realized they'd be better off with Al Gore. They were anxious about what would happen [with respect to gun control] if Al was elected. This one matters a lot to people who otherwise want to vote for us."[42] Democratic Party leaders worry that the Clinton adminis-

Table 3.4. *Fortune* Magazine's "Power 25" Top Lobbying Groups (2000)

Rank	Association	Previous Rank
1	National Rifle Association of America	2
2	American Association of Retired Persons	1
3	National Federation of Independent Business	2
4	American Israel Public Affairs Committee	4
5	Association of Trial Lawyers of America	6
6	AFL-CIO	5
7	Chamber of Commerce of the United States of America	7
8	National Beer Wholesalers Association	19
9	National Association of Realtors	15
10	National Association of Manufacturers	14
11	National Association of Home Builders of the United States	16
12	American Medical Association	13
13	American Hospital Association	31
14	National Education Association of the United States	9
15	American Farm Bureau Federation	21
16	Motion Picture Association of America	17
17	National Association of Broadcasters	20
18	National Right to Life Committee	8
19	Health Insurance Association of America	25
20	National Restaurant Association	10
21	National Governors Association	12
22	Recording Industry Association of America	40
23	American Bankers Association	11
24	Pharmaceutical Research & Manufacturers of America	28
25	International Brotherhood of Teamsters	23

tration's antigun legacy is hurting the party among white men, rural residents, and southerners.

The gun control movement is gaining strength, but for many years it will be no match for the well-funded and well-organized NRA.[43] This is demonstrated by the NRA's success in getting "shall issue" laws passed in at least 28 state legislatures and, after the 1999 Columbine high school massacre, in preventing passage of the federal Gun Show Accountability Act,[44] which would have extended Brady background checks to all firearm sales at gun shows. In 2001, the NRA succeeded in repealing a Florida law that mandated that pawnbrokers keep data on guns and gun purchasers. Even though the pawnbrokers and police favored the controls, the NRA successfully pressed for its elimination.[45]

The NRA's opposition to practically every gun control proposal is substantially explained by its belief that each proposal is a step toward prohibition and confiscation, just what happened in the United Kingdom. In fact, many gun controllers (e.g., the Violence Policy Center's Josh Sugarman and the Communitarian Network's Amitai Etzioni) make no secret of their desire to prohibit all nongovernmental ownership of firearms. A number of bills to disarm the populace have been introduced into Congress during the past two decades (see chapter 10). If prohibition and confiscation were taken off the table by a clear Supreme Court ruling recognizing an individual's right to keep and bear arms, subject only (like all other rights) to reasonable regulation concerning types of weapons and time, place, and manner of carrying weapons, regulation like licensing and registration might be politically possible. But if gun control proponents deny that gun owners have any rights, policy debate on the appropriate regulation of weaponry will continue to take on the character of a life or death, all or nothing, struggle.[46]

The Second Amendment

The regulation of weaponry is not just a technical problem. It is a highly charged ideological and emotional issue that carries a tremendous amount of symbolic baggage. For American society, the debate over gun control is more like the debates over abortion and school prayer than like a debate over automobile safety. Millions of Americans, including a significant percentage of the intellectual elite, believe that guns are bad in themselves and that owning them is at best misguided and at worst pathological. For millions of American gun owners, the right to keep and bear arms is connected to freedom and democracy; it is an article of faith similar to the belief that other Americans have in the centrality of freedom of speech and religion. That many Americans dismiss the right to bear arms as a myth that has no legal or constitutional reality is a challenge to the believers' worldview and an affront to their very status in American society. It is just a short step to seeing the proponents of gun prohibition as "enemies" to be resisted and condemned.

Pro– and anti–gun control proponents sharply disagree about whether the Second Amendment poses an obstacle to gun controls.[47] Gun control proponents argue that the Second Amendment has nothing to do with individual rights; it guarantees only that states can maintain organized militia units. They point to an unbroken line of court decisions that reject Second Amendment challenges to federal, state, and local gun controls.[48] Gun owners' rights advocates cite a large and impressive oeuvre of mostly historical scholarship that demonstrates that the founding fathers and, subsequently, the authors and ratifiers of the Fourteenth Amendment, intended the Second Amendment to protect the individual American's right to be armed.[49]

There is much to be said on both sides of the constitutional debate. The great majority of state constitutions have clauses protecting the right of gun ownership. The only states whose constitutions do *not* contain a right to bear arms are Iowa, California, Maryland, New Jersey, New York, and Minnesota.[50] However, Iowa's, California's, and New Jersey's constitutions explicitly protect the right to "self-defense."[51] Some state constitutions use the same language as the Second Amendment, but several explicitly protect the individual's right to keep and bear arms. Consider Vermont's constitution, enacted in 1777: "That the people have a right to bear arms for the defense of themselves and the State—and as standing armies in time of peace are dangerous to liberty, they ought not to be kept up; and that the military should be kept under strict subordination to and governed by the civil power."[52]

Pennsylvania's constitutional right to bear arms is considered to be the precursor to the Second Amendment.[53] Enacted in 1790, at the time that the Bill of Rights was being ratified, it states: "The right of the citizens to bear arms in defence of themselves and the State shall not be questioned."[54] This language has always been interpreted by Pennsylvania courts to protect the right of all Pennsylvanians, not just militiamen, to possess firearms.[55]

Oklahoma's constitution, enacted in 1907, explicitly protects the right to keep a gun at home, while subjecting the carrying of concealed weapons to regulation: "The right of a citizen to keep and bear arms in defense of his home, person, or property, or in aid of the civil power, when thereunto legally summoned, shall never be prohibited; but nothing herein contained shall prevent the Legislature from regulating the carrying of weapons."

In recent years, a number of states have added gun ownership rights to their constitutions.[56] For example, Wisconsin amended its constitution so that "the people have the right to keep and bear arms for security, defense, hunting, recreation or any other lawful purpose."[57] These state constitutional provisions would not protect gun owners from federal gun controls (assuming such controls were permissible under the federal constitution), but they protect gun owners against some state and local gun controls.

The Second Amendment to the U.S. Constitution states: "A well regulated militia being necessary to the security of a free state, the right of the people to keep and bear arms shall not be abridged." In *U.S. v. Cruikshank*, a nineteenth-century case, the U.S. Supreme Court held that the Second Amendment was only a protection against *federal* infringements of a right to bear arms.[58] But this decision predated the Supreme Court's twentieth-century decisions *incorporating* various Bill of Rights guarantees into the Fourteenth Amendment's due process clause, with the consequence of guaranteeing those rights against violation by state and local governments, as well as by the federal government. It is not at all clear that mid-nineteenth-century judges were oblivious to any right to keep and bear arms. Consider this passage from the Supreme Court's infamous decision in *Dred Scott v. Sandford* (1856),[59] in which the Supreme Court held that slaves and their descendants could claim no rights of citizenship. What is interesting from our perspective is the Court's understanding of what are the rights of citizenship. The Supreme Court pointed out that the framers could not have intended that slaves or their descendants ever be citizens because that

> would give to persons of the Negro race, who were recognized as citizens in any one State of the Union, the right to enter every other State whenever they pleased, singly or in companies, without pass or passport, and without obstruction, to sojourn there as long as they pleased, to go where they pleased at every hour of the day or night without molestation, unless they committed some violation of law for which a white man would be punished; and it would give them the full liberty of speech in public and in private upon all subjects upon which its own citizens might speak; to hold public meetings upon political affairs, *and to keep and carry arms wherever they went.* And all this would be done in the face of the subject race of the same color, both free and slaves, and inevitably producing discontent and insubordination among them, and endangering the peace and safety of the State. (emphasis added)

Yale Law School professor Akhil Amar argues that the right of individuals to be armed was very much the intention of the drafters and ratifiers of the Fourteenth Amendment.[60] After the Civil War, the southern states quickly passed "black codes" that explicitly denied the newly freed slaves the right to keep and bear arms. The debates in Congress in the 1860s over the Civil Rights Act and the Fourteenth Amendment were laced with comments about the need to assure that the freed slaves not be kept disarmed and thereby subservient, and that they be able to enjoy the same right to keep and bear arms as white citizens.

The Supreme Court has rendered only one Second Amendment decision in the twentieth century. In *U.S. v. Miller* (1939), the Court held that, in making it a crime to possess an unregistered sawed-off shotgun, the NFA did not violate the Second Amendment.[61] Gun rights advocates say that the precedential value of the case is only that people are not guaranteed access to gangster weapons, like sawed-off shotguns, and that by negative inference they do have a right to arm themselves with traditional personal firearms. Gun controllers argue that the Second Amendment does not guarantee anybody anything and that *Miller* means that there is no personal right to possess firearms in the U.S. Constitution. Focusing on the amendment's first clause, they argue that the amendment means only that Congress could not abolish the state militia, now the National Guard.[62]

Gun rights advocates believe that the Second Amendment guarantees every law-abiding American adult a right to keep and bear personal firearms. "Implicit in the Bill of Rights, as in the entire structure of the Constitution, are the twin hallmarks of traditional liberal thought: trust in the people; and distrust in government."[63] Some proponents of this interpretation stress that the right to keep and bear arms was meant to guarantee protection against government tyranny.[64] Liberal constitutional law theorist, William Van Alstyne, finds an individual rights view of the Second Amendment in a textual reading of the amendment. He argues that the amendment "speaks to sources of security within a free state, within which . . . 'the right of the people to keep and bear arms shall not be infringed.' " He explains that this language guarantees the individual's right to have arms for self-defense and self-preservation.[65] Harvard Law School Professor Lawrence Tribe, a person closely associated with liberal politics and the Democratic Party, also concludes that "it is impossible to deny that some right to bear arms is among the rights of American citizens."[66]

Perhaps the Supreme Court will take an opportunity to interpret the Second Amendment in a recent Texas case. The U.S. District Court for the Northern District of Texas declared unconstitutional the federal law (18 U.S.C. sec. 922 [g][8]) which makes it a crime to possess a firearm while under a restraining order for domestic violence as applied in a situation where the state divorce court, which issued the restraining order, had made no particularized findings that the defendant posed a threat to his estranged wife. The district court held that the Second Amendment guarantees a personal right to keep and bear arms (*U.S. v. Emerson*, 46 F. Supp. 2d 598 [1999]). Two years later, the 5th Circuit Court of Appeals (Nov. 2001) affirmed, holding that "we find that the history of the Second Amendment reinforces the plain meaning of the text, namely that it protects individual Americans in their right to keep and bear arms whether or not they are members of a select militia or performing active military service or training."

Even if the U.S. Supreme Court ultimately declared that the Second Amendment does not guarantee an individual right to keep and bear arms, which may never happen, the contrary belief is strongly rooted in U.S. and English history, in the constitutions of most U.S. states, and in a mountain of pro-gun scholarship. Many gun owners *believe* that possession of firearms is a right of American citizenship and would not be persuaded otherwise, even by a U.S. Supreme Court decision to the contrary, just as death penalty opponents believe that the Supreme Court was wrongheaded in declaring executions to be constitutionally permissible.* Jeffrey Snyder made the point aggressively in his 1993 *Public Interest* article, "A Nation of Cowards":

> The repeal of the Second Amendment would no more render the outlawing of firearms legitimate than the repeal of the due process clause of the Fifth Amendment would authorize the government to imprison and kill people at will. A government that abrogates any of the Bill of Rights, with or without majoritarian approval, forever votes illegitimately, becomes tyrannical, and loses the moral right to govern.

Conclusion

U.S. federalism, a large and entrenched gun subculture, the lobbying strength of the NRA, and the widespread belief of millions of Americans that the Constitution guarantees their right to keep and bear arms pose major political obstacles to the passage of federal gun controls, other than those directed at punishing criminal use of guns. Beyond that, the fervent belief by a large percentage of gun owners that gun controllers ultimately intend to confiscate all personal firearms means that if any strong gun controls were enacted, they would encounter widespread noncompliance and resistance, including jury nullification. Since approximately 45% of American households contain a firearm, there is nearly a 100% chance that every 12-person jury will contain at least one gun owner, which is all that would be needed to prevent conviction.

The analysis in this book does not depend on which interpretation of the Second Amendment is correct. If the Second Amendment preserves only the state militia and not the individual's right to keep and bear arms, there is no constitutional limitation on federal firearms policy, as long as Congress has authority to legislate under the commerce clause or some other clause. In that case, the policy questions this book addresses are crucial: Are there any practical, feasible, enforceable, and cost-effective

---

*Gun owners' rights proponents also argue that the right of self-defense (embodied in the concept of due process) guarantees the individual a right to possess whatever weapons are necessary to defend one's self successfully. See William Meyerhoffer, "Statutory Restrictions on Weapons Possession: Must the Right to Self Defense Fall Victim."

options for more effective federal regulation of firearms and firearm owners?

If the gun rights advocates are correct, and the Second Amendment
guarantees individual Americans a right to keep and bear arms, gun control is certainly not rendered moot. Because all rights are subject to limitations (i.e., time, place, manner, restrictions on free speech), reasonable
gun controls would be compatible with the Second Amendment. Congress
could still impose all the policy options (except firearms *prohibition*) examined in this book.

II

AMERICA'S DOMINANT GUN CONTROL PARADIGM

In order to assess what gun control options are available to the United States, it is necessary to have a firm grasp on the gun controls we have now. Part II provides an in-depth look at the 1993 Brady Law, the most important federal gun control law since the 1968 Gun Control Act (GCA). The Brady Law extended the model of federal firearms legislation, begun by the 1938 FFA and carried forward by the 1968 GCA, that seeks to keep handguns out of the hands of dangerous individuals. The Brady Law requires federally licensed firearms dealers (FFLs) to submit the names of prospective firearms purchasers to the government so that a background check can be carried out to determine whether the purchaser is ineligible to buy a gun.

Chapter 4 assays the politics of the Brady Law, illuminating the time, effort, and political circumstances required to pass even modest federal gun control legislation. Chapter 5 sets forth the details of the Brady Law and explains the significance of the Supreme Court's *Printz* decision that held one part of the Brady Law unconstitutional. Chapter 6 exposes the gaping holes in the Brady Law's regulatory web, while chapter 7 evaluates the Brady Law's impact on violent crime.

4

The Politics of the Brady Law

The nation's leading gun control group laid nine human-shaped cardboard cutouts on the Capitol lawn—chalk-outlined facsimiles of sprawled murder victims. On a Monday morning in September, Jim and Sarah Brady were turning up the heat on Congress, trying to force a quick vote on a five-business day waiting period for handgun purchases. . . .

Brady, the former White House press secretary . . . groaned as he rose from his wheelchair. He stood unsteadily with a cane before 20 or so reporters and read mechanically from a prepared statement. . . .

"Give members of Congress the chance to stand up for public safety, to stand up for law enforcement, to stand up for these doctors who daily see what bodies riddled with bullets really look like," he said, demanding a vote on the legislation named for him, the Brady bill. . . .

As Brady spoke, earnest staffers from the organization Sarah Brady chairs, Handgun Control Inc., passed out reams of statistics and other printed materials, including a four-foot long scroll detailing handgun horrors. Attached to it, a purple ribbon—HCI's gun control symbol.

—Tom Diemer, "Opponents of NRA Are Chipping away Money,
    Influence Used to Prod Congress"

The 1968 Gun Control Act passed in the wake of the national trauma caused by the assassinations of Robert F. Kennedy and Martin Luther King,

Jr., and horrific rioting in cities across the United States. By contrast, the Brady Law did not result from a cataclysmic event but from persistent lobbying by Handgun Control, Inc. (HCI), by far the most important gun control lobbying organization in American history. To be sure, HCI was able to build on a great deal of public pro–gun control sentiment, including the support of leading print and electronic media and consistently large pro-Brady majorities in public opinion polls (see table 4.1). Nevertheless, it took seven years, from the time it was first submitted to Congress, for the Brady Bill to become law. It probably never would have happened had the Democrats not controlled both Houses of Congress and the White House between 1993 and 1995. Thus, on the one hand, the Brady Law could be cited for the proposition that reasonable, albeit modest, federal gun control is politically possible. On the other hand, the tortuous road that the Brady Law's proponents had to traverse and the negative political fallout for the Democrats could be cited for the proposition that passage of even modest gun control takes monumental effort plus luck and imposes heavy political costs.

The History of HCI: The Growth of a Gun Control Lobby

After Dr. Martin Borinsky was robbed at gunpoint in the early 1970s, he set out to do something about the ready availability of handguns. In 1974, he founded the National Council to Control Handguns (NCCH).[1] In the early years, NCCH's staff consisted of Borinsky, ex-CIA agent Ed Welles, and Nelson T. "Pete" Shields, whose 23-year-old son had been murdered by a serial killer. Shields became executive director in 1976 and chairman of the board in 1978. The organization's name changed to Handgun Control, Inc., in 1980. HCI positioned itself as a moderate alternative to the National Council to Ban Handguns, a coalition of organizations advocating handgun disarmament. HCI soon became the most prominent advocate for gun controls.

In 1981, Shields published *Guns Don't Die, People Do*,[2] a book that laid out HCI's arguments for handgun control. He movingly recounted his son's murder and presented data on the "causal role" of handguns in robberies, rapes, and murders.[3] Shields attributed the extraordinarily high U.S. violent crime rate, compared to western European countries, to America's lax gun policy.[4] He argued that effective gun control could be achieved, without interfering with the interests of hunters and sportsmen, by focusing regulation on handguns. At the end of the book, Shields exhorted readers to write to members of Congress, state and local officials, and "to anyone who will listen" in support of more gun controls.[5]

John Hinckley's 1981 attack on President Ronald Reagan and Press Sec-

Table 4.1. Newspaper Editorials and Op-Ed Pages for and against the Brady Bill, 1990–1999

Newspaper	For	Against
Arizona Republic	Apr. 2, 1993	Dec. 30, 1993
	Dec. 13, 1993	Aug. 5, 1994
Arkansas Democratic Gazette		Jan. 20, 1994
		Feb. 24, 1994
		Mar. 31, 1994
Atlanta Journal-Constitution	Apr. 1, 1991*	
	May 21, 1991	
	Nov. 12, 1993	
	Aug. 12, 1999*	
Baltimore Sun	Jan. 27, 1995	
Boston Globe	May 7, 1991	
	Aug. 23, 1993	
Buffalo News	Feb. 17, 1993	Nov. 13, 1993
	Dec. 11, 1993	Dec. 12, 1993
	July 23, 1998	
Charleston Gazette	Nov. 14, 1994	Sept. 9, 1996
Chicago Sun-Times	Sept. 7, 1993	
	Nov. 12, 1993	
Chicago Tribune	July 18, 1993	
Christian Science Monitor	May 13, 1991*	
Clarion-Ledger (Mississippi)	Sept. 9, 1999*	
Cleveland Plain Dealer		Dec. 19, 1993
Commercial Appeal (Memphis, Tenn.)	Aug. 23, 1993	
Dallas Morning News	Oct. 26, 1993	
Denver Rocky Mountain News	Feb. 9, 1994	
Des Moines Register	Dec. 5, 1993	
Herald (Georgia)	May 21, 1999*	
Houston Chronicle	Feb. 28, 1993*	Mar. 3, 1993
	Nov. 12, 1993*	
	Nov. 15, 1993	
Kentucky Post	Aug. 12, 1999*	
Los Angeles Times	Nov. 10, 1993*	Nov. 24, 1992
Louisville Courier-Journal	Oct. 3, 1992	
Milwaukee Journal Sentinel	Apr. 23, 1999*	
New York Times		May 24, 1990
News & Record (Greensboro, N.C.)		Feb. 18, 1994
		Nov. 21, 1995
Newsday	Nov. 26, 1993	Aug. 25, 1993
	Dec. 24, 1993	
	July 18, 1999*	
Orlando Sentinel Tribune	Apr. 10, 1991	Mar. 10, 1994*
	Apr. 22, 1991	
	May 10, 1991	
	Mar. 27, 1993	
Phoenix Gazette		Sept. 22, 1993

(continued)

Table 4.1. Newspaper Editorials and Op-Ed Pages for and against the Brady Bill, 1990–1999 (Continued)

Newspaper	For	Against
Pittsburgh Post-Gazette	Nov. 16, 1993	Mar. 14, 1993
		June 6, 1993
		Dec. 9, 1993
Rockford Register Star	Sept. 11, 1999*	
Salt Lake Tribune	May 13, 1999*	
San Diego Union-Tribune	May 6, 1991	
	May 10, 1991	
	May 11, 1991	
San Francisco Chronicle		Apr. 5, 1991
		Dec. 10, 1993
Seattle Times		Apr. 7, 1991
		May 23, 1991
		July 1, 1991
		Nov. 30, 1993
St. Louis Post-Dispatch	Aug. 11, 1999*	Apr. 4, 1991*
		Apr. 17, 1993
St. Petersburg Times	Nov. 27, 1993	
Sun-Sentinel (Fort Lauderdale, Fla.)	Nov. 27, 1993	Sept. 24, 1993
		Nov. 21, 1993
		Nov. 28, 1993
		Dec. 1, 1993
Telegraph	June 22, 1999*	
Tennessean (Nashville)	July 19, 1999*	
Times-Picayune (New Orleans)		Aug. 25, 1993
		Nov. 12, 1993
Union Leader		Apr. 8, 1991
		May 10, 1991
University Wire (Minnesota Daily)	Aug. 12, 1998	
USA Today	May 10, 1991	Oct. 1, 1993
	Sept. 1, 1992*	
	Nov. 22,1993*	
	Nov. 26, 1993	
Washington Post	May 10, 1991	Dec. 2, 1999
	May 13, 1991	
	May 30, 1991	
	Dec. 12, 1992	
	Nov. 11, 1993	
	Nov. 16, 1993	
	Nov. 25, 1993	
	Dec. 1, 1993	
Washington Times	Nov. 23, 1993	Apr. 8, 1991
	July 1, 1994	Dec. 19, 1993
		June 8, 1997
Wisconsin State Journal	Sept. 18, 1992	

* = editorials
Source: LEXIS-NEXIS Group (search June 1, 2000).

retary James Brady with a .22-caliber handgun, like the Kennedy and King assassinations, triggered many calls for more gun controls. Reagan, though critically injured, pulled through surgery and recovered his full health. Brady was left paralyzed. Despite the assassination attempt, the Reagan administration remained staunchly anti–gun control. James Brady and his wife, Sarah, remained silent for several years.

In 1983, HCI established the Center to Prevent Handgun Violence (CPHV) as its research and education arm. The CPHV qualified for tax-deductible contributions and foundation grants, which HCI, as a lobbying organization, could not accept. HCI and the CPHV had separate legal identities but the same president and overlapping boards of directors. Charles Orisin, the first president of HCI and the CPHV, implemented a modern mass mailing strategy to increase membership. Ironically, HCI benefited from the existence of the behemoth NRA because the print and electronic news media required a counterweight to the NRA when preparing stories on gun violence and gun control.

In 1985, HCI's fortunes dramatically improved when Sarah Brady joined the organization. She decided to join the campaign for more effective gun controls after her five-year-old son picked up a loaded gun from under the seat in a friend's truck and pointed it at Sarah's head. The cool-headed mother disarmed her son, but this incident, combined with the shooting of her husband four years earlier, persuaded her to become active in the gun control movement.

At Orisin's urging, Brady threw herself into the fight to prevent passage of the NRA–backed Firearms Owners' Protection Act, which sought to roll back the GCA. While FOPA ultimately passed in 1986, the battle transformed Sarah and James Brady into national symbols for the gun control movement. In 1989, Sarah Brady became chairperson of HCI and a full-time campaigner for gun controls. In 2001, HCI changed its name to the Brady Campaign against Handgun Violence.

Sarah and James Brady's importance to the ultimate passage of the Brady Law cannot be exaggerated. James Brady was extremely well liked by the Washington press corps. After the assassination attempt, because of his courage in the face of horrific injuries, journalists held him in even higher regard. At crucial points in the debate over the Brady Bill, James Brady held press conferences and testified before congressional committees. He also campaigned for pro–Brady Law congressmen, such as Mike Synar (D-Okla.).*

---

*The NRA spent $128,397 to thwart Synar's 1992 reelection bid. Synar kept his seat, declaring victory over the NRA, but an NRA-backed candidate defeated him

A lifelong Republican and an attractive, tireless, and articulate speaker, Sarah Brady became an even more important asset to HCI than her husband. In December 1990, *Glamour* magazine proclaimed Sarah Brady one of its "Ten Women of the Year," for her efforts to reduce "the handgun epidemic in the U.S." In 1991, she was instrumental in persuading former president Ronald Reagan to support the Brady Bill. When presidential candidate Bill Clinton (but not President George Bush) endorsed the Brady Bill in the run up to the 1992 election, Sarah Brady endorsed him. In 1996, she addressed the Democratic National Convention.

In 1992, HCI's board chose Richard Aborn to succeed Orisin. The 39-year-old Aborn had been an assistant district attorney in the Manhattan DA's office where, with District Attorney Robert Morgenthau's approval, he had established a small unit to investigate gun trafficking. He left the DA's office for private practice in 1984, continuing to work on gun control issues as an HCI volunteer. In 1988, Aborn was voted on to the HCI and the CPHV boards of directors. In 1991, he moved to Washington to work for HCI as chief lobbyist for the Brady Law; he worked with the Clinton administration and congressional allies to bring the bill out of committee and to a successful floor vote in both Houses.*

Organization of HCI

HCI, the lobbying entity, is divided into several divisions, each with its own director, including Communications, State Legislation, Law Enforcement Relations, and West Coast Operations. The lobbying effort includes drafting legislation, meeting with legislators and staff, and contributing directly to the political campaigns of pro–gun control candidates. It also operates a political action committee, the National Handgun Control Political Action Committee, which promotes the campaigns of pro–gun control candidates. The NRA grades politicians from "A" (completely supports NRA positions) to "F" (completely opposes NRA efforts). HCI uses the NRA grading scheme to guide its political contributions—give to the "F"s, try to defeat any vulnerable "A"s.

The NRA's lobbying expenditures exceed HCI's by more than 10 to 1.[6] In the six years after passage of the Brady Law, the NRA contributed $4.39

---

in the 1994 Democratic primary. Tom Diemer, "Opponents of NRA are Chipping away Money, Influence Used to Prod Congress," *Cleveland (Ohio) Plain Dealer*.

*Aborn served as president until 1996, when he returned to law practice in New York City. His successor was James Guest. Robert Walker, previously head of HCI's legislative section, succeeded Guest.

million to various House and the Senate campaigns, while HCI contributed $543,299.[7] HCI's budget is about $4.3 million a year, while the NRA spends as much as $141.5 million in a single year.[8] (HCI's largest expenditure for a single candidate was $200,000 for President Clinton in the 1996 presidential election.)[9]

The Center to Prevent Handgun Violence (HCI's research, public information, and litigation wing) publishes the quarterly "Washington Report." It sponsors education programs such as Project Lifeline, a campaign involving health professionals that provides public education on handgun violence and promulgates preventive strategies to reduce handgun injuries and deaths. CPHV's Legal Action Project offers free legal representation to victims of gun violence bringing tort suits against handgun manufacturers. It also assists in defending gun control laws, such as the Assault Weapons Ban.[10] The Law Enforcement Relations Department works with police departments to reduce gun-related crimes and injuries. Likewise, the Gun Interdiction Project works with police departments and other criminal justice personnel to eliminate illegal guns.[11] CPHV's Research Department highlights data and studies that demonstrate that guns cause crime and that gun controls work.

Lobbying the Brady Bill to Victory

HCI had several important assets in the battle over the Brady Bill. First, public opinion polls showed that a large majority of Americans favored the Brady Bill. No doubt, incidents like Patrick Purdy's massacre of school children (5 killed, 29 wounded) in January 1989 reinforced pro–Brady Law opinion. Gallup polls from 1988 to 1993 showed that more than 8 out of 10 respondents favored the passage of the Brady Bill (see figure 4.1).[12] Second, by the early 1990s, HCI and the Brady Bill enjoyed the support of all major law enforcement organizations.

Third, the editorial and op-ed pages of the majority of the nation's newspapers supported the Brady Bill (see table 4.1). Although many commentators recognized that the Brady Bill would not *solve* the problem of handgun violence, they argued that it would be an important step in the right direction and urged prompt action.[13] Consider the following:

- "The Brady Bill [is] a measure so sensible that America should be embarrassed for the lawmakers who failed to muster the courage to support it in the past" (*Los Angeles Times*, Nov. 10, 1993).[14]
- "The Brady gun control bill may be the longest languishing, most overdue, most urgently needed piece of legislation before Congress. . . . It is not too much to ask that the government be allowed

Figure 4.1. Gallup Poll: Nationwide Percentage of Americans Who Favor or Oppose a National Law Requiring a Seven-Day Waiting Period to Conduct a Background Check before a Handgun May Be Purchased

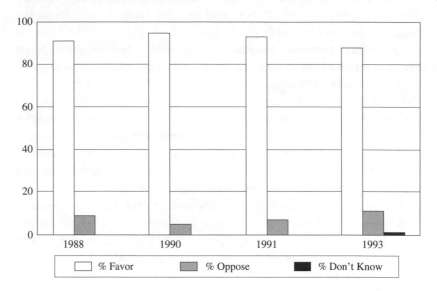

to see if a prospective gun purchaser has killed in the past" (*Boston Globe*, Aug. 23, 1993).[15]

- "Why anyone even listens anymore to the quick-sale handgun hustlers who keep lobbying to weaken the Brady Bill is hard to grasp . . . [the Brady Bill] is a protection for everyone against the obvious terrible dangers of curbside sales of handguns to criminals" (*Washington Post*, Nov. 11, 1993).[16]
- "Though hardly a panacea for urban violence, the Brady Bill provides commonsense regulation for handgun ownership" (*Chicago Sun-Times*, Nov. 12, 1993).[17]
- "Congress needs to go ahead this time and pass the [Brady] Bill. . . . Until something better comes along, it is the best known way to keep handguns out of the hands of those who should not have them" (*Houston Chronicle*, Feb. 28, 1993).[18]

More newspapers criticized the Brady Bill for not going far enough than for going too far.[19] For example, some commentators argued that the bill did not *require* chief law enforcement officers to conduct background checks but merely urged them to do so. Some gun control proponents argued that the Brady Bill would be ineffective and urged repeal of the Second Amendment and prohibition of all civilian ownership of firearms.[20]

Some op-ed writers pointed out that the Brady Law would not prevent criminals from obtaining guns because criminals could get friends and associates to purchase guns for them or they could purchase secondhand guns from nondealers.[21] The NRA predicted that the Brady Law, like other gun controls, would fail; it insisted that money would be better spent on apprehending, prosecuting, and imprisoning violent criminals.[22] Of course, some pro-gun writers warned that the Brady Law was a big step toward handgun prohibition.[23]

HCI's fourth asset was the strong support of some very powerful members of Congress, including Charles Schumer (D-N.Y.) and Senator Howard Metzenbaum (D-Ohio). Like the NRA, HCI did not have to make promises or threats to obtain important legislative support. Many lawmakers hold strong views for and against gun controls because of personal values and experience and/or because of their constituents' beliefs.

In attempting to muster support, HCI tried to shift the focus of debate from "gun control" in principle to the details of the Brady Bill. HCI's lobbyists tried to determine why a legislator was hesitating to support the Brady Bill, then sought a meeting to walk that legislator or his or her aide through the bill, emphasizing its limited impact on law-abiding citizens. If a legislator was worried about alienating a particular group or organization, Aborn and his staff would try to meet with that group.

HCI produced and distributed a great deal of pro–Brady Bill material to legislators, media, nationwide grassroots organizations, and interested individuals. For example, its "Brady Amendment Facts Sheet" labeled the NRA's criticisms "false claims" and sought to rebut them.

1. [The NRA claims that] this law can be extended to include all firearms and be extended beyond seven days.
   Fact: The Brady Amendment applies only to handgun sales and the waiting period could not be extended beyond seven days.
2. A waiting period would never have stopped John Hinckley from shooting the president, Press Secretary James Brady, and two security men.
   Fact: John Hinckley gave a false address on a federal form at a Dallas pawn shop and instantly obtained the handgun used in the assassination attempt. If there had been a waiting period and a background check conducted, it could have been discovered that Hinckley committed a felony by lying about his address on a federal form, and he could have been stopped from purchasing the handgun.
3. The Brady Amendment is de facto registration.
   Fact: The bill would not register or license handguns or handgun owners. Paperwork on approved sales must be destroyed within 60 days.

4. Waiting periods do not prevent criminals from obtaining handguns, because criminals will get guns from other sources.
Fact: The Bureau of Alcohol, Tobacco, and Firearm's study called "Project Identification" found that "the percentage of out-of-state [handgun] purchases is directly proportional to the strength of local firearm regulations." The study found that only 4% of the handguns used in crime in New York City were purchased in the state, most of the rest were purchased in states without waiting periods or background checks.

5. Criminals do not purchase their handguns over the counter and they definitely won't if they have to submit to a waiting period.
Fact: A Department of Justice Study conducted in 1985 called "The Armed Criminal in America" found that at least 21% of criminals obtain their handguns through gun dealers. It has been reported by law enforcement officials across the country that where waiting periods and/or background checks are required, large numbers of criminals and others not qualified to buy handguns have been caught.

6. Police departments would incur major costs by being forced to conduct background checks.
Fact: The Brady Amendment mandates a seven-day waiting period, but it does not mandate background checks. Local police will decide whether or not to conduct background checks and determine the manner in which the checks are conducted.[24]

The fifth HCI asset was the support of numerous state and local organizations working to reduce violence through gun controls and other measures (see table 4.2). In addition to the growing number of organizations solely interested in gun violence, HCI forged alliances with a variety of organizations, such as the American Association of Retired Persons, which supported gun controls among many positions in a broader organizational agenda.[25]

On June 21, 1988, President Ronald Reagan announced his support for waiting periods and background checks for handgun purchasers. In March 1991, on the tenth anniversary of the Hinckley assassination attempt, Reagan, now a former president, endorsed the Brady Bill, thereby providing "cover" for some Republicans who were inclined to vote for the bill.

In the run up to the 1992 presidential election, HCI's chief lobbyist, Gail Hoffman, left HCI to join the Clinton campaign and thereafter functioned as a very effective advocate with candidate Clinton and as a liaison with HCI headquarters. Moreover, thanks in large part to former Ohio attorney general and CPHV board member Lee Fisher, the Democratic Party's 1992 national platform included a pro–Brady Bill plank.

Table 4.2. State and Local Gun Control Organizations

State	Organizations
Alabama	Society against Firearm Endangerment
	Mothers against Violence
Arizona	Handgun Control Activists
California	Californians for Responsible Gun Laws
	Handgun Control, Inc.
	Pacific Center for Violence Prevention
	Women against Gun Violence
	Los Angeles Teens on Target/Youth Alive
	Stop Gun Violence
	Orange County Citizens for the Prevention of Gun Violence
Colorado	Colorado Children's Campaign
	Physician's for Social Responsibility
	SAFE Colorado
	Colorado Coalition against Gun Violence
Connecticut	Connecticut Coalition against Gun Violence
Washington, D.C.	Us Helping Us Network, Inc.
Florida	Florida Coalition to Stop Gun Violence
	MAD DADS of Greater Ocala
Georgia	Georgians against Gun Violence, Inc.
	Georgians United against Gun Violence
Hawaii	Firearms Coalition
	Hawaii Firearms Control Coalition
Illinois	Illinois Counsel against Handgun Violence
	Quad Citizens for Responsible Gun Laws
	Rise High Projects
Indiana	Citizens Concerned about Gun Violence
	GRIEF of Indiana
Iowa	Iowans for the Prevention of Gun Violence
Kansas	Kansans for Handgun Control
	Safe State
Kentucky	Kentuckians' Chapter for Handgun Control
	Kentucky Voice for Crime Victims
Louisiana	Louisiana Ceasefire
Maine	Maine Citizens against Handgun Violence
Maryland	Marylanders against Handgun Abuse
	Rage for Peace
Massachusetts	Americans for a Non-Violent Society
	Citizens for Safety
	Stop Handgun Violence
Michigan	Michigan Citizens for Handgun Control
	SOSAD
	Women against Gun Violence
	Michigan Partnership to Prevent Gun Violence
Minnesota	Citizens for a Safer Minnesota
Missouri	Ad Hoc Group against Crime
	Coalition against Concealed Guns
	Missourians against Handgun Violence
	ENOUGH

(continued)

71

Table 4.2. State and Local Gun Control Organizations (Continued)

State	Organizations
Nebraska	Nebraskans for Responsible Gun Ownership
New Hampshire	Seacoast Advocates for Gun Control
	New Hampshire Ceasefire
New Jersey	Cease Fire New Jersey
New Mexico	New Mexico Ceasefire
	Not Even One
New York	Fellowship of Reconciliation
	Handgun Control, Inc., of New York
	Mothers against Violence
	New Yorkers against Gun Violence
North Carolina	North Carolinians against Gun Violence
Ohio	Handgun Control Federation of Ohio
	LENA
	Ohio Coalition against Gun Violence
Oregon	Oregonians against Gun Violence
Pennsylvania	Pennsylvanians against Handgun Violence
South Carolina	Citizens for a Safer South Carolina
	Alliance for South Carolina's Children
Tennessee	Tennesseans for Responsible Gun Ownership
Texas	Houston Area Violence Prevention
	Physicians for a Violence Free Society
	Texans against Gun Violence
	Zero Accidental Killings
	Texas Crime Prevention Clearing House
Utah	Utahns against Gun Violence
Vermont	Vermonters against Gun Violence
Virginia	Virginians against Handgun Violence
Washington	Mothers against Violence in America
	Washington Cease Fire
Wisconsin	American Trauma Society
	Citizens against Handgun Violence
	Mobilization for Survival
	Wisconsin Anti-Violence Effort

It is time to shut down the weapons bazaars. We support a reasonable waiting period to permit background checks for purchase of handguns, as well as assault weapon controls to ban the possession, sale, importation, and manufacture of the most deadly assault weapons. We do not support efforts to restrict weapons used for legitimate hunting and sporting purposes.

The Brady Bill's opponents stymied the bill by tying it to omnibus crime legislation which was mired down in Congress. Seeking to break this impasse, HCI launched the "Free the Brady Bill Campaign" to persuade Congress to vote up or down on the Brady Bill.[26] HCI mounted press conferences in 13 cities. Aborn and James Brady, standing alongside Mayor David Dinkins, held the lead-off press conference in New York City. On September 1, 1992, Democratic Party presidential candidate Bill Clinton came out in favor of "freeing" and passing the Brady Bill; he reiterated this support throughout the campaign. President Bush took no position.

Law Enforcement Urges Passage

Because most Americans view the police favorably, practically all politicians want to be perceived as "pro-police." (It is a political disaster for a politician or a lobby group to be defined as "anti-police.") Thus, the strong support of the law enforcement establishment for the Brady Bill enabled some hesitant legislators to vote for it.

The Brady Bill's supporters, including the editorial boards of several major newspapers, characterized the battle over the Brady Bill as a referendum on support for the police. For example, a September 1990 *New York Times* editorial said: "Every major law enforcement organization in America formally endorses the Brady Bill, and national polls find overwhelming public support. Yet the National Rifle Association continues to denounce it as an intolerable inconvenience to gun buyers."[27] In November 1993, the *Washington Post* quoted from a letter by leaders of ten law enforcement organizations encouraging senators to reject amendments that would weaken the Brady Bill: "We want you to know that your nation's police are unconditionally and unequivocally opposed to incorporating this NRA substitute version of the Brady Bill into a crime bill. Please stand with law enforcement by voting to table any NRA substitute version."[28] NRA officials acknowledge that the loss of law enforcement support was unfortunate and costly. James Jay Baker, director of the NRA's Institute for Legislative Action during the Brady campaign, said that the defection of police organizations "hurt quite a bit." Paul Blackman, NRA research director during the Brady debate, called it a "key factor."[29]

Final Passage

After the 1992 election, Sarah Brady and Richard Aborn met several times at the White House with Clinton administration officials, once with both the president and vice president, to discuss strategy for passing the Brady Bill. In a speech to a Joint Session of Congress on February 17, 1993, the new president said:

And I ask you to help protect our families against the violent crime which terrorizes our people and which tears our communities apart. . . . And I support an initiative to do what we can to keep guns out of the hands of criminals. Let me say this. I will make you this bargain: If you will pass the Brady Bill, I'll sure sign it.

On October 27, 1993, Rep. Jack Brooks (D-Tex.), chairman of the House Judiciary Committee, split the Brady Bill from the Omnibus Crime Bill, giving House members an opportunity to vote on it separately. Rep. Charles Schumer (D-N.Y.) said, "This is how the political process works: public sentiment and inexorable pressure are outweighing whatever the National Rifle Association can throw in Brady's path."[30] Two days later, the House Subcommittee on Crime and Criminal Justice voted 10–3 to report the bill to the full Judiciary Committee.[31] Rep. James Sensenbrenner (R-Wisc.), the ranking Republican subcommittee member, endorsed the bill once a compromise had been agreed to: the background check by state and local law enforcement officers would be replaced, five years after the bill's passage, by a national instant check system operated by the federal government. On November 4, 1993, the House Judiciary Committee approved the Brady Bill, 23–12.

On November 10, the Brady Bill came up for a vote in the full House. As they had in previous sessions, Republicans offered amendments designed to weaken the bill. Rep. Bill McCollum's (R-Fla.) amendment proposed that the federal five-day waiting period preempt all state and locally mandated waiting periods, thereby invalidating lengthier state waiting periods. Representative George Gekas (R-Pa.) proposed phasing out the waiting period after five years (a "sunset provision"), whether or not the instant check system was operational. The House rejected McCollum's preemption amendment, 257–175,[32] but passed the Gekas amendment, 236–198.[33] The amended bill passed, 238–189.[34]

After a six-and-a-half-year battle, it is not surprising that the final two weeks were marked by intense political maneuvering. On November 19, the Senate overwhelmingly approved a $23 billion crime bill, which included a ban on 19 models of semiautomatic assault weapons,[35] but the Senate failed to end a Republican-led filibuster on the Brady Bill. The Senate also turned down a preemption amendment (that would have struck down all state gun controls stricter than the Brady Bill) similar to the one previously rejected by the House. The next day, the Senate passed the Brady Bill, 63–36,[36] 47 Democrats and 16 Republicans voted "yes"; 8 Democrats and 28 Republicans voted "no." The Senate version phased out the waiting period after four years instead of five, but gave the U.S. attorney general the option of extending the waiting period for an additional five months. House and Senate negotiators essentially accepted the House version of the Brady Bill. Around midnight on November 23, 1993, the House voted in favor of the Brady Bill 238–187.[37]

Still, the prospect of another Senate filibuster loomed. Brady opponents hoped to delay a vote on the Conference Report for as long as possible in the hope that pressure to pass the bill would subside. Senate Majority Leader George Mitchell threatened to reconvene the Senate immediately after Thanksgiving weekend and to remain in session until consideration of the Brady Bill was complete.[38] According to HCI's Richard Aborn:

> The notion that the entire Senate would have to return to Washington after Thanksgiving and stay until the Brady issue was resolved was not terribly inviting. Additionally, and far more importantly, there was a tremendous outburst of anger from Americans across the country. Supporters of the legislation could not believe that despite passage of the Brady Bill and the compromises reached, Senator Dole would continue to delay final passage of the Conference Report.[39]

Once again, the bill rose from the Senate graveyard. Allowing Dole to save face, Mitchell agreed that, in exchange for a vote now, he would allow the Senate to consider modifications when it reconvened in January 1994.* On November 24, 1993, the day before Thanksgiving, the Senate approved the bill with just three senators present in the chamber. Vice President Al Gore joined George Mitchell (D-Maine), Bob Dole (R-Kans.), and Mark Hatfield (R-Oreg.) in the Senate chamber, where Mitchell and Dole announced that the bill passed by unanimous consent. The vice president said, "is there objection? Hearing none, the request is granted and the conference report is agreed to."[40]

Speaking to an empty chamber, Dole said, "after a long, long, hard fight, Jim Brady has won."[41] Senator Mitchell said, "[the Brady Bill] will not by itself end gun violence in America. It is, however, a significant, albeit modest, step forward."[42] At a news conference, James Brady said, "it's an awfully nice Thanksgiving present to the people of America."[43]

The Brady Bill's passage was heralded as a great victory for Handgun Control, Inc., President Clinton, and the Democratic Congress. The *New York Times* said "public pleas to tone down society's violence, and the moral claim for slowing down the domestic small arms race, have overwhelmed a potent gun lobby that in the end went down with a whimper."[44] The *Times* editorial page labeled the Brady Law a "humiliating

---

*Specifically, Dole proposed that the waiting period be phased out in two years if the national instant check system was operational.

loss" for the NRA and called the NRA's defeat more important than the actual bill because the door was now open to more gun controls.

Conclusion

Until the emergence of Handgun Control, Inc., there was no significant national pro–gun control lobbying organization. While HCI has never come close to matching the NRA in membership or resources, it has focused and stimulated gun control interest and activism and provided a respected and constant gun control voice in Washington, D.C. Sarah Brady provided HCI and the gun control movement with a highly visible, popular, celebrity-type spokesperson, who could attract members, resources, allies, and media attention. James Brady gave the bill the face of an innocent, respected, conservative, gravely injured victim of handgun violence. The Brady Bill gave HCI a concrete goal and, in 1993, a major victory. Several months later, the Assault Weapons Ban passed Congress and was signed into law by President Clinton. The politics of gun control had shifted, at least for the moment. HCI used momentum from passage of the Brady Bill and the Assault Weapons Ban to continue organizing and lobbying. In early 1994, it began campaigning for Brady II, a bill that would, among other things, establish comprehensive registration and licensing of handguns and their owners.

Since the mid-1990s, a grassroots gun control "movement" has gained momentum. Every mass killing in schools and other venues produces more calls for gun controls and seems to give rise to new groups. In May 2000, the "Million Mom March" in Washington, D.C., was the largest gun control event ever held in the United States. Unquestionably, there is broad, if diffuse, support for gun control; the question we will be exploring in the rest of the book is whether there is a plausible regulatory strategy worth fighting for.

The long and tortuous battle over the Brady Law demonstrates that achieving even modest federal gun control requires enormous effort and political sophistication and probably Democratic Party control of Congress and the White House. But the battle also shows that passing federal gun control, over fervent NRA opposition, is not impossible. Thus, it behooves us to concentrate on gun control costs and benefits.

5

What the Brady Law Says

The federal government may not compel the States to enact or administer a federal regulatory program. The mandatory obligations imposed on CLEOs [chief law enforcement officers] to perform background checks on prospective handgun purchasers plainly runs afoul of that rule.
—Justice Scalia's majority opinion
  in *Printz v. United States* (1997)

The Brady Act was passed in response to what Congress described as an "epidemic of gun violence." . . . The partial solution contained in the Brady Act, a mandatory background check before a handgun may be purchased, has met with remarkable success . . . the Congressional decision surely warrants more respect that it is accorded in today's unprecedented decision.
—Justice Stevens's dissenting opinion
  in *Printz v. United States* (1997)

Like practically all gun control debates, the Brady Bill debate swirled around symbols and slogans. People tended to declare themselves for or against gun control, in principle. Those "for" gun control favored passage of the Brady Bill. Those opposed to gun control, of course, viewed the Brady Bill unfavorably. Even among partisans with strong views, probably few could explain what the Brady Bill actually said.

The Brady Law built on the regulatory scheme established by the 1938

Federal Firearms Act (FFA) and extended by the 1968 Gun Control Act
(GCA). The GCA required that before selling a firearm, a Federal Firearms
Licensee (FFL) had to obtain from the purchaser a signed "Statement of
Intent to Purchase a Firearm" (Form 5300.35).[1] The purchaser had to swear
that he or she did not have a criminal record, was not a drug abuser, and
didn't fall into any other disqualifying category. The FFL had to verify the
purchaser's in-state residency and age.[2] A purchaser who knowingly provided an FFL with false information about eligibility was guilty of a federal crime punishable by a $10,000 fine, a maximum of 10 years' impris-
onment, or both.* The GCA also made it a federal felony for a person who
had ever been convicted of a felony to possess a firearm; it also made it a
felony for any person (whether or not an FFL) to knowingly transfer a
firearm to a person with a felony record.

The GCA's regulatory scheme had at least two major defects, only the
first of which was addressed by the Brady Law. (1) There was no check
on the truthfulness of the firearm purchaser's affirmation of eligibility;
thus, if the purchaser was willing to lie about his felony record, he could
instantly obtain a firearm. (2) The GCA's regulatory scheme only applied
to sales by FFLs; an ineligible purchaser could, without filling out any
forms, buy a firearm at a gun show or from a private person who was not
an FFL.

The Brady Law mandated that after November 30, 1998, the background checking system would be fully automated, so that FFLs could
obtain an immediate authorization to complete a gun sale. The system in
place prior to the implementation of the automated background checking
system is referred to as "interim Brady"; the system after December 1,
1998, is referred to as "permanent Brady."

Finally, the Brady Law applied only to those states ("the Brady States")
that did not already have a waiting period of at least five days or a handgun licensing or permitting requirement. The new law had no effect on
how guns were sold in 18 states which already had laws at least as strict
as Brady.†

---

*18 U.S.C. § 922 (a) (6) makes it a federal offense to deceive a licensed firearms
dealer in the acquisition of a firearm. See *Huddleston v. U.S.*, 415 U.S. 814 (1974)
(statute applies to defendant redeeming a firearm from a pawnbroker).

†The states affected by the Brady Law, or "Brady States," were Alabama, Alaska,
Arizona, Colorado, Georgia, Idaho, Kansas, Kentucky, Louisiana, Maine, Minnesota,
Mississippi, Montana, Nebraska, New Hampshire, New Mexico, North Carolina,
North Dakota, Ohio, Oklahoma, Pennsylvania, Rhode Island, South Carolina, South
Dakota, Tennessee, Texas, Utah, Vermont, Washington, West Virginia, and Wyo-
ming.

Interim Brady (1993–1998)

The law's major impact in the "Brady states" was the requirement that FFLs notify the chief law enforcement officer (CLEO) in the dealer's jurisdiction of a pending firearm sale. The law instructs the CLEO to make a "reasonable effort" to determine that the prospective purchaser is not ineligible under federal law to purchase a firearm.[3] The FFL had to hold off transferring the firearm to the would-be purchaser until the CLEO approved the sale, or until five business days passed without a response from the CLEO, whichever occurred first. In effect, this meant a limited (up to five business days) waiting period for a firearm purchase. FFLs who knowingly failed to comply with Brady faced up to one year in prison, a fine, or both.[4] Congress mandated that BATF provide FFLs with training on Brady Law compliance, and it authorized BATF audits to assure that FFLs understood the process and maintained proper records. There was no punishment or penalty for a CLEO who failed to fulfill the background checking responsibility. Moreover, the Brady Law provided CLEOs with immunity from civil liability arising from "failure to prevent the sale or transfer of a handgun to a person whose receipt or possession of the handgun is unlawful . . . or for preventing such a sale or transfer to a person who may lawfully receive or possess a handgun."[5]

The law required the prospective handgun purchaser to fill in BATF Form 4473 (the "Firearms Transaction Record" or "Brady Form") with purchaser and firearm information, including name, race, date of birth, residence, type of handgun purchased, and criminal record. The purchaser had to show the FFL photo identification and affirm that neither federal nor state law barred him or her from purchasing or possessing a firearm. Form 4473 also asks the purchaser for optional information: social security number, height, weight, sex, and place of birth. The FFL was required to complete the bottom half of the form, including the FFL's name, address, phone number, license number, and the purchaser's type of photo identification. Under interim-Brady, the FFL had to transmit the Brady form to the CLEO within one day after the prospective purchaser filled out the form. The FFL had to record the name of the CLEO to whom the form was sent and the method of transmission (via phone, fax, in person, other).[6] The five-day period began running from the time the FFL transmitted the form.[7] The law required that the CLEO make a reasonable effort to check whatever state and local recordkeeping systems are available to determine the purchaser's eligibility.[8] Because, with limited exceptions, there are no easily accessible records on drug addicts, hospitalized mental patients, or illegal aliens, the CLEO's job really amounted to determining whether the purchaser had a disqualifying criminal record.[9]

The Brady background check was based on a name check, not on fingerprints or social security number. The CLEO would conduct a name search in criminal records databases to determine whether the purchaser had a criminal record. If the CLEO did not match the prospective purchaser's name to any felony conviction, indictment, misdemeanor domestic violence conviction, or civil restraining orders, he could not block the sale. If the CLEO did not notify the FFL within five business days that the sale was blocked, the FFL could complete the sale. In the event that a rejected purchaser asked for a written explanation, the CLEO had 20 business days to provide it.[10] A still-dissatisfied purchaser could appeal to a designated state agency.

If the sale was approved, the law required the CLEO to destroy the paperwork on the purchase, thereby preventing the formation of a government database on gun owners, that is, a national firearms registry.[11] The FFL, however, was required to retain copies of the BATF form for 20 years and produce it for the police in the event of an investigation tracing the ownership of a firearm believed to have been used in the commission of a crime. (An FFL who goes out of business must turn over his records to the BATF.) The BATF conducts random inspections of FFLs (limited by law to once per year) to audit compliance.

Upgrading State Criminal Records

The Brady Law set November 30, 1998, as the deadline for the National Instant Criminal Background Check System (NICS) to be up and running. At the time that Brady became law, many states' criminal records systems were nowhere near ready to support a computerized background check system.* In addition to being incomplete, the records did not contain information on the final disposition of a large percentage of arrests. The records in many states were not computerized. In other states, records were incomplete due to lengthy delays in entering cases into computer databases. In 1993, many observers did not believe that it would be possible within five years to upgrade state criminal records so that they would be available for automated on-line searching. Some gun control proponents believed that the idea of a computerized instant check system, originally offered by Republicans as an alternative to Brady, was a stalling tactic by the NRA and its congressional

---

*Criminal records are incomplete and inaccurate for many reasons, for example, the decentralized court system, plea bargaining, use of aliases, multiple rap sheets for the same individual, and failure to record case dispositions properly.

allies. The attorney general acknowledged that such a database could not be created "overnight," but only with "significant efforts and expenditures on the part of both the states and FBI."[12]

The U.S. Department of Justice (DOJ) spearheaded an effort to upgrade the quality of state criminal history records. The Bureau of Justice Statistics (BJS) launched the Criminal History Records Improvement (CHRI) program in order to improve the completeness, accuracy, and timeliness of state criminal records.[13] The CHRI program awarded grants, ranging from $112,842 to $521,227, to all 50 states. Some states, such as Arkansas, Florida, and Georgia, used the federal funds to enter final dispositions into the criminal records database. Other states, such as Iowa, designed and implemented an electronic interface between the state's central criminal records repository and its court information system.[14] Maryland, Massachusetts, and a few other states sought to link automated fingerprint systems to their criminal history database.[15]

As part of the Brady Act, Congress authorized the DOJ to allocate $200 million to state and local law enforcement agencies to computerize criminal records to make them accessible electronically in a statewide database. In addition, a National Criminal History Information Program (NCHIP) provided money to state courts for improving criminal records.

Once operational, the NICS would replace the CLEO-based background checking process. Unlike the five-day waiting period, which applied only to handgun sales, NICS checks would apply to rifle and shotgun sales as well. "Permanent Brady" would allow NICS up to three days to block a sale. Of course, there was nothing to prevent states from opting for more stringent gun controls. Brady set the floor, not the ceiling.

Federal Criminal Records

The FBI's criminal record database, the Interstate Identification Index (III), contains information on federal and state felony and some misdemeanor arrests. Prior to Brady, it was the primary database available to criminal justice agencies to determine whether a named individual had a criminal record in a particular state. When a local law enforcement agency wanted to know if a suspect or arrestee had a record in another state, it contacted the FBI, whose III "pointer system" directed the inquirer to those states where the gun purchaser has a criminal record. The Brady Law encouraged the FBI to transform the "III system" into a national criminal record database.

When state and local police make arrests, they are supposed to forward a fingerprint card to their state repository which, in turn, is supposed to send a fingerprint card or digitized fingerprint to the FBI. After the case is disposed of (charges dropped, acquittal, or conviction), the state is responsible for reporting the disposition to the FBI. Ultimately, the criminal record should note a disposition for every arrest. FBI officials responsible for operating the NICS spend significant time chasing down the disposition of prospective gun purchasers' arrests for which there is no disposition information.

The Brady Act required the attorney general to develop computer hardware and software for "linking state record collections into a nationwide system that would enable instant responses to inquiries." Each state was required to have 80% of its criminal records available to the national system within five years after Brady's enactment.[16] The attorney general issued timetables for each state.

The Brady Law required that, beginning six months after its enactment, the attorney general evaluate the state of the nation's criminal records, make recommendations, and provide assistance in making those records accessible through the NICS. After 30 months, the attorney general would have to determine whether 80% of each state's current records were available to the NICS.

In order to "encourage" the states to make progress upgrading their criminal records, the Brady Law authorized the attorney general to reduce a state's annual federal criminal justice grant by up to 50%. Moreover, if the attorney general determined that the national instant check system was not operational after 30 months, the DOJ's administrative funding would be reduced by 5%.

The FBI had to create the NICS from scratch. It established an NICS center in West Virginia and contracted with a private company to handle calls from FFLs regarding a prospective gun purchaser's criminal record. If the contract employees find no criminal record, they approve the sale, usually within a few minutes. If the computer search indicates "a hit," the case has to be turned over to FBI personnel for further investigation. By 2000, NICS employed over 500 persons to run the computerized search program.

The Brady Amendments

The Brady Law was amended twice, between 1994 and 1998, to add to the categories of persons ineligible to purchase firearms. Both additions resulted from successful lobbying by women's groups, not gun control lobbyists. The Violence against Women Act (VAWA), part of the 1994 Violent Crime Control and Law Enforcement Act, was an omnibus effort to protect women from male violence.[17] The law's best-known provision (which the U.S. Supreme Court held unconstitutional)[18] provided female victims of domestic (and other male-sponsored) violence a right to sue their attacker for monetary damages in federal court. For our purposes, the law is important because it made ineligible for firearm ownership persons convicted of a "domestic violence misdemeanor" and persons subject to a court order restraining them from harassing, stalking, or threatening an intimate partner.* VAWA also authorized technical assistance and training programs to assist states in entering data on domestic violence and stalking into the local, state, and national criminal record databases.[19]

The strongest opposition to VAWA's gun control provision came from police organizations that had strongly supported the 1993 Brady Act. They objected that, due to domestic violence convictions, some police officers would lose the right to carry firearms and therefore their capacity to function as full-fledged law enforcement officers. In *Fraternal Order of Police v. United States*, the D.C. Court of Appeals upheld this firearms disqualification.[20]

VAWA placed new and more challenging demands on state records systems, which are far less accurate for misdemeanors than for felonies. It therefore prompted a new round of efforts to improve state criminal records. But there remains a real problem in determining what counts as a domestic violence misdemeanor. In most states, domestic violence assault is not a specific statutory offense; men who abuse their wives and girlfriends are charged with assault or aggravated assault. Therefore, a criminal record would only indicate a misdemeanor assault conviction, not the gender of the victim, the perpetrator's motivation, or the relationship between offender and victim. Creating the kind of domestic assault database, envisioned by VAWA, would thus require substantive criminal law reform or a much more detailed criminal records system. Even then, there would be no easy way to know whether past assault convictions involved a domestic violence situation.

U.S. v. Printz

Even before the Brady Law took effect on February 28, 1994, a few CLEOs, with NRA encouragement and assistance, threatened to go to court to prevent being drafted to carry out background checks on prospective gun purchasers.[21] The NRA announced that it would challenge the law in sev-

---

*As we noted in chapter 3, a federal district court in Texas declared this provision unconstitutional on Second Amendment grounds. *U.S. v. Emerson*, 46 F. Supp. 2d 598 (N.D. Texas 1999). The Fifth Circuit Court of Appeals affirmed the lower court's opinion.

eral states to ensure that a number of district courts would render decisions, thereby assuring several circuit court decisions. The NRA reasoned that the split among judicial circuits would make it more likely that the Supreme Court would choose to resolve the issue. Several sheriffs immediately volunteered to be plaintiffs for these test cases.[22]

On the same day that the Brady Law went into effect, Sheriff Richard Mack of Graham County, Arizona, filed a federal suit challenging its constitutionality. Within months, six more sheriffs, all with NRA financial or legal assistance, brought suits.[23] Most of the sheriffs were represented by NRA–affiliated attorney Stephen P. Halbrook, who ultimately argued the sheriffs' case before the Supreme Court. The sheriffs objected to being required to enforce (via background checks) an unfunded federal regulatory scheme. As Sheriff J. R. Koog, of Val Verde County, Texas, explained, "Congress can't sit up there and tell this lowly little sheriff out here at the end of the world what to do."[24] Some of the plaintiffs, including Sheriff Jay Printz (Montana) and Sheriff Errol Romero (Louisiana), refused to conduct background checks.[25]

The litigation focused attention on how much work CLEOs actually had to perform in order to satisfy the Brady Law. The more work Congress had imposed on the CLEOs, the more likely the courts would see an unconstitutional violation of federalism. The Brady Law provided that the CLEO

> *shall make a reasonable effort* to ascertain within 5 business days whether receipt or possession would be in violation of the law, including research in whatever State and local record keeping systems are available and in a national system to be designated by the Attorney General. (emphasis added)

Apparently anticipating what would become the focus of subsequent litigation, on January 21, 1994, BATF Director John Magaw sent an "Open Letter to State and Local Law Enforcement Officials" that offered an official interpretation of the Law.[26] The 16-page letter specifically addressed four issues: (1) which states are exempt from Brady because of their existing gun control state laws; (2) who should serve as CLEOs for background checking purposes; (3) how FFLs were to notify CLEOs of proposed handgun sales; and (4) what constitutes a "reasonable effort" to determine whether a prospective purchaser is ineligible.[27] On the question of reasonable effort, Magaw acknowledged that the Brady Law "clearly anticipate[d] some minimal effort to check commonly available records."[28] Reasonable effort depended on the nature of the CLEO's jurisdiction; each CLEO could "set its own standards based on its own circumstances, i.e., the availability of resources, access to records, and taking into account the law enforcement priorities of the jurisdiction." These circumstances could also mean that in rural, sparsely populated areas, the CLEO need not conduct any background check if the prospective purchaser's background is personally known to the CLEO.* Director Magaw's interpretation, while certainly relevant, was not binding on the courts' interpretation of the statute.

Lower Court Litigation

Brady's constitutionality was challenged in federal courts by county sheriffs in Arizona, Montana, Mississippi, Texas, Louisiana, Vermont, and North Carolina—states where gun ownership is popular and gun control is not.[29] The NRA attacked the Brady Law as unconstitutional under the Fifth and Tenth Amendments.[30] The Fifth Amendment challenge, which met with very limited success, was based on the statute's criminal penalties. The sheriffs argued that the Brady Law subjected them to criminal liability under an unconstitutionally vague standard; that is, it was not clear what level of background checking might be found inadequate and therefore criminal. Courts found that the Brady Law did not impose any criminal liability on CLEOs and quickly moved on to consider the Tenth Amendment challenge.

The CLEOs argued that Brady's requirement that state and local law enforcement officials check prospective purchasers' eligibility to buy a handgun violated the Tenth Amendment which states that "[t]he powers not delegated to the United States by the Constitution, nor prohibited by it to the States, are reserved to the States respectively, or to the people." According to the plaintiffs, carrying out criminal record background checks consumes time and resources and thereby interferes with their authority to prioritize scarce law enforcement resources.[31] Moreover, they continued, Congress could not insulate itself from the negative political repercussions of a law by placing its enforcement in the hands of state and local officials. The majority of judges who heard these cases were persuaded by the Tenth Amendment argument. District courts in Arizona, Mississippi, Montana, Vermont, and Louisiana held that requiring state law enforcement officials to conduct Brady background checks violated the Tenth Amendment. Table 5.1 shows the lawsuits and their dispositions by date filed.

---

*The letter explained: "Upon being notified [by the FFL], and within 5 days, the CLEO makes a 'reasonable effort' to determine whether the individual is a prohibited person under the law. The CLEO makes a determination based upon information available to him/her. The CLEO finds nothing that would give him/her "reason to believe" that the individual is a prohibited person and, although not required to do so, the CLEO contacts the FFL and tells the FFL it is okay to sell the handgun" ("Open Letter to State and Local Law Enforcement Officials," pp. 4, 10).

Table 5.1. The Cases That Challenged Brady

State/Plantiff	Case	District Court Ruling	Appellate Ruling	Supreme Court Ruling
Montana, Sheriff Jay Printz, Ravalli County, filed Feb. 20, 1994.	*Printz v. United States*, 854 F. Supp. 1503, District of Montana, May 16, 1994.	Held: Brady unconstitutional.		In *Printz v. United States*, the Court ruled, 5–4, that Brady was unconstitutional. 521 U.S. 898, June 27, 1997.
Arizona, Sheriff Richard Mack, Graham County, filed Feb. 28, 1994.	*Mack v. United States*, 856 F. Supp.1372, District of Arizona, June 28, 1994.	Held: Brady unconstitutional.	*Mack* and *Printz* were consolidated into a single appeal, and the Ninth Circuit reversed both district court decisions, holding, in *Mack v. United States*, that Brady was constitutional. 66 F. 3d 1025, Sept. 8, 1995.	
Mississippi, Sheriff Bill McGee, Forrest County, filed Mar. 3, 1994.	*McGee v. United States*, 863 F.Supp. 321, Southern District of Mississippi, June 2, 1994.	Held: Brady unconstitutional. Injunctive relief limited to plaintiff McGee.	In *Koog v. United States* (the consolidated appeal of *McGee* and *Koog*), the Fifth Circuit held that Brady was unconstitutional. 79 F.3d 452, Mar. 21, 1996.	Certiorari denied, June 27, 1997.

Louisiana, Sheriff Errol Romero, Iberia Parish, filed Mar. 7, 1994.	*Romero v. United States*, 1994 U.S. Dist. LEXIS 20653, Western District of Louisiana, Dec. 8, 1994.	Held: Brady unconstitutional.	
Texas, Sheriff J. R. Koog, Val Verde County, filed Mar. 9, 1994.	*Koog v. United States*, 852 F.Supp. 1376, Western District of Texas, May 31, 1994.	Held: Brady constitutional.	
Vermont, Sheriff Samuel Frank, Orange County, filed May 10, 1994.	*Frank v. United States*, 860 F. Supp. 1030, District of Vermont, Aug. 2, 1994.	Held: Brady unconstitutional.	Second Circuit reversed and ruled that Brady was constitutional. 78 F.3d 815, Mar. 15, 1996. Supreme Court vacated the judgment and remanded the case for reconsideration in light of *Printz*, June 27, 1997.
North Carolina, Sheriff Richard Frye, Alamance County, filed Jan. 12, 1995.	*Frye v. United States*, 916 F.Supp. 546, Middle District of North Carolina, Oct. 20, 1995.	Held: Sheriff Frye's motion for a preliminary injunction denied.	

The Montana federal district court was the first to pass on Brady's constitutionality. In *Printz v. United States*, the judge concluded that the law was unconstitutional because the CLEOs were being made to bear its political and financial costs.[32] All but one of the other district courts hearing challenges to the Brady Act agreed.

As the NRA anticipated, the federal circuit courts of appeal divided on the background check's constitutionality. They all recognized the relevance of the Supreme Court's opinion in *New York v. United States*, which held that Congress cannot command state legislatures to carry out a federal regulatory program. However, the circuits differed on the appropriate application of that decision to the constitutionality of the Brady background check. The Ninth Circuit, in *Mack v. United States*, explained that

> it is true that, for a limited period of time, the Act requires state law enforcement officials, the CLEOs, to make reasonable efforts to assist in carrying out the federal program. But the CLEOs are not being commanded to engage in the central sovereign processes of enacting legislation or regulations.[33]

The Ninth Circuit further reasoned that the temporary use of CLEOs to conduct Brady background checks was not "unusually jarring to our system of federalism," in that "the obligation imposed on state officers . . . [was] no more remarkable than, say, the federally-imposed duties of state officers to report missing children or traffic fatalities."[34]

By contrast, the Fifth Circuit, in *Koog v. United States*, held that *New York v. United States* required finding the Brady Act unconstitutional.

> Indeed, Congress' bypass of state legislative processes here constitutes a greater incursion into state sovereignty than forcing the States to enact legislation: a bypass disposes of even the pretext of minimal state discretion that is present when the federal government forces a state to employ its legislative process to achieve a particular end. The Brady Act dispenses with the state legislature altogether and effectively enacts state legislation requiring CLEOs to perform the interim duties under the Act, without even the nominal participation of the States' elected representatives.[35]

The U.S. Supreme Court Weighs In

In June 1996, the Supreme Court decided to hear the case. Fifty-five anti– and pro–gun control organizations, law enforcement organizations, senators, and states, individually and in groups, submitted a dozen amicus (friends of the court) briefs. Those urging the Supreme Court to uphold the Brady Law included the Coalition to Stop Gun Violence and the Educational Fund to End Handgun Violence, Handgun Control, Inc., the Center to Prevent Handgun Violence, the U.S. Conference of Mayors, the Federal Law Enforcement Officers Association, the International Association of Chiefs of Police, the Police Executive Research Forum, the Association of the Bar of the City of New York, 11 senators (Herb Kohl, Paul Simon, John Chafee, Edward M. Kennedy, Diane Feinstein, John Kerry, Frank Lautenberg, Tom Harkin, Bill Bradley, Carol Moseley-Braun, and Bob Kerrey), and 13 states (Maryland, Connecticut, Florida, Hawaii, Iowa, Michigan, Minnesota, Mississippi, Nevada, North Carolina, Oregon, Rhode Island, and Wisconsin). Amici urging that the law be struck down included the NRA, the Gun Owners Foundation, the Law Enforcement Alliance of America, the Council of State Governments, the National Conference of State Legislatures, the Pacific Legal Foundation, and eight states (Colorado, Idaho, Kansas, Montana, Nebraska, South Dakota, Virginia, and Wyoming). Table 5.2 briefly outlines the principal arguments articulated in each brief.

In a 5–4 decision, authored by Justice Scalia, the Supreme Court struck down Brady's mandatory CLEO background checks as violative of both the Tenth Amendment and the Constitution's "dual sovereignty" principle.[36] The majority opinion emphasized that the framers rejected the idea of a central government that would act upon and through the states. They opted instead for a federal system in which the state and federal governments would exercise concurrent authority. "Although the States surrendered many of their powers to the new Federal Government, they retained a 'residuary and inviolable sovereignty,'[37] . . . [that] is reflected throughout the Constitution's text. . . . Residual state sovereignty was also implicit . . . in the Constitution's conferral upon Congress of not all governmental powers, but only discrete enumerated ones, Art.I §8, which implication was rendered express by the Tenth Amendment . . ."[38]

Justice Scalia spent a good portion of the majority's opinion reviewing historical documents that reveal the framers' intent. While acknowledging some precedent for the national government imposing obligations on state judges, Justice Scalia drew a distinction between state judges and state law enforcement officials; state courts, "unlike [state] legislatures and executives, . . . applied the law of other sovereigns all the time."[39] Justice Scalia rejected the dissent's historical evidence that state governments have, at times, assisted with the execution of federal laws as not dispositive; it merely showed that the states sometimes opted voluntarily to cooperate with the federal government. Based on the structure of the Constitution, particularly the interplay between the enumerated powers and

Table 5.2. Amici Curiae, *Printz v. United States*

| | Brady Supporters | | Brady Opponents | |
	Organization	Principal Arguments	Organization	Principal Arguments
	Handgun Control, Inc.; Center to Prevent Handgun Violence; U.S. Conference of Mayors; Federal Law Enforcement Officers' Ass'n; Fraternal Order of Police; Internat'l Ass'n of Chiefs of Police; Major Cities Chiefs; Nat'l Ass'n of Police Organizations; Nat'l Organization of Black Law Enforcement Executives; Nat'l Troopers' Coalition; Police Executive Research Forum	Based on past precedents, Brady should not be deemed unconstitutional because Congress has neither commandeered the state legislature nor overburdened state officials. In addition, Brady has not caused any confusion about political accountability. Brady is consistent with both traditional and contemporary visions of federalism. Even if individual provisions are held unconstitutional, they are severable from the remainder of the act.	National Rifle Association	Congress has impermissibly "shifted the primary burden" of enforcing a federal program to state and local officials. Because Brady cannot be justified as a legitimate exercise of commerce power (nor by any other enumerated power), Congress has violated the Tenth Amendment. The civil cause of action against CLEOs violates the Eleventh Amendment. If the challenged provisions were found to be unconstitutional, they should be deemed nonseverable and the entire act should be voided.
	Coalition to Stop Gun Violence; Educational Fund to End Handgun Violence	Imposition of minor burdens on state officials, even where reallocation of state budgets may be required, is constitutionally permissible. *Printz* can be distinguished from *New York v. United States* because of the "compelling federal interest in combating the national epidemic of gun violence." Any unconstitutional provisions should be severed from the remainder.	Law Enforcement Alliance of America	Brady violates fundamental principles of federalism and the Tenth Amendment. The background check provisions should not be viewed as severable from the rest of Brady.

Amicus	Argument
Association of the Bar of the City of New York	Brady's temporary and minimal imposition on state governments does not violate the Tenth Amendment. "Any construction of the Tenth Amendment that so radically restrains the power of the federal government to enlist the temporary aid of state officers in addressing a dire national problem would disserve both the health and safety of the Nation and the interests of modern federalism."
Senators Herb Kohl, Paul Simon, John Chafee, Edward M. Kennedy, Dianne Feinstein, John Kerry, Frank Lautenberg, Tom Harkin, Bill Bradley, Carol Moseley-Braun, and Bob Kerrey	The Brady Act is distinguishable from the statute struck down in *New York v. United States*, because Brady directs state and local officials "to perform ministerial tasks" and gives rise to no confusion of accountability. In the event that the Court rules that any provisions are unconstitutional, those provisions should be severed from the rest of the law.
Doctors for Integrity in Policy Research; Doctors for Responsible Gun Ownership; Lawyers' Second Amendment Society	These organizations challenged the notion that Brady's "gun control" would actually result in a decrease in crime. They questioned the "scientific data" used to support Brady. Finally, they asserted that claims of Brady being a success are misleading for failing to acknowledge that purchasers, blocked by Brady, would turn to the black market for their handguns.
Pacific Legal Foundation	"Congress has contravened the Tenth Amendment by dragooning state law enforcement officers . . . to act as federal agents in implementing federal policy." *New York v. United States* prohibits congressional commandeering of state resources, no matter how temporary or minor.

(continued)

Table 5.2. Amici Curiae, *Printz v. United States* (Continued)

Brady Supporters		Brady Opponents	
Organization	Principal Arguments	Organization	Principal Arguments
Connecticut, Florida, Hawaii, Iowa, Maryland, Michigan, Minnesota, Mississippi, Nevada, North Carolina, Oregon, Rhode Island, and Wisconsin	Brady should be viewed as part of a system of "cooperative federalism," which acknowledges that states are often called upon to assist in the execution of federal law. In addition, because of the minimal and temporary nature of the imposition on state actors, the Court should not overturn the law.	Gun Owners Foundation	By compelling the participation of CLEOs, Brady violates the Appointments Clause and the Faithful Execution Clause. Brady also violates the Eleventh Amendment immunity of states by subjecting them to suit. Brady's "seizure" of the time and resources of state and local law enforcement personnel is an impermissible Fifth Amendment taking.
		Colorado, Idaho, Kansas, Montana, Nebraska, South Dakota, Virginia, and Wyoming	After *New York v. United States*, it is clear that the federal government may not mandate state enforcement of federal schemes. Brady's burdens on state officials are significant. There is no de minimis exception to the Tenth Amendment. Brady also violates the Guaranty Clause (Art. IV, §4) by clouding state accountability and by imposing on state budgets.
		Council of State Governments; National Conference of State Legislatures	By *requiring* the participation of state CLEOs, Congress overstepped its constitutional authority. Brady "divorced handgun regulation policies from the duty to provide the money and personnel to enforce these policies."

the Tenth Amendment, Justice Scalia concluded that the background check provisions would upset the balance of power between the national government and the sovereign states.

The Court rejected the argument that the Brady Act should be upheld pursuant to Congress's power to enact all laws necessary and proper to carrying out its gun control objectives under the commerce clause. Responding to the dissenters' reliance on the Necessary and Proper Clause (Art. I, Sect. 8), Justice Scalia explained that when a law purporting to regulate commerce "violates the principle of state sovereignty . . . , it is not a 'Law . . . proper for carrying into Execution the Commerce Clause,' and is thus, . . . 'merely an act of usurpation.' "[40]

According to Justice Scalia, *New York v. United States* bound the Court to protect state sovereignty, even when a crisis might seem to call for a national solution. "We adhere to that principle today, and conclude categorically, as we concluded categorically in *New York*: 'The Federal Government may not compel the States to enact or administer a federal regulatory program.' The mandatory obligation imposed on CLEOs to perform background checks on prospective handgun purchasers plainly runs afoul of that rule."[41] In the end, the Court held that "the obligation to 'make a reasonable effort to ascertain within 5 business days whether receipt or possession of a handgun would be in violation of the law, including research in whatever State and local record keeping systems are available and in a national system designated by the Attorney General,' 18 U.S.C. § 922(s)(2) is unconstitutional."*

---

*521 U.S. 898, 933 (1997). Justice Stevens called the Brady Law a "remarkable success." His lengthy dissent made four main points. First, he asserted that the commerce clause provided Congress authority to regulate firearms sales, and that the "temporary enlistment of local police officers" to conduct background checks was justifiable under the necessary and proper clause. Because he viewed Brady as a legitimate exercise of Congress's commerce clause power, he found no Tenth Amendment violation. Second, Justice Stevens pointed to historical evidence that the framers intended for the federal government to rely on state officials to implement national programs. Third, he argued that American federalism does not prevent the federal government from enlisting the aid of state officials in administering federal programs. *New York* "squarely approved of cooperative federalism programs, designed at the national level but implemented principally by state governments. *New York* disapproved of a particular *method* of putting such programs into place, not the existence of federal programs implemented locally." Fourth, Justice Stevens distinguished *New York v. United States* because that case prohibited Congress from mandating that *state legislatures* pass certain laws, while the Brady Act was addressed to state and local executive branch officials.

The Aftermath of *Printz*

The *Printz* decision was a setback for the Brady Law, but it had less impact than at first seemed likely. The same day that the Supreme Court handed down its decision, the BATF sent a letter to FFLs explaining that they were still required to (1) have prospective purchasers fill out the Brady Form; (2) forward the Brady Form to the CLEO (who might decide to conduct a voluntary background check); and (3) hold up the sale of the handgun for five days (unless they received a green light from the CLEO in the meantime).[42] Attorney General Janet Reno sent a letter to state and local officials urging them to continue the background checks voluntarily. She "expect[ed] and hope[d] that the vast majority of law enforcement agencies in America will continue to run these checks voluntarily because they are saving lives, keeping guns out of the hands of criminals and generally are in the best interest of law enforcement."[43] The International Association of Chiefs of Police and the Police Executive Research Forum promised to lobby members in the Brady states to continue the CLEO background checks voluntarily.

Brady supporters emphasized that more than half of the states were not affected by the *Printz* decision because they were not covered by Brady—they conducted their own background checks as a matter of state law.[44] President Clinton reiterated his commitment to have the instant check system operational by November 1998.[45]

In the months following *Printz*, the predictions of Brady supporters were borne out. Chief law enforcement officers in all the Brady states, with the initial exceptions of Arkansas and Ohio, continued to conduct the background checks voluntarily. It took the Department of Justice six months to convince Ohio to require its CLEOs to conduct background checks.[46] In January 1998, Arkansas CLEOs renewed their participation.

The CLEOs' voluntary compliance nullified the *Printz* decision's impact on the Brady Law's operation. The whole matter became irrelevant with the transition to NICS in December 1998. Still, *Printz* has important implications for future federal gun control. For example, a federal licensing or registration scheme could not assign recordkeeping and enforcement responsibilities to state and local officials.

Permanent Brady

"Permanent Brady," which became effective on November 30, 1998, requires an FFL to phone in information about a would-be gun purchaser to the FBI's NICS or the state's "Point of Contact" (POC) system.* There is a financial incentive for them to do so because the FBI bears the expense of the search. The FFL has no choice about which system to use. As of fall 2001, 14 states conducted their own background checks for the purchase of all firearms, while six states conducted their own background checks only for handgun permits and referred dealers to NICS for background checks on purchasers of long guns.

NICS System

In states using the FBI's NICS system, FFLs must dial an 800 number that is routed automatically, depending on volume, to one of two locations. Seventy percent of the calls are directed to Uniontown, Pennsylvania, and 30% to Moundsville, West Virginia. These sites, operated by private contractors, are operational 17 hours a day, seven days a week. The NICS headquarters in Clarksburg, West Virginia, is also equipped to handle NICS checks if more capacity is necessary.

An FFL phones into the NICS system, using for identification an assigned FFL number and a code word (thereby precluding non-FFLs from obtaining on-line criminal record information), and provides the buyer's name, gender, height, weight, date of birth, place of birth, residence, social security number (optional), and type of firearm being purchased. The search is assigned a transaction number.

The NICS searches three databases consisting of 34.7 million criminal records, 700,000 records on wanted persons, and 940,000 records on other prohibited persons. The electronic search takes approximately 8 to 10 seconds. The NICS system can identify a felony arrest but usually not the disposition. (An arrest without a conviction does not bar a gun purchase.) If a disposition is necessary, FBI personnel contact the relevant arresting agency or court.

Approximately 70% of the background checks are completed within 30 seconds, and more than 95% within two hours. If three business days pass without an answer, the FFL may proceed with the sale. (However, if at some later point the NICS discovers a disqualifying conviction, the FBI, BATF, and local police are informed.) During the 1999 calendar year, 72% of the background checks indicated no record and thus permitted the FFL

---

*In addition to checking NICS, the federal government searches the National Crime Information Center (NCIC 2000) and the Interstate Identification Index (III).

to make an immediate firearm transfer. Of NICS checks, 28% triggered further investigation; only 2% of searches resulted in denial.

NICS cannot determine whether a gun purchaser is ineligible because of mental illness hospitalization, drug use or addiction, or illegal alien status because there are no competent databases with this information. Data on ex–mental hospital patients and drug users and addicts do not exist in any coherent or accessible form, and to the extent they do exist, they are not readily available via NICS. Privacy laws in many states protect information identifying patients from hospitals, private doctors, and treatment centers. The Brady Act Task Group, formed shortly after Brady became law and charged with studying the obstacles to creating NICS, concluded that "it will be difficult to obtain this information [on drug use and treatment for mental illness] because of legal restrictions and because of the large number of [state and local hospital] data bases that must be integrated. . . . States would have to change their confidentiality laws in order to make information about mental defectives and mental hospital commitments available to NICS."[47] The mental health community adamantly supports the privacy of mental health records.*

Some officials have proposed providing FFLs with fingerprinting capability and converting NICS to a fingerprint search system to prevent subversion of the system by purchasers using fake names and IDs. Legislation would probably be required to implement this change; it would also entail significant expense. As this book goes to press, a fingerprint search system is not a serious possibility. Another recommendation is that FFLs

---

*In 2001, the Americans for Gun Safety Foundation conducted a major study of NICS's capacity to determine whether firearms purchasers are ineligible to purchase and possess a firearm. It concluded that "most states have done a haphazard and ineffective job in automating these crucial records and have allowed almost ten thousand convicted felons to acquire guns over the last 30 months (as well as an unknown number of domestic violence abusers, illegal aliens, and those mentally ill)." More specifically, the report found: (1) "Twenty-four states have automated less than 60% of their felony criminal conviction records, meaning that investigators must comb through paper records to determine the eligibility of hundreds of thousands of prospective gun buyers"; (2) "Thirty-three states cannot stop those who have been involuntarily committed to a mental health facility from buying a gun, because they do not supply any records to the state and federal databases used to deny purchases"; (3) "Thirteen states cannot stop those with domestic violence restraining orders from obtaining a gun, and 14 states cannot stop those with domestic violence misdemeanors, because they do supply any records to the state and federal databases used to deny firearms purchases"; and (4) "Illegal aliens can easily purchase guns because federal immigration records are poor and background checks do not require Social Security or resident alien registration numbers." See Americans for Gun Safety Foundation, "Broken Records: How America's Faulty Background Check System Allows Criminals to Get Guns," Jan. 2002, p. 2.

be given direct access to the NICS computer system, thus eliminating the NICS centers in West Virginia and Pennsylvania. This proposal faces strong opposition because it would, in effect, make criminal records publicly available. Finally, the FBI would like, through the NICS, to be able to access the states' court records, thereby providing NICS direct access to case dispositions. There is no opposition to that idea, but there are formidable logistical and budgetary impediments.

The POC System

As of fall 2001, 16 states conducted firearms background checks through state-level Point of Contact (POC) systems. Of these, 11 states had partial POCs, that is, the state performs background checks for handgun purchases, while the FBI conducts background checks for long gun purchases.[48] A state POC searches that state's criminal history database, as well as the NICS database. Since the states' criminal records databases contain more information than the FBI's databases, a state background check is typically more thorough and comprehensive than an FBI search. For example, Florida, which conducts its own background checks, can search databases for protection orders and youthful offender records, neither of which are accessible to the FBI. States may provide such information to the FBI, but cost is a deterrent.

Conclusion

The 1968 GCA made it a federal crime for an individual with a felony record (or certain other disqualifications) to possess a firearm. It also made it a crime for any person, including an FFL, knowingly to sell a firearm to a person with a felony criminal record. The GCA required a prospective handgun purchaser to sign a form attesting to his or her eligibility to own and possess a handgun. But the FFL had to take the purchaser's word for it.

The Brady Law provided for an independent check on the purchaser's eligibility. The Brady Act's background check requirement furthered the existing federal handgun regulatory regime's goal of preventing persons with criminal records from purchasing a handgun from FFLs by strengthening the GCA. Interim-Brady imposed a de facto waiting period (up to five days) on prospective handgun purchases. From 1993 to 1998, Interim Brady required the FFL to hold off on the sale (for up to five business days) until the CLEO had an opportunity to check the prospective handgun purchaser's criminal record. Permanent Brady requires that the FFL hold off on the sale of both long guns and handguns for up to three days, while the purchaser's name is run through either the FBI's NICS system or the state's POC system. If the search finds disqualifying information, the FFL is instructed not to make the sale.

In retrospect, the upgrading of state criminal records may prove to be the Brady Law's most lasting achievement. The states used federal grants to modernize their criminal justice records. State and federal criminal records databases have become far more comprehensive and accessible than they were in the early 1990s. This has implications for more informed law enforcement, pretrial detention and release decisions, charging, plea bargaining, and sentencing.

The Supreme Court's 1997 *Printz* decision means that Congress cannot implement future gun controls by assigning regulatory responsibilities to state and local officials. Congress could get some states to cooperate by holding out the carrot of criminal justice grants, but states with strong gun rights' traditions would probably forego federal monies. The only other alternative would be for Congress to expand the BATF or establish a new federal bureaucracy manned by federal personnel.

6

Holes in the Brady Law

Most felons and other ineligibles who obtain guns do so not because the state's screening system fails to discover their criminal record, but rather because these people find ways of circumventing the screening system entirely. . . . Under these circumstances, developing a more intensive and reliable screening process is probably not worth the additional cost.
—Philip J. Cook and James Blose, "State Programs
    for Screening Handgun Buyers"

Regulating gun transfers appears to be a promising method of keeping guns from the hands of youths and criminals, or, at least, of limiting the time that they are armed. When guns are relatively scarce and expensive, youths may be slower to acquire a gun and quicker to sell it.
—Philip Cook, Stephanie Molliconi, and Thomas Cole,
    "Regulating Gun Markets"

While proponents and supporters hailed the Brady Act as an important step toward reducing violent crime, a close look makes that prediction doubtful. The law's most glaring weakness is its failure to require background checks of individuals who obtain "used" firearms via sales, gifts, or loans from a person who is not a Federal Firearms Licensee (FFL). A closely related problem is the failure to cover gun shows, where people interested in purchasing a firearm without being subjected to a background check can easily find an obliging seller. Moreover, an ineligible purchaser can buy a gun from even a diligent FFL using counterfeit ID or a straw purchaser. In short, the Brady Law projects the image of effective regulation without the reality.

Applies Only to Primary Retail Market

While 4.5 million new firearms are sold in the primary market each year, approximately 3.2 million used firearms are sold in the secondary market.[1] According to Senator Charles Schumer, "The secondary market is to guns what the Cayman Islands is to money. It launders the gun so that when it turns up in a crime the trace leads law enforcement to a dead end."* The overwhelming majority of criminals obtain their firearms in the secondary market.[2] (What rational individual, contemplating a crime, would appear before a licensed dealer, show ID, and fill out forms?) Even law-abiding gun owners obtain approximately one-third of their firearms from non-FFLs, often as gifts.[3]

The Brady Law applies only to federally licensed dealers, but *anyone can legally sell a firearm.* A person may not "engage in the business" of importing, manufacturing, or dealing in firearms without a federal license, but individuals, even gun enthusiasts, can sell firearms as a hobby.[4] When Congress enacted the GCA in 1968, it did not define "engaged in the business." In 1986, the Firearms Owners' Protection Act (FOPA) provided a definition:

> the term "engaged in the business" means . . .
> as applied to a dealer in firearms, . . . a person who devotes time, attention and labor to dealing in firearms *as a regular course of trade or business* with the principal objective of livelihood and profit through the repetitive purchase and resale of firearms, *but such term shall not include a person who makes occasional sales, exchanges*

---

*Not surprisingly, guns flow from states with weak gun laws to criminals in states with strong gun laws. For example, in 1998 the BATF successfully traced 4,260 guns used in New York State crimes. Only 32% were bought from FFLs in New York State. Nationwide, roughly two-thirds of the guns used in crime are brought in the state where the crime occurred. But we have to treat data from BATF traces with skepticism because traced guns are not a random sample of all crime guns. Moreover, since Americans move a great deal, and gun owners take their firearms with them, we ought not assume that all, or even most, interstate movement of firearms is carried out by black marketers. See Gary Kleck, "BATF Gun Trace Data and the Role of Organized Gun Trafficking in Supplying Guns to Criminals."

*or purchases of firearms for the enhancement of a personal collec-
tion or for a hobby, or who sells all or part of his personal collection
of firearms.** (emphasis added)

In other words, the FOPA legitimates an unregulated secondary market
in firearms. Occasional gun sellers are explicitly exempted from the federal firearms license requirement. A handgun owner who does not have a
federal license may sell, loan, give, or otherwise transfer his handgun to
another person without filling out forms, informing any state or federal
officials, initiating a background check, or abiding by a waiting period.
An individual could purchase a gun from an FFL and then resell it that
same day, perhaps at a gun show, *no questions asked.* Indeed, he or she
can advertise "handgun for sale" in the newspaper and, that same day,
sell the handgun to anyone who responds. True, it is a federal crime for
a non-FFL to sell or transfer a firearm to an individual whom he knows
is ineligible to possess a firearm, but he is not obliged to question the
purchaser about his eligibility. He need only ask to see some ID showing
in-state residency and proper age.

Likewise, a potential handgun purchaser who, for one reason or another, does not want to buy from an FFL could place a "handgun wanted"
advertisement in the newspaper and purchase a handgun from anyone
who answers the ad. The purchaser would not have to fill out any forms
or comply with any waiting period. While the purchaser of a used gun is
supposed to show the seller an ID proving residency and age, that requirement is probably ignored in many cases.[5]

Brady's impact on the acquisition of handguns by criminals is significantly undermined by criminals' preference for avoiding FFLs. A rational person contemplating crime would prefer to obtain a gun without
having to fill out forms, thereby creating a paper record. What's more, if
he had a disqualifying criminal record, he would be committing a federal felony by lying on the forms and another felony by illegally possessing the gun. It is hardly surprising that a 1986 survey found that five
out of six prison inmates reported obtaining their handguns in the sec-

---

*18 U.S.C. 921 (a) (21) (c). The 1986 amendment made it more difficult to con-
vict unlicensed gun sellers, who commonly defend against charges of selling firearms without a license by claiming to be collectors or hobbyists. It is frequently
difficult to prove that the defendant is "engaged in the business of dealing in firearms." In *Bryan v. U.S.*, 118 S. Ct. 1939 (1998), the U.S. Supreme Court held that
the prosecution need *only* prove that the defendant knowingly engaged in the business of firearms without a federal license. The prosecutor need not prove that the
defendant knew he was violating a particular licensing requirement.

ondary market or by theft,[6] and that "the criminal handgun market is overwhelmingly dominated by informal transactions and theft as mechanisms of supply."[7]

According to sociologists Joseph F. Sheley's and James D. Wright's study of juvenile felons and a control group of inner-city youths,[8] 54% of the inmates and 37% of the control group indicated that they could easily obtain a handgun "off the street." An even higher percentage reported that they could get a handgun from a friend or family member (45% and 53%, respectively).[9] Of the inmates surveyed, 83% owned a gun at the time of arrest, while 22% of the control group admitted to owning a gun at the time of the survey.[10] Sheley and Wright found that the leading sources of handguns were (1) borrowing from a family member or friend (45% of juvenile inmates; 53% of controls); (2) buying "off the street" (54% of inmates; 37% of controls); (3) buying from a family member or friend (36% of inmates; 35% of controls); (4) buying from a drug dealer or addict (36% of inmates; 22% of controls); (5) buying from a gun shop (12% of inmates; 28% of controls); and (6) theft (17% of inmates; 8% of controls).[11]

These numbers, according to Sheley and Wright, understate the extent that urban youths are armed because carrying a gun occasionally was more common than gun ownership for the young men in the study.[12] Sheley and Wright concluded that unregulated purchases and trades between private parties subverts legal measures, designed to prevent dangerous individuals from obtaining guns.[13]

Many criminals obtain handguns by theft. An estimated 500,000 to 1.4 million firearms are stolen annually.[14] According to sociologist Gary Kleck:

> Even if one could completely eliminate all voluntary transfers of guns to criminals, including lawful or unlawful transfers, involving either licensed dealers or private citizens, and even if police could completely confiscate all firearms from all criminals each year, a single year's worth of gun thefts alone would be more than sufficient to rearm all gun criminals and easily supply the entire set of guns needed to commit the current number of gun crimes."[15]

Most gun thefts are not large-scale heists, but small thefts, many occuring in the course of burglaries and other crimes.[16] Professor James Wright and his colleagues found that 40%–70% of convicted felons obtained their most recent handgun through theft.[17] Another study found that 47% of felons had themselves stolen a gun at least once, while 32% had stolen their most recently possessed handgun.[18]

Interim Brady Applied
Only to Handguns

Interim Brady (1993–1998) applied only to handguns. Thus, an individual whose proposed handgun purchase was rejected by the Brady background check could have walked out of the store with a shotgun or rifle.* While most gun crime is committed with handguns, which have the advantage of easy concealability, shotguns and rifles can be sawed down to conceal-able size. This seems like a perverse policy outcome. We would certainly not be better off if criminals switched from handguns to more deadly sawed-off shotguns and rifles.[19]

With the implementation of NICS in December 1998, long gun pur-chasers, just like handgun purchasers, were made subject to a background check. The same ineligibility criteria now apply to purchasers of both handguns and long guns. (However, the problem of substitution of lawful higher calibre guns for prohibited lower calibre guns arises with respect to bans on Saturday Night Specials.)

Gun Shows

Another huge gap in the Brady law is its failure to cover handgun transfers that occur at gun shows. Nationwide, there were 4,442 gun shows (more than 12 per day) in 1998[20] (see table 6.1). Gun shows are held in arenas, civic centers, fairgrounds, and armories.

Anyone can sell a gun at a gun show, but only FFLs must subject their customers to the Brady background check. Non-FFLs can sell firearms at a gun show (and anywhere else) without verifying the eligibility of the person to whom they are selling. In fact, they may attract prospective buyers with placards promising "No background checks required; we need only know where you live and how old you are."[21] BATF investigations reveal numerous federal firearms violations associated with gun shows, such as eligible persons purchasing guns for ineligible purchasers (so-called straw purchasers), FFL sales to out-of-state purchasers, sales by

---

*Indeed, Francisco Martin Duran made just such a substitution. In October 1994, his attempt to purchase a handgun was rejected on account of a prior criminal record. Duran then purchased an SKS semiautomatic rifle from the same FFL and used it to spray the White House with bullets. Jim Kirksey, "Duran Bid to Get a Pistol Rejected," *Denver Post*, Nov. 10, 1994, at A1.

Table 6.1. Ten Leading Gun Show States, 1998

State	Number of Shows
Texas	472
Pennsylvania	250
Florida	224
Illinois	203
California	188
Indiana	180
North Carolina	170
Oregon	160
Ohio	148
Nevada	129

Source: Gun Show Calendar, Krause Publications as quoted in Gun Shows: Brady Checks and Crime Gun Traces, Bureau of Alcohol Tobacco and Firearms (1999), p. 4.

FFLs without background checks, and sales of illegal kits for converting semiautomatic weapons to fully automatic.

Dishonest Dealers

Not all FFLs are conscientious supporters and enforcers of the Brady regulatory scheme.* The Brady Law is circumvented by unscrupulous dealers. According to BATF spokesperson Jerry Singer, "even though the percentage [of dishonest FFLs] might be small, the bad ones can put a lot of firearms out on the street."[22] New York senator Charles Schumer released a report showing that in 1998, 1% of the nation's FFLs were responsible for selling nearly half of traced crime guns.[23] (Of course, to evaluate this statistic properly, we would need to know what percent of all guns in those same areas were sold by those same 1% of dealers.) The study found that criminals obtained firearms through straw purchasers who made re-

---

*Two undercover agents contacted a New Mexico FFL who submitted Agent A's name to NICS. When the request was delayed, the FFL suggested that Agent B purchase the firearm and then transfer it to Agent A. Agent B, also using a counterfeit ID, was cleared immediately, and Agent A used his credit card to pay for the firearm. The FFL then sold Agent A a box of ammunition, assuring him that it was "the best ammunition he had in stock to penetrate a bulletproof vest similar to those worn by police officers" (GAO Report, Firearms Purchased from Federal Firearm Licensees Using Bogus Identification, p. 10).

peat purchases from a small number of FFLs. In just three years (1996–1998), the BATF traced 1,421 *homicide guns* to 140 gun dealers. Seven of eight crime guns bought from these gun dealers changed hands before being used in a crime.* This report confirms that most criminals do not buy guns from FFLs.

Unscrupulous FFLs can frustrate the Brady regulatory scheme by failing to keep records or by keeping sham records. Because there is no database on what firearms have been shipped to a particular dealer, audits of dealer records are time-consuming.† Disreputable dealers might record only a portion of the firearms received from manufacturers and sell the remainder without complying with the Brady Law. The chance of detection by BATF inspectors would be slight, since the BATF inspects dealer records no more than once a year and, on average, less than once in five years.[24]

In fact, only 10% of all FFLs have *ever* been inspected.[25] BATF inspections tend to concentrate on large retail stores, not fly-by-night operators.[26] The audit entails a time-consuming check of the FFL's firearms inventory, acquisition and disposition records, and the Form 4473.[27] With only 1,000 inspectors and 1,200 agents assigned to the firearms division, BATF hardly has the capacity and resources to monitor more than 80,000 firearms licensees. Congress did not appropriate funds for new agents and inspectors for Brady enforcement. Forced to add Brady enforcement to its other responsibilities, the agency responded by diverting resources from tobacco and alcohol enforcement and from headquarters and office operations.[28] Absent the threat of increased BATF inspections, dishonest FFLs may sell, barter, lend, or give away handguns without detection.

The BATF could uncover the unscrupulous FFL's activities only if a number of illegally sold guns were recovered with serial numbers intact and traced to the manufacturer and then to the dealer.[29] In theory, a vio-

---

*According to raw data amassed by the BATF, of the 34,867 guns traced back to these gun stores, in only 4,409 cases (12.6%) was the possessor of the crime gun the retail purchaser. In other words in almost 90% of the traces, the gun-wielding criminal had not obtained the gun from FFL.

†There are too few BATF inspectors to audit 80,000 FFLs. Because of a major BATF effort to eliminate the licenses of FFLs, who had no place of business and were not really in business, the number of FFLs declined dramatically. While the smaller number of dealers makes BATF's auditing job easier, the crack down on fringe FFLs may mean that more guns will be sold by non-FFLs, who are not subject to any regulation. See Christopher Koper, "Federal Legislation and Gun Markets: How Much Have Recent Reforms of the Federal Firearms Licensing System Reduced Criminal Gun Suppliers?" (2001). ("If federal reforms have reduced the availability of guns to criminals, the effect has probably been more modest than suggested by the overall reduction in dealers.")

lation could also be detected by comparing inventory records with sales.[30] FFLs are required to maintain records of all firearms shipped to them by manufacturers. A BATF inspector could compare the number of firearms received from all manufacturers (and wholesalers) with sales records and inventory.[31] An unscrupulous dealer would undoubtedly fail to record illegal sales. But we cannot infer illegal sales from recordkeeping discrepancies. Such discrepancies could also be the product of sloppy recording procedures and incompetent filing and storage of forms.

It is certainly not difficult for an ineligible individual to obtain a gun. Criminals seeking to acquire handguns can simply stroll into a gun show and purchase unlimited numbers of guns from unlicensed dealers. A gun show provides a convenient venue for a criminal to dispose of and purchase guns. From 1991 to 1997, 314 BATF investigations (involving over 54,000 firearms) traced "crime guns"* back to gun shows. Approximately 254 individuals identified in the BATF gun show investigations were checked against data in the Firearms Tracing System and related databases. Of these individuals, 44 had multiple purchase records with an average of 59 firearms per person. A total of 188 "crime guns" were traced back to these individuals, including one individual who had 53 crime guns traced to him.[32] Such an individual is obviously buying guns in order to supply the criminal market.

While the Brady Law aims to prevent a person with a felony record from purchasing a firearm from a licensed dealer, its background-checking system can be circumvented by use of false identity documents. Since the Brady machinery is based on a name check, it is possible for an ineligible person to obtain a firearm by giving a false name. Of course, the would-be purchaser has to show picture ID, but false ID is readily available. Moreover, one cannot expect the FFL or a clerk in the FFL's store to expertly scrutinize identity documents or to confront and rigorously cross-examine customers.

A recent investigation shows just how easily counterfeit documents can be used to avoid the Brady background check. In response to a request from Representative Henry Waxman (D-Calif.), the ranking member of the House Committee on Government Reform, the Government Accounting Office (GAO) created counterfeit drivers licenses using fictitious names, birthdates, and/or social security numbers, using off-the-shelf software, scanner, laminator, and color laser printer.[33] With these counterfeit drivers'

---

*"Crime guns" is a confusing category because it includes the crime of unlawful possession of a weapon. See BATF, *"Gun Shows: Brady Checks and Crime Gun Traces,"* appendix, table 1.

licenses, agents successfully purchased handguns in Virginia, West Virginia, Montana, New Mexico, and Arizona, even though the FFLs followed the Brady system and submitted their names to the NICS. NICS only halts a purchase if it locates a prior record in the name of the person seeking to make the purchase; an ex-felon who uses a counterfeit ID will not be identified as ineligible.[34]

Another strategy for defrauding the Brady system is for a potential purchaser, who knows he is ineligible to purchase a handgun from an FFL, to recruit a "straw purchaser" (a spouse, friend, or fellow gang member, with no disqualification) to purchase the handgun and then transfer it to him. Admittedly, the straw purchaser commits a federal felony in *knowingly* transferring the firearm to an ineligible person, but the risk of apprehension and punishment is small while the incentive (money, future reciprocities) or disincentive (threat) may be large.

Gaps in the Databases

In practically all states, databases on drug addiction and use, mental illness, and misdemeanor domestic assaults are incomplete, if they exist at all. If all users of illicit drugs were known, the number of blocked gun sales would be much greater. Who is a "drug user or addict" for purposes of firearms ineligibility? The Gun Control Act of 1968 neither defines the term nor states how recent the illegal drug use must be. According to BATF regulations, an individual is a "drug user," if there is "current evidence of use."* Possible examples of evidence indicating current drug use include needle marks, participation in drug treatment, or a positive drug test.[35] Accessible databases on participants in drug treatment programs do not exist (and attempts to compile them might well deter drug abusers from seeking treatment). Without such databases, how is an FFL supposed to determine if an individual recently took a urine test? Must the FFL ask the customer to roll up his sleeves to look for suspicious needle marks? An FFL cannot determine whether a person is enrolled in a drug program.

As for the term "addict," does it mean only persons currently abusing drugs or does it include former abusers now in treatment or remission? Is

---

*The National Institute on Drug Abuse defines "current drug user" as a person who has used drugs within the past month. Thus, an individual could be eligible to purchase a gun one week and ineligible the next (Tien and Rich, "Identifying Persons Other Than Felons," p. 16).

an individual who was addicted to cocaine in his twenties prohibited from purchasing a handgun in his fifties? What if he still regularly attends Narcotics Anonymous?

Records on voluntary and involuntary mental hospitalization mostly do not exist; those that do exist are protected by state privacy laws. Many state mental patient databases do not contain patient names, and private psychiatric hospitals do not provide patient information to state mental health agencies. Local court records contain information on adjudications of mental defectives and civil commitments, but very few people are hospitalized involuntarily. Even most severely mentally ill people who are hospitalized these days are voluntary admissions who do not go through any judicial proceedings. In any event, court records that do exist would have to be searched at the local level, a very time-consuming task.

While commanding FFLs not to sell guns to illegal aliens might sound good politically, there is no master database with the names and addresses of illegal aliens. According to a study by James M. Tien and Thomas F. Rich for the Department of Justice, "Unfortunately for the purpose of identifying persons ineligible to purchase firearms, most illegal aliens enter the country clandestinely and have not been apprehended or identified by the INS. Therefore, we do not have records that identify the vast majority of persons who are illegal aliens in this country."[36]

Records of dishonorable discharges from the military have recently become accessible to the NICS. The Defense Manpower Data Center in California maintains a computerized database of all persons discharged from the armed forces.[37] Thus, in theory, it would be possible to determine by an electronic search whether a prospective gun purchaser is ineligible due to a dishonorable discharge. However, as of spring 2001, these records were not readily accessible. Even if they become accessible, the two to four months delay between the date of discharge and the date the discharge is entered into the computer system provides a dishonorably discharged soldier or sailor with a window of opportunity to purchase a firearm.

Brady does not prohibit those with convictions for erratic behavior like drunk driving and disorderly conduct or for violent misdemeanors, other than domestic violence, from purchasing a firearm. Yet, arguably, a person recently convicted of misdemeanor drunk driving or stalking poses as much risk with a gun as a person with a felony conviction for fraud, theft, or tax evasion. A Georgia study found that more than 40% of people buying two or more guns in a single purchase had at least one misdemeanor conviction on their record.[38]

Conclusion

The Brady Law is the federal government's preeminent attempt to prevent presumptively dangerous people from purchasing firearms. However, Brady's supporters have underestimated the ease with which the regulatory system established by the law can be circumvented, and they have overestimated the ability of government agencies to enforce the law. The background check can be stymied by nonexistent or incomplete criminal databases, the use of straw purchasers, counterfeit IDs, and unscrupulous FFLs.

Brady's effectiveness is severely undermined by its failure to cover secondary handgun transfers, including those that take place at gun shows. The existence of a robust informal market (family, friends, and unlicenced dealers) for illegal guns makes it unlikely that the Brady Law has had any significant impact on handgun acquisition and possession by criminals. Since any handgun owner who is not a licensed dealer may sell, loan, give, or otherwise transfer his handgun to another person without filling out the requisite forms, informing any state or federal officials, conducting any background check, or abiding by any waiting period, a criminal can easily obtain a handgun without passing a Brady background check. Furthermore, 500,000 firearms are stolen each year. The thieves may keep the guns themselves, pass them on to friends and colleagues, or sell them to fences.

7

Evaluating the Brady Law

Every time we [enact gun control legislation], the hunter and
the fisherman and the law-abiding sports people are the ones
who get nailed. They are the ones who get hurt. They are the
ones that they enact these Mickey Mouse registration and
regulation requirements upon. And frankly, they wind up the
ones who get hurt . . . This type of legislation amounts to . . .
another form of harassment by a central government which
will not destroy the [Brady] forms . . . and which will use those
to harass and hurt law-abiding people.
—Senator Orrin Hatch (R-Utah)

The gun lobby and its allies in Congress would have us believe
that there is nothing government can do to control the
epidemic of gun violence. This is not true. Here's proof: In the
first seven months of the instant background check required by
[the Brady] law, 100,000 criminals and mentally disturbed
individuals were prevented from buying a gun. This type of
sensible gun law works, and further steps to regulate the flow
of guns and ammunition can work too.
—Senator Barbara Boxer (D-Calif.),
 "No Sanctuary from Gun Violence"

Experience, and I might add common sense, has taught me
that because criminals don't obey the law, gun control will only
limit those who do. It may be old fashioned, but keeping
criminals behind bars still seems [to] be the most effective
approach in fighting crime. Gun control is a completely

> ineffective approach to the lack of safety and security in our communities. Disarming law-abiding citizens only places them at the mercy of those who break the law.
> —Senator Robert Dole (R-Kans.), 1996 letter to NRA

Even before the ink was dry, the Brady Law was hailed as a success. At the bill signing ceremony, President Clinton called the Brady Law "step one in taking our streets back, taking our children back, reclaiming our families and our future."[1] Sarah Brady predicted, "It will begin to make a difference. It will begin to save lives."[2] On the third anniversary of the law's passage, she insisted that "every day criminals do attempt to buy guns, and it's the Brady Law that stops them."[3] In 1998, she declared that "the Brady law has contributed to a major decline in gun related crimes . . . The Brady law is working."[4] The Bradys, members of the Clinton administration, and Democratic legislators have all pronounced the Brady Law an example of successful gun control.

Celebrities have added their voices to the chorus of praise for the Brady Law. Six years after it was signed, Jack Nicholson, Diane Keaton, Gregory Peck (who serves as the honorary chair of the Sarah and Jim Brady Society), and other members of the Hollywood community organized a reception, attended by the Bradys and President Clinton, honoring Clinton's role in the Brady Law's passage.[5] On its spring/summer 2001 U.S. tour, the Irish rock group U2 released a statement praising the Bradys and urging "more people [to] come around to [their] way of thinking."[6]

The only data cited in support of the claim that the Brady Law has reduced violent crime are the number of firearm purchases blocked by background checks. A number of government studies have found that approximately 2%–3% of proposed retail sales by FFLs are blocked by Brady background checks. To Brady Law supporters, this statistic demonstrates that (1) the vast majority of Americans can obtain guns easily; (2) the small minority of ineligible (and presumably dangerous) Americans who try to purchase handguns are prevented from obtaining them; (3) hundreds of thousands, perhaps millions, of Americans with disqualifying criminal and other records are deterred from even trying to purchase guns; and (4) gun crime is reduced because potential gun-wielding criminals are denied the tools of their trade.

This chapter first examines the logic of inferring gun crime reduction from blocked FFL sales. Then, aided by an impressive study by Professors Jens Ludwig and Phil Cook, it assesses whether the decline in violent crime that took place during the 1990s can be attributed to the Brady Law.

Inferring Crime Reduction
from Blocked Retail Sales

There has been a steady stream of government reports presenting favorable accounts of the Brady Law at work. For example, in 1997, the Bureau of Justice Statistics reported that from 1994 to 1996, 7.9 million background checks produced approximately 173,000 rejections or 2.2% of proposed sales.[7] During 1996 alone, approximately 70,000 prospective purchasers were rejected out of 2.5 million (2.8%); 67% of these rejections were based on the purchaser's prior felony record and the remainder for the following reasons: fugitives from justice, 6%; state law prohibition, 5.5%; domestic violence restraining orders, 3.9%; mental defectives, 1.5%; drug users/addicts, 1.2%; and all others, including illegal aliens, juveniles, dishonorable discharges, misdemeanor domestic violence convictions, and renunciation of citizenship, 13.4% (see figure 7.1).

In the first year of permanent Brady (1999), about 8.8 million background checks were performed: 32% for handgun purchases, 66% for long guns and shotguns, and 1% for single purchases of both types of guns. Of these checks, 81,006 (1%) resulted in denials. Of the frustrated purchasers, 17% appealed and 22% of the appeals succeeded.[8] In 2000, 153,000 (2%) of 7,699,000 applications were rejected.[9] A felony record remained the most common reason for rejection (57.6%), even though rejections for other reasons increased.[10]

If the Brady Law prevents 80,000 firearms sales annually, does this mean that 80,000 (nonpossessory) handgun crimes or more (given some offenders' prolific criminality) are prevented? No. Many rejected purchasers would not have committed gun crimes. Many were not left unarmed, since they already owned one or more guns. Still other rejected purchasers would have obtained a gun in the secondary or black market.

It is certainly not realistic to assume that all 80,000 frustrated gun purchasers were bent on committing gun-related crimes. Persons who renounce their American citizenship, for example, typically do so for tax reasons unrelated to gun crimes. Nor is it clear that illegal aliens are likely to be a greater danger with firearms than legal aliens and citizens. Finally, there is some research that shows that, contrary to popular opinion, persons with a history of mental illness are not more crime prone than people without such a history.* The comprehensive "MacArthur Foundation

*A 1999 study found that 61% of the American population believe that schizophrenics are "very" or "somewhat" likely "to do something violent to others." Nu-

Figure 7.1. Trends in Brady Rejections

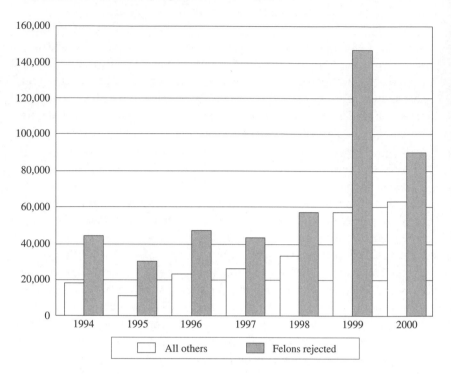

Source: Bureau of Justice Statistics, *Background Checks for Firearm Transfers, 2000*.

Study" of mental disorder and violence found that mental illness by itself is not a strong predictor of future violence. Its study of a sample of outpatients released from mental institutions found that future violence was best explained by prior violence and criminality, childhood experience, alcohol and/or drug dependency, race, and, especially, neighborhood.[11] Controlling for these variables eliminated most of the correlation between mental illness and future criminality.

The MacArthur research also demonstrated that lumping "discharged mental patients" into a single category of people at high risk for future violence is misleading. For example, schizophrenics showed lower levels

_____

merous studies offer conflicting evidence on this point. Some have found a higher incidence of violence among schizophrenics when compared with people suffering from other types of mental illness. Others have found similar or lower rates of violence for schizophrenics (John Monahan et al., *Rethinking Risk Assessment: The MacArthur Study of Mental Disorder and Violence*, pp. 61–62).

of violence than patients diagnosed with bipolar disorder or depression.[12] Psychopaths were more prone to violence than delusional patients.[13] The report advised clinicians that "the same variable could be a positive risk factor for one group, unrelated to violence in another group, and a protective factor against violence in a third group." Thus, even if complete records of mental commitment existed and could be accessed, so that persons with a history of mental illness would be blocked from purchasing firearms from an FFL, any corresponding reduction in gun crime would be purely speculative.

Most people probably assume that persons with a felony record present a greater risk of committing future firearms offenses than persons without a felony record, and that denying "ex-felons" the right to purchase guns prevents some number of gun crimes. However, the Brady Law disqualifies *all persons* with felony records, *no matter what the prior felony and no matter how many years have passed.* According to the Brady Law's logic, a 40-year-old man who was convicted of car theft 20 years earlier is too dangerous to own a firearm. It seems questionable whether a middle-aged man with youthful convictions for joyriding or car theft (not to mention convictions for income tax evasion, fraud, and embezzlement)* poses a higher than average risk of gun violence for the rest of his life.

A study by Wright, Wintemute, and Rivara lends limited support to the assumption that a felony record is a valid predictor of future gun crime.[14] The researchers compared 170 California applicants who were not permitted to make gun purchases because of prior *convictions*, with 2,470 applicants who had felony arrests but no convictions and thus were able to purchase guns. They hypothesized that these two groups were similar with respect to their criminality (the difference between arrest without conviction and arrest with conviction being fortuitous) and thus would have identical patterns of criminal behavior, except if being prevented from purchasing a firearm suppressed the criminality of the group with the convictions.

In the three years after their gun purchase applications, 31% of both groups had accumulated arrests for new offenses. Twenty percent of the group with prior convictions and 19% of the group with prior arrests were convicted of new offenses. From these statistics alone, we might infer that denying the prior convictions group an opportunity to purchase a new handgun from an FFL had no effect on their future criminality. However, because the arrestee group had a significantly higher percentage of arrests

---

*The federal-felon-in-possession law makes an exception for persons convicted of "business-related crimes."

for gun offenses, the authors estimated that the Brady Law prevented approximately 25 gun offenses and 41 violent offenses by members of the prior convictions group.* This modest study should not be overly relied on. The number of gun crime arrests for both groups was very small so that a difference of several arrests for either group would have negated the author's conclusion.

Even if the person prevented from making a gun purchase is a dangerous criminal, he may already own one or more guns; the more criminally minded the person, the more likely it is that he already owns a gun or knows people who can provide him with a gun. Even if the Brady machinery is effective in blocking a would-be criminal's access to a *new* firearm, the rejected purchaser could just as easily commit a gun crime with an old gun. Indeed, he or she could commit a violent crime with a different type of deadly weapon, (e.g., tire iron, knife, or box cutter).†

Hardened criminals are least inclined to purchase guns from FFLs, and they have the best access to other sources of weapons. Studies show that a large majority of prison inmates obtain their guns outside the primary market.[15] Since 1968, FFLs have been required to maintain a record of their customer's identity. Thus, a rational criminal would know that a handgun purchased from an FFL could be traced back to him and prefer to obtain a gun in the secondary market (from a non-FFL seller) or from a gun-runner on the black market.

Who are the individuals who attempt to purchase a firearm from an FFL, knowing that they are not eligible to make the purchase because of a prior criminal record? They would know from the form that they sign when applying to purchase a firearm that lying about their eligibility is itself a federal crime. And they would probably know that by possessing a firearm, they violate the federal felon-in-possession law with its maximum 10-year prison term. It would certainly be interesting to know what offenses such individuals have been convicted of and how many years before. Perhaps many such persons believe that since the conviction took place many years ago and in a different part of the country, it will not

---

*Ludwig and Cook projected that if the results of Wright, Wintemute, and Rivara's study of the California background check were projected to the entire nation, there would have been 44,000 blocked handgun sales in 1996 and 8 homicides prevented. See Jens Ludwig and Philip Cook, "Homicides and Suicide Rates Associated with Implementation of the Brady Handgun Violence Prevention Act," p. 10.

†Frank Zimring has shown an *instrumentality effect* for gun crimes; when the same crime is committed with guns or other weapons, those committed with guns result in more serious injuries and deaths (Franklin Zimring and Gordon Hawkins, *Citizens' Guide to Gun Control*). But see Kleck, *Targeting Guns*.

be discovered. It is implausible that many dangerous ex-felons would ignore the draconian consequences of being identified as ineligible, especially when it is so easy to purchase a firearm in the unregulated secondary market.

What does 80,000 blocked sales per year suggest about the Brady Law's deterrent effect? How many ineligible persons, concerned that the Brady background check will catch them, do not even try to purchase a firearm? There is no basis for even speculating on the answer to this question. We can say that the deterred purchaser, like the rejected purchaser, could easily obtain a gun in the secondary market.

The magnitude of any deterrent effect will depend not only on prospective violators' perception of the *risk* of being identified as ineligible, but also on their perception of the *consequences* of being so identified. Can rejected purchasers expect to be punished for lying on the Brady Form? Though the BATF is authorized to investigate for possible prosecution prospective gun purchasers blocked by NICS, one study showed that BATF headquarters referred only 32% of rejected purchasers to BATF field offices for investigation.[16] According to the General Accounting Office, this low number is the consequence of insufficient evidence and inadequate resources. As a result, only the highest priority cases, those involving attempted purchasers who have a record of violent felonies, serious drug trafficking, or prior firearms convictions, are investigated.[17] The BATF's decision not to investigate two-thirds of rejected gun purchasers belies the notion that a high number of rejections implies an equal number of crimes prevented. If the BATF itself estimates that so few rejected purchasers are a real threat, then how much crime is really being prevented? And, if ineligible persons know that enforcement is so lax, how many are deterred from attempting to purchase a firearm from an FFL?

In November 1998, the Executive Office for U.S. Attorneys (EOUSA), noting that only 50 Brady false-form cases had been prosecuted nationwide in the previous year, urged local offices to increase the number of Brady false-form prosecutions. U.S. attorneys were urged to "incorporat[e such prosecutions] into the respective U.S. Attorney's Office's overall antiviolent crime strategy to remove dangerous offenders from the street."[18]

EOUSA subsequently reported that in fiscal year 1999, 2,272 defendants charged under 18 U.S.C. 922 (a) (6) and/or 18 U.S.C. 922 (g) or 922 (n)* were convicted for firearms-related false statements or felon-in-

*18 U.S.C. 922 (a) (6) makes it unlawful for individuals to knowingly make false statements to FFLs in connection with the attempted purchase of a firearm; 18

possession violations. But EOUSA could not determine how many of these charges came about by following up on denied Brady applications, rather than as felon-in-possession counts in prosecutions of armed felonies.[19] When John Ashcroft became attorney general in 2001, he instructed U.S. attorneys to prosecute those gun purchasers who knowingly provide false information on the purchase forms.

The Brady Law and the Falling Crime Rate: The Cook and Ludwig Study

The rate of violent crime for the nation as a whole and for most of the nation's largest cities has fallen dramatically since the early 1990s. In 1996, the violent crime rate dropped 7%, the greatest decrease since 1961, while the number of robberies dropped by 8%.[20] In 1997, the murder rate fell to 6.8 per 100,000 population, its lowest level in three decades, and the homicide victimization rates of cities with a population of 1 million or more fell to the lowest level in two decades.[21] By 1999, the eighth annual decline in the FBI's Crime Index brought the crime rate to its lowest point since 1978.[22] The figures are similar for gun crimes as well; after peaking in the third quarter of 1993, by the second quarter of 1995, there had been a 23% drop in the rate of criminal firearm injuries and a 10% drop in the firearm-related fatality rate.[23] In fact, the decline in firearm-related crimes outpaced those involving other weapons, so that the *percentage of crimes* involving firearms also decreased.[24]

Could some or all of this decline be attributed to the Brady Law? It seems unlikely given that the precipitous crime drop occurred in both Brady and non-Brady states; New York City, a non-Brady jurisdiction (because it had more stringent gun controls than those imposed by the Brady Law), experienced the largest drop of any U.S. city. In explaining the unprecedented decline in crime, criminologists stress a variety of other factors, including a drop in alcohol consumption, economic prosperity, improved and innovative police tactics, and a massive increase in the prison population.[25] Many criminologists have pointed to the decline of crack use.[26] Alfred Blumstein and Joel Wallman, the editors of a recently published and very well-received study on the nation's crime drop, devoted practically no attention to the Brady Law. They did note that "handgun violence took a sharp downturn at just about the time the Brady Bill be-

---

U.S.C. 922 (g) and 922 (n) make it unlawful for prohibited persons to receive or possess firearms.

came effective. . . . it is not known how many of those [400,000 ineligible] customers eventually bought guns from an unregulated source."[27] But the variables they chose to examine in their book are changes in economics, demographics, the prison population, policing tactics, and drug usage.

Only professors Philip Cook and Jens Ludwig have sought to test empirically the impact of the Brady Law by comparing gun crime trends in the 18 states where the gun purchasing process was unchanged by the Brady Law (because state laws were already as or more stringent than Brady) with gun crime trends in the 32 states where the Brady Law added a waiting period and/or a background check to existing state gun controls. If the Brady Law deterred gun violence after it became effective in 1994, there would have been a greater reduction in gun homicides and suicides by persons over 21 years old in states covered by the Brady Law than in the states unaffected by Brady. Persons under 21 were ineligible to purchase handguns both before and after Brady.

Utilizing the 18 states as the control group and the 32 Brady states as the treatment group, Cook and Ludwig* "exploit[ed] the natural experiment generated by the Brady Act by comparing the change in rate of violence in the Brady treatment states from the pre-Brady to post-Brady period with the change in rates of violence over the same period in the control states."† The authors sought to explain changes in rates of homicide, firearm homicide, suicide, firearm suicide, and the percentage of homicides and suicides committed with a gun. The study held constant state-level changes that might have influenced rates of crime and violence, including consumption of alcohol per capita, percent of population living in a metro area, percent of population below the official poverty line, income per worker, percent African-American, and percent of the population falling into seven different age groups.[28] The trends in firearm homicides and suicides in both treatment and control states were similar during the 1990–1993 pre-Brady period and would be expected to con-

*Professor Cook (Duke University), long recognized as one of the nation's leading criminal justice policy analysts, has undertaken empirical studies on gun violence and gun controls for 25 years. In previous work, Cook has been relatively optimistic about the crime-reducing potential of handgun controls. See Philip J. Cook, Stephanie Molliconi, and Thomas B. Cole, *Regulating Gun Markets*, p. 59.

†Ludwig and Cook, "Homicide and Suicide Rates Associated with Implementation of the Brady Handgun Violence Prevention Act," p. 5. The treatment states were Alabama, Alaska, Arizona, Arkansas, Colorado, Georgia, Idaho, Kansas, Kentucky, Louisiana, Maine, Minnesota, Mississippi, Montana, Nebraska, New Hampshire, New Mexico, North Carolina, North Dakota, Ohio, Oklahoma, Pennsylvania, Rhode Island, South Carolina, South Dakota, Tennessee, Texas, Utah, Vermont, Washington, West Virginia, and Wyoming.

tinue on a parallel course, unless the Brady Law had a significant impact.[29]

The statistical analysis provided *"no evidence that implementation of the Brady Act was associated with a reduction in homicide rates"* (emphasis added).[30] There was no statistical difference in homicide and suicide in the Brady and control states,[31] although the rate of *suicide by handgun* among persons 55 and older decreased in treatment states, where waiting period and background check requirements were both affected by the Brady Law.[32] Nevertheless, there was *no difference in total suicides* in the treatment and control states. In other words, if the Brady Law did have the effect of modestly reducing firearm suicides (by approximately 6%), this effect was completely offset by an increase of the same magnitude in nonfirearm suicide. Apparently, if suicidal people in the Brady states were unable to obtain firearms, they found other ways to kill themselves.

Cook and Ludwig also asked whether or not there was a negative correlation between waiting periods and mortality rates by first comparing the control states with states that experienced change in background checks but no change in waiting periods, and then comparing the control states with the states that experienced a change in both background checks and waiting periods. Because there was no significant difference in homicide or suicide trends, the authors rejected the hypothesis that a waiting period reduced handgun homicide and suicide. This finding is consistent with most previous evaluations of state-level background checks and waiting period laws.[33]

Cook and Ludwig found their results unsurprising, since the Brady Law left the secondary market for guns completely unregulated. They point out that the secondary market is the source of most guns possessed by juveniles and criminals and speculate that the 1968 GCA, which required FFLs to record the identity of gun purchasers, might already have pushed criminals fearful of leaving a paper trail into the secondary market.

Gun control advocates reacted to Cook and Ludwig's pessimistic findings by raising the possibility that the Brady Law may have reduced the flow of guns from traffickers into both Brady and non-Brady states. Cook and Ludwig call the evidence for this hypothesis "sketchy at best."[34] They reason that since both gun and nongun homicides fell during the 1990s, "the same factors that led to fewer murders without guns are presumably responsible for much of the reduction in gun murders as well,"[35] and that attributing this drop to the Brady Law is mere speculation.*

---

*John Lott, an economist, found that those states that passed laws making it easier to carry guns experienced a greater drop in gun crime than states without

Following closely on the publication of Cook and Ludwig's experiment was a new study of Virginia's gun control laws, undertaken by Mark Coggeshall, a graduate student at the University of Maryland.[36] Virginia was exempt from the Brady Law because its gun control laws in 1993 were more stringent than Brady. Its point-of-sale instant background check (passed in 1989) was "designed to minimize access to firearms by persons with troubled criminal, mental health, or substance abuse histories while erecting minimal barriers to access to firearms by persons without such records."* In 1993, Virginia passed a one-gun-per-month limit on firearm purchases.[37]

The Virginia Firearms Transaction Center (VFTC), which administers the background check much in the way that NICS does, processed 1,761,076 firearm transactions from November 1989 through December 1999, and rejected 19,259 applicants (1.1%). A prior felony conviction was the reason for nearly half (49.4%) of the rejections.[38] However, when Coggeshall used the FBI's Supplementary Homicide Reports (SHR), he found a significant *increase* in homicide (primarily by firearm) following the passage of the background check.† Coggeshall concluded that his study "must be discouraging for those who suppose that such systems are formidable instruments of crime control . . . For now, there is no evidence that instant background check systems, even when implemented in earnest, prevent homicides."[39]

Conclusion

That the Brady machinery has prevented 70,000 to 100,000 sales per year does not justify an inference that a comparable number, or any number, of violent crimes has been prevented or deterred. These rejected purchas-

---

such gun laws. Lott found that there was a sharp spike in firearm sales after 1988, when Brady was first proposed, and especially in 1993, the year before it went into effect. Lott believes that more guns produce less crime because criminals fear the risk of encountering armed resistance. Therefore, Brady, in the short run, might have reduced crime by increasing the number of armed citizens (*More Guns, Less Crime*).

*Coggeshall, "Keeping Guns Out of the Wrong Hands," p. 38. In 1995, Virginia also passed an NRA-favored "shall-issue" law that required officials to grant law-abiding applicants permits to carry a concealed weapon.

†The effects of the one-gun-per-month law on SHR data was insignificant, though the shall-issue law was associated with reductions in homicide. Using other homicide data, he found that the three laws had no significant effect on both firearm and nonfirearm homicide. Coggeshall, "Keepings Guns Out of the Wrong Hands," p. 2.

ers may already have owned guns. Other rejected (or deterred) purchasers may have obtained a gun from a non-FFL. They could have accomplished this by placing an advertisement in the paper or by answering a gun-for-sale advertisement. They could have gone to a gun show and purchased a firearm on the spot from a non-FFL without any paperwork or background check. They could have asked a friend or relative, with a clean criminal record, to purchase a gun for them, or they themselves could have purchased a firearm from an FFL using counterfeit ID. They could have stolen a gun. Among prospective gun purchasers rejected or deterred by the Brady machinery, the most dangerous and irresponsible individuals would most persistently try to obtain a gun. For these individuals, the Brady Law hardly presents an impediment.

There are no empirical studies purporting to demonstrate that the Brady Law has reduced gun crime. Cook and Ludwig's research, comparing gun crime rates in Brady and non-Brady states since 1994, shows the opposite, a finding reinforced by Mark Coggeshall's finding that Virginia's instant background check had no effect on firearm homicide. The Brady Law seeks to regulate only gun sales by FFLs, leaving the secondary market unregulated. That fact alone ought to make us skeptical that the law could have much, if any, effect on reducing gun and nongun violent crime.

III

POLICY OPTIONS FOR THE FUTURE

Parts I and II assessed where we've been and where we are now. Part III asks, where do we go from here? Chapters 8 and 9 consider the possibility of further elaborating on the model of keeping guns out of the hands of dangerous persons that was established by the 1938 Federal Firearms Act and carried forward by the 1968 Gun Control Act and the 1993 Brady Law. Chapter 8 examines the possibility of extending Brady background checks to gun shows and to the secondary firearms market generally. Chapter 9 analyzes the feasibility of registering firearms and licensing owners, two strategies that would be necessary to bring the secondary market into the Brady regulatory scheme.

The remaining chapters consider other types of gun control. Chapter 10 takes a hard look at prohibition and disarmament. Chapter 11 examines a whole range of gun control proposals, including mandatory trigger locks, smart guns, banning "bad" guns, limiting gun sales to one per month, safe storage laws, and regulating ammunition. Chapter 12 focuses on the crime control potential of heightened enforcement of current gun controls.

8

Closing the Gun Show and Secondary Market Loophole

Eric Harris and Dylan Klebold had gone to the Tanner gun
show on Saturday and they took me back with them on
Sunday. While we were walking around, Eric and Dylan kept
asking sellers if they were private or licensed. They wanted to
buy their guns from someone who was private and not
licensed because there would be no paperwork or background
check. It was too easy. I wish it had been more difficult. I
wouldn't have helped them buy the guns if I had faced a
background check.
—Robyn Anderson, testimony to the House Judiciary Committee
   regarding the massacre at Columbine, January 27, 2000

Neither the Brady Law nor any other federal law regulates gun sales, loans, gifts, or barters that take place between private individuals, if neither of them is a Federal Firearms Licensee (FFL).[1] In addition, if FFLs transfer guns from their "personal collections," they do not have to initiate background checks on their purchasers. These omissions constitute a huge gap in the Brady Law because the overwhelming majority of criminals obtain their firearms in the secondary market, including at gun shows.[2]

In 1998, there were 4,442 gun shows* in the United States, usually held in arenas, civic centers, fairgrounds, or armories. A gun show is typically

---

*The definition of a gun show for policy-making purposes is important. If gun shows were simply regulated by name, promoters could avoid the regulation by calling their shows "flea markets." The Gun Show Accountability Act (GSAA) de-

a weekend event, drawing 2,500 to 5,000 attendees, who pay a small admission price to browse through the exhibits and examine and purchase firearms that catch their fancy.[3] While gun shows probably account for only a very small fraction (perhaps 2%) of total U.S. gun sales, they are a perfect place for moving guns from law-abiding owners to criminals and vice-versa.[4] This chapter examines the feasibility of subjecting gun show firearms sales, loans and barters, as well as other secondary market transfers, to the Brady background check regimen. In particular, it focuses on the proposed Gun Show Accountability Act (GSAA) that proponents put forward as a plan for "closing the gun show loophole."[5]

Regulating Gun Shows

The Gun Control Act of 1968 (GCA) restricted FFLs to selling firearms at their place of business. But the Firearms Owners' Protection Act of 1986 (FOPA) allowed FFLs to sell firearms at gun shows, leading to an increasing number of these events. FFLs must initiate Brady background checks on gun show purchasers just as they do on purchasers who come into their stores, except for purchasers of guns from an FFL's "personal collection." Thus, FFLs can avoid Brady background checks by declaring certain guns part of their personal collections or by giving guns to relatives or friends who, as non-FFLs, could sell them at a gun show without subjecting the purchaser to a background check. Non-FFLs can sell firearms without background checks, although they do have to see proof of residency and age, since it is unlawful to transfer a firearm to an out-of-state resident, a handgun to anyone under 21, and a long gun to anyone under 18.

The BATF's supervision of gun shows and flea markets is restricted to investigations of "situations where there are specific allegations that significant violations have occurred and where there is reliable information that guns sold at the specific gun show or flea market have shown up in crimes of violence with some degree of regularity."[6] BATF's lack of zealous enforcement has drawn complaints from FFLs, who resent "unfair com-

---

fines gun shows as any "event (a) at which 50 or more firearms are offered or exhibited for sale, transfer, or exchange, if one or more of the firearms has been shipped or transported in, or otherwise affects, interstate or foreign commerce and (b) at which two or more persons are offering or exhibiting one or more firearms for sale, transfer, or exchange." The Hatch/Craig bill defines gun shows more narrowly so that if there are less then 10 exhibitors (undefined), the GSAA would not apply. Senators John McCain and Joe Lieberman introduced a compromise bill (S. 890), the Gun Show Loophole Closing and Gun Law Enforcement Act, into the 107th Congress. Their bill regulates events at which more than 75 guns are offered for sale, except where guns are part of a personal collection.

petition" from non-FFLs. According to Bill Bridgewater, executive director of the National Alliance of Stocking Gun Dealers:

> The BATF has established rules and regulations for these things they call "gun shows." The opportunity for the black marketers is that the BATF doesn't enforce those regulations and there isn't anyone else to do so. Consequently, there are literally hundreds of "gun shows" scattered around the country where you may rent tables, display your wares, sell what you please to whomever you please; the sale that is made with no records, no questions and no papers, earns the highest sales price. There are wide open "gun shows" the length and breadth of the United States, wherein anyone may do as he chooses, including buy firearms for children.[7]

BATF investigations have revealed numerous federal firearms violations associated with gun shows, such as straw purchases, sales by FFLs to out-of-state residents, FFL sales without background checks, and sales of illegal kits used to convert semiautomatic weapons to fully automatic weapons. Criminals seeking to acquire handguns can stroll into a gun show and purchase as many guns as they like from unlicensed sellers. Likewise, gun shows are an ideal place for criminals to sell stolen guns.

The Gun Show Accountability Act

On November 6, 1998, President Clinton charged a task force, led by Attorney General Janet Reno and Secretary of the Treasury Robert Rubin, to come up with a proposal that would close "the gun show loophole."[8] The attorney general and the secretary of the treasury sought input from U.S. attorneys, law enforcement organizations, the BATF, and other individuals and agencies.

In January 1999, the task force recommended that all gun transfers (sales, barters, loans) at gun shows be subjected to Brady background checking; this was to be accomplished by requiring that all gun transfers "go through" an FFL. In other words, a non-FFL seller would have to find an FFL at the gun show to initiate the background check and keep the paperwork on the sale. The FFL could charge a fee for providing this service. President Clinton endorsed the proposal. On February 23, 1999, almost a month before the Columbine massacre, Senator Frank Lautenberg (D-N.J.) and Representative Rod R. Blagojevich (D-Ill.), introduced the administration's proposal into the 106th Congress as the "Gun Show Accountability Act [GSSA]."[9] Two months later, the GSAA became the administration's principal response to the Columbine massacre.

The GSAA defines a gun show as "any event where 50 or more firearms are offered or exhibited for sale, transfer, or exchange, if one or more of the firearms has been shipped or transported in, or otherwise affects, interstate or foreign commerce." It requires gun show promoters to register with the secretary of the treasury and assigns them certain responsibilities. The promoter must notify the secretary of the treasury when and where a gun show will be taking place, check the photo identification of each vendor, keep a list of firearm vendors at the show, indicating whether each vendor is an FFL. The promoter must provide all vendors with information about federal and state gun laws and maintain copies of all the above records at the FFL's permanent place of business. The secretary of the treasury is authorized to review the records and the inventory of any promoter conducting a gun show, either at the show or at the promoter's permanent place of business, without a warrant or showing of probable cause.

The GSAA states that *if any part of a firearm transfer* takes place at a gun show, it is subject to an FFL-initiated background check. However, the bill does not define "part of a transfer" and thus opens a potentially huge loophole. Suppose the physical transfer occurred a day, week, or month after the gun show concluded? Will all transfers first conceived or discussed at a gun show be subject to the GSAA's requirements? Treasury Department regulations would have to deal with this question, but there is no obvious solution.

The GSAA did not include an independent waiting period, just compliance with the Brady Law, which allows NICS up to three business days to block a sale based on the purchaser's criminal record or other disqualification. The FFL brokering the sale is required to maintain records of the manufacturer, model, and firearm's serial number, as well as identifying information about the buyer and seller. Only the information about the firearm must be sent to the BATF's National Tracing Center. However, the FFL must keep the information about the buyer and seller on file and release it to the BATF if requested for a bona fide trace. If, in a five-day period, the FFL brokers more than one sale involving the same seller and buyer, he must file a multiple sale form with the BATF.

Under the GSAA, FFLs would no longer be able to sell guns from their personal collections without initiating a purchaser background check. Furthermore, a person who transfers a gun without a purchaser background check would be guilty of a federal felony carrying a maximum punishment of five years imprisonment.[10] An FFL who violates the law is also subject to having his FFL license suspended or canceled and a $10,000 civil fine. A purchaser could be prosecuted federally for knowingly making false statements on any forms submitted pursuant to the GSAA.

The GSAA enjoyed the support of President Clinton and Attorney General Reno, Vice President Al Gore, and a host of gun control groups, including Handgun Control, Inc., and Americans for Gun Safety (AGS), a new gun control organization that made gun show regulation the centerpiece of its political debut. Other individuals and lobbying groups that are on record as favoring the GSAA include Senator John McCain, various police organizations, and the National Alliance of Stocking Gun Dealers (NASGD).[11]

A few organizations have urged regulation that is more stringent than the GSAA. For example, The Trauma Foundation of San Francisco argued that only FFLs should be permitted to sell firearms at gun shows and that there should be a limit on the total number of firearms sold at a single gun show. The Violence Policy Center (VPC) proposed (1) prohibiting non-FFLs from selling firearms at gun shows, (2) limiting the type of firearms sales that could be made by a non-FFL, and (3) prohibiting the sale of certain types of military hardware.* Amazingly, to my knowledge, none of the gun control groups called for a ban on gun shows.

The Massacre at Columbine

On April 20, 1999, the massacre at Columbine High School in suburban Littleton, Colorado, rocked the nation. Eric Harris, age 18, and Dylan Klebold, age 17, fatally shot 12 classmates and one teacher, as well as themselves; they wounded many others. Three of the four firearms used in the attack were long guns that were purchased for them by a girlfriend at a Denver gun show.[12] The killers also obtained a semiautomatic handgun from an adult who purchased the gun for them at a gun show.[13] (He later pled guilty to knowingly transferring a firearm to underage boys and was sentenced to a six-year federal prison term.)[14] Because the two boys obtained their guns indirectly from gun shows, there was a chorus of demand to pass the GSAA.[15]

During the presidential campaign, Governor George W. Bush supported a background check for firearms transfers at gun shows, but he opposed applying the Brady Law's three-day waiting period to those sales. On June 18, 1999, Representative John Dingell (D-Mich.) offered an amendment allow-

---

*If the GSAA could be enforced it would essentially implement the VPC's recommendations, since it would result in background checks for all purchasers and records of all sales.

ing NICS only 24 hours to conduct a background check on a gun show fire-arm sale. It was defeated.[16]

Senators Orrin Hatch (R-Utah) and Larry Craig (R-Idaho) introduced into the Senate an amendment similar to Dingell's Bill. In addition, the Hatch/Craig Bill narrowed the definition of gun shows so that some events covered by the Lautenberg bill would not be covered.[17] For example, the Hatch/Craig Bill would permit gun show vendors to pool their firearms, reducing the number of individual vendors and thus removing the event from the definition of a gun show. The Democrats opposed Hatch/Craig on the ground that it did not include a requirement that pawnshop oper-ators conduct a background check on customers who redeem their own guns. The Senate passed the Hatch/Craig Bill by a vote of 53–47 on May 14, 1999,[18] but the House version did not pass. Senators John McCain and Joe Lieberman introduced the Gun Show Loophole Closing and Gun Law Enforcement Act of 2001 into the 107th Congress; it attempts to split the difference between the GSAA and the Hatch/Craig bill. As this book goes to press (summer 2002), there is little prospect of passage.

What the GSAA Would Likely Accomplish

The GSAA, like the Brady Law, would be easy to circumvent. The easiest avoidance strategy for the ineligible purchaser would be to have a straw purchaser—a friend, relative, or gang comrade with no criminal record—buy the gun for him. A vendor who is selling a stolen gun or who wishes to avoid the time and expense of finding an FFL to facilitate the sale could walk around a gun show with a placard that reads, "44 Magnum for sale; no questions asked." Upon inquiry, the seller with an eye on the GSAA might explain that he does not have the firearm with him but can show and sell it that evening or some evening the next week, if the purchaser meets him at a designated location.

If a purchaser seeking to avoid a background check negotiates a pur-chase for the next week or the week after, would his transaction come within the GSAA? Does "part of the transfer," under the GSAA, cover sales *first conceived or discussed* at a gun show? The answer depends on reg-ulations that would have to be issued by the secretary of the treasury after passage of the law. To make the GSAA even plausibly effective, those regulations should specify that if *communication* leading to a firearm sale originated within the grounds of a gun show, that communication consti-tutes "part of a transfer," so the transfer must go through an FFL. But such a rule would be impossible to enforce. If both parties denied it, how could the police or BATF ever prove that a firearms sale between two private (non-FFL) individuals had originated in a conversation at a gun show?

What if the purchaser first saw the gun at the gun show but didn't talk to the seller? What if the seller just walked around the show handing out business cards?

Just as the failure to cover non-FFLs sales at gun shows is a loophole for the Brady Law, the failure to cover non-FFLs sales *everywhere except gun shows* is a loophole for the GSAA. The Brady Law did not seek to impose background checks on purchasers who buy used firearms from non-FFLs. Only a small percentage of such sales take place at gun shows. While bringing those sales under the Brady Law's regulatory umbrella might do *some* good, it won't do much good. A person wishing to avoid a background check would retain all kinds of options. And a non-FFL, who wishes to sell firearms without purchasers having to fill out forms and undergo background checks, could still advertise in the newspaper or pass out business cards at a gun show. These loopholes force us to ask whether all secondary firearms sales, indeed all secondary *transfers*, including loans and gifts, ought to be brought under the Brady background-checking system.

If passed, would the GSAA make it more difficult for criminals and other dangerous people to obtain firearms? Yes, but only marginally.[19] Much depends on the motives and attitudes of gun show vendors. If they are anxious not to sell their guns to ineligible persons, access to the background check system, through an FFL, would help them to act responsibly. If they are indifferent or hostile to the Brady machinery, they could easily ignore it, for example, by making the sale after the show has closed. Unless they had the bad luck of selling to an undercover agent, it is very unlikely that their unlawful sale would ever come to light. *A law that regulates secondary transfers, but only those that occur at gun shows, makes little sense, except as a step toward regulating all secondary transfers.* Otherwise, private sellers could use the gun shows to display their guns and give out business cards. They could complete the sales later in the privacy of their homes, cars, or even on street corners.

Private sellers, of course, have many options for selling guns other than at gun shows. Professor William Ruefle of the University of South Carolina's College of Criminal Justice conducted a fascinating field experiment in gun selling.[20] He placed advertisements for a variety of handguns in a local newspaper and was able to sell two dozen guns in a short time without difficulty. Some purchasers from as far as 100 miles away called him and agreed to make the purchase at Ruefle's home or at a convenient rest area along the interstate between their home and his. Professor Ruefle also found that the vast majority of newspapers had no qualms about accepting classified ads for guns even if the newspaper's editorial page supported more gun controls (see tables 8.1 and 8.2).

Table 8.1. Classified Ad Policies for Guns in 184 Major City Newspapers

Will accept gun ads for all types of guns	53% (98)
Will accept gun ads but not for assault weapons	4% (7)
Will accept gun ads but not for semiautomatic guns	2% (3)
Will accept gun ads but not for handguns	12% (23)
Will accept gun ads but not for handguns or assault weapons	7% (13)
Will accept gun ads but not for handguns or semiautomatic guns	2% (3)
Will not accept gun ads	20% (37)
Total	100% (184)

Source: Professor William Ruefle.

Professor Ruefle's subsequent field experiment casts further doubt on the likelihood that gun owners will comply with licensing and registration requirements. He called 42 individuals who had advertised "gun for sale" in the newspaper, telling them he was from out of state and asking if that would cause any problem in purchasing the advertised firearm. Despite it being a crime to knowingly sell a firearm to an out-of-state purchaser, 38 sellers told him that it would be no problem.

State Regulation of Gun Shows

Perhaps, in a few years, we will be able to assess the potential impact of the GSAA, even if it has not been enacted, by looking at a few state gun show laws that have passed. California has a significantly stricter gun show requirement than the GSAA, including a 10-day waiting period on sales, but gun shows continue to flourish there.[21] Santa Clara County (Calif.) attempted to prohibit gun shows by outlawing offers to sell guns on public property.[22] The Ninth U.S. Circuit Court struck down their ordinances on First Amendment grounds. The Ninth U.S. Circuit Court of Appeals affirmed, holding that offers to sell guns were protected commercial speech that the county supervisors could not ban at publicly owned fairgrounds.

> The County has not presented a shred of evidence that any County resident, or anyone else, has somehow gotten the mistaken impression that the County promotes gun usage. Even assuming that some people mistakenly believe that to be true, the County has offered no evidence to substantiate its claim that the practice of holding gun shows at the Fairgrounds either caused or reinforces that mistaken belief. Rather, the record suggests that the addendum is at best an inept response to pressure by residents who strongly support the cause of gun control.[23]

Alameda and Los Angeles counties have been more successful in banning gun shows (by banning possession and sale rather than offers of sale), but litigation is pending.

Table 8.2. Guns Offered for Sale in One Year of Classified Ads

	Atlanta Journal-Constitution (Sunday circulation: 687,397)	San Francisco Examiner (Sunday circulation: 633,513)	Times-Picayune (New Orleans) (Sunday circulation: 316,977)	The State (Columbia, S.C.) (Sunday circulation: 160,381)	Carolina Trader (Fayetteville, N.C.) (weekly circulation: 33,000)
Semiautomatic handguns	30% (102)	Not accepted	25% (166)	21% (16)	19% (396)
Other handguns	12% (40)	Not accepted	13% (85)	12% (9)	14% (305)
Semiautomatic rifles	10% (33)	11% (7)	26% (171)	18% (14)	15% (313)
Other rifles	28% (95)	33% (21)	16% (104)	28% (21)	25% (528)
Semiautomatic shotguns	6% (20)	17% (11)	8% (50)	7% (5)	9% (200)
Other shotguns	14% (48)	39% (25)	13% (86)	14% (11)	18% (392)
Total annual guns offered for sale	100% (338)	100% (64)	100% (662)	100% (76)	100% (2,134)
Total annual guns offered for sale per 10,000 Sunday readers	4.9	1.0	20.9	4.7	646.7

Source: Professor William Ruefle.

On August 9, 2000, New York State passed legislation requiring gun show promoters to notify gun show vendors of their obligation to subject purchasers to background checks prior to the transfer of a firearm.[24] Moreover, the New York law attempts to deal with background check avoidance by providing that "[no] person [shall] offer or agree to sell a firearm, rifle or shotgun at a gun show and then transfer or deliver such weapon at a location other than the gun show for the purpose of evading or avoiding the check."[25] Violation of this law is a class A misdemeanor. There has not yet been a First Amendment challenge.

In the wake of the Columbine massacre, bills were introduced in some pro-gun states to regulate gun shows. Andrew J. McKelvey, a billionaire, started Americans for Gun Safety, which funded referenda in Oregon and Colorado to subject firearms purchasers at gun shows to criminal background checks. Republican Senator John McCain, a long-time ally of the NRA, appeared in commercials on behalf of these proposals.[26] Both proposals passed.

The state-level gun show laws vary from one to another and, of course, will be implemented and enforced by state and local agencies that vary in competence, resources, and commitment. Moreover, all state schemes, like the GSAA, are vulnerable to avoidance by sellers and purchasers.

Subjecting All Secondary Sales to Background Checks

Perhaps 40% to 50% of all handgun transfers, and a much higher percentage of transfers to criminals, occur in the secondary market. Only a small fraction of these transfers takes place at gun shows.[27] Thus, sealing off all gun sales to criminals at gun shows would constitute only a *very small step* toward keeping guns out of criminals' hands.

Could all secondary sales be channeled through FFLs? California has recently mandated just such a requirement.[28] This means that if *S* (seller) wants to give or sell his gun to *B* (buyer), both must appear before *D* (dealer), an FFL, and fill out documents in order to consummate the sale. As under Brady, the FFL must forward the would-be purchaser's name to the NICS for a background check. *S* and *B* would have to delay the sale until they were informed by *D* that the NICS has approved the transaction or until three business days had elapsed.

Of course, if he feared flunking the background check, *B* could evade this scheme, just as he could avoid Brady, simply by having straw purchaser *SP*, a friend with no criminal record, buy the firearm from *D*. But let us assume that *B* has no eligible friends or relatives willing to act as straw purchaser. Let us further assume that, desperate to purchase a handgun, *B* tentatively strikes a purchase agreement with *S*. Would the new law deter *S* (not a licensed dealer) from making the sale? Law enforcement officials would be unlikely to find out that *S* sold this gun to *B* without going to a licensed dealer to initiate a background check because there is no registry of the 250-plus million firearms owned by civilians.[29]

Since there is no gun registry, *S* can realistically discount the possibility that a police officer or BATF inspector will appear at his door demanding that he produce a particular firearm or, if he cannot produce it, that he explain satisfactorily what happened to it. Suppose one day, the police do arrest *B*, an ex-felon, for possessing the handgun that *S* sold to him, and that the police try to persuade *B* to tell them from whom he purchased the gun. *B* might never have known *S's* full name or, having known it, might have forgotten it. *B* might remember *S's* name but refuse to divulge it or *B* might refuse to cooperate. He might lie, saying that he does not remember where he got the gun. If he had a devious sense of humor, *B* might say that he purchased the handgun from an FFL but did not keep the receipt. *He could say anything.*

However, let us suppose that *B*, hoping for leniency, names *S* as the person who transferred the handgun to him. Assume too that the police are able to find *S*. Under interrogation, *S* might break down, admit knowingly selling the handgun to an ineligible purchaser, and throw himself on the mercy of the police, prosecutor, and court. More likely, *S* would either lie or remain silent. Other than B's accusation, no proof exists that *S* sold any handgun to *B*, much less this particular handgun. Even if there were witnesses to the sale, how could they identify a particular handgun as the one that *S* sold to *B* weeks, months, or years before? In fact, if *S* is a street seller, he himself probably has no idea whether he sold *that particular handgun* to *B*. He may have met *B* only briefly, months or years before and have no recollection of him.

If *S* is deceitful and sophisticated, he could admit the transfer, but say he made it lawfully through his friend *C*, who, as far as *S* knows, is or was an FFL (at least that's what *C* told him). *S* might claim that he believed *C* had obtained NICS approval; he had no reason to demand a signed receipt or other proof. If he once had a receipt, he has not kept it all this time. "No, *S* doesn't know where *C* is now." Indeed, even if *C* is found and denies knowing anything about *B's* gun, *S* may call *C* a liar, a person who masquerades as an FFL in order to collect a broker's fee on every street sale of a handgun. These hypothetical scenarios demonstrate that the recent California law that extends the Brady background check to all handgun transfers is unenforceable, even if the police give it high priority, which is very unlikely given competing demands on their resources.

Conclusion

Nothing better symbolizes American exceptionalism in the area of firearms regulations than gun shows. The fact that, even after the Columbine massacre, the U.S. Congress would not pass a federal law requiring a background check on all firearms sales at gun shows demonstrates the status of gun control in American politics. Even after Columbine, except for two California counties that banned gun shows on public property, no city, county, or state banned gun shows altogether. That outlawing gun shows did not emerge as a major national policy proposal illustrates the state of the U.S. gun culture and of contemporary gun control politics.

Examining the GSAA illustrates the deeply embedded resistance to more gun controls. What is the point of the Brady Law's requirement that purchasers of firearms from FFLs be subject to a background check if purchasers can buy firearms from non-FFLs without a background check? What is the purpose of requiring non-FFLs to put their customers through a background check at a gun show, but nowhere else?

If the GSAA is an end in itself, it seems hardly worth the effort. Admittedly, the law would not do any harm and might even prevent a dangerous person, here and there, from obtaining a firearm, at least for a short time. But it is difficult to see how it would have much impact in the long run. A person who wished to purchase a firearm without having to undergo a background check could pick up some business cards at a gun show and consummate the deal after the gun show closed. The would-be purchaser could forego the gun show entirely and just put a "Gun Wanted" advertisement in the local newspaper or on an Internet website. A non-FFL who responded to the advertisement could make the sale without subjecting the purchaser to a background check.

Thus, subjecting all firearms purchasers at gun shows to a background check ought to be a step toward subjecting all firearm purchasers to a background check, regardless of whether the seller has a license and a place of business. But the logistics of implementing and enforcing a universal background check for all firearms purchasers (much less all transferees) are daunting. At a minimum, it would require a comprehensive gun registration program, which we will consider in the next chapter.

9

Comprehensive Licensing and Registration

Like cars, guns are dangerous. Cars are not designed to kill,
and yet are heavily regulated: You must be of a minimum age,
take a training course, pass a proficiency test, get a license,
obtain insurance; and the car must be registered. . . . Guns
carry none of these restrictions. In the interest of saving lives,
Brady II would require gun owners and manufacturers to adopt
safety measures similar to those required of car owners.
—Handgun Control, Inc., "The Gun Violence Prevention Act—
   Brady II Questions and Answers"

Each State should require the registration of all handguns,
rifles, and shotguns. If, after 5 years, some States still have not
enacted such laws, Congress should pass a Federal firearms
registration act applicable to those States.
—Recommendation of President's Commission
   on Law Enforcement and Administration of Justice, 1967

Registration is designed only as a support to any system that
seeks to allow some people, but not others, to own guns. If
registration helped to keep the "good guys" good, it could help
prevent violence, even if not a single criminal were polite
enough to register.
—Franklin Zimring, *Gun Control,*

Just after the Brady Bill became law, handgun control advocates began
pushing a new omnibus gun control bill that would create a comprehen-

sive handgun licensing and registration system. In effect, the proponents of the new bill (popularly called "Brady II") claimed, at one and the same time, that the 1993 Brady Law was a giant step toward reducing gun crime and merely a small step toward that goal. By means of licensing and registration, "Brady II" seeks to extend the Brady Law to the secondary market of handgun transfers between nondealers. Brady II (Gun Violence Prevention Act of 1994) requires states to enact handgun licensing laws meeting minimum federal standards.[1] It also requires that handguns be registered in order to be transferred, thereby establishing a national handgun registry, albeit one that would take decades to mature.[2] This chapter analyzes whether passage of Brady II would finally establish a regulatory system capable of preventing irresponsible persons from obtaining firearms.*

Universal Handgun Licensing

Brady II significantly extends Brady I by making it illegal "for any person to sell, deliver, or otherwise transfer a handgun to an individual who is not [an FFL] unless the transferor verifies that the transferee possesses a valid state handgun license."[3] It makes it unlawful for anyone, other than an FFL, to receive a handgun or handgun ammunition "unless the individual possesses a valid state handgun license."[4] By contrast, currently only 11 states require a permit for handgun purchases. The proposed law

---

*In addition to a licensing and registration system, Brady II contains provisions for (1) a seven-day waiting period; (2) making it a crime to store or leave a firearm any place, where an "unsupervised juvenile" is likely to gain access to firearms, and requiring FFLs to post warning signs to that effect; (3) prohibiting an individual (other than an FFL or one who holds an arsenal license) from possessing more than 20 firearms or more than 1,000 rounds of ammunition; (4) repealing provisions for restoration of firearm possession/purchase privileges under certain circumstances; and (5) limiting handgun purchases to one per month. The proposed act increases the FFL license fee, makes compliance with state and local law a condition precedent to obtaining a license, allows BATF to inspect FFL records up to three times per year, and requires FFL employees to be at least 18 years old and to obtain a handgun license and pass a background check. Furthermore, it prohibits FFLs from transferring a firearm at any location other than the one specified on the license, and requires them to report lost or stolen firearms within 24 hours after discovery. Additionally, the act expands the class of "prohibited weapons" (to include a firearm muffler or silencer, a short-barreled shotgun, a short-barreled rifle, a destructive device, a semiautomatic assault weapon, a Saturday night special, nonsporting ammunition, and a large capacity ammunition feeding device), increases the tax on handguns and handgun ammunition, and prohibits the import or manufacture of any firearm that is not child-proofed (to prevent a child under seven years of age from discharging the firearm).

would prohibit not only handgun sales by an FFL to an unlicensed purchaser but also sales in the secondary market by a nondealer to an unlicensed individual. It would also prohibit gifts and loans of handguns to unlicensed individuals.

Brady II provides that a state handgun license system must "at a minimum," meet the following requirements: (1) licenses shall be issued by the state's chief law enforcement officer (CLEO); (2) they shall contain the licensee's name, address, date of birth, physical description, and a photograph; and (3) licenses shall be valid for a period not to exceed two years.[5] Before issuing a state license, the CLEO must verify that (1) the applicant is at least 21 years old; (2) a resident of the state (the applicant must present an identification document, such as a driver's license, and a document establishing residency, such as a utility bill or lease); (3) the applicant is not prohibited from possessing or purchasing a handgun under federal, state, or local law based on a name and fingerprint-based search in federal and state record systems; and (4) the applicant must present a state handgun safety certificate. According to the proposed bill, a state handgun safety certificate may be issued to residents who have completed a course of not less than two hours of instruction in handgun safety, taught by law enforcement officers and designed by the CLEO and has passed an examination, designed by the CLEO, testing the applicant's knowledge of handgun safety.[6]

In proposing Brady II, Congressman (now Senator) Charles Schumer (D-N.Y.) argued that a comprehensive handgun licensing and registration scheme for handgun owners is needed to complete the regulatory framework begun by the FFA and carried forward by the GCA and the Brady Law. Handgun Control, Inc. (HCI) stated that "licensing of handgun purchasers allows more thorough background checks to be conducted on gun buyers and would help expose gun traffickers by allowing for more accurate tracing of guns found at crime scenes."[7]

Constitutionality

The Supreme Court's decision in *Printz v. United States* almost certainly renders Brady II unconstitutional.[8] The majority opinion explained that the Constitution's framers rejected a central government that would act upon and through the states in favor of a federal system, in which state and federal governments would exercise concurrent authority.

Printz dealt a serious blow to the federal government's ability to enlist state law enforcement personnel to enforce a federal gun control regime. Brady II clearly violates *Printz* because it requires state officials to set up and administer a licensing system, design curriculum for and conduct handgun safety classes, issue safety certificates, and process firearms' license applications. Since a handgun license would be valid for two years, state officials would be involved in a continuous process of reviewing, renewing, and revoking licenses. After *Printz*, Congress must find some other way to implement comprehensive handgun licensing.

One alternative would be for federal law to tie state participation to receipt of federal funds. To receive federal money for additional police, improved law enforcement technology, and new criminal justice programs, states would be required to enact, administer, and enforce the gun controls specified in Brady II. Such incentives are not unusual. For example, Congress has made receipt of federal transportation and highway money contingent on states passing laws requiring a 21-year-old minimum drinking age and the use of seat belts and infant/child car seats.[9] The same strategy could be used to "encourage" state participation in a handgun licensing and registration scheme, but it probably would not succeed. States with strong pro-gun citizenries and lobbies, the very states that now reject strong handgun regulation, would very likely choose to forgo the federal funds. Consider that 23 states did not pass "truth-in-sentencing" legislation, despite the lure of federal law enforcement funds.[10] If even a few states did not participate, this would be a major, probably fatal problem, as handguns could continue to migrate from states with relaxed gun laws to states with strict gun controls. Indeed, the resulting patchwork of strong and weak control states would probably resemble the current situation, in which some states require handgun licenses, while others do not.

Congress could also avoid constitutional problems by creating *a purely federal administrative* handgun licensing and registration system. Such a regulatory scheme, if it could be enforced, would solve the problem of handguns flowing from states with permissive gun laws into states with strict gun laws. However, it would be a complex and expensive undertaking to create a federal nationwide system of handgun licensing and registration. Just consider the size of our motor vehicle registration and licensing system; there is at least one office in every county in the United States.

Brady II and Handgun Licensing

The Brady II licensing scheme would, in effect, precertify prospective purchasers as being eligible to purchase a handgun from FFLs or nondealers. Handgun sellers/transferors would have to verify that the prospective purchaser/transferee has a handgun license, confirm with a CLEO that the license has not been revoked, and fill out and submit registration forms documenting the sale or transfer. A person who sells or transfers a handgun in violation of the Brady II requirements would be subject to a fine, imprisonment of not less than six months or more than three years or both. If a person violates Brady II with respect to five or more handguns during a 30-day period, the penalty increases to a fine, imprisonment of not *less* than three years, or both. An unlicensed person who receives a handgun is subject to the same punishment as the person who transfers the handgun to him. Brady II does not require the millions of current handgun owners to be licensed unless and until they seek to make another handgun purchase or seek to sell or otherwise transfer a handgun.

Brady II extends the Brady Law's background checking scheme to non-FFL sellers. Under Brady I, an individual who is not in the business of selling firearms, can sell or give his firearm to another individual, as long as the seller does not know the purchaser to be ineligible to purchase a handgun. Under Brady II, it is a crime for anyone to sell or otherwise transfer a handgun to an unlicensed person.

What Will Comprehensive Licensing Achieve?

Supporters of Brady II's licensing scheme stress that handgun owners should be regulated at least as stringently as automobile drivers. According to former attorney general Janet Reno:

> I think it should be at least as hard to get a license to possess a gun as it is to drive an automobile. I don't think somebody should have a gun unless they can demonstrate that they know how to safely and lawfully use it, that they're capable of safely and lawfully using it, and that they're willing to safely and lawfully use it.[11]

Brady II seeks to create a driver-licensing–like system for handgun owners by requiring a license to purchase or otherwise receive handguns. However, the driver licensing system is not fully adaptable to guns. Driver licensing sets very low competency standards; it does not seek to screen out ex-felons, drug addicts, or problem drinkers. Its sole focus is on competency. There is no attempt *ex ante* to prevent irresponsible or dangerous people from obtaining drivers licenses. There is no *background check* to determine whether the prospective driver is likely to be dangerous on account of alcohol or drug abuse, mental illness, or criminal record. *Ex ante*, the driver licensing system weeds out practically no one; it only has teeth *after* the driver demonstrates dangerousness by violating the motor vehicle laws or, more likely, after a series of violations. Often, a driver's license is only suspended or revoked after the person has accumulated a serious record of traffic offenses, at which point, injury and even death may already have occurred.

It should not be assumed that this driver licensing system "works." There are more than 40,000 motor vehicle deaths annually (e.g., 43,200 in 1997)[12] and millions of disabling injuries (e.g., 2,300,000 in 1997). A large number of suspended and revoked drivers continue to drive;[13] it is estimated that unlicensed drivers cause one in five traffic fatalities.[14] In New York State, approximately 100,000 persons are convicted of unlicensed operation of a motor vehicle each year, and this is probably a small proportion of the actual number of people who drive without a valid license.[15] New York City even has difficulty keeping dangerous and unlicensed *city employees* off the road. According to a recent study, 1,200 New York City employees who drive vehicles *in the course of their municipal duties* are unlicensed. Furthermore, those with poor records have been permitted to drive on municipal business, including 784 city employees with drunk driving convictions and 1,869 who had two or more accidents.[16] Another intractable problem plaguing the motor vehicle regulatory machinery is the number of drivers with uninsured vehicles. Without valid auto insurance, an automobile may not legally be driven. Nevertheless, it is estimated that uninsured drivers cause approximately one-third of all traffic accidents.[17]

Evading the Brady II Licensing System

A person ineligible for a handgun license could try to evade the Brady II licensing system by persuading a gun owner to sell or "lend" him a handgun, or he could use a counterfeit, stolen, or borrowed handgun license. We can anticipate that if licenses became necessary to purchase handguns from FFLs, counterfeit licenses would become available on the black market, just as fake drivers licenses and other identification documents are now available.[18] A fake license would be especially effective in duping an unsophisticated gun seller.* Furthermore, an unlicensed person could use a licensed straw purchaser to buy a handgun on his behalf. Of course, unlicensed persons could also steal handguns.

Under the Brady II regulatory regime, a handgun transfer to an unli-

---

*A fake driver's license might also be used to obtain a valid handgun license, although this would be less likely to succeed if Brady II's fingerprint-based background check requirement became law.

censed purchaser would not set off any warning bells. As long as the unlicensed purchaser is not caught with the handgun, the unlawful sale
would go unnoticed. There would probably be less risk of an unlicensed
gun owner being caught than an unlicensed driver. In testimony before
Congress, Jo Ann Harris, assistant attorney general, Criminal Division, U.S.
Department of Justice, explained the difficulty of apprehending felons who
unlawfully possess guns, despite it being a federal crime punishable by
up to 10 years in prison.

> The most common way we come across a 922(g) [felon-in-
> possession] violation is when the person has committed another
> crime. It is difficult for law enforcement to learn about and be able
> to prosecute a 922(g) without their having committed another crime
> because it is very difficult to find them in possession.[19]

Because Brady II only requires a handgun owner to obtain a license
before taking possession of a *new* gun, a person arrested for possession of
a handgun without a license might escape punishment by falsely claiming
that he did not need a license because he owned this handgun before
Brady II went into effect. How could that claim be disproved? (Of course,
if the handgun had been manufactured subsequent to passage of Brady II,
that story would not fly.)

Even if he admitted obtaining the handgun after Brady II became effective, federal prosecutors will almost certainly lack the resources or incli-
nation to bring prosecutions against every otherwise law-abiding individual who fails to comply with Brady II's licensing requirements. Consider
that, currently, federal prosecutors do not eagerly accept for prosecution
even *felon-in-possession* (so-called 922[g]) cases, unless the felon is a
hardened criminal.[20] According to Assistant Attorney General Jo Ann Harris, prosecuting every felon-in-possession case would "not be good law
enforcement policy."[21] Furthermore, a study of cases presented to the U.S.
Attorney's Office for the Northern District of Illinois found that only 24%
of prosecutable weapons and explosives offenses were actually prosecuted.[22] In 47% of weapons cases declined for prosecution, the screening
prosecutor's reason was that the case involved a "minor offense." In 1993,
U.S. attorneys' offices nationwide declined to prosecute 27.6% of weapons
offenses.[23] Unfortunately for the prosecution, jurors, especially in southern
and western states, may be unwilling to convict a defendant whose only
crime is unlicensed possession of a handgun.*

---

*Even in Brooklyn, New York, a strong gun control jurisdiction, between 1990
and 1993, juries acquitted 56% of defendants prosecuted for unlicensed possession

If the unlawful handgun transfer did come to light, the transferor (assuming he could be traced and found) might falsely claim that he never sold, lent, or gave the gun to anybody; to the contrary, he did not realize the gun was missing. Brady II requires that within 24 hours after discovering that a handgun has been stolen or lost, the licensee must report the theft or loss to the secretary of the treasury, the CLEO, and local law enforcement. Failure to do so is punishable by a civil penalty of not less than $1,000. Still, the gun owner may argue that because he completely lacks knowledge that the gun had been stolen, he ought to be absolved of any liability, criminal or civil. Another story the transferor may tell is that the person to whom he transferred the handgun did appear to have a valid license and that he did fill out and file all the relevant forms; in other words, he could falsely claim to be the victim of the gun recipient's fraud or a bureaucratic blunder.

Would Brady II make it significantly more difficult for criminals to obtain a handgun? Probably not. First, many criminals already own a handgun or have ready access to one through a friend, family member, or gang associate.[24] Second, many criminals obtain guns by theft or by informal transfers from other criminals, especially drug dealers and addicts.[25] Criminals who are not deterred by existing criminal laws, prohibiting the conduct they regularly engage in, are unlikely to worry about illegally selling or transferring a handgun.

Brady II's Registration System

Under existing law, manufacturers must engrave a serial number on the barrel of each handgun. Manufacturers, wholesalers, and dealers must maintain records of each handgun sale (including serial number, make, model, and the name and address of the purchaser) and supply such information to the secretary of the treasury upon request, in the course of a bona fide BATF or law enforcement investigation. As things now stand, if the FFL maintains records in the manner prescribed by law, if the police find a gun with its serial number intact, it can be traced to its first retail purchaser. After that, there is no paper record of a gun's chain of ownership. That is where Brady II would come in by establishing a comprehensive handgun registration system. This is a completely new policy initia-

---

of a gun. The acquittal rate for all crimes was approximately 35%. David N. Dorfman and Chris K. Iijima, "Fictions, Fault, and Forgiveness: Jury Nullification in a New Context."

tive. Other than the National Firearms Registration and Transfer Record (NFRTR) system for machine guns that has existed since 1934,[26] the federal government has never tried to maintain a firearms registry.*

Recently, Eric M. Larson, a self-described scholar and collector of historic firearms, through exhaustive research, exposed flaws in the NFRTR, the registration system maintained by the BATF for machine guns and other "gangster-type" weapons.[27] (These flaws have been confirmed by BATF audits and have caused Congress to request that BATF "take whatever steps are necessary to ensure that its records are accurate and complete.")[28] Because *reregistration* of these weapons is not required under the National Firearms Act of 1934, more than 100,000 NFA firearms may be registered to people who are dead. Those who inherit the machine guns often do not realize that they have to be registered. In addition, the apparent destruction of some registration/transfer records means that at least some people who believe they have registered their NFA weapons are subject to prosecution and confiscation of their weapons. If handgun registration is to be modeled after the NFRTR system, these flaws would affect a much larger number of citizens. In order to improve the system, handguns would have to be regularly reregistered. This would not only prove an enormous administrative challenge but also might decrease compliance.

Only eight states have attempted to maintain handgun registries, and they have had limited success.† Since 1911, Massachusetts has required the registration of handguns purchased in the primary market. Since 1968, it has required the registration of all handguns.[29] Indeed, Brady II looks a lot like the Massachusetts system of licensing and registration. There has never been a comprehensive evaluation of Massachusetts's registration

---

*As of 1995, there were approximately 240,000 machine-guns registered in the United States. Half of these registered machine-guns were owned by police departments and other government agencies; the other half belonged to private citizens. Gary Kleck, *Targeting Guns: Firearms and Their Control*, p. 108. The Firearms Owners' Protection Act of 1986 prohibited the manufacture or registration of new machine guns. P. L. 99–308, May 19, 1986.

†These states are Hawaii (handguns and long guns); Indiana (voluntary registration); Maryland (owner registration not required, but state maintains record of all sales by FFLs); Massachusetts (handguns); Michigan (handguns); New Jersey (handguns); New York (handguns); and Pennsylvania (owner registration not required, but state maintains record of all sales by FFLs). Registration is required on a local or county basis in Illinois (required by some local governments); Missouri (required by some local governments); and Nevada (required only in Clark County or Las Vegas). Only two states, Hawaii and Louisiana, and the District of Columbia provide for handgun *and* firearm registration. An additional 21 states have record-of-sale laws that prohibit a dealer from selling or otherwise transferring a firearm without making a copy of the sales form.

system, but it appears that no more than 10% of secondary market handgun sales is recorded.[30] The administrative agency in charge of the registration system has been chronically understaffed and short of resources. As of March 1996, approximately 750,000 sales transactions were unentered dating back to 1985, when the agency stopped maintaining a computer database.

In 1994, California passed a law requiring that all handgun sales go through a licensed dealer or law enforcement agency, which was required to forward information about the seller, purchaser, and gun to the California Department of Justice.[31] In the two years after the law became effective, secondary sales generated approximately 25,000 registrations per year. By comparison, dealers submitted approximately 250,000 handgun purchases per year for background check.[32] Since there are approximately as many secondary market handgun sales as primary market sales, the vast majority of sellers and buyers of used firearms did not comply with the law.

Nowhere in Brady II do we find the words *national handgun registry*, but this is what the bill would establish. Brady II would expand the paper trail on every handgun by requiring the manufacturer and all subsequent sellers or transferors (after verifying the prospective buyer's handgun license and eligibility) to fill out a registration form that includes the purchaser's name and address, handgun license number, and information about the handgun, including make, model, and serial number.

Brady II requires "state law [to] provide [that] the CLEO shall furnish information from completed handgun registration forms to federal, state, and local law enforcement authorities upon request." After *Printz*, which rejected federal authority to order state and local background checks, a federally mandated state-based registration system would be unconstitutional.[33]

A post-*Printz* version of Brady II could require that all FFLs and non-FFL handgun transferors send registration information to BATF for storage in a database that would, in effect, constitute a national handgun registry. The 1986 Firearms Owners' Protection Act prohibited the government from retaining firearms transaction records for "any system of registration of firearms, firearms owners, or firearms transactions."[34] Brady II would repeal this provision: "The Director of the Bureau of Alcohol, Tobacco, and Firearms shall centralize all records of receipts and dispositions of firearms obtained by the Bureau and maintain such records in whatever manner will enable their most efficient use in law enforcement." The goal would be to achieve an easily accessible ownership record for every handgun in the United States. Since many owners would not sell their handguns for years, perhaps decades, it would take a long time for the registry to become complete. But, in theory, when fully mature, the system would

look like the registration systems we now have for houses and automobiles, except that Brady II would establish a national registry, not fifty
separate state-based systems.

Goal of the Handgun Registration System

A national registry would play a crucial role in supporting the handgun
licensing system. Indeed, without a record of a gun's ownership, it would
be difficult to prove that a particular individual had sold a specific handgun to a particular person. Without comprehensive registration, many sellers might feel that they could with impunity ignore the duty to sell handguns only to licensed persons. Registration is a strategy for deterring
licensed owners from selling handguns to people who are ineligible to
possess them.

Suppose the police arrest a criminal suspect who is found to have a
handgun manufactured after the effective date of Brady II. If the suspect
does not have a handgun license, he must have obtained this handgun
illegally, but from whom—an unscrupulous FFL? A casual arm's length
seller? A black market gun dealer? A drug dealer? A criminal comrade? A
friend or relative? Without that handgun's history, there would be no way
(other than the suspect's testimony) to figure out who sold or gave the
handgun to the criminal suspect. In theory, registration provides the paper
trail enabling the police to identify the handgun's last owner. Investigators
could confront the last registered owner, demanding to know how it is
that a handgun registered to him is now in the hands of a criminal; there
is no record of the handgun having been transferred or any record of the
handgun having been reported as stolen or lost.[35]

Solving Crimes

Would a national handgun registry help prevent or solve crime? Suppose
the police could send the serial number of a gun recovered at a crime
scene to the proposed National Tracing Center, which could immediately
identify the registered owner.* The police would then have a suspect.

---

*BATF has maintained a National Firearms Tracing Center since 1974, so
it seems odd that Brady II proposes to establish just such a center. In 1996, the
National Firearms Tracing Center responded to approximately 130,000 trace re-

This crime-solving potential is diminished by a few realities. If the gun is recovered at the scene, it is usually because the police have arrested the person holding it. In the overwhelming majority of crimes, where an offender successfully flees the scene of the crime, the gun is never recovered.

A savvy criminal could defeat the tracing system by obliterating the serial number with a file or some other tool.[36] Currently, an estimated 20% of guns submitted to the BATF are untraceable for this reason.[37] Sheley and Wright reported that their juvenile inmate respondents listed firepower, quality of construction, and untraceability as the three most desirable qualities for a gun. It remains to be seen whether the secretary of the treasury could come up with a foolproof scheme for marking guns with unremovable serial numbers. Perhaps new technology, such as a computer chip containing a serial number, could prevent destruction of a gun's identity. Of course, handguns manufactured before the new technology came on line would still be vulnerable to obliteration of the serial number and would continue to be untraceable.

Identifying Black Marketeers

BATF's National Firearms Tracing Center has been used mostly for gathering intelligence about the origins and interstate migration of crime guns, not for solving individual gun crimes.[38] At best, tracing identifies the manufacturers and FFLs whose guns are disproportionately used in crime.[39] This goal could be achieved without expanding the current regulatory system. Under existing laws and regulations, unless the serial number has been obliterated, a firearm can be traced back to its manufacturer and from the manufacturer to the wholesaler, then to the FFL retailer, and finally to the first purchaser.

Handguns move from the legitimate market into the hands of criminals through thefts, purchases in the secondary market, loans and gifts from family members, friends, and criminal comrades. Some corrupt FFLs specialize in selling handguns to criminals or to traffickers who, in turn, sell

---

quests. The center's main purpose has been to gather intelligence on the origins (manufacturers and dealers) of crime guns and on patterns of interstate migration of guns. The traces are of little use in solving individual crimes. See Office of Juvenile Justice and Delinquency Prevention, "Section IV: Strategies to Interrupt Sources of Illegal Guns, Promising Strategies to Reduce Gun Violence," 1999, available at: http://ojjdp.ncjrs.org/pubs/gun violence/sect04.html; David B. Kopel, "Do Federal Gun Traces Accurately Trace Street Crime?"

them to criminals. The BATF reported that in 1996, about 60% of successfully traced crime guns originated with 1% of all FFLs. The current tracing system can identify corrupt FFLs.* It is hard to see how Brady II would significantly improve the investigation of black marketeers and gun runners.

Evading the Registration System

The biggest impediment to implementing a national handgun registry is obtaining compliance from handgun owners. There is no doubt that any gun registration system would be met by massive resistance because of the fear that registration would lead the way to confiscation. Tanya K. Metaksa, the former director of the NRA's Institute for Legislative Action, has articulated an attitude toward registration that is likely to be widely shared.

> Time after time, firearms registration systems have led inexorably toward firearms confiscation. The lessons of history are vivid in the minds of gun owners who value their rights. From gun confiscation schemes launched by the former Soviet Union against Lithuania to turn-guns-in-or-go-to-jail policies in California, gun lists become gun losses, and gun owners know it.[40]

Given many gun owner's hostility to registration and their belief that a registration system would later be used to confiscate all handguns (as occurred in Britain),[41] there would certainly be significant noncompliance.†

---

*BATF's "Project Detroit" traced all guns confiscated by Detroit police from 1989 to 1990. It resulted in successful prosecutions against 10 FFLs. The BATF estimated that these dealers supplied over 3,000 firearms to black marketeers. The BATF subsequently continued its efforts to crack down on corrupt FFLs and black marketeers through Project LEAD, an automated program that assembles information from gun traces and multiple purchase forms submitted by FFLs. In 1996, BATF recommended 2,230 trafficking defendants for prosecution (whether these cases were prosecuted is not known). Eric Larson, "The Story of a Gun," *Atlantic Monthly*, Jan. 1993, 68. BATF, "Crime-Gun Trace Analysis Reports," 1997.

†Canada passed a law on December 5, 1995, requiring federal firearms licenses for all gun owners by December 31, 2000. In October 2000, not even one-quarter of the estimated number of owners had complied. In July 2001, Canadian officials estimated that of the 2.3 million gun owners, 2 million have applied for licenses, with the remaining 300,000 citizens owning about 7 million guns illegally. Critics countered that 5 million gun owners, owning approximately 20 million guns have failed to comply. See Lorne Gunter, "Canadian Gun Registration Push Fails," *Edmonton Journal*, Oct. 13, 2000; Doug Smith, "Law in Canada to Mean Red Tape," *Minneapolis-St. Paul Star Tribune*, July 15, 2001.

Indeed, if a current handgun owner decided to sell and wanted to avoid the registration requirement, he could easily find a buyer of like mind, and so on down the line. A single handgun could be sold again and again without being registered and with little risk of detection.

In recent years, several states and municipalities passed laws mandating the registration of assault rifles. These laws were overwhelmingly ignored. In Boston and Cleveland, the rate of compliance with bans on assault rifles is estimated at 1%.[42] Out of the 100,000 to 300,000 assault rifles estimated to be in private hands in New Jersey, 947 were registered, an additional 888 rendered inoperable, and 4 turned over to the authorities.[43] In California, nearly 90% of the approximately 300,000 assault weapons owners did not register their weapons.

Even if a significant percentage of law-abiding handgun owners complied with the registration law, we can be certain that *handgun-owning criminals would not comply*, because in so doing they would be admitting to felony possession of a firearm. There are already large numbers of handguns in circulation in the criminal subculture. A criminal could use the same unregistered gun throughout his career and, when he "retired," he could sell or give it to a relative, friend, or criminal associate. Therefore, even a well-functioning registration system might, for many decades have little impact on the availability of handguns in the criminal subculture.

Would a new generation of criminals find it difficult to obtain unregistered handguns? Some criminals claim that it is as easy to buy a gun on the streets as it is to buy fast food. One Chicago gang member stated, "[I]t's like going through the drive-through window. 'Give me some fries, a Coke, and a 9-millimeter.' "[44] The 500,000 firearms that are stolen each year provide an enormous pool of handguns that, even under Brady II, could not be traced to their new owners. Rifles and shotguns that are cut down could not be traced because they are not subject to registration. Criminals might also be able to purchase unmarked handguns that are smuggled into this country from abroad. Some number of never-registered handguns would, of course, continue to be sold by gun dealers, drug dealers, and gun owners hostile to the idea of handgun registration.

Enforcing the Registration Law

Brady II does not require the registration of handguns until the owner decides to sell or otherwise transfer his handgun to another person. Even if compliance with the registration requirement is high, it would take decades for the existing stock of handguns to be registered. If the rate of noncompliance is high, the value of the registration system would be seriously undermined; yet compliance would depend, to a large extent, on gun owners' voluntary registration. While Brady II calls for imprisonment of not less than six months or more than three years for gun owners, who transfer their firearms without filing the appropriate registration forms, U.S. attorneys would probably be reluctant to expend much resources to prosecute otherwise law-abiding gun owners for failure to register. Finally, even if U.S. attorneys were willing to prosecute, we can anticipate that in states where registration compliance is low, prosecutions for nonregistration would be very unpopular with jurors.

Conclusion

Even if all ineligible persons could be prevented from obtaining handguns *from FFLs*, enforcing a licensing scheme in the secondary market would require a herculean enforcement effort. One reason to be pessimistic is the existence of tens of millions of unregistered handguns currently in private hands. Were it ever to appear likely that Congress was going to pass Brady II, there would almost certainly be a rush to buy handguns before the registration system became effective, just as there was a rush to buy handguns before Brady's five-day waiting period went into effect,[45] and a rush to buy assault rifles before new sales were banned. By the time Brady II took effect, there would likely be more than 100 million handguns in private hands, perhaps millions stockpiled for future sales at a large premium. The regulatory tools, enforcement resources, and political consensus for licensing and registration on this scale simply does not exist.

Handgun control advocates envision a registration system that would resemble automobile registration. Every automobile is registered with a state Department of Motor Vehicles. An owner cannot get license plates without registering the vehicle. When the vehicle is sold, the seller must provide the state DMV with the details of the sale and must turn in his license plate. The new owner must register the vehicle and apply for a new license plate.

The system is fairly easy to enforce. Every car must have a license plate. A car without a license plate is easily spotted and stopped and the driver ticketed; the car can be removed from the road. Car owners do not "resist" the registration requirement; they feel no risk of impending car confiscation.

What if an owner just sells or gives the car to someone else, not bothering with the forms and license plate? The seller would remain the owner of record and would be liable for maintaining insurance on the vehicle and for accidents in which the car is involved. Obviously, the seller has a strong interest in avoiding such liability. Likewise, the buyer would hardly wish to pay for the car and not get an ownership document in return.

One rationale for the auto registration system is that it allows the government to tax automobiles efficiently. A second rationale is that the registration system makes it more difficult to steal cars. The victim of a car theft reports it to the police. If a police officer sees a car with the license plate of the stolen vehicle, he will stop and apprehend the driver; the car can be returned. Moreover, if the thieves are "joyriders" and abandon the vehicle, the police can locate the owner through the registration system.

Still, the deterrent potential of the vehicle registration system is fairly weak. Over 1 million autos are reported stolen every year; the majority are never recovered.[46] The thieves may put new license plates on the vehicle, bring it to a different state, or have it broken down for parts in a "chop shop."

In contrast to cars, handguns can last for 100 years or more, and a handgun registration system would have to be launched when there are already 100 million or more unregistered handguns in private hands. There can be no doubt that handgun registration would be strongly and massively resisted because of the fear that once there is a handgun registry, the next step in the gun control project would be handgun confiscation.

Even with significant compliance by handgun owners, the Brady II registration system would take decades to mature into a comprehensive system. During that period, the license requirement would be difficult to enforce since it relies heavily on efficient registration. If significant compliance could not be achieved, the whole regulatory scheme would be severely undermined. The result could be a bureaucratic apparatus collecting paper but to no constructive end, much like the handgun registration system in Massachusetts and in some foreign countries.*

---

*New Zealand, for example, has found firearms registration to be unworkable. Review of Firearms Control in New Zealand: Report of an Independent Inquiry Commissioned by the Minister of Police ("The Thorp Report"), 1997.

10

Prohibition and Disarmament

Argument is pursued concerning the obvious—should a minor, a convicted criminal, one who is mentally ill, an alcoholic, or a drug addict have the right to possess a gun? Our edicts do not fuss with such trivialities. Negative licensing of guns with sporting purposes, excluding a few defined categories from the right to possess a firearm, is an excessively cautious, only marginally useful mechanism, other than as a wedge to more rational legislation. We seek a disarmed populace.
—Norval Morris and Gordon Hawkins,
   The Honest Politician's Guide to Crime Control, 1969

In the area of *Policy* we recommend that . . . there be a complete and universal federal ban on the manufacture, importation, sale, and possession of handguns (except for authorized police and military personnel).
—Surgeon General's Workshop on Violence and Public Health,
   1985, U.S. Department of Health and Human Services

All small arms and light weapons which are not under legal civilian possession and which are not required for the purposes of national defense and internal security, should be collected and destroyed by States as expeditiously as possible.
—*UN Report*, August 1999

If the Brady Law, even with amendments, is not likely significantly to reduce gun crimes and injuries, what about prohibiting all firearms or at

least all handguns? Does prohibition mean "just" forbidding the importation, manufacture, and sale of firearms or does it include a ban on possession? Would disarmament provide exceptions for three-quarters of a
million federal, state, and local police and twice as many contract and in-
house private security personnel? What about owners and employees of
small businesses in dangerous neighborhoods? How would any version of
firearms prohibition avoid the implementation and enforcement problems
(including corruption) that bedeviled National Alcohol Prohibition and
plague the present-day war on drugs?

A History of Handgun Prohibition

In the United States, proposals for universal handgun prohibition are relatively recent, although most of the western states in the mid-nineteenth
century had laws against *carrying* concealed weapons. Efforts to prevent
people from owning or possessing firearms altogether first arose in the
Black Codes passed by the southern states after the Civil War. The former
Confederate states passed laws to prevent former slaves from exercising
any rights, especially the right to own firearms. The Civil Rights Act of
1866 and the Fourteenth Amendment were both aimed at reversing the
disarmament and subjugation of the former slaves.[1] In the latter decades
of the nineteenth century and early decades of the twentieth century, some
politicians advocated that aliens be denied the right to keep and bear arms.
Some New Dealers favored the idea of handgun prohibition and tried un-
successfully to have handguns covered by the 1934 NFA.

Until the 1960s, no politician or criminologist seriously urged prohibition of handguns, much less all firearms. The 1930–1931 Wickersham
Commission, the first national commission on crime, did not even place
"guns" or "firearms" in its index. Rather, that commission focused on the
emergence of organized crime groups that trafficked alcoholic beverages
and corrupted government agents. While the commission criticized law
enforcement officers for "too free and easy use of firearms," it did not
even mention possible options for regulating private citizens' access to
guns.

The 1967 President's Commission on Law Enforcement and the Administration of Justice assigned a task force to gun violence. That task force
concluded that federal firearms regulation, particularly the 1938 Federal
Firearms Act, had "an extremely limited effect."[2] It found that only eight
states required firearms permits, although some counties and cities had
more restrictive gun controls. Nevertheless, would-be purchasers in re-

strictive jurisdictions could easily obtain a gun by traveling to a permissive jurisdiction to make a purchase.

The President's Commission recommended outlawing "military-type firearms" (bazookas, machine guns, and other "military-type" devices); prohibiting certain categories of dangerous individuals from possessing any firearms ("habitual drunkards, drug addicts, mental incompetents, persons with a history of mental disturbance, and persons convicted of certain offenses"); creating a federal registration system for rifles, shotguns, and handguns; requiring persons to obtain permits to possess or carry handguns; banning mail-order sales of handguns; and delaying interstate sales of rifles and shotguns to give local law enforcement officials an opportunity to block the sale.

The President's Commission criticized the NRA for lobbying against regulations that do nothing more than "inconvenience" the legitimate gun owner. In short, the commission favored strengthening existing firearms laws, while recognizing the importance of "affording citizens ample opportunity to purchase weapons for legitimate purposes."

Until 1970, no major criminologist called for prohibiting handguns. For example, Sutherland and Cressey, authors of *Principles of Criminology*, the leading criminology textbook for much of the twentieth century, only touched on firearms in a general discussion of the increasing number of deaths resulting from interaction between police and criminals. Handguns were not mentioned, although the authors criticized the "war on crime" mentality that had led to an arms race between police and civilians. They did not recommend banning or even restricting firearms availability.[3]

In their influential 1970 book, *The Honest Politician's Guide to Crime Control*, Norval Morris and Gordon Hawkins did propose a general prohibition of handguns to the public; only the police and "security services" would be permitted to have handguns. Morris and Hawkins made five recommendations, labeled "ukases," for accomplishing this goal.[4]

First, they proposed annually renewable licensing for firearms owners. But licenses would only be available to police, undefined "security services personnel," and any persons who "can show good cause" (left undefined) to have a gun. Depending on how "good cause" is defined, their disarmament proposal might leave a great deal or very little weaponry in private hands. Shotgun and rifle licenses would be available to hunters and target shooters who are members of registered gun clubs. However, "sporting associations" would be responsible for storing their members' long guns. The authors did not explain how prohibition would be enforced, specify a punishment for unlicensed gun possession, or discuss how law enforcement officials would deal with problems that surely would arise in disarming tens of millions of Americans. They did acknowledge that it might take up to ten years to achieve a disarmed citizenry.

Morris's and Hawkins's second "ukase" banned purchasing firearms through the mail, except for federally licensed dealers. (The 1968 GCA had already achieved this.) Third, Morris and Hawkins proposed an additional sentence, up to 10 years, for using a firearm or imitation firearm to resist arrest.

Fourth, the authors proposed a sentence enhancement of up to five years imprisonment for possessing an unlicensed firearm in the commission of any crime. Fifth, they urged prohibition of possession of "military weapons" by anyone other then the armed forces. (The 1968 GCA had also accomplished this by adding "destructive devices" to the NFA list of "gangster weapons.")

Morris and Hawkins rejected the anticipated objection that their plan would disarm law-abiding citizens, but not criminals. They argued that "it is most implausible to assume that the individuals involved in the majority of murder cases are so determined to kill that . . . they will deliberately evade whatever restrictive legislation passed." Apparently, they assumed that most murderers are first-time offenders who resort to lethal force on the spur of the moment.* They did not say whether they anticipated armed robbers and other hard core criminals to disarm voluntarily.

In order to facilitate compliance with their disarmament plan, Morris and Hawkins suggested regular amnesties for gun owners to surrender firearms in exchange for at or above market-level compensation. In order to identify violators, Morris and Hawkins proposed to install "portable and discriminatory monitors capable of identifying a concealed gun on persons passing through a door or a footpath." They also recommended that a "trace element" be added to the metal of new guns so that they would be detectable by monitoring devices.

Congressional Prohibition Proposals

In 1973, Representative Ronald Dellums (D-Calif.) introduced the first federal handgun prohibition bill.[5] It aimed to prevent lawless and irresponsible use of firearms by prohibiting "the importation, manufacture, sale,

---

*This widely shared assumption has been effectively rebutted by Daniel Polsby and Don Kates, "American Homicide Exceptionalism" (1998).

purchase, transfer, receipt, possession, or transportation of *handguns*."*
Because the bill prohibited handgun *possession*, all handgun owners
would have to give up their arms or face the consequences.

Dellums's prohibition and disarmament bill proposed a $5,000 fine
and/or a prison sentence up to five years for persons convicted of possessing handguns or handgun ammunition. Pistol clubs could store handguns for licensed members, but such clubs themselves would have to be
licensed by the secretary of the treasury. Firearms could only be transported with the approval of a law enforcement agency.

Under Dellums's proposal, handguns could only be sold by licensed
dealers and only to licensed pistol club members, importers, manufacturers, and other dealers. Federal and state law enforcement personnel and
state licensed security guards would continue to be lawfully armed. The
federal government would offer to purchase all privately owned handguns
for either $25 or the market value of the gun, whichever was higher.

Only a few days after Dellums introduced his bill, Rep. John Bingham
(D-N.Y.) introduced a similar bill to "prohibit the importation, manufacture, sale, purchase, transfer, receipt, possession, or transportation of
handguns, except for or by members of the armed forces, law enforcement
officials, and as authorized by the secretary of the treasury, licensed importers, manufacturers, dealers, antique collectors and pistol clubs."[6] Representatives Bingham and Dellums reintroduced their bills several times
over the next few years, but neither bill ever made it out of committee.

In June 1992, Senators John Chafee (R-R.I.), Claiborne Pell (D-R.I.), and
Alan Cranston (D-Calif.) introduced legislation to ban the sale, manufacture, and possession of handguns, with exceptions for law enforcement
personnel and licensed target clubs. Senator Chafee exhorted his colleagues: "It is time to act. We cannot go on like this. Ban them!"[7] The bill
did not provide compensation to those who surrendered their handguns.[8]

In 1993, Representative Major Robert Owens (D-N.Y.) proposed that it
be "unlawful for a person to manufacture, import, export, sell, buy, transfer, receive, own, possess, transport, or use a handgun or handgun am-

---

*It also provided for a registration scheme for long guns. An application had to
be filed with the Treasury Department within 180 days of purchasing a long gun.
The treasury secretary would be responsible for the exact details of the application,
but it would have to include biographical information on both buyer and seller,
including the seller's license number (if a licensed dealer), as well as the gun's
serial number, make, model, caliber, and gauge. Upon receipt of a valid application
and a fee of one dollar, the secretary of the treasury would send the owner a certificate of registration. The gun owner would have to carry this certificate whenever
he carried the firearm.

munition."[9] He exempted military personnel, registered security service guards, and licensed handgun clubs and their members. In addition, licensed manufacturers, importers, and dealers "as necessary" were exempted in order to satisfy the limited remaining market. The bill proposed to reimburse gun owners, who voluntarily surrendered their firearms to a law enforcement agency within 180 days. Violators would face a maximum fine of $5,000 and five years imprisonment.

Other Disarmament Proposals

The Communitarian Network, an organization led by noted sociologist Amitai Etzioni, issued a high profile proposal for handgun prohibition in 1991. "The Case for Domestic Disarmament" condemns "vanilla pale measures that have been taken thus far with regard to firearms" and calls for prohibiting handguns for everyone except military and law enforcement agencies, licensed pistol clubs, security services, and collectors.[10] This manifesto was signed by 75 prominent academics, politicians, and other national leaders, including Independent Party presidential candidate John Anderson, former Illinois senator Adlai Stevenson III, former FCC chairman Newton Minow, former San Antonio mayor (and later secretary of housing and urban development) Henry Cisneros, and many prominent academics such as Benjamin Barber (Rutgers), John Coffee (Columbia), John Gardner (Stanford), Mary Ann Glendon (Harvard), Albert O. Hirschman (Princeton), Charles Moskos (Northwestern), Philip Selznick (Berkeley), Lester Thurow (MIT), and dozens of others. If handgun disarmament was once considered a fringe idea, after promulgation of this manifesto, it could no longer be so considered.

The Communitarian Network called a ban on handguns "one measure sure to gain monumental benefits in the short run." It argued that domestic disarmament is the remedy for accidental gun discharges, impulsive uses, and gun violence. According to the manifesto, criminalizing all private possession of handguns will reduce deadly crime simply by making it harder for people to arm themselves.

Etzioni and his colleagues would permit very limited exceptions to the disarmament plan. Gun collectors could keep only those weapons that they render nonfunctional, for example, by pouring cement into the barrel. Hunters could have rifles and shotguns, as long as they do not have sights and cannot fire "powerful" bullets. The communitarians, with some sarcasm, encouraged "super-patriots" to join the National Guard.

The Communitarian Network urged that disarmament be implemented quickly. Acknowledging that it would be costly to buy up all existing fire-arms, it argued that this would be better and cheaper than devoting more resources to enforcing current legislation. It suggested implementing and testing its plan in the northeast region of the country.

The Communitarian Network's proposal leaves many questions about implementation and enforcement unanswered. For example, what punish-ment would be meted out to handgun owners who do not turn over their handguns? Who would enforce handgun prohibition?

A few other gun control organizations have also endorsed various forms of handgun prohibition. The Coalition to Stop Gun Violence (CSGV), pre-viously the National Coalition to Ban Handguns, seeks to "ban handguns and assault weapons from importation, manufacture, sale and transfer by the general American public," except for military, police and security per-sonnel, and gun clubs.[11] CSGV proposes a series of steps leading up to the handgun ban. It calls for restrictive licensing of gun dealers and owners and higher licensing fees, high taxes on handguns and ammunition, strict liability for gun manufacturers and dealers, regulating firearms as con-sumer products, limiting individuals to one handgun purchase per month, and banning Saturday Night Specials. This is not a disarmament plan, since it permits handgun *possession* (although encouraging voluntary dis-armament). It also does not cover rifles or shotguns because, according to the coalition, those weapons do not pose the same threat as handguns.

In its model "Cease Fire" legislation, the Violence Policy Center (VPC) calls for a "handgun phase out." Manufacture and sale of new handguns would be prohibited. Existing handguns would have to be surrendered upon the owner's death.[12] Presumably, the VPC would ban *transfers* of existing handguns, but this is not mentioned. There also is no explanation of how sales or other transfers in violation of the prohibition would be prevented or, if discovered, punished.* The VPC argues that implementing its proposal would cost far less than maintaining the status quo. But it does not discuss enforcement costs.

The 55,000-member American Academy of Pediatrics (AAP) urges us to "protect children from injuries and deaths caused by handguns by pro-hibiting the manufacture, sale and possession of handguns."[13] The AAP's proposal exempts any U.S. agency or department, licensed gun collectors, licensed gun clubs, as well as private security agents.

---

*The VPC plan would give BATF comprehensive regulatory authority to set and monitor saftey standards for the production of firearms, restrict the availability of certain classes of firearms, and "take immediate action to stop the sale and distri-bution of firearms or firearms products found to be imminent hazards."

On May 20, 1999, in response to a school shooting in Conyers, Georgia, Physicians for Social Responsibility (PSR), a 15,000-member organization established in the 1960s, stated that "it is time for the U.S. to join other civilized nations and enact a ban on handguns." Citizens should "send a clear message to Congress that we are not willing to tolerate the insane laws that allow such tragedies to happen." The organization does not offer any plan or strategy for attaining its goal. Instead, it calls on Congress "to design and implement an effective disarmament program."

A number of newspapers have endorsed handgun prohibition or disarmament *in principle*, but without any recognition of implementation and enforcement problems. In April 1999, a *Washington Post* editorial, "Why Not Ban Handguns?," urged President Clinton to "stand up for a national ban on the general sale, manufacture and ownership of handguns."[14] A May 1999 *Chicago Daily Herald* editorial exhorted municipalities to ban the sale of handguns and assault weapons and suggested that they buy up the local handgun inventory.[15]

The Feasibility of Prohibition

Prohibition proposals come in different styles and sizes. Prohibiting manufacture of handguns would be the easiest form of prohibition to implement and enforce. The Census of Manufacturers for 1997 shows that there were one hundred and ninety-one small arms manufacturing companies with combined sales of $1.2 billion. The locations of these manufacturers are known. The federal government could order them shut down, subject them to prohibitive taxation ("tax them to death"), or expose them to ruinous tort liability. Their decommission would be easy to monitor. Of course, the government would need to permit at least one private company to continue producing enough handguns for the police and whatever other groups would still be lawfully armed. Alternatively, the government could set up its own handgun manufacturing plant to supply the legitimate market.*

Closing down legitimate manufacturers would be a boon to black mar-

---

*Congress might even be able to close the handgun manufacturers down without compensation as was done to the alcoholic beverage producers during National Alcohol Prohibition (see Andrew Sinclair, *Prohibition—The Era of Excess*, 154–178). More likely, because of fairness concerns (and the manufacturers' political clout), lawmakers would compensate the companies and their employees many billions of dollars for, in effect, the nationalization of their business.

ket producers. Clandestine handgun manufacturers would spring up, just as thousands of illegal stills operated during alcohol prohibition, and hundreds or thousands of clandestine labs now produce unlawful mood and mind-altering drugs like amphetamine and ecstasy. Even today, "zip guns" are produced or assembled in small workshops within the United States.* These black market manufacturers, already illegal, operate outside any regulatory scheme for recordkeeping, serial numbers, safety locks, or taxation.

Implementing a prohibition on *importation* of handguns would be even more difficult. Without (or with sharply diminished) domestic U.S. sources for new handguns, there would be a greater economic incentive for smugglers to bring in handguns from abroad. Is there any reason to believe that customs officials and other law enforcement personnel would be more successful in preventing handgun smuggling than in preventing drug smuggling? I think not. Contraband handguns, like illicit drugs, would enter the country illegally in seaborne containers, trucks, cars, planes, and by mail. (Currently, there are firearms black markets in Western Europe, where handguns smuggled from Eastern Europe and the former Soviet Union are easily obtainable in Amsterdam, Brussels, and other cities.)[16]

Prohibiting the Sale of Handguns

All handgun prohibition proposals discussed in this chapter include a ban on the *sale* of handguns. A sales prohibition would necessarily have to prohibit every type of commercial transfer, lest the ban be circumvented by leasing and renting. But even that expanded proscription would be incomplete. Banning just *commercial transfers* would not prevent handguns from being transferred by nondealers to new owners as gifts or barter. Therefore, an effective "sales" prohibition should encompass a ban on gifts and lending as well.

No doubt once a sales prohibition seemed like a realistic possibility,

---

*David Kopel, "Crime and Punishment Symposium: A System in Collapse: Peril or Protection? The Risks and Benefits of Handgun Prohibition," *St. Louis University Public Law Review* 12 (1993): 318. Even in some less developed countries, villagers produce "a crude, but fully functional, copy of such a handgun using tools considerably less sophisticated than those contained in millions of American households."

some people (including profiteers and ideological opponents of the prohibition) would purchase large quantities of handguns in order to supply the post-sales prohibition demand.

Prohibiting Possession of Handguns

Proponents of handgun prohibition ought to see little point in banning the manufacture and sale of handguns without also banning *possession*. Failure to ban possession would leave the existing private sector stock of handguns intact. Moreover, if handgun possession was undisturbed, following the model of National Alcohol Prohibition, there would be a tremendous opportunity for blackmarketeers to meet the demand for handguns with weapons imported from abroad or produced in clandestine workshops. The new handguns and handgun possessors would blend in with the existing handguns and their possessors. The moral coherence of this form of prohibition would be weak; tens of millions of owners would be allowed lawfully to possess guns, while younger people would be treated as criminals for doing the same thing.

Criminalizing the possession of handguns, along with the manufacture and sale, would conform the gun prohibition paradigm to the regime that currently covers illicit mind- and mood-altering drugs. Prohibition that includes a ban on possession would commit the country to disarming the citizenry. The Dellums and Bingham bills say that 180 days after the law becomes effective, it would be a crime to possess a handgun. In one fell swoop, tens of millions of Americans would be prosecutable, unless they surrendered or destroyed their arms.

We can get a sense of the magnitude of the compliance problem by looking at the success of our current prohibition on possession that applies to persons with a felony record. Hundreds of thousands, perhaps millions, of ex-felons currently possess handguns illegally, despite the federal felon-in-possession law's threat of a 10-year maximum federal prison sentence. We can also obtain a perspective on compliance by looking at what happened when, in 1995, several states required *registration* of assault rifles. In California, only 10% of about 300,000 assault weapons owners registered their weapons.[17] Cleveland and Boston achieved an estimated 1% compliance rate. Denver authorities registered 1% of 10,000 assault rifles.[18] The estimated 100,000 to 300,000 New Jersey assault rifle owners registered 947 assault rifles, rendered 888 inoperable, and turned over 4 to law enforcement personnel. It should be emphasized that these assault rifle laws were implemented in states that had produced legislative majorities for such gun controls. A federal registration requirement would have to be enforced in states where handgun prohibition could not command a legislative majority. In those states, noncompliance would be an even greater problem, and police and prosecutors, charged with enforcing the prohibition, would have to confront jurors' hostility.*

Prohibition would face constitutional litigation all over the country. Most gun owners (rightly or wrongly) believe that they are exercising a constitutional right.[19] Even a Supreme Court decision, rejecting the contention that the Second Amendment guarantees law-abiding individuals the right to keep and bear arms, would not shake millions of citizens' belief that gun ownership is a right of American citizenship.

Enforcement Problems

Who would enforce handgun disarmament and with what degree of vigor? National Alcohol Prohibition was enforced by a small number of U.S. Treasury Department agents and by state and local police departments. Criminal justice and organized crime scholar Humbert S. Nelli writes that "Prohibition overburdened the criminal justice system and undermined respect for the nation's law." Another author recalled that "organization and methods . . . were hopelessly inadequate."[20] Professor McBain of Columbia Law School wrote in 1928 that "the large-liquor drinking public has been indifferent to, if not positively in favor of, the corruption that helps to keep the stimulating stream flowing without interruption . . . the [police] force from the beginning has been thoroughly spoils-ridden."[21] In many cities, the police were contemptuous of alcohol prohibition and did not enforce it; corruption flourished. History has repeated itself with the contemporary drug war.

After the Supreme Court's decision in *Printz*, rejecting federal authority to order state and local officials to conduct background checks, National Handgun Prohibition might have to be a completely federal program.[22] What kind of a federal enforcement agency would be needed to investigate and deter unlawful handgun possession? Currently, most illegal handguns are seized as a consequence of street or car stops made by local law enforcement agents; a frisk reveals the gun.[23] Routine car and street stops are

---

*David Kopel says that "perhaps no laws in American history have been more universally ignored than the 'assault weapon' prohibition." He argues that the threatened ban on assault weapons led to the greatest civilian armament in history. "Gun factories worked furiously to produce a two-year supply of rifles and an estimated 10-year supply of ammunition. The magazine, *Guns and Ammo,* provided instructions on burying guns" (*Guns: Who Should Have Them?* p. 186).

not the province of federal agents, who lack general street-level policing authority and experience. Perhaps BATF could be expanded into a super nationwide street-level police agency with tens of thousands of new agents? Such a move would have to overcome the opposition of the NRA, gun owners, some members of Congress, and others who excoriate BATF agents as "jack-booted minions."* It would also have to overcome those who oppose expanding federal power and expending a great deal of federal funds. Undoubtedly, there would be opposition and resistance from fringe elements, who for years have warned of a colossal and despotic federal government. The number of militia groups would probably grow, with the potential for Waco-type standoffs and shootouts.[24]

These potential problems suggest that *passive enforcement* might be a better alternative. BATF agents might make no special effort to identify and arrest handgun possessors. They could simply make arrests when handguns come to light in the course of investigations of other crimes. Of course, that is not much different than the way federal and state felon-in-possession laws are currently enforced.

Some prosecutors, for political or practical reasons, would hesitate to prosecute unlawful possession cases, just as prosecutors today do not prosecute every drug possession case. They would face serious difficulties convicting defendants with no criminal record who claim to possess a gun for self-defense or sport. Currently, federal prosecutors decline to prosecute a high percentage of charges even against persons *with felony records* when, though possessing firearms illegally, the arrested person has committed no other crime.[25] It would be much more difficult to convince federal or state prosecutors to bring charges against otherwise law-abiding persons for merely violating National Handgun Prohibition. Even if prosecutors brought charges, it would be difficult to get unanimous guilty verdicts from jurors who, in many states, would be inclined to nullify the unpopular law.

Perhaps enforcing unpopular, or at least controversial, handgun disarmament could be made easier by setting the punishment low. If illegal possession of a handgun were treated as a misdemeanor or administrative violation, punishable by a small fine, say $250 or $500, jury trials could be avoided altogether. However, under that scheme, people who were

---

*Apparently, this phrase was first uttered by Harlon Carter, NRA executive vice president, in 1980. "Gun prohibition is the inevitable harbinger of oppression . . . it can only be pursued by 'no-knock' laws under which jack booted minions of government invade the homes of citizens; by 'stop and frisk' laws under which the person of citizens can be searched on the streets at the whim and suspicion of authority." See Osha Gray Davidson, *Under Fire*, p. 46.

committed to keeping their handguns would be no more deterred from violating the gun law than from violating the speed limit.

Coping with the Black Market

National Handgun Prohibition, whether actively or passively enforced, would have to contend with a black market.[26] If the lawful supply of firearms was shut down, consider how easily guns could migrate into the black market. In the United States, there exists a black market in handguns that are stolen, purchased for unlawful sale, or otherwise diverted from lawful owners to criminals. According to Gary Kleck, "There appears to be stronger evidence pointing to theft as a major source of guns for criminals than illicit trafficking." Perhaps half of the guns obtained by criminals have been stolen at some time in the past, though not necessarily by the criminal who most recently possessed it and used it in a crime. Kleck estimates that as many as 750,000 guns are stolen each year.[27] Of the inmates interviewed by sociologists James Wright and Peter Rossi in 1986, thirty-two percent said that they stole their most recently acquired handgun; 46% stated that their most recently acquired handgun was "definitely stolen," while another 24% said the gun was "probably stolen."[28] Even in countries with strong prohibitory regimes (like Japan and Holland), criminals are able to obtain handguns relatively easily on the black market.

We can reasonably estimate that there would be a stock of some 100 million or more handguns in private hands by the time National Handgun Prohibition was enacted (assuming booming sales in the 4–5 years leading up to prohibition). The handgun black market would be supplied by imports, stolen handguns, handguns illegally produced in clandestine workshops, and handguns given away or sold by lawful owners, who oppose the law or who, for a profit, are willing to risk getting caught.

Exemptions

Any handgun disarmament plan has to face the question of exemptions: Who will be permitted to continue to possess a handgun? Exemptions are infectious; each one triggers demands for more. The more exceptions, the weaker disarmament's legitimacy.

Even the most fervent prohibitionists do not suggest that federal, state, and local law enforcement agents would have to give up their handguns.[29] Apparently, they accept that armed police will be necessary, at least during a lengthy transitional period, when criminals (who today ignore felony sentences for illegally possessing handguns) would continue to possess and use handguns (as well as knives and other lethal weapons). The police would surely need handguns to apprehend and protect themselves from such criminals. But if the police go about armed, private citizens might well take it as a sign that the social environment is dangerous and conclude that they, too, need handguns for protection. Should they then be prosecuted for wanting to protect themselves and their families? Of course, there will be a proportionally small, but numerically sizeable (and vocal), minority who will perceive the attempt by the government to monopolize firearms as a giant step toward an authoritarian state.

Will only the police remain armed or will other groups also obtain exemptions? What about other law enforcement officials (prison guards, court officers, probation and parole officers) and private police, especially those who guard banks, nuclear installations, museums, and high-end jewelry stores? What about campus police? School police? It is hard to believe that as long as many criminals remain armed, we could expect persons charged with many private security functions, to operate without handguns.

There are more private police in the United States, engaged in protecting persons (e.g., university students) and property (e.g., factories, stores, and homes) than there are public police. Are we prepared to deny them firearms? If not, what is left of the disarmament regime? If private security guards are permitted to bear arms, what about the owners, managers, and employees of gas stations, convenience stores and retail liquor stores, whose proprietors and employees typically function as their own (in-house) security personnel? Would they be entitled to armed defense only if they are wealthy enough to hire a security company?

The two best-known U.S. handgun prohibition initiatives of recent times* illustrate the potential for exemptions to swallow a disarmament rule. In June 1981, Morton Grove, a suburb of Chicago with a population of 27,000, enacted a ban on the possession and sale of handguns.[30] One year later, San Francisco enacted a similar ban. Each was riddled with exceptions.

The Morton Grove ordinance exempted:[31]

1. Peace officers
2. Wardens and other jail and penitentiary personnel

---

*There are others. Washington, D.C., bans the possession of all handguns purchased after 1976 (see D.C. Code §§6-2311). Chicago has a similar provision, as do several of its suburbs, including Evanston, Oak Park, and Wilmette.

3. Members of the active and reserve armed forces and National Guard
4. Special agents employed by a railroad or a public utility to perform police functions: guards of armored car companies; watchmen and security guards actually and regularly employed in the commercial or industrial operation for the protection of persons employed and private property related to such commercial or industrial operations
5. Agents of the Illinois Legislative Investigating Commission
6. Licensed gun collectors
7. Licensed gun clubs
8. Those possessing antique firearms
9. Those transporting handguns to persons authorized to possess them
10. Those transporting handguns from one gun club to another

The vaguest of the Morton Grove exemptions is "Peace Officers." The state courts had interpreted the term to include *"any employee of a public entity responsible for maintaining public order* (emphasis added)."*

The San Francisco ordinance provided even more exemptions:[32]

A. Public law enforcement personnel
B. Military personnel while employed in the performance of their duties
C. Those using handguns at target ranges
D. Those transporting target shooting handguns
E. Licensed collectors
F. Those who qualify for licenses to carry concealed weapons, and licensed handgun sellers
G. Armored vehicle guards who obtained a Firearms Qualification Card
H. Patrol special officers, assistant patrol special police officers, animal control officers or zookeepers, humane officers, and harbor police
I. Guards or messengers of common carriers, banks, and other financial institutions engaged in the course of their duties; guards of contract carriers operating armored vehicles; private investigators, private patrol operators, and alarm company operators; uni-

---

*According to the NRA, this prohibition scheme achieved little compliance. Two years after the law's enactment, more then 80% of the households that held handguns before the ban still possessed them. Of an estimated 3,000 handguns in Morton Grove prior to the ban, 20 were turned in. See NRA-ILA Research and Information, "Fact Sheet—The War against Handguns."

formed security guards or night guards employed by any public agency; uniformed security guards, regularly employed and compensated as such by persons employed in any lawful business
J. Any person engaged in any lawful business, or any officer, employee, or agent authorized by such person for lawful purposes connected with such business, possessing a handgun within such person's fixed place of business.

This San Francisco ordinance, eventually struck down by the California Supreme Court on preemption grounds (i.e., state law forbids municipalities from making laws on the subject), allowed members of many groups to retain their handguns. The last exception is the broadest; it permitted most businesses to be protected by armed guards.

The Constitutionality of Handgun Prohibition

National Handgun Prohibition would face intense constitutional attack. During the several years that it would take for the issue to reach the Supreme Court, there would be numerous federal district court decisions. If, as seems likely, some of these lower federal courts struck down handgun prohibition as unconstitutional, it would create an unsettled and ambiguous legal environment, strengthening the resolve of gun rights advocates. It would also trigger an extraordinary demand for handguns in those jurisdictions where they could still be legally purchased.

If the Supreme Court struck down National Handgun Prohibition as violative of the Second Amendment, the only other possible strategy for prohibitionists would be repeal of the Second Amendment by a constitutional amendment. Because of the super-majority required to amend the Constitution (three-quarters of the states), this would be even harder to accomplish politically than federal handgun prohibition itself. If the Supreme Court upheld the constitutionality of a National Handgun Prohibition, the disarmament law would be valid, but difficult issues of implementation, enforcement, and punishment would have to be faced.

Conclusion

"Prohibition" is a slogan. What it means and how it would be implemented and enforced are questions that have hardly begun to be addressed. The devil is in the details. What groups and individuals would be exempted from the prohibition? Would all firearms be prohibited or just handguns? National Handgun Prohibition could apply to manufacture, importation, sale, or possession. Ending manufacture of new guns would be easiest to implement, but more than 100 million handguns would by then be in private hands, augmented by imports and the production of small clandestine shops. Prohibiting possession would require disarming the citizenry; whether done quickly or over a long period, it would be a monumental challenge, fraught with danger. Millions of citizens would not surrender their handguns. If black market activity in connection with the drug laws is any indication, a decades-long "war on handguns" might resemble a low-grade civil war more than a law enforcement initiative.

11

Other Gun Control Strategies

One would assume that the most sensible approach to "gun safety" would be the one that offers the greatest opportunity to reduce firearms death and injury. If that is the standard, then current "gun-safety" measures—which include trigger locks, safety training, and safe-storage laws—fail miserably.
—Josh Sugarman, director, Violence Policy Center,
   Every Handgun Is Aimed at You

You can't have it two ways. If you really safeguard your gun so that innocent people in your house—your children or visitors or someone else—can't get hurt with it, then they won't be able to get that gun for the kind of emergency that they bought it for in the first place.
—Joseph McNamara, San Jose police chief

History will not be kind to the Court's ruling. The California Supreme Court today discovered a tortured path to granting the gun industry a special immunity from legal accountability that has no justification in law or public policy. . . . We call on the California legislature to act immediately to right this wrong and repeal the special interest statute invoked by the Court to deny justice to these victims of assault weapon violence.
—Dennis Henigan, director, Brady Center's Legal Action Project,
   commenting on the California Supreme Court's decision
   in *Merrill v. Navegar*

So far we have considered three gun control strategies: first, leaving guns generally available for private ownership, but endeavoring to keep them out of the hands of high risk users; second, prohibiting manufacture and sale of all firearms or just handguns; and third, prohibiting possession (i.e., disarmament) of all firearms or just handguns. In this chapter we deal with a range of other gun control proposals. Unlike licensing, registration, and prohibition, many of these proposals are aimed at preventing accidental injuries rather than at preventing violent crime.

Making Guns Safer

Some gun control advocates urge a number of strategies—trigger locks, smart guns, and safe storage laws—aimed at making guns and gun possession safer. These strategies are not directed at reducing the criminal misuse of firearms, but at reducing firearms accidents.

Trigger Locks

Recently, a number of gun control proponents and organizations have urged that gun manufacturers be required to sell their guns with a trigger lock, which when engaged makes the firearm inoperable (see table 11.1). Senator John Kerry (D-Mass.), co-sponsor of a recent proposal to set minimum standards for gun safety locks, believes that "accidental shootings can be prevented by simple safety measures, one of which is the use of an effective gun safety lock."[1] Former president Bill Clinton also endorsed mandatory trigger locks.[2] As of summer, 2002, five states have passed safety lock laws, and several other states are considering them. A 1997 settlement of a lawsuit between several cities and Smith & Wesson, the nation's largest firearms manufacturer, calls for that company to sell trigger locks with all its firearms.[3]

The Bush administration has made child safety locks a centerpiece of its firearms policy by proposing to allocate $75 million in matching grants to states that provide gun owners with child-safety devices or trigger locks;[4] $65 million will go toward assisting state and local governments with the purchase and distribution of safety locks. The remaining $10 million will be spent on promoting the program to the public.[5]

In theory, trigger locks will prevent accidental firearms deaths by making it impossible for a child to discharge a gun. (Of course, *very young* children lack the hand size, grip, and strength to fire most guns.) Unfortunately, some parents will continue to act irresponsibly by discarding the locks.[6] Nothing prevents a purchaser from throwing the lock away or dis-

Table 11.1. Trigger Locks

	How It Works	General Problems	Ready for Use in Sudden Emergency?	Can It Be Easily Defeated?	Price Range	Notable Differences from Other Locking and Storage Devices
Trigger locks	Locks placed on or around trigger, preventing trigger from being pressed.	If used on a loaded gun, may cause accidental discharge. Some guns have fired even with trigger lock on. Quality of locks varies greatly—some have been subject to recalls.	No. The user must unlock the device with a key or combination, which may be difficult under stressful circumstances or in the dark. User may have to search for key.	Can be defeated with pliers, wire-cutters, and other common tools.	Starts around $10 and can go above $30 for battery powered combination locks.	None noted.
Cable locks	A cable is run through the magazine tunnel, barrel, or action of the firearm with each end locking to an ordinary padlock. This prevents bullets from being chambered or fired.	Quality of locks varies greatly—some have been subject to recalls.	No. Same delays as with a trigger lock. Additional time needed to load the gun.	Can be defeated by wire-cutters.	Between $10 and $15.	Unlike a trigger lock, a gun outfitted with a cable lock cannot be loaded or discharged while the lock is in place.

(continued)

Table 11.1. Trigger Locks (Continued)

	How It Works	General Problems	Ready for Use in Sudden Emergency?	Can It Be Easily Defeated?	Price Range	Notable Differences from Other Locking and Storage Devices
Internally installed combination locks (Saf-T-Lok)[1]	A kit that can be permanently installed on the firearm to prevent the gun from firing, unless the user correctly depresses three individually programmed buttons in any order.	The lock is known to malfunction, causing ammunition to feed improperly.	Saf-T-Lok manufacturer says the owner can disarm the device in three seconds in total darkness. Critics believe that this timeframe, although short, is too long to make the Saf-T-Lok useful. The lead attorney for Handgun Control, Inc., and Maryland governor Parris Glendening were both unable to disengage the lock at separate press conferences. The owner may also forget the correct combination.	Forcibly removing the Saf-T-Lok from a firearm will irreparably damage the gun. Simple combination and a feature that allows for the combination to be entered short of one digit for even more rapid use, might make this lock less child-resistant.	$69.95 for revolvers and $89.95 for pistols.	Use of a combination system eliminates problem of keys. Device can be safely used on a loaded gun.

174

Device	Description	Reliability	Can be used in an emergency?	How defeated	Cost	
Hammer-locking devices	Device prevents the hammer from striking the firing pin and igniting a round of ammunition. Two popular hammer locks include a removable hammer (Saf-T-Hammer) and a lock that blocks the motion of the hammer (Taurus Security System).[2]	Difficult to disengage, requiring the use of a toothpick-sized screw driver (in the case of the Saf-T-Hammer) that could be easily lost and requires some dexterity to use.	No. Both types of locks require fine movement to disengage, making them unsuitable for use in a sudden emergency.	Removable hammers can be easily circumvented with a single motion. They are no longer sold on their parent company's website.[3]	Taurus provides devices free of charge to owners of Taurus guns.	Can be used on a loaded gun.
Magazine disconnects	Prevents a gun from firing if the magazine is not engaged.	Foolproof. If no magazine is engaged, gun won't fire. Might not be child-proof if magazine is kept near the gun.	Depends on where magazine is stored.	Magazine disconnects can be easily defeated with one snip of a metal cutter.	Magazine disconnects are installed by the manufacturer, and cost $0.25 to $0.50 to insert.	None.
Gun lock boxes and gun safes	A safe designed to hold loaded handguns.	None noted.	No. User must open the safe before using a firearm.	Some models can be defeated with screw drivers and other household tools by children.	Price ranges from $50 to more than $1,000.	None.

1. See http://www.saf-t-lok.com/ for more information.
2. See http://www.taurususa.com/keylock.html for more information.
3. See http://www.saf-t-hammer.com for more information.

Source: Compiled from Leonardatos, Blackman, and Kopel, "Smart Guns/Foolish Legislators."

abling it. Indeed, many gun purchasers do not lock their guns because they want them available for rapid deployment in the event of a self-defense emergency. Furthermore, the trigger lock requirement will only apply to new guns, not to the more than 80 million handguns already in private homes. (However, some proposals call for distributing locks free of charge to all gun owners.)

Some *pro–gun control* activists are ambivalent toward, or even oppose, trigger locks because they fear that if guns are rendered childproof, more people would acquire them.[7] Many firearms safety trainers also warn that trigger locks and personalized ("smart") firearms might create an unjustified sense of security and lead to unsafe practices.[8] Only empirical research will tell us whether safety locks reduce firearms accidents. There's certainly enough plausibility in the hypothesis to support most of the trigger lock initiatives.

Trigger locks might prevent some suicides if the individual contemplating suicide does not have easy access to the key or combination and is not determined enough to choose an alternative method of self-destruction. Perhaps trigger locks would also have a limited crime control impact if thieves who seek to steal guns for personal criminal use or resale are unable to open or break the lock. However, most of the locks currently on the market can easily be cut or broken.[9] Gun owners' rights activists argue that trigger locks might actually spawn a large *increase* in crime if potential victims can less easily employ a gun to defend themselves.[10]

Smart Guns

Gun controllers have urged that manufacturers be required to adopt "smart gun" technology[11] that would permit the firearm to fire only for the owner whose identity the weapon had been programmed to recognize (see table 11.2).[12] Smart guns are an exciting prospect. They would give consumers a choice to be armed without endangering their children or their suicidal relatives or friends. However, no smart guns suitable for the general market have been produced.

The U.S. Patent Office has issued several patents for gun personalization technologies, but the only commercially available models are the Magna-Trigger and other magnetic coding devices that have been on the market for decades.[13] The Magna-Trigger allows a gun to fire only when it is held by a user wearing a magnetic ring. The device, however, is not very smart because it can be defeated easily with any magnet.

Truly smart gun technology must permit a firearm to fire reliably without delay under stressful conditions.[14] The federal government has awarded three small research grants totaling $1.1 million to manufacturers

Table 11.2. Personalized Firearms

	How It Works	Stage of Development	Features and General Problems	Dependent on Battery Power?	Subject to Electronic Interference?
Radio Frequency Identification Device (RFID)	Gun will not fire unless user is wearing a ring or wristband that transmits the proper code to receiver in firearm. Several users (a family or police unit) can be equipped with the same wristband or ring.	Prototype. No publicly announced progress since Nov. 1998.	Wristband or ring can be lost. If ring or wristband is stored close to firearm, the device may not be childproof. The maximum distance between the ring and the firearm at which the firearm will still fire is uncertain, meaning that a gun may still discharge in a struggle if not held by the owner or is stored close to the transmitter.	Yes	Yes. Cell phones, radio waves, and other devices may interfere with the proper functioning of the system.
Remote control	A handheld transmitter that would enable or disable a particular firearm.	Unknown. Not currently on the market.	Ineffective if users leave firearm enabled.	Yes	Yes
Bar codes and magnetic stripes	A firearm would be equipped with a scanner programmed to recognize a unique barcode or magnetic stripe. The barcode or stripe must be accurately placed with respect to the scanner for the device to work.	Unknown. Not currently on the market.	Precise alignment necessary for a successful scan may be difficult to accomplish in stressful circumstances. The unreliability of the scanner, which would be comparable to that of a grocery store check-out, makes this device unsuitable for emergency use.	Yes	No

(continued)

177

Table 11.2. Personalized Firearms (Continued)

	How It Works	Stage of Development	Features and General Problems	Dependent on Battery Power?	Subject to Electronic Interference?
Touch memory	The firearm is activated by contact between a specific part of a ring worn by the user with a specific spot on the gun.	Unknown. Not currently on the market.	Inclement weather, gloves, blood, and oil could interfere with the electronic connection between ring and sensor. The precise alignment between ring and sensor may be difficult to achieve rapidly.	Yes	No
Biometric technologies	Scanners installed in the firearm activate the gun once it recognizes an authorized user's fingerprint or voice.	Prototype. Not currently on the market.	Can be slow to operate. Affected by environmental factors such as noise, grime, and gloves.	Yes	No
Magnetic coding devices (Magna-Trigger)	A magnetic ring worn by the user enables the gun to fire. The device is purchased separately from a firearm and can only be installed by a company gunsmith. It fits most Smith & Wesson revolvers.	Magna-Trigger has been commercially available for several years.	Can be easily circumvented with any magnet.	No	No

Source: Compiled from Leonardatos, Blackman, and Kopel, "Smart Guns/Foolish Legislators."

for research and development,* but so far, firearms manufacturers have not been able to produce such a weapon.

Perhaps, some day smart guns will be available, and gun control proponents will persuade Congress to pass a federal law (or states to pass state laws) requiring all new firearms to utilize smart gun technology.[15] The smart guns we are imagining might have some effect on gun crime, since many criminals use stolen guns. But this is complete speculation since we do not know how easily, if at all, smart guns could be deprogrammed by thieves or the ease with which criminals could obtain their guns in other ways.

Safe Storage Laws

Fourteen states—California, Connecticut, Delaware, Florida, Hawaii, Iowa, Maryland, Minnesota, New Jersey, North Carolina, Rhode Island, Texas, Virginia, and Wisconsin—have Child Access Prevention (CAP) laws, which criminalize the failure to store guns safely; that is, it is a crime to locate a loaded gun such that the owner knows or should know that a child may gain access to it.[16] Because such laws are really not enforceable until after a tragic accident occurs, and because most handgun owners keeping a gun for self-defense want to have ready access to it, compliance with these laws is likely to be low. Nevertheless, such laws may prevent a few shooting accidents.

CAP proponents admit that the law's primary purpose is to prevent accidental shootings by children, but they speculate that such laws might also prevent a significant number of criminal shootings.[17] To support this prediction, proponents point to a few well-known shootings. For example,

---

*In 1997, the National Institute of Justice awarded a $500,000 grant to Colt Manufacturing Company for the development of a personalized gun prototype based on a radio frequency identification device. The prototype showed that the technology is feasible, could fit inside a pistol, and could recognize an authorized user within an acceptable time frame. Research and development continues. See http://nij.ncjrs.org/portfolio/XSearch_Details.asp?strGrantNumber=1997LBVXK006 (visited June 28, 2001). In 2000, Smith & Wesson won a $300,000 grant to test "the feasibility of an electronic fire handgun with code-based combination lock, a separate fingerprint module that communicates with an electric fire handgun, and an analysis of the existing Smith & Wesson technology and design of the next generation prototype." This grant was made with an eye toward the eventual goal of fitting a completely integrated biometric system in a handgun. See http://nij.ncjrs.org/portfolio/XSearch_Details.asp?strGrantNumber=2000RDCXK001 (visited June 28, 2001). Another firm was awarded a $300,000 grant for an ultrasonics-based technology.

the children responsible for the 1998 Jonesboro, Arkansas, school shooting, Mitchell Johnson (13) and Andrew Golden (11), at first attempted to take a parent's gun, but it was locked up.[18] They then stole four pistols and three rifles from Andrew's grandfather.[19] Perhaps if these guns had been locked up, their rampage would not have been carried out. On the other hand, maybe the boys would have persevered by finding the key to the parents' secured gun cabinet or obtained guns elsewhere.

Pro-gun commentators suggest that safe storage laws, like trigger lock mandates, may *increase* crime because the deterrence effect produced by the perception of widespread armed self-defense will decline.[20] Perceiving that citizens will not be readily able to defend themselves, criminals may become more brazen. Some gun control advocates oppose safe storage laws because they fear that if people come to believe that guns can be safely stored at home, more people will purchase guns.

Manufacturer Civil Liability

As of fall 2001, 33 local governments, including New Orleans, Miami-Dade County, Atlanta, Cincinnati, and seven cities and counties in California, have filed lawsuits against gun manufacturers and distributors.* The cities allege that gun manufacturers' and distributors' methods of marketing and distributing firearms create a public nuisance. According to the plaintiffs, defendant gun manufacturers produce, market, and distribute substantially more guns than they could reasonably expect to sell to law-abiding customers and, therefore, knowingly facilitate a criminal gun market. Plaintiffs further claim that the defendant manufacturers knowingly do business with FFLs that sell guns to criminals.

The public nuisance claim seeks to vindicate the public's right to a city, county, or state free from gun violence and its associated costs.[21] For example, Camden County, New Jersey's suit against 22 manufacturers and distributors charges that

> defendants market, distribute and promote handguns, a lethal product, with reckless disregard for human life and for the peace, tran-

---

*The Legal Action Project arm of the Center to Prevent Handgun Violence (a Handgun Control, Inc., affiliate renamed Brady Center) provides pro bono legal assistance to attorneys bringing lawsuits against gun manufacturers, as well as to individual victims of gun-related injuries. These suits against gun manufacturers include city suits based on public nuisance claims, as well as victims suits based on negligence or strict liability theories. See the Legal Action Project's website at http://www.gunlawsuits.com/

quility and economic well-being of Camden County. They have knowingly created, facilitated and maintained an oversaturated handgun market that makes handguns easily available to anyone intent on crime, including legally prohibited purchasers. This constitutes a public nuisance by unreasonably interfering with public safety and health, undermining New Jersey's gun laws, and causing grave injury and damage to Camden County.[22]

To take another example, various city suits brought by California municipalities, later combined into one large suit, *People of the State of California v. Arcadia Machine & Tool, Inc.*,[23] alleges that 39 gun manufacturers, 6 distributors, 5 dealers, and 3 associations create a public nuisance by supplying an illegitimate firearms market that causes widespread harm and imposes large costs on California cities, counties, and citizens.[24] Similarly, Atlanta, Bridgeport, Cincinnati, and St. Louis have sued manufacturers, alleging unsafe and defective firearms designs and unfair and deceptive advertising.

The remedy sought by the municipal plaintiffs includes monetary damages to reimburse the cities and counties for funds expended to fight gun crime (e.g., the police force) and care for gun victims (e.g., in public hospitals). Many suits seek punitive damages. Some ask for injunctive relief,[25] including mandatory gun safety devices and warning systems, tightened distribution standards, and support for public education campaigns on gun violence.[26] The goals of this litigation are compensating victims, bankrupting the firearms manufacturers, and reducing violent crime.

The Clinton Administration's Department of Housing and Urban Development (HUD) threatened to bring a suit against the gun manufactures on behalf of public housing authorities seeking reimbursement for security and other costs of gun violence. (While it is questionable whether courts would have recognized HUD as having standing to bring such a suit, the matter became moot when Smith & Wesson, the nation's largest gun manufacturer, split with the other defendant manufacturers and, as a result of negotiations brokered by HUD attorneys, settled with 15 of the 30 plaintiff cities in March 2000.)

In exchange for being dropped from the 15 suits, Smith & Wesson agreed to produce all future guns with trigger locks. (The company was already doing so prior to the settlement.) Smith & Wesson agreed to install smart-gun technology* within three years. The agreement also prohibits

*The settlement provides that "the manufacturer parties to this Agreement shall each commit two percent of annual firearms sales revenues to the development of

Smith & Wesson from selling its products at gun shows if any dealers at those shows sell guns without conducting background checks. (Of course, it is unlawful for FFLs to sell firearms at gun shows or anywhere else without submitting the purchaser to the NICS background check system, unless the firearms are from the dealer's personal collection.) Smith & Wesson later clarified its interpretation of that provision by stating that it applies only to Smith & Wesson firearms sold by FFLs. Disagreement between the company and the government has prevented finalization of the settlement.*

Fifteen city and county plaintiffs did not join in the settlement. They objected to Smith & Wesson's unwillingness to pay monetary damages and to its refusal to turn over documents regarding its distribution and marketing practices. Thus, while many gun controllers hailed the Smith & Wesson settlement as a landmark agreement, it did not really change Smith & Wesson's business practices, nor did it bring an end to all pending lawsuits against the manufacturer. Importantly, no other firearms manufacturer signed the agreement. Still, [then] President Clinton hailed the settlement as a "powerful example of responsibility"[27] by Smith & Wesson and predicted that it would have a domino effect on the entire industry.[28]

Unlike gun control via legislation, gun control via manufacturer liability provides a way to circumvent the political obstacles to gun control. This is an advantage for gun control advocates, who cannot command a political majority in Congress and in most states. However, like many efforts to achieve political change through the courts, the gun manufacturer liability litigation has, to some extent, galvanized and mobilized pro-gun forces. Many gun owners have called for a boycott of Smith & Wesson

---

a technology that recognizes only authorized users and permits a gun to be used only by authorized persons. Within 36 months of the date of the execution of this Agreement, this technology shall be incorporated in all new firearm designs, with the exception of curios and collectors' firearms."

*Fox Butterfield and Raymond Hernandez, "Gun Maker's Accord on Curbs Brings Pressure From Industry," New York Times, March 30, 2000, p. A1. The NRA criticizes the Smith & Wesson settlement accompanying the "Code of Conduct" for manufacturers on the grounds that it would ban almost all semiautomatic pistols, ban the manufacture of all small handguns, potentially require the recall of every handgun made, require gun dealers to create a fund that encourages future lawsuits, potentially replace a handful of product liability lawsuits with hundreds of other lawsuits, surrender firearms design and distribution to antigun politicians, remove the issue of gun control from the normal democratic process, and circumvent the constitutional guarantees of the Second Amendment. Jeff Reh, "The Smith & Wesson Settlement and the 'Code of Conduct'—Why We Have Not Signed," NRA-ILA Research and Information, available at: http://www.nraila.org/research/20000905-FederalFirearmLicenses-001.shtml (visited June 28, 2001).

weapons. The NRA has lobbied for state laws barring municipalities from suing firearms manufacturers, as well as for laws limiting private suits. Twenty-seven states enacted legislation prohibiting cities from bringing tort claims against gun makers.* For example, Arizona law now provides:

> The governing authority of any political subdivision or local or other governmental authority of the state is precluded and preempted from bringing suit to recover against any firearms or ammunition manufacturer, trade association, or dealer for damages for injury, death, or loss or to seek other injunctive relief resulting from or relating to the lawful design, manufacture, marketing, or sale of firearms or ammunition. The authority to bring such actions as may be authorized by law shall be reserved exclusively to the state.[29]

Tort suits by victims of gun violence have been less successful than the city suits. Practically all courts have rejected plaintiffs' claims that the firearm manufacturers be held liable via theories of products liability or strict liability for abnormally dangerous activities.[30] In an early (1985) case, the Maryland Court of Appeals carved out an exception, however, for small, cheap handguns—the so-called Saturday Night Specials. In *Kelley v. R. G. Industries, Inc.,*[31] the court found the defendant handgun manufacturer liable for the plaintiff's injuries caused by a Saturday Night Special. However, the Maryland legislature responded to the *Kelley* case by enacting legislation prohibiting such liability,[32] but establishing an administrative procedure for reviewing handgun designs and banning models that failed the criteria.

Since *Kelley*, many victims of gun violence have brought claims against gun makers on theories of strict liability for design defect[33] and/or negligent marketing.[34] The design defect theory is frequently used in cases of accidental shootings involving children and teenagers. Plaintiffs allege that guns without locks and other safety features are defective products.[35] The negligent marketing theory mirrors the public nuisance and negligence claims brought by the municipal plaintiffs. Private plaintiffs utilizing this legal theory allege that manufacturers negligently promote and distribute guns in ways that facilitate criminals obtaining them, and that criminally inflicted firearms injuries are a direct result of this negli-

---

*Alabama, Alaska, Arizona, Arkansas, Colorado, Florida, Georgia, Idaho, Indiana, Kentucky, Louisiana, Maine, Michigan, Missouri, Montana, Nevada, North Dakota, Ohio, Oklahoma, Pennsylvania, South Carolina, South Dakota, Tennessee, Texas, Utah, Virginia, and Wyoming have passed legislation protecting the firearms industry from suit. Wyoming has taking the additional step of asking its attorney general to provide legal support to gun manufacturers if suits against them are brought.

gence.[36] Courts have almost always dismissed these suits, although a recent Illinois appeals court has reversed the dismissal of a suit against Smith & Wesson and other manufacturers (*Ceriale v. Smith & Wesson*, Dec. 31, 2001).

In *Merrill v. Navegar*, the California Supreme Court (Aug. 6, 2001) dismissed a victims' (relatives) suit against the manufacturer of TEC-9 "assault pistol," which was used on July 1, 1993, by Gion Luigi Ferri to kill eight people and wound six at a San Francisco law office. The court held that "the legislature has declared as a matter of public policy that a gun manufacturer may not be held liable in a product's liability action . . . on the basis that the benefits of its product do not outweigh the risk of injury posed by [the product's] potential to cause serious injury, damage or death when discharged."

One case (*Hamilton v. Accu-Tek*) by a victim against gun manufacturers has so far produced a jury verdict for the victims. In January 1995, 49 victims of handgun violence sued 49 firearms manufacturers for fraud, design defect, ultrahazardous activity, and negligent marketing. Judge Jack Weinstein allowed the case to proceed to trial on the plaintiffs' negligent marketing theory. After a four-week trial, three manufacturers were held liable to two plaintiffs, even though the shooter had no recollection how he obtained the gun, which was never found.[37]

The district court's decision was based on certain novel interpretations of New York State's personal injury law. Thus, the federal appeals court certified two legal questions to New York's highest court.[38] The New York Court of Appeals answered both questions unfavorably to the victims, thereby negating their trial victory.[39]

If city or victim suits were to succeed, in the manner of the cigarette litigation, they might force some or all firearms manufacturers out of business. Even unsuccessful lawsuits impose significant costs on gun manufacturers, whose business has been suffering, in any event, from declining sales. Thus, the suits may have contributed to the bankruptcy of Davis Industries and Lorcin Engineering and perhaps to Colt's decision to stop producing some of its less profitable handgun models.[40] Of course, the collapse of the legitimate firearms industry would not necessarily mean a world without guns or even a world with fewer guns. If all legitimate manufacturers closed down, new firearms would be available via smuggling from abroad and clandestine shops in the United States. Marijuana, amphetamines, cocaine, and heroin cannot be legally grown, manufactured, or sold in the United States. Yet, despite the expenditure of billions of dollars and massive criminal justice resources, these drugs are still plentiful.

The gun owners' rights lobby at the state level has succeeded in persuading several state legislatures to pass laws prohibiting product liability suits by private persons against gun manufacturers. In 1999, for example, Alaska passed a law preventing most lawsuits by firearms victims against manufacturers. The law states that

> [a] civil action to recover damages or to seek injunctive relief may not be brought against a person who manufactures or sells firearms or ammunition if the action is based upon the unlawful sale, manufacture, or design of firearms or ammunition. However this section does not prohibit a civil action resulting from a negligent design, a manufacturing defect, a breach of contract, or a breach of warranty.[41]

Other states with similar legislation include California, Colorado, Idaho, Kentucky, Louisiana, Maryland, Montana, North Carolina, South Dakota, and Texas.

Banning Dangerous Guns

Prohibiting certain types of especially dangerous firearms has been a part of federal gun control policy since the National Firearms Act (NFA) of 1934. One reason supporting such policies is the belief that certain types of firearms are especially useful for crime and therefore especially attractive to criminals. There has been little, if any, support for this belief. The other reason is that some weapons pose too great a risk of destruction, that is, there has to be a dividing line between weaponry suitable only for armies and weaponry suitable for sporting and self-defense purposes. The NFA sought to eliminate machine guns, sawed-off shotguns, and certain other firearms and destructive devices by subjecting them to a huge tax and a registration requirement.[42] The 1968 GCA banned civilian possession of "destructive devices," for example, military weapons like bazookas and hand grenades. In 1986, manufacture of machine guns was prohibited; existing machine guns could continue to be sold legally, as long as they were properly registered with the National Firearms Registration and Transfer Record (or NFRTR) that is maintained by BATF.[43]

Assault Weapons

The 1994 Assault Weapons Ban[44] prohibited some military-looking or menacing semiautomatic rifles on the basis of cosmetic features, like bayonet mounts, folding stocks, and plastic pistol grips.[45] Nineteen weapons were banned by name and the BATF was authorized to add other models to the blacklist if they possessed a combination of militaristic design features. Only new assault weapons (post-1994) were banned; pre-1994 weapons could be possessed and transferred lawfully. Gun rights proponents claim that they cannot figure out which guns are illegal and which are not, and that when they can figure it out, they see no functional distinction between lawful and unlawful guns. Not surprisingly, they disparage the moral coherence of a law that makes it a felony to possess a post-1994 assault weapon but treats possession of a pre-1994 assault weapon as perfectly lawful?*

Little, if any, crime control payoff can be expected from this "bad guns" strategy. For one thing, very little gun crime is committed with shotguns, rifles, or assault rifles. All long guns combined, including assault weapons, account for less than 10% of murders and manslaughters committed with firearms.[46] Only a tiny fraction of crimes are committed with assault rifles.† Moreover, any crime-reducing effect of the assault rifle ban is diminished if people who would have purchased banned models purchase lawful long guns or handguns that operate in the same way. Banning some models simply shifts purchasers to unbanned models. For example, after the 1994 Assault Weapons Ban, manufacturers began producing firearms functionally identical, but cosmetically different, to the banned assault weapons. The massive increase in assault rifle sales in the run-up to the 1994 law, plus the appearance of new modified rifles after the ban, suggests that the impact of the "ban" was to put more semiautomatic rifles into private hands.[47]

The 1994 Assault Weapons Ban also banned manufacture and import of ammunition clips or magazines that hold more than 10 rounds.[48] This limitation on the bullet capacity of magazines is meant to address the crazed gunman mowing down schoolchildren or railroad commuters. There's no reason to oppose such a restriction, but the potential payoff seems quite small. Are rampaging criminals and madmen less dangerous with a 10-bullet magazine than with a 15-bullet magazine? Perhaps marginally, since the second or two that it takes to expel an empty 10-bullet

---

*Admittedly, we are used to safety and emission standards that apply only to new vehicles, but these are regulations of manufacturers, not car owners. Driving a vehicle that doesn't meet safety standards is a traffic violation. The assault rifle ban makes ownership of a post-1994 assault rifle a *felony* offense.

†A frequently cited newspaper "study," which showed that assault rifles turn up in BATF gun traces more than their share of the total gun stock, would predict, is flawed for several reasons: (1) which guns are sent to BATF for tracing is dependent on local police who are more likely to send in strange looking assault weapons than "ordinary" guns, and (2) so-called crime guns sent to BATF for tracing include guns that are unlawfull *possessed*.

magazine and insert a replacement might give the victims or the police a tiny window of opportunity to seize the aggressor and stop the attack.

Saturday Night Specials

In the 1960s and, to a lesser extent, in the 1990s, there was a substantial move to ban cheap, poorly made handguns, so-called Saturday Night Specials, because they were said to be favored by criminals and to have no legitimate purpose.[49] In 1968, Congress banned the *importation*, but not the domestic production, of Saturday Night Specials. The importation of the component parts of Saturday Night Specials was not banned until 1986; again, domestic guns and parts were left untouched, leaving the impression that this type of gun control is actually protectionist trade policy.

The drive to ban cheap handguns has made more headway in a few state legislatures than in Congress.* As of 2000, seven states had some version of a Saturday Night Special law.† Ironically, however, recent studies have shown that cheap handguns are not disproportionately used in crime, criminals preferring better made and higher calibre weapons.

Some gun control proponents, including Philip Cook and Jens Ludwig, see raising the price of handguns through taxation, especially the cheapest models, as a good strategy for keeping handguns out of the hands of ju-

---

*Foreign imports were prohibited based on factoring criteria, e.g., size, meltdown temperature, and so on. See Franklin Zimring, "Firearms and the Federal Law: The Gun Control Act of 1968." Yet, domestic importers were not prohibited from importing parts of the banned foreign handguns and assembling them into finished products in the United States.

†Jon Vernick and Stephen Terret, "A Public Health Approach to Regulating Firearms as Consumer Products." In *Kalodimos v. Village of Morton Grove*, 470 N.E.2d 266 (1984), the Illinois Supreme Court upheld Morton Grove, Illinois's handgun ban on the ground that the ban was a valid exercise of the town's police powers and did not violate state or federal constitutions because it did not ban all guns. Available at: http://www.nraila.org/FactSheets.asp?FormMode=Detail&ID=17 (visited July 6, 2001). Most laws define Saturday Night Specials as handguns of (comparatively) small size, that melt at a (comparatively) low temperature, and that weigh (comparatively) little. Whatever the definition, some manufacturers will react by designing new models that closely resemble the banned guns but avoid the prohibition. Hawaii, Illinois, Minnesota, and South Carolina have adopted melting-point laws designed to remove Saturday Night Specials from the streets. While melting-point laws do not affect all Saturday Night Specials, they target the cheapest handguns that are made of the least expensive materials. California, Maryland, and Massachusetts have established standards, which most Saturday Night Specials do not meet, for banning low quality handguns.

veniles and impecunious adults. They argue that because dangerous persons' demand for guns is not rigidly inelastic, every price increase will lead some would-be purchasers to rethink their intent to purchase. But guns would probably have to become much more expensive to significantly reduce demand. New semiautomatic handguns currently can be purchased from retailers for as little as $70; many models sell for less than $125. Used handguns can be purchased from retailers, pawnshops, and at gun shows for less. Thus, a handgun costs about as much as a pair of sneakers. Purchasing a new or used gun, even every year or two, is a much smaller expense than even very casual drug use. Consequently, to significantly, impact demand, the tax would have to be extremely high.

Some proponents of banning Saturday Night Specials argue that such guns pose unreasonable risk of accident because they misfire, jam, or fire when dropped and are so inaccurate as to pose a serious risk to third parties. If true, such firearms should be banned on consumer safety grounds; meanwhile, their manufacturers should be vulnerable to tort suits.* But this has nothing to do with *crime control* unless the possessors and would-be possessors of prohibited Saturday Night Specials are disarmed when these guns are outlawed. However, the costs to society of gun crime might actually increase if criminals switched from low quality guns that jam and fire inaccurately to higher quality more accurate guns.

Regulating Ammunition

Ammunition is even less regulated than firearms. Under current law, ammunition manufacturers and importers must obtain federal licenses, but retailers do not need a license.[50] As far as federal law, any grocery store or sports shop can sell bullets.[51] Purchasers must be over 18 to purchase long gun ammunition and over 21 to purchase handgun ammunition.[52] Convicted felons are prohibited from buying ammunition. Knowingly selling ammunition to ineligible persons is a federal crime. But there is no background check.

From time to time, gun control proponents have proposed regulating or banning ammunition. Some politicians and commentators have argued

---

*The federal government, however, cannot regulate Saturday Night Specials on consumer safety grounds as the Consumer Product Safety Commission is legally prohibited from setting gun safety standards. (The American Handgun Standards Act of 1997 [S. 70 and H.R. 492] proposed by Sen. Barbara Boxer [D-Calif.] and then Rep. Charles Schumer [D-N.Y.] would impose the more stringent quality and safety standards required of imports on domestically manufactured handguns.)

that a total ammunition ban would be easier to implement than a firearms ban.[53] While firearms disarmament would require *taking away* guns from tens of millions of people, ammunition prohibition would *only* require keeping people from *acquiring* bullets. It is estimated that 10 billion rounds of ammunition are produced in the United States alone each year. Proponents of a total ammunition ban believe that gun crime would sharply decline as gun owners consumed the supply of pre-ban ammunition. Former senator Daniel Patrick Moynihan (D-N.Y.), the most prominent proponent of ammunition regulation, estimates that the existing ammunition supply would last no more than five years at current rates of consumption.[54]

If government could keep the citizenry from obtaining bullets, it could prevent gun crimes with loaded guns. But that is a big *if*. It would be extremely difficult, if not impossible, to effectively ban ammunition. Moynihan neglects to account for ammunition reloaders, a common mechanical device that reloads spent casings with gunpowder, primer, and bullets at rates up to a thousand rounds per hour.[55] Gun owners without such devices could turn to black market bullets produced by foreign manufacturers, clandestine domestic ammunition manufacturers, or to a neighbor with a reloader. Our experience with alcohol and drug prohibitions should make us skeptical about whether ammunition could effectively be kept out of the hands of millions of people who want to possess it. We certainly have not been able to prevent people from getting illicit drugs, despite the fact that every aspect of growing, manufacturing, wholesaling, retailing, trafficking, and possessing is illegal, and that such drugs are rapidly consumed and constantly require replenishment. By contrast, an ammunition user might only have to buy ammunition once a decade; modern ammunition has a useful life that is nearly as long as that of a modern firearm.

Ironically, armed criminals require very little ammunition since they usually achieve their objective just by threatening deadly force. A few dozen bullets might last a highly active criminal a lifetime. By contrast, target shooters expend huge amounts (thousands of rounds a month) of ammunition. A total ban on ammunition would eliminate all shooting competitions, even the Olympic shooting team, unless some exceptions could be crafted. But the existence of exceptions would create opportunity for spillage of ammunition from the legal sector to the banned sector.

Total ammunition prohibition is not the only option. Former senator Moynihan and others have proposed prohibiting especially dangerous bullets. In the 1980s, Congress prohibited "cop killer" or armor-piercing ammunition, defined by the materials used in the round.[56] Los Angeles has recently banned handgun ammunition above .46 caliber, rifle rounds above .40 caliber, tracer or incendiary bullets, and "ammunition designed for use in Saturday Night Specials or other junk guns." Former senator Moynihan proposed selectively prohibiting certain types of ammunition, for instance, the .25, the .32, and the 9mm—because they are fired from Saturday Night Specials and assault weapons.[57]

The ammunition targeted by Moynihan's proposed ban does *not* correspond closely to the calibers most commonly used in crimes.[58] According to BATF crime gun trace data from 1999, the 9mm, .22, .38, and .380 are the top four most frequently traced caliber handguns, accounting for a combined 63.2% of all traces.[59] Unfortunately because these are also the most common types of ammunition, it would be difficult to ban them. Furthermore, gun owners could circumvent Moynihan's proposal by using kits that switch gun barrels, thereby allowing a gun to fire different calibers of ammunition.[60] This proposal could also have the effect of shifting criminals to other, possibly more lethal, firearms that would be unaffected by the ban.

Moynihan also proposed huge taxes on .25-, .32-, and 9mm-caliber ammunition, thereby rendering such ammunition unaffordable.[61] This strategy could also be stymied by the use of mechanical reloaders, use of firearms unaffected by the ban, and reliance on the black market.

Some activists and policy analysts have urged that ammunition purchasers be subject to background checks.[62] Why not limit bullet sales to FFLs and make purchasers pass a background check? In April 2001, the Los Angeles City Council passed an ordinance requiring an annual background check in order to obtain a permit to purchase ammunition.[63] This is a sound idea, but its effectiveness will be undermined in all the ways that the Brady Law itself is undermined, especially by straw purchasers and by transactions in the secondary market.

Some commentators have proposed limiting the amount of ammunition an individual could buy in a given time period—possibly 1,000 rounds per month,[64] thereby balancing the need to restrict potential black-market ammunition trade with legitimate gun-usage. A thousand rounds per month would hardly pose a scarcity problem for would-be criminals or for anyone who simply wants to keep a loaded gun ready.

One Gun Per Month

Brady II would limit firearm purchasers to one handgun per month.[65] This gun control strategy is aimed at preventing gun trafficking and at disrupting the black market in firearms. A one-gun-per-month rule might well make it harder for black marketers to build up an inventory, but they could still acquire guns on the secondary market or by using multiple straw purchasers or by dealing with unscrupulous FFLs.[66] (Black marketers could obtain FFL licenses themselves or get a relative, friend, or fellow gang member to obtain an FFL license.) Federal law, to some extent, already regulates volume purchases. An FFL must notify BATF of any multiple purchases.[67] BATF claims that investigating volume purchasers is currently a high priority. Thus, illicit firearms traffickers should already be deterred from making volume purchases from an FFL, unless the FFL is known to be corrupt.

Virginia has had a one-handgun-per-month law since 1993.[68] (Maryland and California have adopted similar laws.) The Virginia one-handgun-per-month law allows narrow exceptions for collectors who pass a stringent background check (Virginia State Police issued 2,739 multiple handgun purchase permits between 1993 and 1999) and for individuals whose guns are lost or stolen. The one-gun-per-month limit is enforced through the mandatory background check system—a record is generated in the background check system that records who has bought a gun and when—so that a purchaser cannot circumvent the system by buying guns from several different FFLs.[69]

The only study to evaluate Virginia's one-gun-a-month law on crime rates was carried out by Mark B. Coggeshall, a University of Maryland graduate student. He found that the law had no effect on homicides in Virginia, but he did not research its impact on gun crime in other states; perhaps traffickers are less able to purchase guns in Virginia and sell them in New York? A 1996 study of BATF firearms trace data by Douglas Weil and Rebecca Knox found a 66% reduction in "the likelihood that a crime gun seized in the northeast would be traced to Virginia relative to gun dealers elsewhere in the southeast for guns purchased after the 1-gun-a-month law took effect." For gun traces originating anywhere in the nation, Virginia scored a 36% reduction.[70] In 1998, Virginia fell from the most common origin state for crime guns prior to the passage of the purchase limit law to the eighth most common origin state.[71]

One handgun per month makes sense because of low implementation and enforcement costs. Very few legitimate users would be inconvenienced by such a limit. Perhaps such laws, adopted nationally, as Brady II requires, would disrupt the flow of guns to criminals, but I have seen no estimates of the nationwide crime reduction that might be anticipated.

Prohibiting Stockpiling

It has been proposed that citizens be restricted in the number of firearms they can own or possess. For example, Brady II would "limit" an individual to 20 guns, with an exception for bona fides collectors. New York State already makes possession of 20 or more firearms a class D felony, which carries a maximum punishment of 20 years in prison.[72] Perhaps this policy is directed at illegal traffickers? Anyone other than an FFL found in possession of more than 20 guns is, in effect, presumed to be an illegal trafficker.

Would limiting arsenals to 20 guns reduce violent crime? The existence of large arsenals is not part of the crime problem. A lone gunman can do as much damage with one or two guns as with 20. Even a single gun can be reloaded in under two seconds with a fresh clip (magazine). Ten gang members could do as much harm with 10 or 20 guns as with a hundred. Groups of evil-intentioned people are highly dangerous whether each group member has a single firearm or half a dozen. A vigorous campaign against multiple gun ownership would shift law enforcement attention to groups like the Branch Davidians (the Waco cult) and set up the possibility of more Waco-type confrontations.[73] Crime reduction should be the main focus of U.S. firearms policy, not hypothetical threats from eccentric groups, whose apocalyptic worldviews might be confirmed by government harassment.

Any limitation on arsenals would be extremely difficult to define, implement, and enforce. Is the unit we are seeking to limit the individual, family, household, commune, gang, or friend-group? Would each *individual* be entitled to possess some maximum number of firearms at a single location or everywhere? Would each *family* (including any people sharing living quarters) be limited to a number of guns? How would we determine whether a batch of guns belong to an individual or to all his family members? Wouldn't a significant exception have to be carved out for collectors? Who qualifies as a collector?

Buy-Backs and Exchanges

Gun exchange programs, which offer goods or cash for guns, have become a popular grass-roots response to urban violence.[74] These programs, which are usually run by local businesses or other community groups in cooperation with law enforcement, aim to reduce the number of guns in circulation. Police time and gun-disposal expenses are the only public costs involved.* The majority of gun exchange program costs are funded

---

*Sen. Barbara Boxer (D-Calif.) and then Rep. Charles Schumer (D-N.Y.) both proposed bills in the 103rd Congress that would increase the amount of the char-

privately.* Sponsors frequently contribute goods—sports tickets, apparel, groceries, toys—or money in exchange for guns.

The most successful gun buy-back program, which occurred in Baltimore more than 20 years ago, brought in 13,000 firearms. Nationwide, it is estimated that exchange programs have attracted more than 76,700 firearms during the 21-year period from 1974 to 1995 (at a cost of over $3 million or roughly $62 per firearm).[75] By contrast, during the same 21 years, more than *80 million* guns were produced in the United States.

Some form of immunity from prosecution is a condition of all gun exchange programs. While proponents of absolute immunity believe that such legal protection is necessary to get guns off the streets, criminals are effectively being offered a legal method to dispose of a crime gun. Some programs have offered limited immunity, excusing participants from possession charges, but not for any crimes they may have committed with their gun.

Communities have also taken different approaches to which guns they will accept at exchanges; compensation is sometimes based on the value and "killing power" of the gun. Most programs, however, do not distinguish between the firearms they accept. By failing to make this distinction, they end up paying cash or goods for cheap or broken guns. Participants can easily use cash awards to purchase newer, better guns. A 1997 National Institute of Justice Study, which also evaluated three studies of gun buy-backs, concluded that gun buy-back programs have little, if any, crime control value.[76]

Ballistic Fingerprinting

When a gun is fired, it leaves a unique marking, or "ballistic fingerprint," on the shell casing. Recently, New York and Maryland enacted legislation that requires manufacturers to test-fire new guns and send samples of the bullets and shell casings to wholesalers and retailers who, upon sale of the gun, must send the bullets and shell casing to the state police, along

---

itable tax deduction available to companies participating in gun exchange programs (S. 1840 and H.R. 3771). Their bills would have allowed companies to deduct the fair market value of the donated goods instead of the cost-deduction currently allowed. President Clinton proposed a $15 million program to sponsor local gun exchanges.

*Ramsey County, Minnesota, Toledo, Ohio, and St. Louis, Missouri, have used seized assets to fund their gun buy-back programs. Connecticut bailed out an exchange program in 1994 when private funding dried up. Joshua Kaufman, "Gun Control or Gimmick."

with the name of the person who purchased the gun. In theory, if bullets or shell casings were found at a crime scene, they could be traced in the ballistics database and linked to the gun's owner; similar legislation has been proposed in several other states. And the FBI and BATF have resources to link their ballistics database with state crime labs to improve the chances that when a shell is found at a crime scene, it can be linked to other crimes and perhaps to the gun and its owner. The problem, of course, is that 80 million existing handguns are not in the databases. Smith & Wesson and Glock are currently installing systems to produce digital images of ballistics material for all their handguns. These companies' databases will be accessible by law enforcement agencies.

Proponents believe that ballistic fingerprinting will prove to be a valuable law enforcement tool because, while guns are rarely found at crime scenes, bullets and shell casings often are. Once the system is in place, police could find a casing, feed its picture into a computer, and perhaps come up with the name of the gun's owner.

Skeptics, including the NRA, argue that so-called ballistic fingerprinting won't work because a gun's markings change every time the gun is fired and because the gun's markings can be altered by any instrument inserted into the barrel.[77] The system would also be defeated if the gun were stolen or passed on by the first owner to whom it was initially registered. Indeed, gun owners' rights organizations criticize ballistic fingerprinting as a de facto firearms registration system.

Ballistics fingerprinting is worth trying because the implementation and enforcement costs are low. Time will tell if the system proves useful in solving gun crimes.

Conclusion

Some advocates of gun control argue that the FFA-GCA-Brady model of trying to keep guns out of the hands of potentially dangerous persons is *just one type* of policy initiative, and not a very strong one at that. They imply that there are all sorts of superior policy options and casually tick off proposals (e.g., safety locks, ammunition control, buy-backs). A close look reveals that, at best, these proposals might reduce accidental firearms injuries and deaths; none has the potential for major crime reduction.

I believe that the FFA-GCA-Brady model will be the dominant gun control option available to American society for the foreseeable future, and that the feasibility of gun control ought to be judged by the feasibility of keeping guns out of the wrong hands. The Brady Law was a step toward elaborating the federal gun control model that originated in the 1930s and was carried forward in the 1960s. It ought not to be regarded as some half-hearted legislation that was just a prelude to *real gun control*. That model can continue to be elaborated and fine-tuned, but, in the final analysis, it will be the centerpiece of U.S. gun control.

Safety locks, smart guns, and safe storage laws ought to be seen as proposals seeking to protect consumers and their families from unsafe guns or perhaps from safe guns stored unsafely. Mostly, guns do work as they are intended to, but there's no reason not to demand that manufacturers continue to employ new safety technologies, where it is reasonable to do so. The NRA and other gun owners' rights organizations preach gun safety to owners and users and sponsor educational training programs.

While trigger lock proposals seek to regulate manufacturers, safe storage laws seek to regulate individual gun owners, a tougher challenge. Indeed, such laws are not really enforceable. The police will not be able to determine whether a firearm is safely stored. And even if somehow they did identify an unsafely stored weapon, criminal prosecution is hardly likely and punishment, if imposed at all, would be very light. Therefore, such laws really amount to little more than exhortations to gun owners to be safety conscious. Most gun owners are already safety conscious, but those who are currently blasé about loaded weapons in the home may not be easily persuaded to change their behavior.

Product liability suits against manufacturers are partly directed at safety but are primarily a strategy for achieving prohibition. The legal theories on which this litigation is predicated have so far not persuaded courts or legislatures, but if the legal ground suddenly shifted, black market importers and manufacturers would probably step in to satisfy the demand for new guns. Proposals to ban ammunition (or tax it to death) similarly really seek to achieve prohibition and are also subject to critique on the basis of implementation and enforcement problems and costs, as well as on the probable formation of a black market. Nevertheless, requiring ammunition purchasers to pass a background check is a good idea.

Currently, the efficacy of ballistic fingerprinting is unclear. If it works, it would provide the police an additional investigative tool. It is an idea worth pursuing, but the payoff in terms of cases solved is not likely to be great, so it will be important to weigh the costs of computer hardware and software against the value of a small number of additional solved crimes.

Gun buy-back programs are directed at eliminating firearms from private hands, but they have proven ineffective. The one-gun-per-month limit on firearms purchases is directed at disrupting the flow of guns from traffickers to the criminal market. Because there are so many ways for criminals to obtain guns, it is hard to anticipate a large crime-reducing payoff from a one-gun-per-month limit, but the strategy ought to be adopted because it is easily implemented without large logistical or enforcement costs.

12

Creating Gun-Free Public Spaces

The most effective way to reduce illegal gun-carrying is to encourage the police to take guns away from people who carry them without a permit. This means encouraging the police to make street frisks. . . . Innocent people will be stopped. Young black and Hispanic men will probably be stopped more often than older white Anglo males or women of any race. But if we are serious about reducing drive-by shootings, fatal gang wars and lethal quarrels in public places, we must get illegal guns off the street.
—James Q. Wilson, "Just Take away Their Guns"

The killing of Amadou Diallo was neither an act of racist violence nor some fluke accident. It was the worst-case scenario of a dangerous and reckless style of policing. Policymakers should dispense with confrontational stop-and-frisk tactics before more innocent people are injured and killed.
—Timothy Lynch, director, Cato Institute, Project
　on Criminal Justice, "We Own the Night"

The history of gun control in the United States has been one of discrimination, oppression, and arbitrary enforcement. The need for self-defense is far more critical in the poor and minority neighborhoods ravaged by crime and without adequate police protection. Enforcing gun prohibitions, furthermore, will only lead to vast increases in civil liberties violations, including illegal searches and seizures.
—Stefan Tahmassebi, NRA's General Counsel's Office,
　"Gun Control and Racism"

Gun control encompasses a much broader range of strategies than just *preventing* "dangerous" people or *prohibiting* all people from obtaining firearms. It includes strategies for apprehending, prosecuting, and punishing people who illegally possess, carry, or use guns in the commission of crimes. In recent years, there have been many initiatives to make punishment of illegal gun possession and gun crime more certain and more severe. These initiatives are primarily the province of state and local criminal justice agencies, but Congress and the U.S. Department of Justice have played an increasingly larger role. It would make sense to make illegal gun carrying in public the centerpiece of U.S. gun control policy. There is much more support for allowing people to defend their homes and businesses with a gun than there is for allowing people to carry concealed weapons on public streets and in open-to-the-public buildings. Carrying concealed weapons in public impacts on community life much more than keeping loaded guns in the house or at a business. Could we not forge a consensus around keeping our public spaces free of concealed weapons?

Apprehending, Prosecuting, and Punishing Illegal Gun Possession

The federal "felon-in-possession" law and similar laws in practically every state make it a crime for a person with a felony conviction to *possess* a handgun. Violators may be identified in the course of routine police work. For example, a police officer may stop someone for jumping a subway turnstile, pat him down, and find a firearm, or a police officer may make a routine vehicle stop (e.g., for speeding) and see a firearm under the seat. Police are constitutionally permitted to make an arrest for any crime, even a traffic violation. Once police make an arrest they can search the arrestee, the passenger compartment of the arrestee's car, and any packages inside it.[1] The more citizens who are stopped and frisked, the more illegal gun possession will be uncovered. (However, an aggressive stop-and-frisk policy will also result in a large number of frisks that do not turn up a weapon and thereby, perhaps, fuel resentment against the police.) Whether prosecutors will prosecute, juries convict, and judges sentence for illegal gun possession when it is not associated with an assault, robbery, or other predatory crime is another question. There is plenty of evidence to suggest that a significant number of pure gun possession arrests are not prosecuted or, if they are prosecuted, that they result in a light sentence, even when severe mandatory punishment is prescribed.[2]

Suspects, arrested for murder, robbery, rape, drug trafficking, or other crimes, may also face an additional charge under the federal felon-in-possession law or a state equivalent. The unlawful gun possession count may be used as a chip in plea bargaining, thereby resulting in a more severe sentence. There is little, if any, political or ideological opposition to punishing armed felons very severely; indeed, all the political momentum is in the direction of meting out draconian sentences for violent felonies,[3] especially those committed with firearms.

Identifying and apprehending people who are illegally carrying guns is a local police function. While many states have made it easier for law-abiding citizens to obtain a license to carry a gun in public, cities like New York, Washington, Chicago, and Boston issue very few carry licenses; most people who carry guns in those cities are doing so unlawfully. In New York, carrying an unlicensed gun is punishable as a class D felony, which carries a maximum sentence of seven years in prison. For years, Massachusetts and a few other jurisdictions have had mandatory jail sentences for unlawful gun possession, but the law is often evaded through plea bargaining.[4]

In the 1990s, various city police departments made illegal gun possession a higher priority. Officers would look for any lawful reason to stop more motorists and pedestrians in order to search for guns.* The New York City Police Department (NYPD), for example, considers its aggressive street policing against unlawful gun carrying an important factor in the city's huge decrease in violent crime since the early 1990s.[5] NYPD officials believe that by making more street stops, carrying out more frisks, seizing more guns, and prosecuting more unlawful gun possession cases, they

---

*In its famous *Terry v. Ohio*, 392 U.S. 1 (1968) decision, the U.S. Supreme Court held that law enforcement officers may temporarily detain an individual for questioning based on reasonable suspicion that a crime has occurred or is about to occur. Officers can conduct a limited physical search for weapons ("pat-down frisk") if they have reason to believe that the individual detained is armed with a weapon. (The U.S. Supreme Court held that "pretextual stops" [e.g., suspecting that a motorist might be a gun trafficker, the officer stops the car for a defective light and carries out search] are constitutional in *When et al. v. United States*, 517 U.S. 806 [1996].)

The *Terry* Court acknowledged that stops and frisks could constitute a "great indignity" that might arouse "strong resentment" (*Terry* at 27). In 1993, Justice Scalia wrote, "I frankly doubt . . . whether the fiercely proud men who adopted our Fourth Amendment would have allowed themselves to be subjected, on mere *suspicion* of being armed and dangerous, to such indignity" *Minnesota v. Dickerson*, 508 U.S. 366, 381 (1993) (Scalia, J., concurring); Timothy Lynch, "We Own the Night: Amadou Diallo's Deadly Encounter with New York City's Street Crime Unit," p. 4; see also William J. Stuntz, "*Terry*'s Impossibility," *St. John's Law Review* 72 (1998): 1213.

increased the risk of being apprehended for unlawfully carrying an unlicensed gun, thereby deterring potential offenders from carrying guns in public.*

The hypothesis that heightening the perception that illegal gun carrying will be punished will lead to fewer gun crimes and violent crimes finds support in a highly publicized Kansas City (Mo.) field study in the early 1990s.[6] For six months the police department sought to seize as many illegal guns as possible in one of the city's highest crime rate areas. While the police seized only 29 more guns during the experimental six months than in the previous six months, the anti-gun initiative was pronounced successful because gun crime dropped significantly in the experimental area compared with the control neighborhood. The evaluators concluded that people who would have carried guns into the area to commit crimes were deterred by the highly publicized policy of focusing on unlawful gun carrying in the experimental area.

Aggressive street policing to identify and punish unlawful carrying of concealed weapons carries risks as well as opportunities. It has the potential to heighten friction and conflict with minority citizens, who inevitably disproportionately bear the brunt of stepped-up street policing. This can and has led to hostility toward police, diminished witness cooperation, and increased rejection of police trial testimony.[7]

In 1999, criticism of the NYPD reached a crescendo when four plain clothes officers, members of the Street Crime Unit, killed Amadou Diallo, an unarmed West African immigrant.[8] The officers claimed that Diallo fit the description of a serial rapist and that Diallo started to run when they ordered him to freeze. In the darkness they thought he was reaching for a gun and fired forty-one times, killing him in the fusillade.†

Almost at the same time as the Diallo controversy, the NYPD and other

---

*This is consistent with then New York Transit Police Commissioner William Bratton's initiative to reduce New York City subway crime. Bratton had the police concentrate on stopping fare beaters and other minor offenders and frisking those who were stopped: 1 out of 21 individuals who was stopped had a gun or a switchblade; 1 out of 7 had an outstanding bench warrant. The number of felonies dropped 75% (robberies 64%) from 1990 to 1994. William Bratton (with Peter Knobler), *Turnaround: How America's Top Cop Reversed the Crime Epidemic*, pp. 130–76; George Kelling and Catherine M. Coles, *Fixing Broken Windows: Restoring Order and Reducing Crime in Our Communities*, pp. 114–37 and 151f. Cf. Jeffrey Fagan and Garth Davies, "Street Stops and Broken Windows: Terry Race and Disorder in NYC" (2000).

†After an investigation, which began immediately after the shooting on February 5, 1999, the police officers were indicted on charges of second degree murder, depraved indifference to human life, and reckless endangerment. On February 26, 2000, after a four-week trial, the four officers were acquitted on all counts.

police departments were hit with a wave of criticism for "racial profiling"—namely, stopping and frisking black males more than members of other racial or ethnic categories because of the belief that they might be carrying guns or drugs or committing other crimes. On March 18, 1999, in response to "deep public concern about the impact of 'stop and frisk' tactics upon minority communities and individuals," the Office of the New York State Attorney General (OAG) launched a major study of NYPD stopping and frisking.[9] The OAG report, released on December 1, 1999, found that minorities, especially blacks, were stopped at higher rates than whites, relative to their percentages within New York City population. Moreover, precincts where racial minorities constituted the majority of the population tended to have higher frequencies of stopping and frisking than predominantly white precincts. The report found that stops of minorities were less likely to result in arrests than stops of whites; the lower "yield rate" suggests that police stop African-Americans on the basis of less suspicion. While the NYPD's gun seizure program may have contributed significantly to the decline of gun crime, especially in minority neighborhoods, its racially disparate stops and frisks may have further delegitimized the police in the eyes of the minority community, weakening minority citizen participation in fighting crime.[10] It is crucial that aggressive street policing be carried out consistent with respect for the individual's and community's legitimate privacy and autonomy concerns. That this is possible is confirmed by a VERA Institute of Justice study of two Bronx, New York, police precincts where both crime and citizen complaints about police had declined. The VERA researchers found that this impressive result had been achieved by commanders who emphasized techniques of treating citizens professionally and respectfully. This is precisely what needs to be achieved.[11]

Technology to the Rescue? Millivision

Is it possible to stop and frisk more efficiently, so that there are far fewer innocent people frisked? In 1994, the eminent criminologist James Q. Wilson published an essay in the *New York Times Magazine,* calling for development of gun detection technology that police officers could use to scan individuals for concealed weapons.[12] "What is needed is a device that will enable the police to detect the presence of a large lump of metal in someone's pocket from a distance of 10 or 15 feet." Such technology would greatly enhance the identification and seizure of unlawful guns. Wilson's essay caught the attention of former president Bill Clinton and then attorney general Janet Reno. As a result, the National Institute of

Justice awarded $2.15 million to three companies to develop gun detection technology that would enable police officers to determine instantly whether an individual is carrying a gun.*

"Millivision" is the best gun detector so far devised.[13] The Millivision Handheld Scanner is a portable scanner that reads the unique electromagnetic radiation emitted by all inanimate objects and animate beings, transmits them into electrical signals, and projects an image on an attached screen. The device is programmed to receive the high frequency waves emitted by human beings. Consequently, objects blocking the waves emitted from a human body are displayed as bright shapes against the black background outline of the body. Millivision poses no health risks because, unlike X-ray machines and metal detectors, it does not direct any form of radiation or energy at individuals; instead, it passively reads electromagnetic waves naturally emitted by people. Scanning and image projection occur simultaneously. Although, in a sense, Millivision "sees" through clothing, Dr. G. Richard Huguenin, executive vice president of the Millitech Corporation (now Millivision LLC), testified before Congress in 1994 that it "does not reveal intimate anatomical details."[14] Moreover, an internal algorithm can instruct the machine to scan only for gun-shaped metal objects so that a person who is carrying nothing, or even a chunk of metal that could not be a gun, can be cleared without a body image being displayed on the screen. A highly sophisticated criminal or terrorist might be able to fool the system by taking his gun apart so that its shape is disguised, or by wrapping it in tinfoil to conceal its shape (which might still raise suspicion and trigger a frisk).

The Millivision model that could best help police enforce concealed carry laws is a hand-held, camera-like device (it could also be mounted on a police car), which scans individuals from a close distance, twelve feet or less. Because Millivision is not sensitive to light, it could be used day or night and in all weather conditions.

It should be emphasized that Millivision is still under development. Moreover, Millivision's potential can only be realized if it survives con-

---

*The three companies awarded grants in 1995 were the Millitech Corporation (now Millivision, LLC), Raytheon Company, and the Idaho National Engineering and Environmental Laboratory (INEEL). While Millivision and Raytheon employ different technologies, the two companies' portable devices are functionally similar. They seek to scan persons passively from a distance. INEEL, on the other hand, has developed a stationary detection portal, like an advanced magnetometer used in airports. INEEL, which licensed the detector to Milestone Technology, hopes that its device will eventually identify different types of handguns by storing information about the magnetic makeup of specific weapons.

stitutional attack.[15] Whether courts allow this new surveillance technology depends on how and where Millivision is used.

Gun detection technology could be used in lieu of a traditional pat down frisk that a police officer conducts after having ascertained reasonable suspicion that criminal activity is afoot.[16] This would pose no constitutional problem because it would be a lesser invasion of privacy than a hands-on frisk.[17] However, in order to reap the advantages that Professor Wilson envisions, Millivision would have to be used to scan crowds or a flow of pedestrians, not just individuals stopped on suspicion of crime. Whether Millivision deployed in that way would pass constitutional muster depends, in the first place, on whether it constitutes a *search*. Under the Fourth Amendment, if a Millivision scan constitutes a search, it would be constitutional only if it was found to be reasonable. Searches and seizures are presumed to be unreasonable unless carried out pursuant to a warrant supported by probable cause or pursuant to a well-delineated exception to the warrant requirement. If Millivision does not constitute a search, law enforcement officials could legally scan everyone for weapons.

The use of surveillance technology, like flashlights, binoculars, and cameras, that merely enhances police officers' sensory perception has been held not to constitute a search for Fourth Amendment purposes.[18] But Millivision does more than enhance sensory perception. It does not just "put police officers artificially closer [to whom or what they are observing]; it does not just illuminate what would be visible anyway but for distance or darkness."[19] Millivision would enable officers to determine whether someone is concealing a gun. This would provide the police with a qualitatively new capability. Under U.S. Supreme Court precedent, these factors would support, although not compel, the conclusion that Millivision is a search.[20]

The Supreme Court has held that using trained dogs to signal that a person is carrying illegal drugs does not constitute a search because it is unintrusive and discloses only limited information—whether the sniffed individual is carrying drugs. The Court stressed that a canine sniff "does not require opening luggage. It does not reveal the nature and identity of noncontraband items that otherwise would remain hidden from public view . . . [T]he sniff discloses only the presence or absence of narcotics, a contraband item."[21] Perhaps the Court would find dog sniffs a compelling analogy, although Millivision *looks* through clothes and (despite the company president's denial) might reveal some anatomical details, as well as objects other than guns.

The Court has upheld warrantless chemical testing of substances under the same theory as dog sniffs. Thus, for example, postal inspectors do not conduct a search when they subject powder found on an envelope to chemical testing to determine if it is cocaine. A technique that "looks" only for contraband "compromises no legitimate privacy interest."[22] If it works the way its promoters claim, Millivision reveals only whether a person is carrying a gun. The targeted individual may not even be aware that he or she had been scanned. Thus, the Supreme Court might find that, like canine sniffs and chemical tests, a Millivision scan is not a search and thus does not implicate Fourth Amendment rights. However, if Millivision reveals anatomical features, or even all sorts of under-the-clothing objects, the analogy to a canine sniff or a chemical test breaks down.

In June 2001, in *Kyllo v. United States*, the Supreme Court held that the use of heat-sensing technology deployed from outside a house to identify grow lights associated with marijuana growing inside the house constitutes a Fourth Amendment search.[23] The Court noted that "where, as here, the Government uses a device that is not in general public use, to explore details of the home that would previously have been unknowable without physical intrusion, the surveillance is a search and is presumptively unreasonable without a warrant." While the *Kyllo* decision emphasized the strong expectation of privacy in the home, *Kyllo* makes it more likely that the Court would refuse to permit a Millivision scan without probable cause, reasonable suspicion, or at least a general reasonableness justification; that would be especially true if the scanner reveals information other than the presence of a gun.

If a Millivision scan constitutes a search, it would be permissible if it served a "special need" other than the goals associated with enforcing the criminal law. The special needs doctrine has been held to permit urine testing of railroad employees and student athletes for drugs, searching probationers' homes, requiring airline passengers to pass through magnetometers, and requiring drivers to stop briefly at roadblocks to check license, insurance, and sobriety.[24]

Perhaps the Supreme Court would conclude that protecting police officers and the general citizenry from the risk posed by armed individuals in public places counts as a special need distinct from enforcing the criminal laws. The Court could analogize removing deadly weapons from the sidewalks to removing drunk drivers from the roads and removing drug-using employees from transportation jobs.* However, the police have tra-

---

*In his dissenting opinion in *Michigan Dept. of State Police v. Sitz*, 496 U.S. 444 (1990), Justice Stevens compared the injuries inflicted with guns to the injuries caused by drunk drivers: "In 1988 there were . . . 8,291 fatalities in which somebody other than the intoxicated driver was killed in an accident involving legally intoxicated persons. . . . By contrast, in 1986 there were a total of 19,257 murders and

ditionally had greater leeway in regulating the roads than the sidewalks, and while drunk drivers are per se dangerous, the same is not true of all gun possessors, for instance, those who have licenses.

On the one hand, Millivision would allow police officers to determine instantly and from a safe distance whether an individual is armed, thereby reducing the risk of the police mistaking an unarmed person for someone who is armed and potentially dangerous; such mistakes are fraught with danger. On the other hand, Millivision scanning is much more like routine police investigation than drug testing which, if positive, usually results in assigning the drug-using employee to a treatment program. Police on routine patrol seek to protect the public from dangerous persons and situations. If the police uncover unlawful gun possession, they will make an arrest.

Admittedly, it is possible that routine use of Millivision would *increase* tension between the police and the minority community because the police would probably use the scanning device more often in minority neighborhoods. Indeed, Professor Wilson predicted that "young black and Hispanic men will probably be stopped more often than older white Anglo males or women of any race."[25] But it is more likely that Millivision, at least as its promoters describe it, would reduce racial tensions and conflicts associated with aggressive frisking and racial profiling, since it would allow the police to screen for guns without frisking unarmed people. Unarmed people might not even realize that they had been scanned. A well-functioning Millivision scanner could therefore be a great help to the police in keeping the streets free of unlawful firearms, while reducing the number of unpleasant interactions between the police and the citizenry.

The "Shall Issue" Laws

The possibility of ratcheting up street-level policing to seize more unlawful guns is complicated by the passage of state "shall issue" laws, which require the state licensing authority to issue a license or permit to carry a concealed weapon to all adult applicants who are not ineligible on ac-

---

nonnegligent manslaughters. Of these, approximately 11,360 were committed with a firearm, and another 3,850 were committed with some sort of knife. From these statistics, it would seem to follow that someone who does not herself drive when legally intoxicated is more likely to be killed by an armed assailant than by an intoxicated driver. The threat to life from concealed weapons thus appears comparable to the threat from drunken driving."

count of a criminal record or some other disqualifying characteristic.[26] A typical shall issue statute states:

> Not later than 60 days after the date of the application, the judge of the probate court *shall issue* the applicant a license to carry any pistol or revolver if no facts establishing ineligibility have been reported and if the judge determines the applicant has met all qualifications, is of good moral character, and has complied with all the requirements contained in this code section.[27] ["Qualifications" are the absence of a disqualifying criminal record or other Brady Law ineligibility factor. "Requirements" are the submission of fingerprints and payment of a small fee.]

Passage of state-level shall issue laws has been an NRA priority for almost two decades.[28] From the mid-1980s to the mid-1990s, 22 states passed such laws;* as of 2002, 33 states have them.[29] However, since 1996, no state has passed a shall issue law and proposals have been defeated in several states.[30] In Missouri, despite $3.7 million spent by the NRA, voters narrowly defeated the shall issue proposal.[31] School shootings may have persuaded shall issue proponents in other states that the time is not right for lobbying efforts.[32]

There is some state-to-state variation in how shall issue laws are administered. In Georgia, for example, officials have discretion to refuse to issue a concealed weapon permit to an applicant who lacks "good moral character," even if the applicant is otherwise eligible. Similarly, Oregon permits denial of a license

> if the sheriff has reasonable grounds to believe that an applicant has been or is reasonably likely to be a danger to self or others, or to the community at large, as a result of the applicant's mental or psychological state, as demonstrated by a past pattern of behavior or participation in an incident involving unlawful violence or threats of unlawful violence.[33]

---

*Only seven states prohibit carrying concealed weapons (Illinois, Kansas, Missouri, Nebraska, New Mexico, Ohio, and Wisconsin prohibit carrying concealed firearms, but licenses are available to a narrow class of persons). Twelve states and the District of Columbia provide for discretionary issuing of permits or licenses to carry a concealed weapon based upon a showing of occupational or personal safety needs (Alaska, California, Colorado, Hawaii, Iowa, Maryland, Massachusetts, Michigan, Minnesota, New Jersey, New York, and Rhode Island). How liberally such permits are issued varies by state, county, and municipality (see John R. Lott, Jr., *More Guns, Less Crime*, pp. 144–45). In restrictive licensing states, like New York and California, applicants must demonstrate that they have "good cause" or even "extraordinary need" for a concealed carry permit.

The licensing office carries the burden of proving the applicant unqualified.

Texas requires an applicant for a concealed carry permit to fill out a postcard request for an application, complete the application package, submit recent color passport photographs and fingerprints taken by a law enforcement agency, complete a certified 15-hour training course, and pass both a written test about nonviolent conflict resolution and a practical shooting test. The total cost, including application fee, safety course, and fingerprinting, is about $150.[34] In Washington state, applicants for a concealed carry permit must tender a $60 application fee and a picture identification card along with their application to a county courthouse or police precinct.[35] In Tennessee, applicants are required to carry liability insurance or post a surety bond of at least $50,000.[36]

Private businesses, in the majority of shall issue states, are free to set their own policies on whether patrons and employees may carry concealed weapons on the premises.[37] Many businesses ban guns on their premises, though in doing so they may be making themselves vulnerable to lawsuits, in the event that an act of violence occurs that arguably could have been prevented if the license holder had been armed.* Depending on the state, government buildings, places of worship, hospitals, playgrounds, amusement parks, schools, airports, financial institutions, and charitable organizations are off limits to persons carrying guns.[38]

The administration of shall issue laws can vary from county to county in the same state. In Virginia's, circuit courts have the responsibility for issuing concealed carry permits. Before 1995, gun rights advocates charged that courts in Virginia's two most populous counties rarely issue concealed carry permits based on a legal loophole.[39] The law had no time limit for processing applications. Courts intent on frustrating the law just sat on the applications. Eventually the legislature responded, eliminating the loophole and requiring that permits be granted in a timely manner to eligible applicants.

In a jurisdiction that issues concealed carry permits more or less on demand, police probably could not justify a policy of suspicionless Mil-

---

*On the one hand, establishments which prohibit concealed weapons could be liable for acts of violence that might have been prevented had a permit holder been allowed to have her gun with her at the time of the incident. On the other hand, liability could attach if a shooting occurs at a business, where patrons and employees are allowed to carry concealed guns on the premises. Employers might be liable if an employee intentionally or accidentally shoots a gun. These issues are discussed in detail in Mack, "This Gun for Hire: Concealed Weapons Legislation in the Workplace and Beyond," p. 7.

livision scanning on the ground that they need to identify armed persons. In effect, hasn't the legislature in a shall issue jurisdiction made the judgment that, for most persons, carrying a concealed weapon is not dangerous? In a shall issue jurisdiction knowledge that a pedestrian is carrying a concealed handgun should raise no more suspicion than knowledge that a pedestrian is carrying keys or a wallet.

Punishment as Gun Control

The NRA frequently opposes new gun control proposals with the argument that the Department of Justice (DOJ) doesn't enforce existing laws, especially when it comes to prosecuting violent criminals and that, if convicted, such criminals are not adequately punished. (The NRA relentlessly urges that criminals be locked up and law-abiding people be left alone.) While neither the BATF nor any other federal agency is in a position to increase gun seizures and arrests by means of street-level policing (a local function), federal prosecutors could prosecute armed felons more aggressively.

In 1991, Attorney General Richard Thornburgh announced Project Triggerlock to encourage U.S. attorneys to use federal statutes to "protect the public by putting the most dangerous offenders in prison for as long as the law allows."[40] The program targets violent repeat offenders who violate federal firearms laws.[41]

Janet Reno, the Clinton administration's attorney general, claimed to have given high priority to enforcing the felon-in-possession law, the career-criminal law, and other laws that send gun-carrying criminals to prison for long terms. During her tenure (1993–2000), the DOJ urged U.S. attorneys to collaborate with state and local law enforcement agencies to target criminals who use guns. In 1994, the DOJ introduced the Anti-Violent Crime Initiative (AVCI), a collaborative effort to develop firearms and violent crime prosecution strategies.[42] The AVCI encouraged each U.S. attorney to meet with federal, state, and local law enforcement agencies to form, or improve, violent crime working groups. The federal government moved aggressively into the battle against street crime.

Project Exile, launched by DOJ in 1997,[43] began as a collaborative effort among state, local, and federal prosecutors and law enforcement officers to vigorously enforce federal gun laws in Richmond, Virginia. All gun crimes that violate federal firearms laws are prosecuted in federal court, where defendants face five-year mandatory minimum sentences. Those convicted are supposedly "exiled" to distant federal prisons. A $400,000 advertising campaign using billboards and bus advertisements announces that "an illegal gun gets you five years in federal prison." Radio and TV spots echo the message. Richmond public schools, Boys and Girls Clubs, local newspapers, and police officers distribute business cards that warn about the consequences of carrying a gun.[44]

After the implementation of Project Exile, more than 400 people were sentenced to prison and 700 guns were confiscated.[45] Richmond experienced a sharp decline in homicides. There were 160 murders in Richmond in 1994, 94 in 1998, and 74 in 1999. Rapes, robberies, and assaults also dropped significantly; crimes involving guns decreased by 65%. Overall, violent crime fell 42% from 1994 to 1999.[46] Police officers report that far fewer arrestees are armed, and that when confronted by police, suspects often volunteer that they are not armed. Moreover, the police claim that Richmond residents are more comfortable reporting information about suspects to authorities because they believe gun-toting criminals will be sent to prison for long terms.[47] Federal prosecutors claim that witnesses are much more willing to testify against Project Exile defendants because they believe that the defendants will be convicted and sentenced to long prison terms.

Project Exile has proved extremely popular. Similar federal enforcement programs with such names as Operation Ceasefire and Project Disarm have been launched in other cities.[48] In 2000, the U.S. House of Representatives, by an overwhelming margin, passed "Project Exile: The Safe Streets and Neighborhoods Act of 2000" (H.R. 4051). It provided $100 million to be distributed to states that adopt the Project Exile program. The bill's critics argue that it is merely symbolic—$100 million over a five-year period is not nearly enough to fund advertising campaigns and hire additional federal prosecutors.

Handgun Control, Inc.'s Sarah Brady said, "It is cynical to refer to this legislation as 'The Safe Streets and Neighborhoods Act of 2000' when it does so little to make our country safer. The American people are expecting more from their elected officials than lip-service. They want action. And, the American people understand that we can have both enhanced prosecution and stricter gun laws. This is not an either/or. The American public wants both. Unfortunately, H.R. 4051 falls far short of that goal."[49] Other critics worry that increased federal prosecutions of street criminals will distract federal prosecutors from distinctly federal crimes (including, after September 11, 2001, terrorism and cyberterrorism) and clog federal courts.

The claims for the effectiveness of Project Exile have not been evaluated in Richmond or other jurisdictions. It is not even clear whether, or by how much, federal prosecutors increased felon-in-possession prosecutions during the 1990s. While Justice Department officials report that prosecutions for federal gun crimes increased 25% between 1998 and 1999, federal firearms prosecutions actually decreased between 1992 and 1998. The DOJ argues that while prosecutions may have declined for lower-level gun offenders, prosecutions resulting in sentences of five years or longer increased by more than 25% between 1992 and 1997.[50] Much in this confusing debate depends on how "gun offender" is defined. An increase in federal armed robbery convictions, for example, would not demonstrate greater federal attention to getting guns off the street. Local prosecutors have always given high priority to career criminals and armed offenders. Admittedly, federal sentencing law is draconian, but it is unclear whether federal law enforcement treats an armed rapist with a felony record more severely, and if so by how much, than state law. In my judgment, the acid test is whether federal officials have actually cracked down on unlawful gun possession. *Has there been an increase in federal prosecutions for unlawful firearm possession, when there is no other prosecutable offense?* As table 12.1 shows, there are very few such prosecutions.

Since 1993, violent crime has fallen precipitously in almost all large cities in the United States. The causes of this extraordinary decline remain unclear.[51] Some criminologists point to the waning of the crack epidemic; others focus on mass incarceration, changing demographics, strong economy, growth of private security sector, or vague "cultural" variables. The NYPD believes that a greater number of stop and frisks has been decisive. Some scholars are even claiming that the increasing number of abortions is an important factor.[52] There is simply insufficient evidence from which to conclude that federal initiatives like Project Exile have played an important role.

Table 12.1. Total Federal Prosecutions for Specific Firearms Offenses, 1996–1998

Reason for Prosecution	1996	1997	1998
Unlawful firearm possession by a person with a prior domestic violence crime conviction	0	21	56
Unlawful possession of a handgun or handgun ammunition by a juvenile	27	3	8
Unlawful transferring of a handgun or handgun ammunition to a juvenile	9	5	8
Unlawful possession/discharge of a firearm in a school zone	4	5	8
Providing false information on Brady Act (background check) form	0	0	1

Source: Senate Committee on the Judiciary, "Crimes Committed with Firearms: A Report for Parents, Prosecutors, and Policy Makers," Sept. 15, 1999.

Conclusion

Leaders and members of both political parties, gun control groups, and the NRA support catching and severely punishing armed offenders. A number of police initiatives (Kansas City [Mo.], New York City, Richmond) aimed at getting armed criminals off the street claim to have been successful. This is the kind of gun control that can be implemented and that is more closely linked to reducing crime than diffuse controls aimed at preventing people from obtaining guns in the first place.

Such initiatives are "promising," but whether claims of success can be validated empirically remains to be seen. Armed offenders have always been treated seriously by all levels of law enforcement. Gun control strategies that focus on "criminals" have never been contentious. However, it is certainly possible that in the past, some armed offenders have fallen through the cracks for one reason or another. Better information technology, specialized units, and more federal attention to gun crime are making it much less likely that an offender who uses a gun will get off lightly.

What is contentious are gun controls seeking to punish "law-abiding" people (who have not committed any crime, except illegal gun possession) for unlawful firearm *possession*. Their possession might be unlawful because, in a state like New York, law-abiding citizens cannot obtain a license to possess or carry a gun, unless they can persuade the chief law enforcement officer in their municipality that they have good cause to do so. Their possession might also be unlawful because they have a license to own but not to carry. The police and prosecutors, and especially juries, may be hesitant to punish the illegal gun possessor who may be armed due to fear of an estranged lover or because she works the night shift in a dangerous neighborhood.

Any effort to get armed individuals (whether "criminals" or "law-abiding") off the streets will have to rely on more stops and frisks.* The more stopping and frisking, the more guns will be uncovered and the more gun carrying will be deterred. But more stopping and frisking is not so easy to accomplish. First, there is the Fourth Amendment to contend with. Second, street stops and frisks set up the possibility for confrontations

---

*In an April 1, 2000, *New York Times* op-ed piece, Columbia Law Professor Richard Uviller wrote, "The only way to reduce gun crime is to go after the unlawful guns secretly carried by dangerous people. And the only way to do that is for the police to approach suspicious people, to expand traffic stops to include a search for guns and yes, even to stop cars and people, lawfully, as a pretext for a gun frisk" (p. A29).

between law enforcement and the public, especially members of the minority community. Racial profiling for purposes of crime control, drug control, and gun control has been widely condemned. Stopping everybody as frequently as minority citizens have been stopped would certainly not be popular. *Perhaps* technology will provide a way to remove illegal guns from the streets without exacerbating police/citizen frictions. But Millivision is not currently an option. Even if it turns out to be technically feasible, its constitutionality is dubious, especially in states with shall issue laws. Thus, it is essential that the police become skilled in carrying out stops and frisks consistent with a citizen's dignity. Of course, to achieve this goal, any taint of racial discrimination in the choice of individuals to stop must be eliminated. VERA's field experiment with a Bronx precinct gives us reason for optimism that progress toward this goal is possible.

The shall issue laws represent an expansion of gun owners' rights and a concomitant setback for rational gun control, especially in our cities. Gun control proponents ought to make repeal of these laws a top priority. Perhaps the best strategy toward that end would be to press for local control over gun regulation. Then urban areas might be able to marshal support to eliminate the shall issue laws or, at a minimum, to require proof of "good character" in the application process.

13

Conclusion: The "Problem" Reconsidered

1. America has always been a relatively violent nation. Considering the tumultuous historical forces that have shaped the United States, it would be astonishing were it otherwise.
2. Since rapid social change in America has produced different forms of violence with widely varying patterns of motivation, aggression, and victimization, violence in America has waxed and waned with the social tides. The decade just ending [the 1960s], for example, has been one of our most violent eras—although probably not the most violent.
3. For remedial social change to be an effective moderator of violence, the changes must command a wide measure of support throughout the community.
4. Official efforts to impose change that is resisted by a dominant majority frequently prompt counter-violence.
5. Finally, Americans have been, paradoxically, both a turbulent people but have enjoyed a relatively stable republic. Our liberal and pluralistic system has historically both generated and accommodated itself to a high level of unrest, and our turmoil has reflected far more demonstration and protest than conspiracy and revolution.
—National Commission on the Causes and Prevention of Violence, 1970

As this book draws to a close, it will be useful to return to the beginning: what is the problem for which gun control is the solution? Passing gun control laws is not an end in itself. Defeating the NRA is not an end in itself. Gun control only makes sense as a means toward reducing accidental and intentional deaths, injuries, and crimes. Most accidental and intentional injuries are not inflicted with guns, although most suicides and homicides are. This statement ought to lead us to think about violence reduction and accident reduction in a broader context.

Violence is a multifaceted and deeply entrenched phenomenon in American society. Violence implicates our history, including slavery and the near genocide of Native Americans, our economic system, including the widening gap between the wealthy and the poor; our social organization, including a multiplicity of ethnic, racial, and religious groups; our culture, including extreme emphasis on individual achievement and material success; our family values, including extremely high rates of teenage pregnancy and families without fathers; our patterns of drug use, including a tremendous amount of alcohol and drug abuse and a close relationship between alcohol, drugs, and violence; our mental health, including high levels of anxiety, stress, depression, and serious pathology; and our criminal justice system, especially penal institutions that breed and amplify violence.

There are many reasons why individuals act violently, ranging from the completely instrumental to completely expressive. There is no single type of violence and no single remedy. Because probing this complex and unsavory phenomenon of American society reveals many unhappy truths about our society and ourselves, it is understandable that many people prefer to blame violence on guns and illicit drugs, inanimate objects that can deflect attention from more troubling "causes." Perhaps it is best to think of guns as both a consequence of the violent strain in our culture, as well as a contributing cause. In any event, gun controls can only be one part, probably only a small part, of remedying the multifaceted violence problem. The broader effort must involve individuals, families, schools, churches, media, corporations and political institutions and especially those neighborhoods that are the locus of the most intense violence. To change the patterns of violence in a violent society will require more than a better gun policy, it will require changing society.

Toward More Responsible Gun Ownership and Use

Gun "control" should be about reinforcing a norm of responsible gun ownership and use. We should approach the use of guns with the same mindset that we approach alcohol consumption and driving. These are dangerous activities that must be approached with maturity and caution. We talk about "responsible drinking" and "safe driving," not about drinking and driving controls. Firearms accidents are clearly a gun problem just as automobile accidents are a car problem. It ought to be cause for optimism that accidental firearms deaths have been decreasing for decades, despite a steady increase in the number of firearms. If there were no firearms, no swimming pools, and no automobiles, the number of accidental deaths would greatly decrease. But eliminating swimming pools, cars, or guns are not realistic options.

Consumer safety is an option and should be a priority. Unsafe firearms should not be sold and manufacturers should be held to reasonable and appropriate safety standards. Obviously, firearms' owners, especially those with young children, should be encouraged to store their firearms safely and to maintain them in good condition, which the vast majority do. Requiring manufacturers to provide safety locks with their products is a sound idea, but coercing firearms' owners, by threat of criminal sanction, to keep their guns unloaded or to lock them up would defeat the self-defensive purpose of gun ownership for many owners. It is also unenforceable.

Dealing with Gun Crime

Gun crime is by far our most serious firearms problem. However, gun crime itself is not a single phenomenon or homogeneous category. Breaking gun crime down into several broad categories helps us to think about (1) the extent to which the availability of guns causes crime, and (2) the potential and limits of various gun controls. First, there is gun crime committed by career offenders, including professional bank robbers, members of Cosa Nostra, drug cartels, drug distribution networks, and street gangs. It is simplistic to label guns the *cause* of this kind of criminality, although guns certainly make such groups more dangerous. There is no possibility that any gun control policy could succeed in denying the members of these groups access to firearms. Indeed, even in Japan, where there is very little private ownership of guns, members of the Yakuza and other organized crime groups have no difficulty obtaining firearms.[1] In the United States, career criminals possess, carry, and use guns, despite the threat of draconian punishment under state and federal felon-in-possession laws and of sentence enhancements for committing crimes with a gun.

Second, there is "disorganized" gun crime, like carjacking and armed robbery of stores, gas stations, and pedestrians, carried out by individuals alone or in twos or threes. This is the kind of street crime that terrifies the public. The people who commit such crimes are often young, poor, and heavily involved with drugs. They may kill people in botched robberies or for no apparent reason. They often kill one another. Their stray bullets may kill or injure bystanders. From their own experiences in juvenile detention centers, reformatories, adult jails and prisons, and in the criminal subculture, individuals in this category have many sources—family members, friends, gang associates, drug dealers, and professional fences—from whom they can purchase or borrow handguns. It seems highly unlikely that any gun control regime could prevent such individuals from obtaining firearms.[2] They rarely purchase guns from FFLs, so more stringent regulation of licensed retail sellers would have little, if any, impact. Why would gun controls be any more effective in keeping guns out of the criminal subculture than drug controls in keeping illicit drugs out of the drug subculture?

Professors Cook and Ludwig suggest, almost in passing, that if the price of firearms increased* (via enforcement and regulatory strategies or by taxation), some poor young offenders would not have the money or choose not to spend their money on a gun.[3] I have no objection to increasing the tax on handguns, if for no other purpose than to fund victims' services, but I fear that the demand for firearms will prove far more inelastic than Cook and Ludwig imagine. Young men, albeit poor, living in tough neighborhoods will come up with an additional $10, $20, or $30 to purchase a firearm if they perceive that it is essential to their survival, status, or criminal opportunities. Indeed, several researchers, including, most recently, Anthony Braga and his colleagues in Boston, have found that street criminals do not prefer cheap guns. According to Braga et al., gang members in Boston prefer relatively expensive high caliber handguns rather than the cheapest guns.[4] Guns are not expensive, cost no more than a fancy pair of sneakers, and far less than even casual use of drugs. In any event, an impecunious youth living in a tough neighborhood can likely share or borrow a gun. This kind of criminality must be addressed by targeting gun criminals with vigorous policing, prosecution, and long incarcerative sentences, and by effective social welfare programs and employment and education initiatives. "Supply side" gun strategies hold very little promise.

Third, there are gun crimes committed by friends, spouses, and lovers

---

*For decades we have heard that enforcing the drug laws more severely could drive up the price of illicit drugs and, in effect, drive poor people out of the market. For all our billions of dollars and massive law enforcement efforts, drugs have not become more expensive, and drug use by poor youth remains high.

against one another. It is here that gun controls have the most promise. Undoubtedly, there are shootings which are predominantly situational; without the presence of a gun, such incidents would not occur or they would result in less injury. But the frequency of spontaneous lethal violence by essentially law-abiding individuals is frequently exaggerated. The great majority of people who kill their "acquaintances" have substantial criminal records. Most of the victims also have criminal records. Some victims coded as "acquaintances" are actually members of rival gangs or drug networks or are rivals within the same group. A high percentage of the "relationships" that spawn lethal violence have been marred by a long history of conflict and violence. The reality of such killings is hardly captured by the term "situational."

Even killings of intimate partners are rarely the product of a mere lover's quarrel or a jealous rage. Most serious and lethal domestic violence is not the result of an argument that got out of hand between an otherwise harmonious couple. Far more frequently, a domestic violence killing is the culmination of months or years of abuse and beatings, that is, the product of a relationship spiraling ever downward.[5] (One thinks of Nicole Brown Simpson, predicting that her ex-husband would someday kill her.) These are not the kind of situations where absence of a gun means that the conflict will blow over and the marriage return to happy homeostasis. (Nicole Brown Simpson, of course, was stabbed to death.) It would be a mistake to assume that killings between intimates are usually the result of spur-of-the-moment explosions of violence. Some defendants have planned their murderous conduct over a substantial period of time. They may have coolly decided that their spouse or business partner is worth more dead than alive. They may have stalked a former lover for months. They may have harbored a murderous plan for years. Even a momentary murderous rage can be so powerful that the aggressor will not stop short of killing the victim, with or without a gun. People who live in the same household have many opportunities and many weapons to kill one another—for example, with knives, bottles, cords, bats, poisons, or even bare hands.

Of course, men with domestic violence convictions or restraining orders *ought to be prevented* from purchasing and possessing firearms, at least while their relationship with the victim continues to simmer. But this is easier said than done in contemporary American society, where there are so many routes to obtaining a gun. It would not be wise to put much faith in the efficacy of a gun control scheme to protect the vulnerable partner. It makes more sense to invest in safe houses for the victims of domestic violence.

Is there any way to prevent people without a criminal record from obtaining guns? A Brady background check will not exclude people who do not have a prior criminal record from making purchases in the primary market, much less at gun shows and in the secondary market generally. As we have seen, it would be a tremendous, probably insoluble, logistical and enforcement challenge to regulate secondary firearms sales. And even if that were somehow accomplished, the market in stolen and trafficked guns would remain.

A waiting period could prevent a person in a murderous rage from running out of the house, job site, or bar and, on the spot, purchasing a firearm from an FFL, then rushing back home to use it on his spouse or lover. A waiting period imposes a time period of several days or longer during which tempers can cool, so that by the time the gun is obtained, the motivation to kill will have evaporated. Perhaps a waiting period also makes an important symbolic statement: a gun purchase is a serious matter and it should be undertaken soberly, more slowly, and more deliberately than the ordinary consumer purchase.

My guess is that cases in which an enraged killer runs to a store, buys a gun, and immediately shoots his victim are *extremely rare* (I have never seen any data on the frequency of such events), but the cost of implementing a waiting period is very low. Interim Brady established a de facto waiting period of five (business) days. Permanent Brady allows NICS up to three days to approve a sale, but most sales are approved immediately. A person without a disqualifying record can walk into a gun store and leave with a gun in under an hour.

Many states (like California and Florida) have additional waiting periods. But waiting periods do not apply to gun purchases from non dealers. The enraged individual could instantly borrow a gun from a friend or colleague or from someone advertising in the local paper. Of course, a waiting period would have no effect on an enraged individual who already owns a gun or who can lethally deploy a knife, baseball bat, or some other weapon. Moreover, the NRA has a point in noting that, in some cases, a waiting period could deny a firearm to a person under immediate threat who has no other viable means of self-defense. Thus, a waiting period ought to be linked to a law enforcement commitment to protect the individual facing a serious threat.

A fourth category of gun crime involves rampages, such as what happened at Columbine High School and at the Jewish Community Center in Granada Hills, California. The enormity of these tragedies understandably provokes calls *to do something*. But what? Those who commit such atrocities usually develop their plans over many months and may be indifferent to or even hoping for their own death. Thus, they can take whatever time is necessary to obtain a firearm from a dealer or nondealer, or they can steal a gun. The two students who carried out the indiscriminate murder

of classmates at Columbine High School planned to and did kill themselves after shooting as many of their schoolmates as possible. It is difficult
to imagine any regulatory regime that could have prevented them from
obtaining the firearms necessary to achieve that goal. Probably the only
way, if there is a way, to prevent such tragedies is obtaining and acting on
information about students or others who are behaving curiously, talking
about revenge killings, or otherwise signaling an impending rampage.
Sadly, we probably also need armed security personnel and perhaps a few
armed teachers able to respond effectively in the event that a rampage
occurs.

Concentrating on Armed Offenders

The purpose of this book is to refocus the gun control debate on realistic
options. To debate gun control strategies that have no relation to our current predicament is a distraction that triggers divisive argument. By far,
the easiest firearms policy for the United States is to provide severe punishment for every defendant who uses a firearm in the commission of a
crime. There are no interest groups that oppose tough treatment for gun
offenders. Indeed, the NRA, the police, and victims groups all support
long prison terms for individuals who commit crimes with guns. We
should retrace a line that has been drawn in the sand for a long time: gun
crime will be severely punished. Enforcing that message vigorously and
consistently in federal and state court should be our top priority in the
area of gun violence. Specialized prosecution units and even specialized
gun courts (that only deal with defendants charged with gun crimes)
would help to assure that no armed offender falls between the cracks.
Offenders who use guns should not get probation and not qualify for early
release from prison.

Smarter problem-solving policing has the potential to prevent some of
the most serious gun crime. Under Operation Ceasefire, the Boston police
made it clear to gang members that any armed violence would be met with
the strongest possible local, state, and federal law enforcement response.
The Harvard team evaluating this initiative concluded that the deterrent
message paid large dividends.[6] Likewise, devoting extra police resources
to "hot spot" policing in neighborhoods plagued by gun violence makes a
great deal of sense.[7] The general principle should be to focus and concentrate police resources on the people, situations, and locations where gun
violence occurs most frequently rather than to spread law enforcement's
anti-violence resources thinly over the whole population and all locations.
Investment in ballistic fingerprinting is worthy of serious consideration. It

may assist in apprehending some number of gun-wielding offenders who otherwise would escape arrest. It certainly makes sense to maintain contact and at least limited surveillance over individuals who have abused or threatened their intimate partners. Such people obviously present an enhanced risk of serious violence, especially in the short term.

More vigorous enforcement of the felon-in-possession laws, especially against individuals who have committed violent crimes in the recent past, should be a priority. But there are practical obstacles to severely punishing simple possession. Over the last several decades, federal prosecutors have declined to prosecute the majority of such cases, probably because of excessive caseloads and because some of these cases look like victimless crimes. Upon taking office, Attorney General John Ashcroft promised to make enforcing the gun laws his top priority (of course, that was before the terrorists destroyed the World Trade Center and part of the Pentagon).* Still, the "ex-felon" charged with unlawful possession may, truthfully or untruthfully, claim to have had the gun to protect himself from deadly enemies. Unfortunately, this claim may have a ring of truth. Fear for their personal security is neither uncommon nor unreasonable in some of our worst neighborhoods (and toughest schools). If the unlawful possession laws are viewed as too harsh and are not enforced, it makes sense *to reduce* the sentences associated with such crimes. *A modest punishment that is routinely enforced is far better than a draconian threat that is rarely applied.*

Preventing Access to Firearms: A Dose of Realism

The most unrealistic control policy for the United States is prohibition of private ownership of firearms or just handguns. Demanding disarmament, as the Communitarian Network, the Surgeon General's Task Force, and others have done, serves no useful purpose and only fans the flames of a culture war between gun owners and gun controllers, who in fighting with one another forget that the violent crime problem is the source of our concern.

*On January 23, 2002, Attorney General Ashcroft officially launched Project Safe neighborhoods, America's Network against Gun Violence. He announced that nearly $70 million in Justice Department funding will go to state and local prosecutors' offices to hire additional prosecutors to handle gun violence cases. Ultimately, the administration promises to fund 580 new state and local prosecutors and 94 additional assistant U.S. attorneys to combat gun crime.

Furthermore, talk of disarmament is counterproductive; it reinforces the resolve of gun owners to resist all gun controls because they are steps down a path to involuntary disarmament. Any serious effort to pass a firearms disarmament plan would trigger massive gun acquisition and expand and radicalize a resistance movement. The last thing the U.S. government needs is endless conflict with a huge segment of the citizenry that has never committed a gun crime. A war on civilian gun ownership would undermine crime prevention by unnecessarily diverting resources from preventing and solving crime.

If prohibition must continue to hold a place on the firearms policy agenda, it would make sense to always hold proposed gun prohibition up to the light and compare it with National Alcohol Prohibition and contemporary drug prohibition. Prohibiting manufacture and importation of new guns would be a much easier form of prohibition to implement than disarmament. Assuming that a congressional majority could be achieved (a huge assumption), it would be possible for the federal government to close down firearm or ammunition manufacturers or to achieve the same result through confiscatory taxation. Gun manufacturers could also be put out of business by common law courts if civil juries granted sizeable damage awards in municipal and victims' suits against manufacturers. These options are politically and legally unrealistic, but even if they could be implemented they would substitute a black market for the legal market we now have. As long as there is demand for new firearms and ammunition, a black market forms; indeed, there are such black markets in the United States, Western Europe, and Japan. Like drugs, guns and bullets would be manufactured in clandestine shops and imported from abroad. Unlike drugs, gun ownership enjoys the support of a substantial segment of the population that might view such activity as morally justified. With 300 million guns (my estimate after the mass buying that would occur in the several years while the prohibitionist legislation wended its way to passage) being held lawfully, prosecuting people for selling new guns, rather than used guns, would likely face hostility on grounds of hypocrisy or logic, as well as policy.

The dominant American twentieth-century firearms policy of trying to keep guns out of the hands of dangerous individuals by regulating federally licensed dealers has reached a dead end. It would be very difficult to elaborate this strategy beyond the Brady Law. And the Brady Law itself, passed to give teeth to the Federal Firearms Act and Gun Control Act can be easily circumvented by ineligible purchasers. They need only find a straw purchaser willing to buy a gun for them, or buy a gun themselves at a gun show or from a nondealer who is selling a gun through a newspaper ad or by word of mouth. Closing the gun show loophole, by extending Brady to all gun show sales, would be another weak measure, if all other secondary sales by nondealers remain unregulated. Extending the Brady background check to ammunition purchases is probably sensible although an ineligible person would have no trouble circumventing the scheme.

National *restrictive licensing* is politically and administratively unrealistic. Congress would have to pass a law making guns available only to people who could demonstrate "good cause" for owning a handgun or a firearm; a huge federal agency would be necessary to administer the scheme. How would a national restrictive licensing system treat the tens of millions of gun owners who do not have "good cause" to own a gun? If these gun owners were required to disarm, the national licensing system would be little different from disarmament and, like disarmament, would present enforcers with monumental problems.

If the federal licensing plan gave a license to all current gun owners, we would have something like a national *permissive licensing* scheme; practically anyone could lawfully purchase a gun and ammunition as long as he or she filled out an application form and paid a small fee. That is more or less the way drivers licensing works. The system initially does not weed out antisocial individuals, including criminals, drug, and alcohol abusers. The auto licensing system only has bite, that is, a suspension or revocation, after the driver has committed serious driving violations. (That's analogous to moving against the gun owner after he has been arrested for committing an armed crime, as we do now.) Moreover, the auto licensing system's bite is not very hard. Denial or revocation of a license to drive does not prevent the denied or revoked individual from continuing to drive. Tens of thousands of dangerous and antisocial drivers continue to drive, even after their licenses have been suspended or revoked. The criminal justice system does not seem to have the will or the capacity to punish or incapacitate such individuals. Would the criminal justice system function differently with respect to unlicensed gun owners? Probably the best strategy would be to make unlicensed gun possession by a nonfelon punishable by a $1,000 fine, that could be meted out quickly and without a jury trial. Seizure of the unlawfully possessed weapon could also be made part of the punishment.

Registration of firearms would be even more complicated to implement and enforce than licensing because of the difficulty of bringing secondary market transfers into the registration system. People would have to be persuaded to register the guns they currently own, as well as any new guns they receive from their parents or friends. Criminals would certainly not comply. Noncompliance would also be very high among law-abiding gun owners, who perceived the registration system to be the precursor to general confiscation. Only a Supreme Court decision declaring that the Second Amendment guarantees law-abiding adults a right to keep and bear arms would make significant compliance with a firearms registration system *possible*, and even then success could not be assured; many gun owners, at least for several years, would worry about a future Supreme Court decision reversing the earlier one or that a gun control majority might be able to pass a constitutional amendment.

So what options are we left with? The Brady background check could be extended to ammunition purchases, gun shows, and the secondary market generally. But starting from where we are now, it would be very difficult to bring gun shows, much less all nondealer transfers, into the Brady framework by channeling all gun transfers through an FFL. It would be extremely difficult to enforce such a plan effectively. Evasion would be simple; nondealer sellers and buyers could just ignore the requirement.

It would be much simpler just to outlaw gun shows. Why permit an institution that seems tailor-made for selling stolen guns and for avoiding the Brady background check? Limiting gun purchases to one per month is also a realistic and cost effective idea that would impose little, if any, cost on law-abiding users and might disrupt somewhat the trafficking of guns to the criminal market. We should continue to support the research and development of smart guns that could prevent guns from being used by thieves, minor children, and family members bent on suicide.

The Shall Issue Laws

Rather than cutting back on "keeping and bearing arms," we seem to be moving in the other direction, toward a policy of permitting people who have no disqualifying record to carry firearms with them at all times. Passage of right to carry laws makes implementing some gun controls much more difficult. Facilitating citizens being armed in public is a dangerous experiment, especially for our big cities. True, John Lott's research finds that laws giving private citizens a right to a gun carry permit, as long as they have no disqualifying record, reduces crime. However, at the time he did his research, only a small percentage of citizens in the shall issue jurisdictions had obtained licenses. Lott claims that more gun-carrying citizens means less crime, but in New York City, without a right to carry law, crime fell in the 1990s more than in any other U.S. city.[8] Indeed, the NYPD tried mightily to get guns off the street. I do not think that Lott's conclusions are well-documented enough to warrant a nationwide hard-to-reverse experiment of encouraging the citizenry to go about armed. Neither, however, should they be scoffed at or ignored. After all, Chicago,

New York, and Washington D.C., which issue very few concealed carry permits, are still plagued by high rates of violent crime. Their laws may be counterproductive if criminals arm themselves with ease, while law-abiding citizens lack adequate self-defense. Perhaps these highly restrictive licensing jurisdictions should issue more permits to "reliable" citizens. But reliable ought to mean "good character," not just "absence of a criminal conviction."

In New York and other big cities, I believe that peoples' insecurity would rise to unbearable levels if they perceived that a good percentage of the people walking next to them on the street, sitting next to them on a subway train, or waiting on line with them at a parking garage were armed with a concealed handgun. This insecurity probably arises from the fact that life in big cities is so anonymous, and that there is little trust among people who do not know one another. The people next to us are strangers who, for all we know, might be dangerous. Trust takes time and confidence to develop. Perhaps, in small towns where people know one another, there is enough assurance in the reliability of one's neighbor and fellow citizen to allay the fear that one's fellow citizen might be a dangerous criminal.

Policy Devolution

One size fits all does not make sense for many social and legal policies, especially firearms. My observations about the unsuitability of shall issue policies for big cities underlines my belief that firearms policy ought to be made at the local level. The firearms traditions in small town and urban America are different. Level of trust and anonymity is different. The level of policing is different. The federal government should certainly support, provide technical expertise, and *evaluate* licensing and registration schemes at the state and local levels.[9] There is much that could be learned from evaluating the efforts of jurisdictions that have a solid political consensus to implement such initiatives. If it turns out that they can be done well in one jurisdiction, that alone will encourage other jurisdictions to follow suit.

Admittedly, allowing for decentralized gun regulation according to local preference allows negative externalities. Some communities wishing to ban private possession of firearms in public places, for example, will find their ambition undermined by a neighboring community's policy of allowing liberal access to firearms. This criticism can be raised against many decentralized policies, even levels and patterns of police deployments and criminal sentencing. Perhaps the best response is that a community that wishes to enforce its "no guns on the streets" law is free to do so, aggressively arresting and prosecuting unlicensed gun carriers.

All this might leave some readers with a feeling of despair. But there is more reason for optimism now then there was one or two decades ago. Violence has decreased dramatically in the last decade in the United States, despite the continued increase in the stock of civilian guns. This means that firearms accessibility is not the only thing, and not the most important thing, driving gun crime. Criminologists and policy makers should not be distracted by unrealistic proposals and slogans for "gun control." Rather, they should look to building on other anti-crime strategies and constructive social welfare policies that might be contributing to this unprecedented decrease of violent crime and gun crime.

Notes

Preface

1. John Keplan's wonderful article, "Controlling Firearms" (1979), has stimulated my thinking along those lines.

Chapter 1

1. Legal Community against Violence, "Addressing Gun Violence through Local Ordinances," 2000 supplement, pp. 8–9. Available at: http://www.lcav.org/content/localordinance.asp.

2. All numbers from National Safety Council, *Accident Facts*, http://www.nsc.org/lrs/statinfo/af2.htm.

3. Ibid.

4. See http://www.guncite.com/gun_control_gcgvintl.html.

5. See Ronald V. Clarke and Pat Mayhew, "The British Gas Suicide Story and Its Criminological Implications," in *Crime and Justice: A Review of Research*, ed. Michael Tonry and Norval Morris (1988), 10:79–116.

6. D. Gunnell et al., "Method Availability and the Prevention of Suicide: A Reanalysis of Secular Trends in England & Wales, 1950–1970," *Social Psychiatry Psychiatric Epidemiology* 25 (2000): 437–43.

7. Jennifer Warren, "Soltys Is Charged in Death of Fetus Arraignment: A Seventh Murder Count Is Added against Suspect Accused of Slaying Six Relatives," *Los Angeles Times*, Sept. 5, 2001, Metro desk, B1; Pat Doyle, "Iowa Man Bludgeoned Family, Prosecutors Say Seven Deaths Are Sioux City's Worst Mass Killing," *Minneapolis-St. Paul Star-Tribune*, Sept. 2, 2001, 9A; Emily Gersema, "$7 Million Bail Set for Man Accused of Killing Seven in Iowa," *Seattle Times*, Sept. 2, 2001, A2.

8. Ford Fessenden, "They Threaten, Seethe and Unhinge, Then Kill in Quantity," *New York Times*, Apr. 9, 2000, sec. A1, col. 1.

9. Office of Juvenile Justice and Delinquency Prevention, *Promising Strategies to Reduce Gun Violence* (Washington, D.C.: U.S. Department of Justice, 1999).

10. Fessenden, "They Threaten, Seethe and Unhinge," A1, col. 1.

11. Don B. Kates and Daniel Polsby, "The Myth of the 'Virgin Killer': Law-Abiding Persons Who Kill in a Fit of Rage," paper delivered at the annual meeting of the American Society of Criminology, San Francisco, Nov. 2000; David Kennedy et al., "Homicide in Minneapolis: Research for Problem Solving," *Homicide Studies* 2 (1998): 263, 269; Delbert Elliott, "Life Threatening Violence Is Primarily a Crime Problem: A Focus on Prevention," *University of Colorado Law Review* 69 (1998): 1081–98; Marvin Wolfgang, *Patterns in Criminal Homicide* (Philadelphia: University of Pennsylvania Press, 1958). See also Philip J. Cook and Jens Ludwig, *Gun Violence: The Real Costs* (New York: Oxford University Press, 2000), p. 23.

12. "Also, it may not be inferred that the remaining twenty to twenty-five percent of murderers are ordinary law-abiding people. There are two reasons why only seventy to eighty percent of murderers have prior adult criminal records. First, ten to fifteen percent of murderers are juveniles who, by definition, cannot have such records. Second, wife murderers generally have long prior histories of violence which have not resulted in arrest because they attacked spouses and other family members." Don Kates, Jr., "Gun Control: Separating Reality from Symbolism," *Journal of Contemporary Law* 20 (1994): 353, 378.

13. There is a massive scholarly literature on violence in America. See, e.g., Ted Robert Gurr, *Violence in America: The History of Crime* (Thousand Oaks, Calif.: Sage, 1989); Richard Hofstadter and Michael Wallace, *American Violence: A Documentary History* (New York: Knopf, 1970); Fox Butterfield, *All God's Children: The Bosket Family and the American Tradition of Violence* (New York: Avon, 1996); James Gilligan, *Violence: Reflections on a National Epidemic* (New York: Vintage, 1997); Franklin Zimring and Gordon Hawkins, *Crime Is Not the Problem: Lethal Violence in America* (New York: Oxford University Press, 1997).

14. "Homicide Trends in the U.S.," Bureau of Justice Statistics, Jan. 1999, available at: http://www.ojp.usdoj.gov/bjs/homicide/homtrend.htm

15. Kleck, *Targeting Guns: Firearms and Their Control* (Hawthorne, N.Y.: De Gruyter, 1997).

16. Don B. Kates and Daniel D. Polsby, "Long-Term Nonrelationship of Widespread and Increasing Firearm Availability to Homicide in the United States," *Homicide Studies* 4 (2000): 185–201.

17. The regions are made up of the following states: New England (Connecticut, Maine, Massachusetts, New Hampshire, Rhode Island, Vermont), Middle Atlantic (New Jersey, New York, Pennsylvania), East North Central (Illinois, Indiana, Michigan, Ohio, Wisconsin), West North Central (Iowa, Kansas, Minnesota, Missouri, Nebraska, North Dakota, South Dakota), South Atlantic (Delaware, District of Columbia, Florida, Georgia,

Maryland, North Carolina, South Carolina, Virginia, West Virginia), East South Central (Alabama, Kentucky, Mississippi, Tennessee), West South Central (Arkansas, Louisiana, Oklahoma, Texas), Mountain (Arizona, Colorado, Idaho, Montana, Nevada, New Mexico, Utah, Wyoming), Pacific (Alaska, California, Hawaii, Oregon, Washington). Bureau of Justice Website.

18. Franklin Zimring and Gordon Hawkins, *The Citizen's Guide to Gun Control* (New York: Macmillan, 1987).

19. Kleck, *Point Blank: Guns and Violence in America* (Hawthorne, N.Y.: De Gruyter, 1991).

20. Arthur Kellerman and Donald Reay, "Protection or Peril: An Analysis of Firearm-related Deaths in the Home," *New England Journal of Medicine* 314 (1996): 1557.

21. Ibid.

22. Victims felt that 63% of the time "self-protective measures" (not necessarily gun self-protection) were helpful. Only 9.2% of the time did they feel that these measures were harmful. According to the respondents, 36.3% of the time, protective measures taken by others helped, 9.7% of the time they hurt. Criminal Victimization in the U.S. Statistical Tables: Full Report, Table 72 (p. 79).

23. Jens Ludwig, "Gun Self-Defense and Deterrence," in *Crime and Justice: A Review of Research* 27 (Chicago: University of Chicago Press, 2000), p. 375.

24. Philip S. Cook and Jens Ludwig, "Defensive Gun Uses: New Evidence from a National Survey," *Journal of Quantitative Criminology* 14 (1998): 111–31.

25. David Hemenway and Deborah Azrael. "Survey Research and Self-Defense Gun Use: An Explanation of Extreme Overestimates," *Journal of Criminal Law and Criminology* 87 (1997): 1430.

26. Kleck, *Targeting Guns*, pp. 6, 149.

27. "Handgun Hunting: Getting Started in the Sport," *Sports Afield*, 224 (Feb. 2001).

28. Kleck, *Targeting Guns*, pp. 148–49.

29. Jens Ludwig, "Gun Self-Defense and Deterrence," in *Crime and Justice: A Review of Research* 27 (Chicago: University of Chicago Press, 2000), p. 366.

30. Lott, *More Guns, Less Crime*, 2d ed. (Chicago: University of Chicago Press, 1998), p. 37.

31. Jens Ludwig, "Concealed Gun-Carrying Laws and Violent Crime: Evidence from the State Panel Data," *International Review of Law & Economics* 18 (1998): 239, 241–42, 251 (finding that shall-issue laws have resulted, if anything, in an *increase* in adult homicide rates). Lott responds to Ludwig's criticism in *More Guns*, at 128, 147–48.

32. Dan A. Black and Daniel S. Nagin, "Do Right-to-Carry Laws Deter Violent Crime?" *Journal of Legal Studies* 27 (1998): 209, 218 (arguing that

Lott's results are highly sensitive to small changes in the model and sample). Lott answers Black and Nagin in John R. Lott, Jr., "The Concealed Handgun Debate," *Journal of Legal Studies* 27 (1998): 221, 242; see also Lott, *More Guns*, at 128.

33. Zimring and Hawkins, "Concealed Handguns: The Counterfeit Deterrent," *The Responsive Community* 59 (1997): 50. Lott answers Zimring and Hawkins in *More Guns*, at 150.

34. Zimring and Hawkins, "Concealed Handguns," at 52. Lott answers this argument in *More Guns*, at 152.

35. Zimring and Hawkins, "Concealed Handguns," at 57–58.

36. Albert W. Alschuler, "Two Guns, Four Guns, Six Guns, More Guns: Does Arming the Public Reduce Crime?" *Valparaiso University Law Review* 31 (1997): 365, 367–70 (arguing that some of Lott's findings do not make commonsense: "something's *wrong*"). Lott answers Alschuler in Lott, *More Guns*, at 144, 148.

37. David McDowall, Colin Loftin, and Brian Wiersema, "Easing Concealed Firearms Laws: Effects on Homicide in Three States," *Journal of Criminal Law & Criminology* 86 (1995): 207, 224.

38. Michael D. Maltz, *Bridging Gaps in Police Crime Data* (Washington, D.C.: U.S. Department of Justice, Office of Justice Programs, Sept. 1999).

39. See, e.g., National Commission on the Causes and Prevention of Violence, *To Establish Justice: To Insure Domestic Tranquility* (New York: Praeger, 1970).

Chapter 2

1. Title 18 Criminal Code 18 U.S.C. ch. 340, 1101 stat. 489, 69th Cong. See also Franklin E. Zimring and Gordon Hawkins, *The Citizen's Guide to Gun Control* (New York: Macmillan, 1987), p. 132.

2. Zimring and Hawkins, *Citizen's Guide*, p. 140.

3. Gerald D. Robin, *Violent Crime and Gun Control* (Cincinnati, Ohio: Anderson, 1991), p. 19.

4. Zimring and Hawkins, *Citizen's Guide*, p. 133.

5. But see Office of the Inspector General, *Special Report on Allegations Concerning the Bureau of Alcohol, Tobacco and Firearms' Registration and Record Keeping of the National Firearms Registration and Transfer Records*, OIG-99-099, October 26, 1998; and *Audit Report on Allegations Concerning the Bureau of Alcohol, Tobacco and Firearms' Administration of the National Firearms Registration and Transfer Record*, OIG-99-018, December 18, 1998.

6. Zimring and Hawkins, *Citizen's Guide*, p. 133.

7. *Federal Firearms Act*, ch. 850, 52 Stat. 1251 (1938).

8. Ibid.

9. Zimring and Hawkins, *Citizen's Guide*, p. 133.

10. Robin, *Violent Crime and Gun Control*, p. 23.

11. Ibid.

12. Bureau of Alcohol, Tobacco, & Firearms, "Commerce in Firearms in the United States," Feb. 2000.

13. 27 C.F.R. 178.11 (1997).

14. Zimring and Hawkins, *Citizen's Guide*, p. 134.

15. See *Huddleston v. U.S.*, 415 U.S. 814 (1974).

16. Robin, *Violent Crime and Gun Control*, p. 23.

17. 18 U.S.C. A. App. § (1202 [a]), recodified with amendments at 18 U.S.C. § 924 (e) (1).

18. P.L. No. 99–570 § 1402 (a) (1986).

19. P.L. 100–690, 100th Cong., 2d sess., 102 Stat. 4181, 4359–62.

20. FOPA, 1 (b), 100 Stat. 449 (1986) (codified at 18 U.S.C. 926 [1986]).

21. 18 U.S.C. sec. 926 (1994). See David T. Hardy, "The Firearms Owners' Protection Act: A Historical and Legal Perspective," *Cumberland Law Review* 17 (1986/1987): 585–682.

22. 18 U.S.C. 926 (a) (3).

23. *Firearms Owners' Protection Act*, P.L. 99–308, 457 (1986).

24. 18 U.S.C. sec. 921 (a) (17) (B)

25. Gary Kleck, *Targeting Guns: Firearms and Their Control* (Hawthorne, N.Y.: De Gruyter, 1997).

26. The Undetectable Firearms Act of 1988, P.L. 100–649, 100th Cong., 2d sess., 102 stat. 3816; 18 U.S.C. 922 (p).

27. P.L. 100–690, 100th Cong., 2d sess., 102 Stat. 4181.

28. 18 U.S.C. § 922 (q).

29. *U.S. v. Lopez*, 115 S. Ct. 1624 (1995).

30. Ibid., at 1631.

31. P.L. 104–208, sec. 657, 110 Stat. 3009–369 through 3009–371 (1996), 18 U.S.C. § 922 (q). See (2) (a) Csupp. IV (1998).

32. P.L. 103–322, 18 U.S.C. § 922 (g) (8).

33. P.L. 104–208, 18 U.S.C. § 921 (a).

34. BATF Department of the Treasury, "Commerce in Firearms in the United States," Feb. 2000.

35. *The Violent Crime Control and Law Enforcement Act of 1994*, 18 U.S.C. sec. 921 et seq.

36. There is a great deal of legal material available on state and local firearms law. Windle Turley and James E. Rooks's *Firearms Litigation: Law, Science & Practice* (Colorado Springs, Colo.: Shepard's/McGraw-Hill, 1997), is a good place to start. There are books or manuals on practically every state's gun law; for example, Alan Korwin, *The Arizona Gun Owners Guide* (Bloomfield Pub., 1994); see also http://www.gunbookstore.com/law.htm.

37. Alan Gottlieb, *The Rights of Gun Owners* (Bellevue, Wash.: Merril, 1981), p. 95.

38. Bureau of Justice Statistics, Survey of State Procedures Related to Firearms Sales (1996); see also Turley and Rooks, *Firearms Litigation*.

39. Wright, Rossi, and Daly, *Under the Gun: Weapons, Crime, and Violence in America* (Hawthorne, N.Y.: De Gruyter, 1983), p. 248.

40. Gottlieb, *Rights of Gun Owners*, p. 95.

41. NRA-ILA Research and Information, Compendium of State Firearms Laws.

42. Ibid.

43. For example, the California Gun Free School Zone Act of 1995, Cal. Pen. Code § 626.9.

44. NRA-ILA Research and Information, Compendium of State Firearms Laws.

45. Bureau of Justice Statistics, *Survey of State Procedures Related to Firearms Sales* (1996).

46. NY Penal Law 400 (McKinney Supp. 1994).

47. Susan Novak, "Why the New York System for Obtaining a License to Carry a Concealed Weapon Is Unconstitutional," *Fordham Urban Law Journal* 26 (1998): 121.

48. Mass. Ann. Laws ch. 140, 128A (1995).

49. James B. Jacobs and Kimberly A. Potter, "Comprehensive Handgun Licensing & Registration: An Analysis & Critique of Brady II, Gun Control's Next (And Last?) Step," *Journal of Criminal Law & Criminology* 89 (1999): 106–7; Robin, *Violent Crime and Gun Control*, p. 52.

50. Philip J. Cook et al., "Regulating Gun Markets," *Journal of Criminal Law & Criminology* 86 (1995): 59.

51. John R. Lott, Jr., *More Guns, Less Crime* (Chicago: University of Chicago Press, 1998), p. 43.

Chapter 3

1. 1999 Gallup Poll from the *Sourcebook of Criminal Justice Statistics*, 2000. While the Gallup Poll is most often cited in books on gun control, other surveys have produced higher and lower estimates. For instance, on the low end of the spectrum, the 2000 General Social Survey (GSS) published by the National Opinion Research Center estimates that only 28.4% of households have firearms. On the high end, John Lott, Jr., estimates ownership rates well above 50%.

2. This figure is calculated by taking an average of nine polls since 1989. For information on these polls, see the *Sourcebook of Criminal Justice Statistics*, table 2.66 at http://www.albany.edu/sourcebook/1995/pdf/t266.pdf.

3. Hal Quinely, Feb. 6, 1990, memorandum reporting results from Time/CNN poll of Gun Owners, Yankelovich Clancy Shulman survey organization, New York.

4. Gary Kleck, *Point Blank: Guns and Violence in America* (New York: Aldine, 1991), appendix 1, p. 458.

5. Philip J. Cook and National Institute of Justice, "Research in Brief," May 1997, p. 2.

6. Gary Kleck, *Targeting Guns: Firearms and Their Control* (New York: Aldine, 1997), p. 70.

7. 1998 General Social Survey of Gun Ownership.

8. The 1996 National Survey of Fishing, Hunting, and Wildlife—Association Recreation Report, p. 26.

9. Kleck, *Targeting Guns*, p. 102.

10. www.zapdata.com

11. This statistic can be calculated two ways: (1) take the number of guns and divide it by the average number of guns per household or (2) take the number of households and multiply that by the percent claiming to own a firearm. The resulting survey estimates differ widely. This book has chosen a generally accepted middle number between the two extremes: 42% of U.S. households own 275 million firearms. Population statistics come from the *U.S. Census Bureau, Statistical Abstract of the U.S. 2000*. Gun ownership statistics come from a number of surveys discussed in other footnotes and endnotes.

12. See Jacobs and Potter, "Comprehensive Handgun Licensing & Registration: An Analysis & Critique of Brady II, Gun Control's Next (and Last?) Step," *Journal of Criminal Law and Criminology* 89 (1999): 106.

13. But see James Lindgren and Justin Heather's devastating critique in "Counting Guns in Early America," unpublished manuscript, available on Professor Lindgren's web site, http://www.law.northwestern.edu/faculty/fulltime/Lindgren/Lindgren.html. These authors have made serious charges regarding the integrity of Professor Bellesiles's work. See also "FORUM: Historians and Guns" *William and Mary Quarterly* 59 (January 2002): 203–68; Cf. Lee Kennett and James Anderson, *The Gun in America: Origins of a National Dilemma* (1975).

14. www.zapdata.com

15. Ibid. The average manufacturer employs 23 people and has an average sales of $8.2 million. However, there are a few very large manufacturers such as Smith & Wesson and Berreta. Most manufacturers are located in Texas and California, although there are also many manufacturers in Montana and other western states. Connecticut, New Hampshire, and New York have the largest number of persons working in the industry.

16. www.amfire.com/main.html

17. 2001 National Survey of Fishing, Hunting, and Wildlife—Association Recreation Report, p. 27.

18. Ibid., p. 9.

19. U.S. Census Bureau, *Statistical Abstract of the U.S. 2000*.

20. See http//www.nrahq.org/shootingrange/findlocal.asp.

21. http://www.pla-net.net/rcomer/"Internet Shooting Directory."

22. http://www.goal.org/home7.shtml

23. Audit Bureau of Circulation, averages for six months ending June 30, 2000. See http://abcas1.accessabc.com/cgi-shl/pbcgi60.exe/ECIRC/uo_ecirc/f_magform?

24. *U.S. v. Lopez*, 115 S. Ct. 1624 (1995); *U.S. v. Printz*, 521 U.S. 898 (1997); *U.S. v. Morrison*, 120 S. Ct. 1740 (2000).

25. William J. Vizzard, *In the Cross Fire: A Political History of the BATF*. (Boulder, Colo.: Rienner, 1997).

26. U.S. Department of Justice, *Report to the Deputy Attorney General on the Events at Waco, Texas*, Feb. 28 to Ap. 19, 1993, p. 110.

27. U.S. Department of the Treasury, *Report of the Good Ol' Boys Roundup Policy Review* (Washington, D.C.: Government Printing Office, Ap. 1996).

28. *Firearms Owner's Protection Act*, 18 U.S.C. § 923 (g) (1) (B) (ii) (I).

29. The best study is Osha Gray Davidson, *Under Fire: The NRA and the Battle for Gun Control* (Iowa City: University of Iowa Press, 1998).

30. Robert J. Spitzer, *The Politics of Gun Control* (New York: Chatham House, 1998) p. 108.

31. Davidson, *Under Fire*, p. 40.

32. Ibid., p. 39.

33. 18 U.S.C. 922(a)(1)(A).

34. 18 U.S.C. 923(g)(1)(A).

35. 18 U.S.C. 923(g)(1)(B)(ii)(I).

36. Gregg Lee Carter, *The Gun Control Movement* (New York: Twayne, 1997).

37. Evelyn Theiss, "Clinton Blames Losses on NRA," *Cleveland Plain Dealer*, Jan. 14, 1995, p. A1.

38. Brad O'Leary, "Fire Power: Surprising Results and Election Returns Show That the National Rifle Association Had a Lot More to Do with November 8 Than Most Pundits Realize," Campaigns & Elections, Inc., Dec.–Jan. 1995.

39. Ibid.

40. Juliet Elperin, "Rejuvenated NRA Arms for Election Year Showdown," *Fortune*, Mar. 5, 2000, p. A2.

41. Susan Page, *Arizona Republic*, Aug. 13, 2001, p. A4. (Also listed on the Fortune web site under "Fortune Lists.")

42. Ibid., p. A4.

43. *Fortune* magazine ranked the NRA the most powerful lobby in the nation, and Gun Control, Inc., the most powerful voice for gun control, 60th. *Fortune*, Dec. 6, 1999.

44. James B. Jacobs and Daniel Heumann, "Extending Brady to Gun Shows and the Secondary Market," *Criminal Law Bulletin* 37 (May–June 2001): 248–62.

45. Kevin Krause and Mark Hollis, "Police Defend Firearm Tracker Detectives' Group Fights NRA for Right to Search for Gun Transactions on Pawnshop Databases," *Fort Lauderdale Sun—Sentinel*, June 24, 2001.

46. See discussion in Don B. Kates, "Bigotry, Symbolism, and Ideology in the Battle over Gun Control," *Public Interest Law Journal* 2 (1992): 31, and "Gun Control: Separating Reality from Symbolism," *Journal of Contemporary Law* 20 (1994): 353, and the following from Robert J. Cottrol and Raymond T. Diamond, "Public Safety and the Right to Bear Arms," in *After 200 Years: The Bill of Rights in Modern America*, ed. D. Bodenhamer and J. Ely (Bloomington: Indiana University Press, 1993).

47. There is a vast legal literature on the Second Amendment. The interested reader would do well to browse through the following law review symposia: *Tennessee Law Review: A Second Amendment Symposium Issue* 62, no. 3 (spring 1995); *Chicago Kent Law Review Symposium on Second Amendment: Fresh Looks* 76, no. 1 (2000); *Seton Hall Constitutional Law Journal: Symposium on Second Amendment* 10 (summer 2000); *Constitutional Commentary* 16 (1999).

48. *U.S. v. Miller*, 307 U.S. 174(1939), see *Quilici v. Village of Morton Grove*, 695 F.2d 261 (7th Cir. 1982), cert. denied, 464 U.S. 863 (1983), and *U.S. v. Day*, 476 F.2d 562 (6th Cir. 1973); *U.S. v. Kraase*, 340 F.Supp. 147 (E.D. Wis. 1972); and *U.S. v. Gross*, 313 F.Supp. 1330 (S.D. Ind. 1970) among numerous cases involving constitutionality that are collected at National Rifle Association, "Fact Sheet—The Second Amendment in Court" (July 29, 1999). http://nraila.org.

49. See Don Kates, "Handgun Prohibition and the Original Meaning of the Second Amendment," *Michigan Law Review* 82 (1983): 203; Janet Malcolm, *To Keep and Bear Arms: The Origins of an Anglo-American Right* (Cambridge, Mass.: Harvard University Press, 1994); Sanford Levinson, "The Embarrassing Second Amendment," *Yale Law Journal* 99 (1989): 637; William Van Alstyne, "The Second Amendment and the Personal Right to Arms," *Duke Law Journal* 43 (1994): 1236; Eugene Volokh, "The Commonplace Second Amendment," *New York University Law Review* (1998): 793; and Akhil Amar, *The Bill of Rights: Creation and Reconstruction* (New Haven: Yale University Press, 1998).

50. http://www.law.ucla.edu/faculty/volokh/beararms/statecon/htm

51. Robert Dowlut and Janet Knoop, "State Constitutions and the Right to Keep and Bear Arms," *Oklahoma University Law Review* 7 (1982): 177.

52. VT Const. ch. I, Art. 15.

53. Dowlut and Knoop, "State Constitutions and the Right to Keep and Bear Arms."

54. PA Const. Art. 1, '21 (1790).

55. Robert Dowlut, "Federal and State Constitutional Guarantees to Arms," *Dayton Law Review* 15 (1989): 59. E.g., *Wright v. Commonwealth*, 77 Pa. St. 470 (1875).

56. Other states include Delaware, Nebraska, North Dakota, and West Virginia.

57. WI Const. Art. I, 25 (1998); Jim Stingl, "Gun Amendment Handily Wins Approval, Wisconsin becomes 44th State with Measure," *Milwaukee*

Journal Sentinel, Nov. 4, 1998, p. 16. The amendment passed with an overwhelming 72% vote.

58. *U.S. v. Cruikshank*, 92 U.S. 542 (1875); *Presser v. Illinois*, 116 U.S. 252 (1886).

59. *Dred Scott v. Sandford*, 60 U.S. 393 (1856).

60. Amar, *The Bill of Rights*, pp. 257–66.

61. *U.S. v. Miller*, 307 U.S. 174 (1939).

62. Interestingly, this interpretation does not seem to have occurred to any constitutional commentator or court before the end of the third decade of the twentieth century. David Kopel, "The Second Amendment in the Nineteenth Century," *Brigham Young University Law Review* (1998): 1359.

63. David Hardy, "The Second Amendment as a Restraint on State and Federal Firearms Restrictions," in *Restricting Handguns*, ed. Don Kates (Great Barrington, Mass.: North River, 1979), p. 184.

64. Ibid.

65. Van Alstyne, "The Second Amendment and the Personal Right to Arms."

66. Lawrence H. Tribe, *American Constitutional Law*, 3rd ed. (New York: Foundation, 2000), pp. 901–2, n. 221.

Chapter 4

1. Pete Shields. *Guns Don't Die—People Do* (New York: Arbor House, 1981), pp. 22–23; Robert J. Spitzer, *The Politics of Gun Control*, 2d ed. (New York: Chatham House, 1998), p. 114.

2. Shields, *Guns Don't Die*, at 22.

3. Ibid., at 29.

4. Ibid., at 60.

5. Ibid., at 67.

6. Tom Diemer, "Opponents of NRA Are Chipping away Money, Influence Used to Prod Congress," *Cleveland (Ohio) Plain Dealer*, Oct. 12, 1993, p. 42.

7. Ibid., p. 43.

8. Ibid.

9. Juliet Elperin, "Rejuvenated NRA Arms for Election Year Showdown," *Washington Post*, Mar. 5, 2000, p. A2.

10. Glenn Utter, *Encyclopedia of Gun Control and Gun Rights* (Phoenix, Ariz.: Oryx, 2000), p. 54.

11. Ibid., p. 55.

12. Susan Yoachum, "200 Million Weapons Already in Private Hands," *San Francisco Chronicle*, July 13, 1993, p. A1.

13. "Brady Bill 1, NRA 0," *Christian Science Monitor*, May 13, 1991, p. 20.

14. Editorial, "Gun Control Watch; Brady Bill Vote," *Los Angeles Times*, Nov. 10, 1993, p. B6.

15. Editorial, "Slow Draw on the Brady Bill," *Boston Globe*, Aug. 25, 1993, p. 10.

16. Editorial, "Brady Bill: The Senate Can Seal It," *Washington Post*, Nov. 11, 1993, p. A22.

17. Editorial, "How They Voted on the Brady Bill," *Chicago Sun-Times*, Nov. 12, 1993, p. 35.

18. Editorial, "Brady Bill: Measure Is Reasonable Handgun Control," *Houston Chronicle*, Feb. 28, 1993, p. 2.

19. Richard Cohen, "Weak Endorsement for Weak Gun Bill," *St. Louis Post-Dispatch*, April 4, 1991, p. 3B.

20. Thomas Baldino, "Time to Repeal the 2nd Amendment," *Arizona Republic*, Dec. 30, 1993.

21. Bob Stump, "Crime: Misguided Brady Bill Targets the Wrong People," *Phoenix Gazette*, Oct. 1, 1993, p. B15.

22. Ibid.

23. Charley Reese, "Brady Bill II: A Conspiracy to Deprive Honest Americans of Liberty," *Orlando Sentinel*, Mar. 10, 1994, p. 9.

24. Handgun Control, Inc., "Briefing Paper on the Brady Amendment," pp. 2–3.

25. Gregg Lee Carter, *The Gun Control Movement* (New York: Twayne, 1997), p. 101.

26. Interview with Richard Aborn, June 21, 2000.

27. Editorial, "The Brady Bill and New York Guns," *New York Times*, Sept. 13, 1990, p. A26.

28. Editorial, "Brady Bill—Don't Lose It Today," *Washington Post*, Nov. 16, 1993, p. A20.

29. Telephone interview with Paul Blackman, July 20, 1999.

30. Clifford Krauss, "Gun Bill Is Unsnagged, Making Passage More Likely," *New York Times*, Oct. 28, 1993, p. A23.

31. H.R. Rep. 103–344 (1993).

32. Brady Handgun Violence Prevention Act of 1993: Roll Call Vote No. 560 (139 *Cong. Rec.* H9131; Date: Nov. 10, 1993).

33. Brady Handgun Violence Prevention Act of 1993: Roll Call Vote No. 559 (139 *Cong. Rec.* H9123; Date: Nov. 10, 1993).

34. Brady Handgun Violence Prevention Act of 1993: Roll Call Vote No. 564 (139 *Cong. Rec.* H9088; Date: Nov. 19, 1993).

35. Violent Crime Control and Law Enforcement Act of 1993: Roll Call Vote No. 384 (139 *Cong. Rec.* S16288; Date: Nov. 19, 1993).

36. Brady Handgun Violence Prevention Act of 1993: Roll Call Vote No. 394 (139 *Cong. Rec.* S16710; Date: Nov. 20, 1993).

37. Brady Handgun Violence Prevention Act of 1993: Roll Call Vote No. 614 (139 *Cong. Rec.* H10905; Date: Nov. 22, 1993).

38. Richard Aborn, "The Battle over the Brady Bill and the Future of Gun Control Advocacy," *Fordham Urban Law Journal* 22 (1995): 417, 427.

39. Ibid., p. 427.

40. 139 *Cong. Rec.* S17091 (daily ed. Nov. 24, 1993).

41. 139 *Cong. Rec.* S17092 (daily ed. Nov. 24, 1993).

42. Ibid.

43. Clifford Krauss, "Gun Control Act Wins Final Battle as GOP Retreats," *New York Times*, Nov. 25, 1993, p. A1.

44. Editorial, "At Last, the Brady Law," *New York Times*, Nov. 25, 1993, p. A26.

Chapter 5

1. 27 C.F.R. 178.130.

2. 18 U.S.C. 922 (b) (3).

3. 18 U.S.C. 922 (s).

4. 18 U.S.C. 922 (a) (5).

5. 18 U.S.C. 922 (s) (7).

6. Bureau of Alcohol, Tobacco, and Firearms, "One-Year Progress Report: Brady Handgun Violence Prevention Act," Feb. 28, 1995, appendix.

7. 18 U.S.C. 922 (s) (1) (A) (ii) (I).

8. 18 U.S.C. 922 (s) (2).

9. A felony record is defined as "a crime punishable by imprisonment for a term exceeding 1 year." 18 U.S.C. 922 (g) (1).

10. 18 U.S.C. 922 (s) (6) (B).

11. Ibid.

12. Office of Justice Programs, U.S. Department of Justice, "Attorney General's Program for Improving the Nation's Criminal History Records and Identifying Felons Who Attempt to Purchase Firearms," March 1991.

13. Bureau of Justice Assistance, "Early Experiences with Criminal History Records Improvement," May 1997, pp. 3–4.

14. Ibid., pp. 2–3.

15. Office of Justice Programs, U.S. Department of Justice, "Attorney General's Program for Improving the Nation's Criminal History Records," pp. 5–6.

16. *Brady Handgun Violence Prevention Act*, House Report No. 103–344, (1993), p. 1988.

17. *Violent Crime Control and Law Enforcement Act of 1994*, P.L. 103–322.

18. See *United States v. Morrison, 529* U.S. 598 (2000).

19. Bureau of Justice Statistics, U.S. Department of Justice, "National Criminal History Improvement Program," 1996, pp. 4–5.

20. See *Fraternal Order of Police v. United States*, 355 U.S. App. D.C. 359 (1999).

21. See Mark Shaffer, "Sheriff Targets Gun Curb," *Arizona Republic*, Feb. 21, 1994, p. B1. See "NRA Plans Legal Challenge to 'Brady Bill,' " United Press International, Feb. 23, 1994.

22. See "NRA Plans Legal Challenge to 'Brady Bill' "; "NRA Readies

Assault on Handgun Law," *Washington Times*, Feb. 25, 1994, p. A11. Pat Flannery, "Anti-Brady Momentum Accelerates: Symington Emphasizes States' Rights Argument," *Phoenix Gazette*, Feb. 25, 1994, p. B1; "NRA Will Try to Shoot Brady Law Full of Holes," *Seattle Post-Intelligencer*, Feb. 25, 1994, p. A3.

23. *See* Sam Howe Verhovek, "Five Rural Sheriffs Are Taking the Brady Law to Court," *New York Times*, Apr. 25, 1994, p. A10; Michael Kirkland, "NRA Says It Will Help to Challenge Brady Gun Control Law," United Press International, Feb. 28, 1994.

24. Verhovek, "Five Rural Sheriffs . . . ," p. A10.

25. Ibid. Joan McKinney, "Iberia Parish Sheriff Asks NRA for Advice on Defying Brady Law," *Advocate*, Mar. 4, 1994, p. 1A; Dirk Johnson, "Brady Ruling Heartens Opponents of Gun Control," *New York Times*, May 24, 1994, p. A12.

26. Bureau of Alcohol, Tobacco, and Firearms Director John Magaw, "Open Letter to State and Local Law Enforcement Officials," Jan. 21, 1994.

26. Ibid., pp. 4–5.

28. Ibid., p. 9.

29. Verhovek, "Five Rural Sheriffs . . . ," p. A10; Johnson, "Brady Ruling Heartens Opponents of Gun Control," p. A12.

30. Kirkland, "NRA Says It Will Help to Challenge Brady Gun Control Law."

31. See Johnson, "Brady Ruling Heartens Opponents of Gun Control," p. A12; McKinney, "Iberia Parish Sheriff Asks NRA . . . ," p. 1A.

32. 854 F. Supp. 1503, 1517–18 (D. Mont. 1994).

33. 66 F. 3d 1025, 1031 (9th Cir. 1995).

34. 66 F 3d. 1025, 1029–30 (9th Cir. 1995) (citations omitted).

35. 79 F. 3d. 452, 460 (5th Cir. 1996).

36. 521 U.S. 898, 918 (1997).

37. 521 U.S. 898, 918–19, quoting from Fed. No. 39, 245 (J. Madison).

38. 521 U.S. 898, 919 (1997).

39. 521 U.S. 898, 907 (1997).

40. 521 U.S. 898, 923–24 (1997).

41. 521 U.S. 898, 933 (1997), quoting from *New York v. United States*, 505 U.S. 144, 187 (1992).

42. Bureau of Alcohol, Tobacco, and Firearms, "Open Letter to All Federal Firearms Licensees," June 27, 1997. Downloaded from http://www.atf.treas.gov/firearms/bradylaw/letter/htm (last updated August 25, 1998).

43. Office of the Attorney General, "Letter to Law Enforcement Colleagues," June 27, 1997. Downloaded from http://atf.treas.gov/firearms/bradylaw/attorn.htm (last updated August 25, 1998).

44. See Lizette Alvarez, "Lawmakers See Minor Defeat Over Checks of Gun Buyers," *New York Times*, June 28, 1997, p. A1.

45. See "Washington News," United Press International, June 27, 1997;

Frank J. Murray, "Supreme Court Throws Out Crucial Part of Brady Law," *Washington Times*, June 28, 1997, p. A1.

46. See "A Tighter Rein on Guns," *Cleveland Plain Dealer*, Jan. 5, 1998, p. 8B.

47. Brady Act Task Group, *National Instant Criminal Background Check System* (1994), pp. 3–4.

48. Federal Bureau of Investigation, Criminal Justice Information Services Division, "National Instant Background Check System—The First Seven Months, Nov. 30, 1998–June 30, 1999."

Chapter 6

1. Gary Kleck, *Targeting Guns: Firearms and Their Control* (Hawthorne, N.Y.: De Gruyter, 1997), p. 87.

2. Philip J. Cook, Stephanie Molliconi, and Thomas Cole, "Regulating Gun Markets," *Journal of Criminal Law and Criminology* 86 (Fall 1995): 59, 69.

3. Philip J. Cook and Jens Ludwig, *Guns in America, Summary Report* (Washington, D.C.: Police Foundation, 1997).

4. See 18 U.S.C. § 922 (a) (1) and 923 (a).

5. William Ruefle, "No ID, No Wait, No Questions Asked: Classified Ads, Private Gun Sales and the Brady Act," unpublished manuscript, 2000.

6. Joseph F. Sheley and James D. Wright, *Gun Acquisition and Possession in Selected Juvenile Samples*, National Institute of Justice Research in Brief, no. 9 (Dec. 1993).

7. James D. Wright and Peter H. Rossi, *The Armed Criminal in America: A Survey of Incarcerated Felons* (Washington, D.C.: National Institute of Justice, 1985), p. 2.

8. Sheley and Wright focused on juvenile felons and inner-city juveniles "because these groups are popularly thought to engage in and experience violence at rates exceeding most other groups." Sheley and Wright, *Gun Acquisition and Possession*, p. 1.

9. Ibid., p. 6.

10. Sheley and Wright, *In the Line of Fire: Youth, Guns and Violence in Urban America* (New York: De Gruyter, 1995), pp. 42–43.

11. Sheley and Wright, *Gun Acquisition and Possession*, p. 4.

12. Ibid., p. 5.

13. Ibid., p. 10.

14. Kleck, *Targeting Guns*, pp. 92–93.

15. Ibid.

16. Sheley and Wright, *Gun Acquisition and Possession*, p. 6; Kleck, *Targeting Guns*, p. 91.

17. James D. Wright, Peter H. Rossi, and K. Daly, *Under the Gun: Weap-*

ons, Crime and Violence in America (Hawthorne, N.Y.: De Gruyter, 1983), pp. 193–97.

18. Wright and Rossi, *The Armed Criminal in America.*

19. Kleck, *Targeting Guns*, p. 136.

20. Gun Show Calendar, Krause Publications, as quoted in Bureau of Alcohol, Tobacco, and Firearms, "Gun Shows: Brady Checks and Crime Gun Traces," 1999, p. 4.

21. Ibid., p. 6.

22. Don Terry, "How Criminals Get Guns: In Short, All Too Easily," *New York Times*, Mar. 11, 1992, p. A1.

23. Charles Schumer, "A Few Bad Apples: Small Number of Gun Dealers the Source of Thousands of Crimes," 1999.

24. *Firearms Owners' Protection Act of 1986*, 18 U.S.C. 926 (1994).

25. Bureau of Alcohol, Tobacco, and Firearms, *Operation Snapshot: Final Report* (1993).

26. Ibid.; Cook et al., "Regulating Gun Markets," at 74–75.

27. Telephone interview with Bill Bowers, Technical Advice, BATF Firearms Programs Division, Sept. 5, 2000.

28. Telephone interview with William Earle, Deputy Associate Director, Regulatory Programs, BATF.

29. William J. Vizzard, *In the Crossfire: A Political History of the Bureau of Alcohol, Tobacco and Firearms* (Boulder, Colo.: Rienner, 1997), p. 61.

30. Telephone interview with William Earle.

31. Ibid.

32. Bureau of Alcohol, Tobacco, and Firearms, "Gun Shows: Brady Checks and Crime Gun Traces," pp. 8–9.

33. General Accounting Office, "Firearms: Purchased from Federal Firearm Licensees Using Bogus Identification," Mar. 2001.

34. Ibid., p. 2.

35. James Tien and Thomas Rich, *Identifying Persons Other Than Felons Ineligible to Purchase Firearms: A Feasibility Study* (Washington, D.C.: U.S. Dept. of Justice, (1990), p. 16.

36. Ibid., p. 63.

37. Ibid., p. 70.

38. Mark Sherman and R. Robin McDonald, "Numbers Offer Glimpse of Gun Sales in Georgia, but Much Remains Hidden," *Atlanta Journal-Constitution*, Feb. 17, 1994, p. A1.

Chapter 7

1. Nancy Mathis, "Emotional Ceremony Marks President's Signing of Brady Bill," *Houston Chronicle*, Dec. 1, 1993, p. A1.

2. Ibid.

3. Press Release, Handgun Control, Inc., "Sarah and Jim Brady Join Law Enforcement to Commemorate Third Anniversary of Brady Law" (Feb. 28, 1997).

4. Press Release, Handgun Control, Inc., "Statement of Sarah Brady on President Clinton's Support for Strong Brady Law" (Aug. 6, 1998).

5. Press Release, Handgun Control, Inc., "President Clinton, Celebrities Joined Sarah and Jim Brady in Los Angeles" (Nov. 30, 1999).

6. "A Special Message from U2 at the National Tribute to Jim and Sarah Brady, June 14, 2001," available at: http://www.bradycampaign.org (last visited Jun. 25, 2001).

7. Bureau of Justice Statistics, *Presale Handgun Checks, 1996* (Sept. 1997), p. 1.

8. General Accounting Office, *Gun Control: Implementation of the National Instant Criminal Background Check System* (Feb. 2000), p. 3.

9. Bureau of Justice Statistics, *Background Checks for Firearm Transfers, 2000* (July, 2001), p. 1.

10. Ibid.

11. John Monahan et al., *Rethinking Risk Assessment: The MacArthur Study of Mental Disorder and Violence* (New York: Oxford University Press, 2001).

12. Ibid.

13. Ibid.

14. Mona A. Wright, Garen J. Wintemute, and Frederick P. Rivara, "Effectiveness of Denial of Handgun Purchase to Persons Believed to Be at High Risk for Firearm Violence," *American Journal of Public Health* 89 (Jan. 1999): 88–90.

15. Gary Kleck, *Targeting Guns: Firearms and Their Control* (Hawthorne, N.Y.: De Gruyter, 1997), p. 87.

16. According to the BATF, every request to purchase that is denied does not necessarily indicate that there has been a violation of federal law, as only those rejected purchasers who *knowingly* supply false information can be prosecuted. However, the BATF is authorized to investigate all individuals whose applications are denied, even if there has been no criminal act (GAO Report, *Gun Control*, p. 39).

17. General Accounting Office, *Gun Control*, p. 41.

18. Ibid.

19. Ibid.

20. "U.S. Violent Crime Rate Takes Sharp Drop," available at: http://www.cnn.com/US/9706/01/fbi.violent.crime/ (June 1, 1997).

21. Bureau of Justice Statistics, "Homicide Trends in the United States" (Jan. 1999), pp. 1–3.

22. "Crime in the United States, Section II: Crime Index Offenses Reported, Crime Index Total," available at: http://www.fbi/gov/ucr/Cius_99/99crime/99c2_01.pdf

23. Garen Wintemute, "Guns and Gun Violence," in *The Crime Drop*

in America, ed. Alfred Blumstein and Joel Wallman (Cambridge: Cambridge University Press, 2000), p. 67.

24. Ibid.

25. See generally "Symposium, Why Is Crime Decreasing?" *Journal of Criminal Law and Criminology* 88 (1998); see also Philip B. Heymann, "The New Policing," *Fordham Urban Law Journal* 28 (2000): 407.

26. Bruce D. Johnson, Andrew Golub, and Eloise Dunlap, "The Rise and Decline of Hard Drugs, Drug Markets, and Violence in Inner-City America," in *The Crime Drop in America*, ed. Blumstein and Wallman, pp. 187–89.

27. Alfred Blumstein and Joel Wallman, "The Recent Rise and Fall of American Violence," in *The Crime Drop in America*, ed. Blumstein and Wallman, p. 5.

28. Jens Ludwig and Philip Cook, "Homicide and Suicide Rates Associated with Implementation of the Brady Handgun Violence Prevention Act," *Journal of the American Medical Association* 284 (Aug. 2000): 587.

29. Ibid., p. 586.

30. Ibid., p. 589.

31. Ibid., p. 588.

32. Ibid., p. 589.

33. Ibid., p. 590.

34. Philip J. Cook and Jens Ludwig, "Has the Brady Act Been Successful?" *Charlotte Observer*, Aug. 15, 2000, p. A12.

35. Ibid.

36. Mark B. Coggeshall, "Keepings Guns out of the Wrong Hands: Effects of Gun Control on Homicide in Virginia" (master's thesis, University of Maryland, 2001) (on file with author).

37. Ibid., p. 1.

38. Ibid., p. 10.

39. Ibid., p. 162.

Chapter 8

An earlier version of this chapter appeared as James B. Jacobs and Daniel M. Heumann, "Extending Brady to Gun Shows and the Secondary Market," *Criminal Law Bulletin* 37(3) (May–June 2001): 248–62.

1. It is a criminal offense for any person to sell a firearm to a person he knows to be ineligible. 18 U.S.C. sec. 922 (a) (1) and 923 (a).

2. Philip J. Cook, Stephanie Molliconi, and Thomas B. Cole, "Regulating Gun Markets," *Journal of Criminal Law and Criminology* 86 (Fall 1995): 59, 69. (Of adult inmate respondents, 43% report purchasing their firearms; of these, only ⅓ purchased their guns in the primary market, i.e., a gun store or pawnshop.)

3. Bureau of Alcohol, Tobacco, and Firearms, "Gun Shows: Brady Checks and Crime Gun Traces," 1999, p. 4.

4. David Kopel and Linda Gorman, "The Truth about Gun Shows," Independence Institute, Sept. 11, 2000 available at: www.I2i.org/suptdocs/backgrounders/gunshows.htm

5. *Gun Show Accountability Act of 1999*, 106th Cong., 1st sess., H.R. 902.

6. Bureau of Alcohol, Tobacco, and Firearms, Statement of Richard J. Davis, Assistant Secretary of the Treasury, 1979, p. 360, available at: http://www.cs.cmu.edu/afs/cs.cmu.edu/user/wbardwel/public/nfalist/atf_hearing1a.txt

7. Kristen Rand, *Gun Shows in America: Tupperware Parties for Criminals* (Washington, D.C.: Violence Policy Center, July 1996), p. 3.

8. Glenn H. Utter, *Encyclopedia of Gun Control and Gun Rights* (Phoenix, Ariz: Oryx, 2000), p. 63.

9. *GSAA*, H.R. 1903, S.B. 443.

10. Under current law, an FFL's failure to carry out a Brady background check is a misdemeanor, 18 U.S.C. § 922.

11. U.S. Newswire, "Ten National Law Enforcement Groups Call on Congress to Close the Gun Show Loophole," Oct. 20, 1999.

12. Bill McAllister and David Olinger, "Clinton Wins Changes from Major Gun Maker," *Denver Post*, Mar. 18, 2000, pp. 25–26.

13. United Press International, "Columbine Parents Atty. Predicts More," May 27, 1999, p. 4.

14. News Services, *St. Louis Post-Dispatch*, May 9, 2000, p. 11.

15. James Dao, "In Turnaround, McCain Does Ad Urging Background Checks for Buyers at Gun Shows," *New York Times*, Oct. 4, 2000, p. 18.

16. U.S. Newswire, "Ten National Law Enforcement Groups Call on Congress to Close the Gun Show Loophole."

17. The Hatch/Craig Amendment to GSAA, CR S5309, 106th Cong., 1st sess. The Hatch/Craig Bill fails to define the term "exhibitor," so that vendors could pool their firearms to circumvent the background check requirement.

18. S. 5146, *Cong. Rec.* 145 (May 14, 1999).

19. James B. Jacobs and Kimberly Potter, "Keeping Guns out of the Wrong Hands," *Journal of Criminal Law and Criminology* 86 (1995): 93.

20. William Ruefle, "Buyers and Sellers in the Secondary Firearms Market: A Field Study of Anonymous Cash and Carry Gun Sales" (paper delivered at Conference on Guns, Crime & Punishment in America, University of Arizona College of Law, January 26–27, 2001).

21. The Hatch/Craig Amendment to GSAA, CR S5309, 106th Cong., 1st sess.

22. Legal Community against Violence, "Addressing Gun Violence through Local Ordinances," 2000 Supplement. These ordinances have

been challenged in pending litigation. See *Great Western Shows, Inc. v. County of Los Angeles*, Dist. Ct. N. CV. 99-09661R AP.

23. *Nordyke v. Santa Clara County*, 110 F. 3d 707 (1997), at p. 716.

24. New York State Division of Criminal Justice 200, "Closing the Gun Show Loophole," available at: http://criminaljustice.state.ny.us/pio/gunbill.htm

25. N.Y. Ann. Laws, ch. 189 (Aug. 9, 2000).

26. James Dao, "The 2000 Campaign: The Gun Issue," *New York Times*, Oct. 5, 2000, p. A29.

27. Cook et al., "Regulating Gun Markets," pp. 59, 69.

28. Cal. Pen. C. 12071 (b) (3) bans the sale of any firearm, except through licensed dealers.

29. Gary Kleck, *Point Blank: Guns and Violence in America* (Hawthorne, N.Y.: De Gruyter, 1991), p. 18.

Chapter 9

1. *Gun Violence Prevention Act of 1994*, 103d Cong., 2d sess., H.R. 3932 (Mar. 1, 1994); 103d Cong., 2d sess., S. 1882 (Mar. 1, 1994).

2. *Gun Violence Prevention Act of 1994*, 104th Cong., 1st sess., H.R. 1321 (Mar. 24, 1994); 104th Cong., 1st sess., S. 631 (Mar. 27, 1995).

3. H.R. 1321, § 101.

4. Ibid.

5. H.R. 1321, § 101(Y) (5) (A).

6. H.R. 1321, § 101(Y) (5) (B).

7. Handgun Control, Inc., Press Release, "Statement of Sarah Brady, Chair, Handgun Control, Inc. Re: Our Country's Claim to Shame" (May 5, 1997).

8. *Printz v. United States*, 521 U.S. 98 (1997).

9. *South Dakota v. Dole*, 107 S. Ct. 2793 (1987).

10. General Accounting Office, *Truth in Sentencing: Availability of Federal Grants Influenced Laws in Some States* (1998).

11. Stephen Labatib, "Administration Floats Proposal for Licensing All Gun Owners," *New York Times*, Dec. 10, 1993, p. A1.

12. National Safety Council, *Accident Facts* 1997, available at: http://www.nsc.org/lrs/statinfo/af2.htm. Disabling injury is defined as disabling beyond the day of injury.

13. James B. Jacobs, *Drunk Driving: An American Dilemma* (Chicago: University of Chicago Press 1989), p. 120.

14. Emily Sachar, "Unlicensed Drivers' Bill Near," *Newsday*, June 16, 1993, p. 7.

15. *New York State Statistical Yearbook* (1994), p. 455.

16. Paul Moses, "City Lets 1,200 Drive with No License," *Newsday*, Sept. 6, 1996, p. A33.

17. Michael DeCourcy Hinds, "Uninsured Drivers Create Other Kinds of Wreckage," *New York Times*, Sept. 3, 1990, p. A1.

18. Subcomm. on International Law, Immigration, and Refugees of the House Comm. on the Judiciary, *Implementation of Employer Sanctions: Hearings on H.R. 521*, 103d Cong., 1st sess., 1994, 282 (statement of Dan Stein, executive director, Federation for American Immigration Reform, noting ready availability of phony identification documents); Art Barnum, "Curbing Fakes: State Targeting Traffic in Phony Driver's Licenses," *Chicago Tribune*, Sept. 13, 1993, p. D1; William Branigan, "New Law Fails to Stem Flow of Mexicans into California," *Washington Post*, June 23, 1988, p. A30 (discussing "booming market" in phony identification papers); Jeffrey Roberts, "ID Cards Used to Buy Guns Illegally," *Denver Post*, Jan. 17, 1994, p. A1.

19. Subcomm. on Crime and Criminal Justice of the House Judiciary Comm., *Prosecution of Federal Gun Crimes: Hearings*, 103d Cong., 1st sess., 1994, 50 (hereinafter Prosecution of Federal Gun Crimes).

20. Daniel C. Richman, "*Old Chief v. United States:* Stipulating Away Prosecutorial Accountability," *Virginia Law Review* 83 (1997): 939, 982–85.

21. *Prosecution of Federal Gun Crimes*, at 50 (testimony of Jo Ann Harris, assistant attorney general, Criminal Division, U.S. Dept. of Justice).

22. Richard S. Frase, "The Decision to File Federal Criminal Charges: A Quantitative Study of Prosecutorial Discretion," *University of Chicago Law Review* 47 (1980): 246, 258.

23. Ann Pastore and Kathleen Maguire, Bureau of Justice Statistics, *Sourcebook of Criminal Justice Statistics, 1995* (Washington, D.C.: U.S. Government Printing Office, 1996), at 465, table 5.16.

24. Kleck, *Targeting Guns* (Hawthorne, N.Y.: De Gruyter, 1997), pp. 86–88; Joseph F. Sheley and James D. Wright, *Gun Acquisition and Possession in Selected Juvenile Samples* (Dec. 1993); Marianne W. Zawitz, "Guns Used in Crime" (July 1995).

25. Sheley and Wright, *Gun Acquisition and Possession*, at 6; Kleck, *Targeting Guns*, at 90–91.

26. *National Firearms Act of 1934*, 26 U.S.C. 5861(d) (1994); 18 U.S.C. 922(o) (1994) (prohibiting transfer or possession of machineguns). 27 C.F.R. 178.101–105 (1996).

27. Eric Larson, Prepared Statement before the Subcommittee on Treasury, Postal Service and General Government of the House Committee on Appropriations, May 1, 2001.

28. *Special Report on Allegations Concerning the Bureau of Alcohol, Tobacco and Firearms' Registration and Recordkeeping of the National Firearms Registration and Transfer Records*, OIG-99-099, October 26, 1998; and *Audit Report on Allegations Concerning the Bureau of Alcohol, Tobacco and Firearms' Administration of the National Firearms Registration and Transfer Record*, OIG-99-018, December 18, 1998; *Treasury,*

Postal Service, and General Government Appropriations Bill, 2001, 106th Cong., 2d sess., H.R. 4871 (July 18, 2000), "Firearms Database Accuracy," H.R. Report No. 106–756, pp. 23–24.

29. Mass. Ann. Laws. ch. 140, sec. 128A (1995).

30. I have drawn on an unpublished NYU Law School seminar paper by Caleb Pollack entitled "Massachusetts Gun Laws and a National Solution to Gun Control."

31. Cal. Penal Code § 12072 (d); § 12082 (a); § 12084

32. Interview with Ann Overoye, analyst, Dealer Record of Sale Section, Firearms Division, California Department of Justice (Apr. 3, 2001).

33. *Printz v. United States*, 521 US 98 (1997).

34. 18 U.S.C. sec. 926 (a) (3) (1994).

35. No later than 24 hours after a handgun licensee discovers that a handgun has been stolen from or lost by the licensee, the licensee is required to report the theft or loss to the secretary of the treasury, the chief law enforcement officer of the state, and appropriate local authorities.

36. Sheley and Wright, *Acquisition and Possession*, at 5.

37. David M. Kennedy, Anne M. Piehl, and Anthony A. Braga, "Youth Violence in Boston: Gun Markets, Serious Youth Offenders and a Use-Reduction Strategy," *Law and Contemporary Problems* 59 (Winter 1996): 147, 174.

38. Bureau of Alcohol, Tobacco, and Firearms, "Memorandum for Treasury Secretary Robert Rubin," Feb. 3, 1997.

39. Using these trace data to make criminological conclusions about "crime guns" and patterns of trafficking is a different matter. Gary Kleck has shown why gun traces ought not to be used for research purposes. The biggest problem is that traced guns are by no means a random sample of crime guns. See Gary Kleck, "BATF Trace Data and the Role of Organized Gun Trafficking in Supplying Guns to Criminals," *St. Louis University Public Law Review* 18 (1999): 23–46; see also David Kopel and Paul Blackman, Research Note, "Firearms Tracing Data from the BATF: An Occasionally Useful Law Enforcement Tool but a Poor Research Tool," *Criminal Justice and Policy Review* 11(1) (2000): 44–62.

40. http://www.concentric.net/rweller/news418.htm]

41. Firearms (Amendment) Act of 1997, *Current Law Statistics*, vol. 1 (London: Sweet & Maxwell, 1997).

42. David B. Kopel, *The Samurai, the Mountie, and the Cowboy: Should America Adopt the Gun Controls of Other Democracies?* (Buffalo, N.Y.: Prometheus, 1992), p. 231, n. 210.

43. David B. Kopel and Christopher C. Little, "Communitarians, Neorepublicans, and Guns: Assessing the Case for Firearms Prohibition," *Maryland Law Review* 56 (1997): 438, at 459.

44. Don Terry, "How Criminals Get Their Guns: In Short, All Too Easily," *New York Times*, Mar. 11, 1992, at A1.

45. Kim Bell, "Brady Bill Triggered Jump in Pistol Sales, Police Officers

Say," *St. Louis Post-Dispatch*, Jan. 18, 1994, p. B1; Steve Bates, "Gun Shops Get Shot in the Arm, Brady Bill Fears Said to Spur Surge in Sales," *Washington Post*, Nov. 27, 1993, p. B1.

46. Uniform Crime Reports, *Crime in the United States, 1996* (Nov. 1997).

Chapter 10

1. Don Kates, "Towards a History of Handgun Prohibition in the United States," in *Restricting Handguns: The Liberal Skeptics Speak Out*, ed. Don B. Kates, Jr. (Great Barrington, Mass.: North River, 1979). See also Don Kates, "Handgun Banning in Light of the Prohibition Experience," in *Firearms and Violence: Issues of Public Policy*, ed. Don B. Kates, Jr. (Cambridge, Mass: Ballinger, 1984), pp. 139–65; Stephan B. Tahmassebi, "Gun Control Would Not Reduce Crime against the Poor and Minorities," in *Gun Control (Current Controversies)*, ed. Carol Wekesser (San Diego: Greenhaven, 1992), p. 61.

2. U.S. President's Commission on Law Enforcement and Administration of Justice, *The Challenge of Crime in a Free Society* (Washington, D.C.: Government Printing Office, 1967), p. 240.

3. Edwin H. Sutherland and Donald Cressey, *Principles of Criminology* (Philadelphia: Lippincott, 1978), pp. 271, 657–689; Kates, "Towards a History of Handgun Prohibition in the United States."

4. Norval Morris and Gordon Hawkins, *The Honest Politician's Guide to Crime Control* (Chicago: University of Chicago Press, 1969), p. 64.

5. H.R. 2582, 93rd Cong., 1st sess. (1973).

6. H.R. 3547, 93rd Cong., 1st sess. (1973).

7. Sen. John H. Chafee (D-R.I.), "In View of Handgun's Effects, 'There's Only One Answer: A Ban,'" *Minneapolis Star-Tribune*, June 15, 1992, p. 13A, available at: http://www.gunscholar.org/gunban.htm

8. S. 2913, 102nd Cong., 2nd sess. (1992).

9. H.R. 3132, 103rd Cong., 1st sess. (1993).

10. Amitai Etzioni and Steven Hellend, "The Case For Domestic Disarmament," available at: http://www.gwu.edu/ccps/pop_mdisarm.html, originally released as Amitai Etzioni and Steven Hellend, "The Case for Domestic Disarmament," *Responsive Communitarian Quarterly*, Nov. 18, 1991.

11. Coalition to Stop Gun Violence, available at: http://www.gunfree.org/csgv/csgvsumm.htm

12. Violence Policy Center, "Cease Fire: A Comprehensive Strategy to Reduce Firearms Violence," 1994, available at: http://www.vpc.orf//fact_sht/ceasefs_htm

13. American Academy of Pediatrics, "Protection of Children from Handguns Act," written Aug. 1990, reaffirmed June 1995, revised Oct. 2000, available at: http://www.aap.org/policy/m938.html

14. Editorial, "Why Not Ban Handguns?" *Washington Post*, Apr. 26, 1999, p. A18.

15. Editorial, "Ban Local Sale of Handguns," *Chicago Daily Herald*, May 24, 1999, p. 6.

16. See, generally, Lora Lumpe, ed., *Running Guns: The Global Black Market in Small Arms* (London: Zed Books, 2000).

17. James B. Jacobs and Kimberly A. Potter, "Comprehensive Handgun Licensing & Registration: An Analysis & Critique of Brady II, Gun Control's Next (And Last?) Step," *Journal of Criminal Law and Criminology* 89 (1999): 106, 110.

18. David B. Kopel and Christopher C. Little, "Communitarians, Neorepublicans, and Guns: Assessing the Case for Firearms Prohibition," *Maryland Law Review* 56 (1997): 438, 458.

19. David T. Hardy and Don B. Kates, Jr., "Handgun Availability and the Social Harms of Robbery: Recent Data and Some Projections," in *Restricting Handguns*, pp. 118–139.

20. Andrew Sinclair, *Prohibition* (New York: Little, Brown, 1962), p. 183.

21. Howard Lee McBain, *Prohibition, Legal and Illegal* (London: Macmillan, 1928), pp. 156–157.

22. *Printz v. United States*, 521 U.S. 898 (1997).

23. Sutherland and Cressey, *Criminology*, p. 271.

24. Kopel and Little, "Communitarians, Neorepublicans, and Guns."

25. Daniel C. Richman, "Old Chief v. United States: Stipulating Away Prosecutorial Accountability," *Virginia Law Review* 83 (1997): 939.

26. Peter Reuter, *Disorganized Crime: The Economics of the Visible Hand* (Cambridge, Mass.: MIT Press, 1983).

27. See Gary Kleck, "BATF Gun Trace Data and the Role of Organized Gun Trafficking in Supplying Guns to Criminals," *Saint Louis University Public Law Review* 18 (1999): 39, 42.

28. James Wright and Peter Rossi, *Armed and Considered Dangerous: A Survey of Felons and Their Firearms* (Hawthorne, N.Y.: De Gruyter, 1994), pp. 185, 193–197.

29. See, for example, Nicholas Dixon, "Why We Should Ban Handguns in the United States," *St. Louis University Public Law Review* 12 (1993): 243.

30. Gerald D. Robin, *Violent Crime and Gun Control* (Cincinnati: Anderson Publishing and Academy of Criminal Justice Sciences, 1991), p. 31.

31. James B. Jacobs, "Exceptions to a General Prohibition on Handgun Possession: Do They Swallow up the Rule?" *Law and Contemporary Problems* 49 (Winter 1986): 11–12. For the complete text of the Morton Grove Ordinance, see Morton Grove, Ill., Code s 132.102(E)([1]–[10])(1981).

32. San Francisco, Cal., Municipal Code pt. II, ch. VIII, art. 35 s3507 (A)-(J) (1982).

Chapter 11

1. *Child Handgun Injury Prevention Act*, H.R. 1014, 107th Cong., 1st Sess. (Mar. 2001).

2. House Doc. 106-1, 1999 State of the Union; *NBC Today Show*, "President Bill Clinton Discusses Need for Gun Control in Light of Recent Shootings" (Mar. 2, 2000), transcript.

3. Cynthia Leonardatos, Paul H. Blackman, and David B. Kopel, "Smart Guns/Foolish Legislators: Finding the Right Public Safety Laws, and Avoiding the Wrong Ones," *Connecticut Law Review* 34 (2001): 157.

4. *Criminal Justice Newsletter*, 31(10):1.

5. "A Blueprint For New Beginnings: A Responsible Budget for America's Priorities," available at: http://www.whitehouse.gov/news/usbudget/blueprint/bud09.html (visited July 5, 2001). President Bush has also proposed that Congress allocate $9 million annually for a dedicated juvenile gun crimes prosecutor in every U.S. attorney's office.

6. "NRA Fact Sheet on Mandatory Storage/Trigger Lock Legislation," available at: http://www.mynra.com/default.sph/Ibn.class/second_page?destUrl=http://www.nraila.org (viewed on July 5, 2001).

7. Josh Sugarman, *Every Handgun Is Aimed at You: The Case for Banning Handguns* (New York: New Press, 2001); P. M. Barrett, "There's a Catch: A Simple Invention Points up Complexity of Gun Control Suits," *Wall Street Journal,* April 23, 1999, pp. A1, A6. (The pro–gun control Violence Policy Center also fears that locking and personalization devices will give parents false confidence in the safety of firearms, leading them to leave loaded firearms within reach of children.) Johns Hopkins Center for Gun Policy and Research and National Opinion Research Center, "1996 National Gun Policy Survey: Questionnaire with Weighted Frequencies (1997). (Finding that a large number of people who do not currently own guns would consider buying a personalized gun.)

8. Leonardatos, Blackman, and Kopel, *"Smart Guns,"* p. 13. See W. Kip Viscusi, *Fatal Tradeoffs: Public and Private Responsibilities for Risk* (New York: Oxford University Press, 1992), pp. 234–42, and J. S. Wilde, *Target Risk* (Toronto: PDE Publications, 1994), ch.6.3 ("childproof" safety caps on pill bottles led to an increase in child poisonings).

9. Leonardatos, Blackman, and Kopel, *"Smart Guns,"* p. 168.

10. NRA literature is inconsistent on trigger locks; see: http://www.mynra.com/default.sph/Ibn.class/second_page?destUrl=http://www.nraila.org supporting trigger locks and http://www.mynra.com/default.sph/Ibn.class/second_page?destUrl=http://www.nraila.org opposing trigger locks (visited July 5, 2001).

11. Cynthia Leonardatos et al., *Personalized Guns: Reducing Gun Deaths through Design Changes*, 2nd ed. (Baltimore: Johns Hopkins Center for Gun Policy and Research, 1998).

12. Ibid.

13. Leonardatos, Blackman, and Kopel, "Smart Guns," p. 29.

14. See http://support.jhsph.edu/departments/gunpolicy/documents/Personguntech.PDF for information on available personalization technology (visited June 30, 2001). Mossberg, a shotgun manufacturer, has reported some progress in personalization technologies, but Glock has abandoned research and development on personalization technologies.

15. 106 H.R. 4066, proposing funding for research on gun personalization. 2000 H.R. 5472; 106 H.R. 5472, proposing a requirement that firearms manufacturers spend a minimum of 2% of annual firearms sales revenues on research into personalized firearms and a ban on the import, design, manufacture, or sale of handgun models (other than those models in manufacture at the time of the bill's passage) 36 months from the passage of the bill.

16. Cal. Penal Code 12035; Conn. Gen. Stat. Ann. 29–37i; Del. Code Ann. Tit. 11, 1456; Fla. Stat. Ann. 784.05; Haw. Rev. Stat. 134-10.5; Iowa Code 724.22; Md. Ann. Code art. 27, 36K; Minn. Stat. Ann. 609.666; N.J. Stat. Ann. 2C:58-15; N.C. Gen. Stat. 14-315.1; R.I. Gen. Laws 11-47-60.1; Tex. Penal Code Ann. 46.13; Va. Code Ann. 18.2–56.2; Wis. Stat. 948.55.

17. Andrew J. McClurg, "Child Access Prevention Laws: A Common Sense Approach to Gun Control," *St. Louis University Public Law Review* 18 (1999): 47, 58.

18. Sam Howe Verhovek, "Bloodshed in a Schoolyard: The Overview," *New York Times*, Mar. 27, 1998, p. A1.

19. Rick Bragg, Dirk Johnson, John Kifner, and Sam Howe Verhovek, "From Wild Talk and Friendship to Five Deaths in a Schoolyard," *New York Times*, Mar. 29, 1998.

20. John R. Lott, Jr., and John E. Whitley, "Safe Storage Gun Laws: Accidental Deaths, Suicides, and Crime," working paper #237, March 28, 2000, Yale Law School Program for Studies in Law, Economics, and Public Policy.

21. David Kairys, "The Origin and Development of the Governmental Handgun Cases," *Connecticut Law Review* 32 (Fall 2000): 1163, 1173.

22. Second Am. Compl. and Jury Demand ¶ 15, in *Camden County Board of Chosen Freeholders v. Beretta U.S.A. Corp.*, 123 F. Supp. 2d 245 (2000).

23. *People of the State of California v. Arcadia Machine & Tool, Inc.*, Judicial Coordination Proceeding No. 4095 (Superior Court of California, County of San Diego), May 25, 1999.

24. Ibid.

25. See, e.g., *Camden County Board of Chosen Freeholders v. Beretta U.S.A. Corp.*, 123 F. Supp. 2d 245 (2000).

26. See, e.g., *City of Cincinnati v. Beretta U.S.A. Corp.*, No. A9902369 (Court of Common Pleas, Hamilton County, Ohio), case dismissed October 7, 1999, aff'd Ohio Court of Appeals, 1st Appellate District, August 11, 2000, Appeal Nos. CC-990729.

27. Michael Romano, "U.S. Makes Handgun Deal; Smith & Wesson OK's Restrictions," *Chicago Tribune*, March 17, 2000, p. 9.

28. James Dao, "Under Legal Siege: Gunmaker Agrees to Adopt Curb," *New York Times*, Mar. 18, 2000, p. A1.

29. Arizona Revised Statutes, Title 12, Chapt. 6, art 12–714.

30. Andrew O. Smith, "The Manufacture and Distribution of Handguns as an Abnormally Dangerous Activity," *University of Chicago Law Review* 54 (1987): 369.

31. 304 Md. 124, 487 A.2d 1143 (1985).

32. The Maryland legislature established a Handgun Roster Board, which publishes a roster of handguns approved for sale.

33. See, e.g., *Dix v. Beretta U.S.A. Corp.*, 2002 WL 187397 Cal. App. 1 Dist).

34. See, e.g., *Hamilton v. Accu-tek*, 62 F. Supp. 2d 802 (EDNY 1999).

35. Timothy D. Lytton, "Lawsuits against the Gun Industry: A Comparative Institutional Analysis," *Connecticut Law Review* 32 (2000): 1247, 1257.

36. Ibid at 1257.

37. 62 F. Supp. 2d 802 (EDNY 1999).

38. *Hamilton v. Accu-tek*, 222 F. 3d 36, 39 (2d Cir. 1999).

39. *Hamilton v. Accu-Tek*, USCOA, 2 No. 36, at 8 (May 2001).

40. Mike Allen, "Colt to Curtail Sale of Handguns," *New York Times*, Oct. 11, 1999. p. A1.

41. 1999 AK S.B., 77

42. 27 CFR Part 179 details the types of firearms that must be registered in the National Firearms Registration and Transfer Record under the NFA.

43. See 27 CFR Part 179 for types of firearms that must be registered under the NFA. See 27 CFR 179.84–179.87 and 179.62–179.67 for methods of legally acquiring an NFA firearm.

44. *Violent Crime Control and Law Enforcement Act of 1994*, PL 103, 322.

45. David Kopel, ed., *Guns: Who Should Have Them?* (Amherst, N.Y.: Prometheus, 1995).

46. Ann Pastore and Kathleen McGuire, Bureau of Justice Statistics, *Sourcebook of Criminal Justice Statistics, 1998* (1999), table 3.119.

47. Jeffrey A. Roth and Christopher S. Koper, *Impacts of the 1994 Assault Weapons Ban: 1994–1996* (Washington D.C.: National Institute of Justice, 1999).

48. Jon Vernick and Stephen Terret, "A Public Health Approach to Regulating Firearms as Consumer Products," *University of Pennsylvania Law Review* 148 (2000): 1193–1211.

49. Robert Sherill, *The Saturday Night Special* (1937); Philip J. Cook, "The 'Saturday Night Special': An Assessment of Alternative Definitions from a Policy Perspective," *Journal of Criminal Law and Criminology* 72 (1981): 1735–1745; T. Markus Funk, "Gun Control and Economic Discrim-

ination: The Melting-Point Case In-Point," *Journal of Criminal Law and Criminology* 85 (1995): 764–806; "NRA Fact Sheet: Saturday Night Specials," available at: http://www.nraila.org/FactSheets.asp?FormMode= Detail&ID=61 (visited July 7, 2001).

50.   18 U.S.C. 921 (a)(17) and 922 (b)(5), 27 CFR 178.11.

51.   An example of lack of regulation of ammunition sales is a coupon issued by a Baltimore Burger King: "Good for one free box of ammo with gun purchase or 10 percent off." "Bullets and Burgers at Baltimore Restaurant," *San Francisco Chronicle*, Apr. 6, 1996, p. A3. K-Mart recently stopped selling ammunition. "Ammunition Sales to End," *New York Times*, June 29, 2001, p. A19.

52.   27 CFR 178.125. "No records are required for ammunition other than armor piercing ammunition. Disposition records must be kept by licensed manufacturers, importers, and collectors for transactions in armor piercing ammunition." BATF Online Firearms FAQ http://www.atf. treas.gov/firearms/faq/faq2.htm#a5 (viewed July 16, 2001).

53.   LA City Council Document 99–1581. Council member Mike Hernandez: Ban Sale of Firearm Ammunition in City of LA, 1999.

54.   139 Cong. Rec. S. 612 (daily ed. Jan. 21, 1993) (statement of Sen. Daniel Patrick Moynihan). But see Scott D. Dailard, "The Role of Ammunition in a Balanced Program of Gun Control: A Critique of the Moynihan Bullet Bill," *Journal of Legislation* 20 (1994): 19, 24–25, for a disagreement with the senator's estimate.

55.   Brendan J. Healey, "Plugging the Bullet Holes in U.S. Gun Law: An Ammunition-Based Proposal for Tightening Gun Control," *John Marshall Law Review* 32 (1998): 1–34, 25.

56.   See http://www.atf.treas.gov/firearms/legal/armor.htm for a complete summary of current laws relating to armor-piercing ammunition (visited July 16, 2001). Lisa J. Steele, "No Bad Bullets," *Criminal Law Bulletin* 37 (May–June 2001): 263.

57.   Violent Crime Prevention Act of 1992 (S. 178) proposes to "prohibit the manufacture, transfer, or importation of .25 caliber, .32 caliber, and 9 millimeter ammunition." Dailard, *"The Role of Ammunition,"* p. 23.

58.   Dailard, "The Role of Ammunition," p. 31.

59.   *Crime Gun Trace Reports (1999) National Report, General Findings*, p. 9. available at: http://www.atf.treas.gov/firearms/ycgii/1999/gen-findings.pdf (Visited July 10, 2001).

60.   See, e.g., http://www.22lrconversions.com/, http://www.22lr conversion.com/riflekit.htm, http://www.tcarms.com/contpistol/index. html, and http://www.bultransmark.com/products/mags-convkit.htm Caliber is the nominal diameter of a projectile of a rifled firearm or the diameter between lands in the rifled barrel. In the United States, caliber is usually expressed in hundredths of an inch, in Britain, in thousandths, in Europe, in millimeters.

61.   *The Real Cost of Ammunition Act of 1993* (S. 179) would impose

a 1000% sales tax on the regulated calibers. It would also impose a 10,000% excise tax on Winchester's hollow point 9mm "Black Talon" cartridge and the .50-caliber "Desert Eagle."

62. *Ammunition Safety Act of 1997*, 105th Cong. S. 553, 1st sess. (Sen. John Kerry's [D-Mass.] proposal for adding bullets to Brady among other ammunition-related proposals); *Gun Violence Prevention Act of 1994*, 103d Cong, S. 1982 (Sen. Howard Metzenbaum's [D-Ohio] instituting a handgun licensing scheme that prohibits the sale of ammunition to anyone without a handgun license); *Ammunition Safety Act of 1995*, 104th Cong, S. 433 (Sen. John Kerry's [D-Mass.] proposal for extending Brady background checks to ammunition purchases); 104th Cong, H.R. 1403 (1995) (Rep. Joseph Kennedy's [D-Mass.] proposal to add ammunition to Brady).

63. The council also voted to ban various types of "offensive ammunition," including handgun rounds above .46 caliber, rifle rounds above .40 caliber, and a variety of other ammunition including rounds commonly used in Saturday Night Specials. See http://www.lacity.org/council/cd11/press/ammunition%20purchase.pdf (visited July 3, 2001).

64. Healey, "Plugging the Bullet Holes in U.S. Gun Law," pp. 15, 24.

65. *Handgun Control and Violence Prevention Act of 1995*, 104th Cong; H.R. 1321, 1st sess., 104th Cong, S. 631

66. Brady II does not include a regulatory mechanism to make sure that the handgun purchase limit cannot be circumvented by shopping at different FFLs. The Virginia handgun-a-month law avoids this problem by entering every sale into a database that is searched by the state's background check system.

67. 18 U.S.C. 923(g)(3), 27 CFR 178.126a. An FFL selling more than one handgun to an individual over a period of five consecutive business days must report the transaction on BATF Form 3310.4 (Report of Multiple Sale or Other Disposition of Pistols and Revolvers). The form must be sent to the BATF in addition to a state police or local law enforcement agency by the end of the day of the second sale. The dealer must keep a copy of the form. Persons who buy one gun from several different FFLs could go undetected under this system.

68. Virginia Acts of Assembly 1993, Ch. 486; Virginia Code Ann. §18.2-308.2:2. Maryland has also implemented a one handgun-a-month law (Md. Ann. Code, Art. 27 at § 442A).

69. Mark B. Coggeshall, "Keeping Guns Out of the Wrong Hands: The Effects of Gun Control on Homicide in Virginia," (master's thesis, University of Maryland, 2001).

70. Douglas S. Weil and Rebecca C. Knox, "Effects of Limiting Handgun Purchases on Interstate Transfer of Firearms" *Journal of the American Medical Association* 275 (1996): 1759–1761.

71. Mark Johnson, "Gun-A-Month Law Has Mixed Results in Virginia, Maryland," *Virginian-Pilot & Ledger Star*, Oct. 9, 1998, p. A4.

72. NY Penal Law § 265.02 (5) (I)

73. Lawrence Sherman et al., "Preventing Crime: What Works, What Doesn't, What's Promising."

74. Martha Plotkin, ed., *Under Fire: Gun Buy-Backs, Exchanges and Amnesty Programs* (Washington, D.C.: Police Executive Research Forum, 1996).

75. Joshua Kaufmann, "Gun Control or Gimmick?" (NYU School of Law, student paper on file with author), pp. 15–16.

76. Lawrence W. Sherman et al., "Preventing Crime: What Works, What Doesn't, What's Promising," National Institute of Justice Report to Congress, July 1997; David M. Kennedy, Anne M. Piehl, and Anthony A. Braga, "Gun Buy-Backs: Where Do We Stand and Where Do We Go?" in Plotkin, ed., *Under Fire*, pp. 141–71.

77. National Center for Policy Analysis, "Will Ballistic Fingerprinting Work?" available at: http://www.ncpa.org/pi/crime/pd032900e.html; Americans for Gun Safety Foundation, "Ballistic Fingerprinting," available at: http://w3.agsfoundation.com/s_finger1.html

Chapter 12

1. *New York v. Belton*, 453 U.S. 454 (1981).

2. See, e.g., Richard Frase, "The Decision to File Federal Criminal Charges: A Quantitative Study of Prosecutorial Discretion," *University of Chicago Law Review* 47 (1980): 246; James B. Jacobs and Kimberly A. Potter, "Keeping Guns out of the 'Wrong' Hands: The Brady Law and the Limits of Regulation," *Journal of Criminal Law and Criminology* 86 (1995): 93, 110.

3. David Garland, *The Culture of Control* (Chicago: University of Chicago Press, 2001).

4. Glenn Pierce, "The Bentley Fox Gun Law's Short-Term Impact on Crime in Boston" (1981); Colin Loftin, Milton Heumenn, and David McDowall, "Mandatory Sentencing and Firearms violence: Evaluating an Alternative to Gun Control," *Law and Society Review* 17 (1983): 287–318.

5. In 1994, the NYPD issued Police Strategy No. 1: Getting Guns off the Streets of New York, which set forth "the Department's plan to eradicate gun violence by stepping up efforts to find and seize illegal firearms." See Elliot Spitzer, "The New York City Police Department 'Stop and Frisk' Practices," Office of the Attorney General of New York, Dec. 1, 1999, p. 53. See also "New York City Rings in the New Year with the Lowest Crime in over a Quarter Century," Mayor's Press Releases #691–96, Dec. 31, 1996, availabe at http://www.nyc.gov/html/om/html/96/sp691–96.html ("Police attribute the steep crime declines to strategic changes in the police department's crime-fighting approach since Mayor Giuliani took office, including intensified enforcement of misdemeanors and other quality-of-life

offenses, a highly focused attack on felony crime achieved through the CompStat process, and the impact of the anti-drug initiatives mounted in 1996").

6. Lawrence Sherman, James W. Shaw, and Dennis P. Rogan, *The Kansas City Gun Experiment* (Washington, D.C.: National Institute of Justice, 1995).

7. Lawrence Sherman, " 'Policing for Crime Prevention,' Preventing Crime: What Work's, What Doesn't, What's Promising," report by the National Institute of Justice (1996), available at: http://www.ncjrs.org/works/chapter8.htm.

8. Michael Cooper, "Officers in Bronx Fire 41 Shots, and an Unarmed Man Is Killed," *New York Times*, Feb. 5, 1999, p. A1.

9. Elliot Spitzer, "The New York City Police Department 'Stop and Frisk' Practices."

10. Jeffrey Fagan and Garth Davies, "Street Stops and Broken Windows: Terry, Race, and Disorder in NYC," *Fordham Urban Law Journal* 28 (2) (2000): 457–504.

11. Robert Davis and Pedro Mateu-Gelabert, *Respectful and Effective Policing: Two Examples in the South Bronx* (New York: VERA Institute of Justice, 1999).

12. James Q. Wilson, "Just Take away Their Guns," *New York Times Magazine*, Mar. 20, 1994, p. 47.

13. See, generally, *Hearings on Reducing Gun Violence, before the Subcommittee on Crime & Criminal Justice of the House Judiciary Committee*, 103d Cong. 2nd sess. (1994) (prepared statement of "Millivision" designer Dr. G. Richard Huguenin, president, Millitech Corp.), available in 1994 WL 14190555 [hereinafter Huguenin Statement]. See also Steven Salvador Flores, "Gun Detector Technology and the Special Needs Exception," *Rutgers Computer and Technology Law Journal* 25 (1999): 135, at 138. G. Richard Huguenin, "The Detection of Concealed Weapons, Explosives, and Other Contraband with Passive Millimeter Wave Imaging," *American Society of Industrial Security* (Sept. 1997), p. 1; George Dery III, "Remote Frisking down to the Skin, Government Searching Technology Powerful Enough to Locate Holes in Fourth Amendment Fundamentals," *Creighton Law Review* 30 (1997): 353, 356; David A. Harris, "Superman's X-ray Vision and the Fourth Amendment: The New Gun Detection Technology," *Temple Law Review* 69 (1996): 1, 7–8 and n. 38; Erik Milstone, "New Devices Let Frisks Go Undercover," *American Bar Association Journal* 82 (1996): 32.

14. Huguenin Statement. But see Joyce Price, "X-ray Camera Could Reveal Criminal Intent," *Washington Times*, Aug. 13, 1996, pt. A, p. A1 (quoting Don Haines, lobbyist for the ACLU, as saying, "I'm familiar with the millimeter wave technology, and it's an incredible invasion of privacy. . . . It produces a virtual 3-D image, and you can see the contours of breasts, buttocks and genitals").

15. See, generally, Wayne R. LaFave, 1 *Search & Seizure* (3d ed., 1999) § 2.2 (2000) (Pocket Part); Dery III, "Remote Frisking," pp. 353, 356; Harris, "Superman's X-ray Vision," pp. 1, 7–8 and n. 38; Flores, "Gun Detector Technology and the Special Needs Exception"; T. Wade McKnight, "Passive, Sensory-Enhanced Searches: Shifting the Fourth Amendment Reasonableness Burden," *Louisiana Law Review* 59 (1999): 1243; Alyson L. Rosenberg, Note, "Passive Millimeter Wave Imaging: A New Weapon in the Fight against Crime or a Fourth Amendment Violation," *Albany Law Journal of Science & Technology* 9 (1998): 135; Laura B. Riley, Note, "Concealed Weapon Detectors and the Fourth Amendment: The Constitutionality of Remote Sense-Enhanced Searches," *UCLA Law Review* 45 (1997): 281; Merrick D. Bernstein, Note, "Intimate Details: A Troubling New Fourth Amendment Standard for Government Surveillance Techniques," *Duke Law Journal* 46 (1996): 575; Jason Lazarus, Note, "Vision Impossible? Imaging Devices—The New Police Technology and the Fourth Amendment," *Florida Law Review* 48 (1996): 299; Jerome H. Skolnick and Abigail Caplovitz, "Guns, Drugs, and Profiling," *Arizona Law Review* 43(2) (2001): 413–37.

16. *Terry v. Ohio*, 392 U.S.1 (1968).

17. Harris, "Superman's X-ray Vision," p. 15.

18. LaFave, 1 *Search & Seizure* § 2.2 (b) (c). For a discussion of how courts have analyzed sensory enhancing technology in the context of what constitutes a search, see David E. Steinberg, "Making Sense of Sense-Enhanced Searches," *Minnesota Law Review 74* (1990): 563; Lewis R. Katz, "In Search of a Fourth Amendment for the Twenty-first Century," *Indiana Law Journal* 65 (1990): 549; Clifford S. Fishman, "Technologically Enhanced Visual Surveillance and the Fourth Amendment: Sophistication, Availability, and the Expectation of Privacy," *American Criminal Law Review* 26 (1988): 315.

19. Harris, "Superman's X-ray Vision," p. 24.

20. *Dow Chemical v. United States*, 476 U.S. 227, 238 (1986) (noting that use of highly sophisticated technology cuts in favor of finding a search), and at 236 (noting that aerial photography of a factory, rather than a residence or person, cuts in favor of finding that no search occurred).

21. *United States v. Place*, 462 U.S. 696 (1983).

22. *United States v. Jacobsen et al.*, 406 U.S. 109 (1984).

23. *Kyllo v. United States*, 121 S.Ct. 2038 (2001).

24. See *Indianapolis v. Edmond*, 531 U.S. 32 (2000) for a list of judicially recognized special needs.

25. Wilson, "Just Take away Their Guns," p. 47.

26. Clayton E. Cramer and David B. Kopel, " 'Shall Issue': The New Wave of Concealed Handgun Permit Laws," *Tennessee Law Review* 62 (1995): 679, 686.

27. Ga. Code Ann. § 16-11-129 (a) (1992 & Supp. 1994).

28. Franklin Zimring and Gordon Hawkins, "Concealed Handguns:

The Counterfeit Deterrent," *The Responsive Community* 59 (1997): 46, 48. See also Handgun Control, Inc., "Concealed Weapons, Concealed Risk," available at: http:www.handguncontrol.org/ccwmyth.htm (claiming, "After its stunning losses on the Brady Bill and the assault weapon ban in 1993–94, the NRA needed a win and turned its attention to state legislatures. By 1995, the NRA made the liberalization of state-level CCW [Concealed Carry Weapons] laws its top political priority"); Serge F. Kovaleski, "NRA Officials Take Aim at Ousting Clinton in Fall; Concealed Weapons Laws Also Top Priority," *Washington Post*, Apr. 21, 1996, p. A4 (reporting that NRA calls passing state shall issue laws its top priority); James B. Sweeney, "Concealed Weapons Bill Passes Assembly," *San Diego Union & Tribune*, Feb. 1, 1996, p. A1; "Concealed Weapons Act Up for a Vote," National Public Radio, Domestic News, Morning Edition, Apr. 18, 1995, available in 1995 WL 2968067.

29. John M. Bruce and Clyde Wilcox, *The Changing Politics of Gun Control* (Lanham, Md.: Rowman & Littlefield, 1998), pp. 143–44, table 8; Todd Barnet, "Gun Control Laws Violate the Second Amendment and May Lead to Higher Crime Rates," *Missouri Law Review* 63 (1998): 155, 181, and n. 127 (listing legislative cites for 30 state shall issue laws). Although Vermont does not have a shall issue law, its courts have interpreted the state constitution to allow individuals to carry concealed weapons provided they have no "intent or avowed purpose" of injuring others with the weapon. See *State v. Rosenthal*, 55 A.2 (Vt. 1903).

30. "Despite the best efforts of the NRA, the 'shall issue' policy has been rejected by a bipartisan group of legislators in more than 10 states." Statement of Senator Carl Levin, 106th Cong. 1st ses. Cong. Rec. (May 27, 1999), available at: http://levin.senate.gov/floor/052799.htm See also, Robyn Tysver, "In the Legislature," *Omaha World Herald*, Jan. 11, 2000, p. 12 (reporting that Nebraska shall issue law died in the state legislature); Ronald Brownstein, "Along the Great Divide Gun Issues Split U.S. into Distinct Political Zones," *Albany (N.Y.) Times Union*, June 20, 1999, p. B1 (reporting that shall issue bill died in Michigan state legislature due to overwhelming public opposition); Lee Leonard, "Concealed Carry Bill Running Out of Time," *Columbus Dispatch*, June 20, 1999, p. 1D (reporting Ohio shall issue bill "lost momentum" and is "going nowhere in the foreseeable future"); Conrad DeFiebre, "Gun Carrying Measure Fails," *Minneapolis–St. Paul Star-Tribune*, Mar. 21, 1996, p. 1A (reporting that Minnesota shall issue law was defeated); Julie Forster, "Ten States Considering Legislation to Make It Easier to Carry Concealed Weapons," *West's Legal News*, Mar. 21, 1996, available at 1996 WL 259120 (reporting that New Mexico shall issue law died due to lack of support in state senate).

For dates of enactment of each state's shall issue law, see "Right to Carry," NRA website, http://nraila.org/research/19990729-RighttoCarry-001.html.

31. See Jo Mannes, "Groups Petition for Concealed Weapons, Defeat of Proposition B," *St. Louis Dispatch*, Feb. 11, 2000, p. C1 (noting that although NRA bankrolled the campaign for shall issue law, voters rejected the proposal); Scott Charton, "Missouri Concealed Carry Ban Upheld by Voters," *Topeka Capital Journal*, Apr. 7, 1999 (reporting that voters rejected shall issue law and noting that the ban on concealed carry in Missouri dates back to era of Jesse James); Mark Wiebe, "Leavenworth's Ruff Serious about Concealed Carry," *Kansas City Star*, Apr. 15, 1999, p. 1 (reporting that defeat of Proposition B contributed to Kansas shall issue law dying in the state legislature).

32. Michael Grunwald and Robert Suro, "Firearms Fight Isn't Over Yet, Efforts Nationwide Seek More Controls," *Washington Post*, June 20, 1999, p. A1 (reporting that school shootings seem to have curbed public support for shall issue laws); Brownstein, "Along the Great Divide Gun Issues Split U.S." (reporting that shooting in Columbine led to overwhelming opposition to proposed concealed carry law in Michigan); Vanessa O'Connell, "The Colorado Shooting, NRA Scales Back Its Convention," *Wall Street Journal*, Apr. 22, 1999, p. B1 (reporting that the sponsor of Colorado shall issue legislation withdrew the bill in the wake of Columbine tragedy).

33. Or. Rev. Stat. § 166.293 (2) (1993).

34. "Getting a Concealed Handgun License," Texas Department of Public Safety, available at http://www.txchia.org/txchia/getchl.htm and http://www.txdps.state.tx.us/administration/crime_records/chl/faq.htm.

35. King County Sheriff Concealed Weapons Permits, available at: http://www.metroke.gov/sheriff/conceal.htm.

36. Tenn. Code Ann. § 39-1315(b)(1)(1994).

37. Richard Dahl, "Packing Heat," *American Bar Association Journal* 82 (1996): 72–75; see also Donnie E. Martin, "Concealed Carry Legislation and Workplace Violence: A Nightmare in Employers' Liability," *Defense Counselors Journal* 65 (1998): 100; Raneta Lawson Mack, "This Gun for Hire: Concealed Weapons Legislation in the Workplace and Beyond," *Creighton Law Review* 30 (1997): 285; Frank Bass, "Firing Line: Cities and Companies Say No to Concealed Handguns," *Wall Street Journal*, Dec. 20, 1995, p. T1.

38. For a detailed discussion of authority to prohibit firearms from specific locations and institutions in shall issue states, see Cramer and Kopel, " 'Shall Issue'," pp. 686–701. See also Albert R. Karr, "A Special News Report about Life on the Job and Trends Taking Shape There," *Wall Street Journal*, Nov. 17, 1998, p. A1; Dahl, "Packing Heat," p. 72; Andrea Gerlin, "Concealed Gun Laws Give Businesses the Jitters," *Wall Street Journal*, Mar. 5, 1996, p. B1; Carlos Tejada, "Police Officers Say Right to Bear Arms Applies on Roller Coasters," *Wall Street Journal*, June 21, 1996, B1; Laura Johannes, "For Some, It's the Best Law since the Bans on Smoking," *Wall Street Journal*, Nov. 15, 1995, p. T2.

39. Cramer and Kopel, " 'Shall Issue'," pp. 694–95.

40. Tracy Thompson, "Gun Crimes Targeted by Prosecutors: National Efforts Seen as Partly Political," *Washington Post*, April 11, 1991, p. A14.

41. U.S. Senate Committee on the Judiciary, "Crimes Committed with Firearms: A Report for Parents, Prosecutors, and Policy Makers," Sept. 15, 1999, available at: http://www.senate.gov/judiciary/guns106.htm.

42. U.S. Department of Justice, Statement Concerning Firearms Prosecutions, Before the Subcommittee on Criminal Justice Oversight and Youth Violence, March 22, 1999, available at: http://www.vpc.org/graphics/doj01.pdf.

43. See, e.g., "Project Exile, U.S. Attorney's Office—Eastern District of Virginia, Profile No. 38," website http://ojjdp.ncjrs.org/pubs/gun_violence/profile38.html; Bob Kemper, "Law Leaves Criminals Gun-Shy: Richmond's Bad Guys Don't Want to Carry," *Chicago Tribune*, Mar. 26, 2000, p. 1; Victoria Irwin, "A Gun Control Plan That Even the NRA Can Love, *Christian Science Monitor*, Apr. 12, 2000, p. 1; Tom Campbell, "Court Affirms Project Exile," *Richmond-Times Dispatch*, Jan. 21, 2000, p. B1. "NRA Praises U.S. House for National Project Exile Passage," U.S. Newswire, Apr. 11, 2000, available at 2000 WL 4143775 (reporting "According to Syracuse University, federal prosecutions of gun laws decreased by almost 50 percent during the Clinton-Gore administration, while federal referrals to state authorities for prosecutions decreased by 30 percent."); Meredith Fischer, "NRA Official Criticizes Justice Over Project Exile," *Richmond-Times Dispatch*, Jan. 25, 2000, p. B1 (quoting Wayne LaPierre, "What people don't realize is that with all the political talk in Washington, there is a complete lack of federal enforcement of gun laws in this country"); Daniel C. Richman, " 'Project Exile' and the Allocation of Federal Law Enforcement Authority," *Arizona Law Review* 43 (2001): 2. See also "Federal Prosecutions Take a Nosedive," NRA website, http://www.nraila.org/research/19990706-Crime&CriminalJustice-001.html (presenting statistics regarding fewer federal gun crime prosecutions during Clinton administration).

44. Melissa Healy, "Making a Federal Case out of Guns: Officials in Richmond, Va., Are Sending Criminals Away on Illegal Possession Charges to Far-Flung Institutions, Away from Street Contacts. Ads Are a Key Component to the Program," *Los Angeles Times*, Jan. 20, 2000, p. A1. The NRA donated $100,000 for the ad campaign.

45. Bob Kemper, "Law Leaves Criminals Gun-Shy," p. 1. The first wave of offenders sentenced under Project Exile in 1997 will likely be released in 2002. Richmond Police Chief Jerry Oliver announced Project Embrace in 2000, a program designed to help released convicts integrate successfully back into Richmond society. See Mark Holmberg, "Richmond on Top of Crime, 'It's a Phenomenal Turnaround,' Renaissance Executive Director Says," *Richmond-Times Dispatch*, Jan. 3, 2000, p. B1.

46. Holmberg, "Richmond on Top of Crime," p. B1.

47. Healy, "Making a Federal Case Out of Guns," p. A1.

48. Matt Gryta, "War on Armed Criminals Declared in County," *Buffalo News*, Dec. 16, 1999, p. B5 (reporting that Rochester, Buffalo, and Philadelphia have adopted Project Exile programs modeled after Richmond program); James H. Burnett III, "5 People sent to U.S. Court in First Weeks of Gun Crackdown," *Milwaukee Journal and Sentinel*, Jan. 21, 2000, p. 1A (reporting Operation Ceasefire, modeled after Richmond Program, has begun in Milwaukee); Barry Bortnick, "Anti-Gun Violence and Blitz Coming," *Denver Gazette*, Feb. 23, 2000, p. 5 (reporting that Project Exile, modeled after Richmond Program, has begun in Denver); Michael James and Caitlin Francke, "Larger Federal Role Sought in Sentencing Violent Criminals, Tough Anti-Gun Efforts Succeed Where Local Court Systems Fail," *Baltimore Sun*, Feb. 19, 2000, p.1A (reporting that Project Disarm, modeled after Richmond program, has begun in Baltimore); "Battling Gun Crime," *Detroit News*, Apr. 2, 2000 (reporting that Detroit lawmakers are considering starting a program similar to Richmond's Project Exile); "Federal Program Targeting Armed Felons to Expand," Associated Press, *Times Union Albany*, Apr. 2, 2000, p. B2 (announcing Project Exile program will be started in Albany, N.Y.); Healy, "Making a Federal Case out of Guns," p. A1 (reporting that major cities in California are developing programs modeled after Richmond program). Some programs are also modeled after a Boston gun control project (sometimes referred to as Operation Ceasefire) that focuses on parole officers searching the homes of adolescents on probation or parole looking for guns, as well as on an advertising campaign warning about the repercussions of gun crimes. Some anti-gun programs modeled after the Boston program do not rely on federal prosecutions or mandatory minimum sentences. See Tanya Eiserer, "Project Directed at Youths, Omaha Copies Boston Effort in Hopes of Reducing Gun Violence among the Young," *Omaha-World Herald*, Dec. 19, 1999, p. 1B; Fred Kaplan, "Brooklyn Adopts Boston Plan," *Boston Globe*, Oct. 14, 1999, p. A14.

49. Handgun Control, Inc., "American Public Wants Enforcement, Gun Safety Legislation," U.S. Newswire, Apr. 11, 2000, available at 2000 WL 4143739 (reporting that while Handgun Control, Inc., supports Richmond's Project Exile, the national bill is symbolic and deflects attention from real gun control).

50. U.S. Department of Justice, Statement Concerning Firearms Prosecutions. Cf. Patrick Walker and Pragati Patrick, "Trends in Firearms Cases from Fiscal Year 1989 through 1998, and the Workload Implications for the U.S. District Courts," Administrative Office of the U.S. Courts, Apr. 4, 2000, available at www.uscourts.gov/firearms/firearms00.html.

51. Al Blumstein and Joel Wallman, eds., *The Crime Drop in America* (Cambridge: Cambridge University Press, 2000), see especially chap. 7.

52. John J. Donohue and Steven D. Levitt, "The Impact of Legalized Abortion on Crime," *Harvard Quarterly Journal of Economics* 116 (2001): 379–420; but see John Lott and John Whitley, "Abortion and Crime: Un-

wanted Children and Out-of-Wedlock Births," working Paper #254, Yale Law School Program for Studies in Law, Economics and Public Policy, 2001.

Chapter 13

1. See David Kopel, *The Samurai, the Mountie, and the Cowboy* (Buffalo: Prometheus, 1992).

2. James D. Wright, Peter Rossi, and Kathleen Daly, *Under the Gun: Weapons, Crime and Violence in America* (Hawthorne, N.Y.: Aldine, 1983).

3. Philip J. Cook and Jens Ludwig, *Gun Violence: The Real Costs* (New York: Oxford University Press, 2000).

4. Anthony Braga et al., "Problem-Oriented Policing, Deterrence and Youth Violence: An Evaluation of Boston's Operation Ceasefire," *Journal of Research in Crime and Delinquency* 38 (2001): 195–225.

5. Jill Davies with Eleanor Lyon and Diane Monti-Catania, *Safety Planning with Battered Women: Complex Lives/Difficult Choices* (Thousand Oaks, Calif.: Sage, 1998), p. 97; Jacquelyn Campbell, " 'If I Can't Have You, No One Can': Power and Control in Homicide of Female Partners," in *Femicide: The Politics of Woman Killing*, ed. J. Radford and D. Russell (New York: Twayne, 1992), pp. 99–113.

6. Braga et al., "Problem-Oriented Policing, Deterrence and Youth Violence."

7. Lawrence Sherman, James W. Shaw, and Dennis P. Rogan, *The Kansas City Gun Experiment* (Washington, D.C.: National Institute of Justice, 1995).

8. Jeffrey Fegon and Franklin Zimring, "Declining Homicide in New York: A Tale of Two Trends" (1998).

9. See, e.g., Colin Loftin et al., "Effectives of Restrictive Licensing of Handguns on Homicide and Suicide in the District of Columbia" (1991).

Bibliography

Aborn, Richard. "The Battle over the Brady Bill and the Future of Gun Control Advocacy." *Fordham Urban Law Journal* 22 (1995): 417.

Alschuler, Albert W. "Two Guns, Four Guns, Six Guns, More Guns: Does Arming the Public Reduce Crime?" *Valparaiso University Law Review* 31 (1997): 365.

Amar, Akhil. *The Bill of Rights: Creation and Reconstruction.* New Haven, Conn.: Yale University Press, 1998.

Americans for Gun Safety Foundation. "Broken Records: How America's Faulty Background Check System Allows Criminals to Get Guns." Available at: http://www.agsfoundation.com (Jan. 2002).

Anderson, Elijah. *Code of the Street: Decency, Violence and the Moral Life of the Inner City.* New York: Norton, 1999.

Barnet, Todd. "Gun Control Laws Violate the Second Amendment and May Lead to Higher Crime Rates." *Missouri Law Review* 63 (1998): 155.

Bellesiles, Michael. *Arming America: The Origins of the National Gun Culture.* New York: Knopf, 2000.

Bernstein, Merrick D. Note, "Intimate Details: A Troubling New Fourth Amendment Standard For Government Surveillance Techniques." *Duke Law Journal* 46 (1996): 575.

Bijlefeld, Marjolijn. *The Gun Control Debate: A Documentary History.* Westport, Conn.: Greenwood, 1997.

Black, Dan A., and Daniel S. Nagin. "Do Right-to-Carry Laws Deter Violent Crime?" *Journal of Legal Studies* 27 (1998): 209.

Blumstein, Alfred, and Joel Wallman. "The Recent Rise and Fall of American Violence." In *The Crime Drop in America*, edited by Alfred Blumstein and Joel Wallman. Cambridge: Cambridge University Press, 2000.

Brady Act Task Group. *National Instant Criminal Background Check System.* 1994.

Braga, Anthony, et al. "Problem-Oriented Policing, Deterrence and Youth

Violence: An Evaluation of Boston's Operation Ceasefire." *Journal of Research in* Crime and Delinquency 38 (2001): 195.

Bratton, William, and Peter Knobler. *Turnaround: How America's Top Cop Reversed the Crime Epidemic*: New York: Random House, 1998.

Britt, Chester L., David D. Bordua, and Gary Kleck. "A Reassessment of the D.C. Gun Law: Some Cautionary Notes on the Use of Interrupted Time Series Designs for Policy Impact Assessment." *Law and Sociology Review* 30(2) (1996): 361.

Bruce, John M., and Clyde Wilcox. *The Changing Politics of Gun Control.* Lanham, Md.: Rowman & Littlefield, 1998.

Bruce-Briggs, B. "Views on Gun Control Legislation." *The Public Interest* 45 (1976): 37.

Buffaloe, Jennifer Y. Note, "Special Needs and the Fourth Amendment: An Exception Poised to Swallow the Warrant Preference Rule." *Harvard Civil Rights–Civil Liberties Law Review* 32 (1997): 529.

Bureau of Alcohol, Tobacco, and Firearms. "Crime Gun Trace Analysis Reports: The Illegal Youth Firearms Markets in Seventeen Communities." Washington, D.C., July 1997.

Bureau of Alcohol, Tobacco, and Firearms. "Commerce in Firearms in the United States." Washington D.C., Feb. 2000.

Bureau of Alcohol, Tobacco, and Firearms. List of States Subject to the Five Day Waiting Period or States Having Alternative Systems as Defined in the Law. Available at: <http://www.atf.treas.gov/core/firearms/information/brady/bstat.htm>

Bureau of Alcohol, Tobacco, and Firearms. *Operation Snapshot: Final Report.* Washington, D.C.: U.S. Department of the Treasury, 1993.

Bureau of Alcohol, Tobacco, and Firearms. "Open Letter to State and Local Law Enforcement Officials," sent by Director John Magaw, Jan. 21, 1994.

Bureau of Alcohol, Tobacco, and Firearms. "One Year Progress Report: Brady Handgun Violence Prevention Act." Washington, D.C.: U.S. Department of the Treasury, Feb. 1995.

Bureau of Alcohol, Tobacco, and Firearms. "Open Letter to All Federal Firearms Licensees," June 27, 1997. Available at: http://www.atf.treas.gov/firearms/bradylaw/letter.htm (last modified Aug. 25, 1998).

Bureau of Alcohol, Tobacco, and Firearms. "Gun Shows: Brady Checks and Crime Gun Traces." Washington, D.C.: U.S. Department of the Treasury, 1999.

Bureau of Alcohol, Tobacco, and Firearms. "Commerce in Firearms in the United States." Washington, D.C.: U.S. Department of the Treasury, Feb. 2000.

Bureau of Justice Assistance. "Early Experience with Criminal History Records Improvement." Washington, D.C.: U.S. Department of Justice, May 1997.

Bureau of Justice Statistics. "National Criminal History Improvement Program." Washington, D.C.: U.S. Department of Justice, 1996.

Bureau of Justice Statistics. *Survey of State Procedures Related to Firearm Sales*. Washington, D.C.: U.S. Department of Justice, 1996.

Bureau of Justice Statistics. *Presale Handgun Checks, 1996*. Washington, D.C.: U.S. Department of Justice, Sept. 1997.

Bureau of Justice Statistics. *Presale Handgun Checks*. Washington, D.C.: U.S. Department of Justice, June 2000.

Bureau of Justice Statistics. "Homicide Trends in the United States," Jan. 1999. Available at: www.ojp.usdoj.gov/bjs/homicide/homtrend.htm (last visited August 23, 2001).

Bureau of Justice Statistics. *Background Checks for Firearm Transfers, 2000*. Washington, D.C.: U.S. Department of Justice, July 2001.

Butterfield, Fox. *All God's Children: The Boskett Family and the American Tradition of Violence*. New York: Avon Books, 1996.

Campbell, Jacquelyn. " 'If I can't have you, no one can': Power and Control in Homicide of Female Partners." In *Femicide: The Politics of Woman Killing*, edited by J. Radford and D. Russell. New York: Twayne, 1992.

Carter, Gregg Lee. *The Gun Control Movement*. New York: Twayne, 1997.

Clarke, Ronald V., and Pat Mayhew. "The British Gas Suicide Story and Its Criminological Implications." In *Crime and Justice: A Review of Research*, edited by Michael Tonry and Norval Morris. Vol. 10. Chicago: University of Chicago Press, 1988. 79–116.

Coggeshall, Mark. "Keeping Guns out of the Wrong Hands: Effects of Gun Control on Homicide in Virginia." Master's thesis, University of Maryland, 2001.

Cook, Philip J. "The 'Saturday Night Special': An Assessment of Alternative Definitions from a Policy Perspective." *Journal of Criminal Law and Criminology* 72 (1981): 1735.

Cook, Philip J. "The Technology of Personal Violence." In *Crime and Justice: An Annual Review of Research*, edited by Michael Tonry and Norval Morris. Vol. 14. Chicago: University of Chicago Press, 1991. 1–71.

Cook, Philip J., and National Institute of Justice. "Research in Brief." Washington, D.C.: U.S. Department of Justice, May 1997.

Cook, Philip J., and James Blose. "State Programs for Screening Handgun Buyers." *Annals of the American Academy of Political and Social Science* 455 (May 1981): 80.

Cook, Philip J., and James A. Leitzel. " 'Perversity, Futility, Jeopardy': An Economic Analysis of the Attack on Gun Control." *Law and Contemporary Problems* 59 (1996): 91.

Cook, Philip J., and Jens Ludwig. *Guns in America: Results of a Comprehensive Survey of Gun Ownership and Use*. Washington, D.C.: Police Foundation, 1996.

Cook, Philip J., and Jens Ludwig. *Guns in America, Summary Report.* Washington, D.C.: Police Foundation, 1997.

Cook, Philip J., and Jens Ludwig. "Defensive Gun Uses: New Evidence from a National Survey." *Journal of Quantitative Criminology* 14 (1998): 111.

Cook, Philip J., and Jens Ludwig. *Gun Violence: The Real Costs.* New York: Oxford University Press, 2000.

Cook, Philip J., Stephanie Molliconi, and Thomas Cole. "Regulating Gun Markets." *Journal of Criminal Law and Criminology.* 86 (1995): 59.

Cottrol, Robert J., and Raymond T. Diamond. "Public Safety and the Right to Bear Arms." In *The Bill of Rights in Modern America: After 200 Years,* edited by D. Bodenhamer and J. Ely. Bloomington: Indiana University Press, 1993.

Cramer, Clayton E., and David B. Kopel. " 'Shall Issue': The New Wave of Concealed Handgun Permit Laws." *Tennessee Law Review* 62 (1995): 679.

Dahl, Richard. "Packing Heat." *American Bar Association Journal* 82 (1996): 72.

Dailard, Scott D. "The Role of Ammunition in a Balanced Program of Gun Control: A Critique of the Moynihan Bullet Bill." *Journal of Legislation* 20 (1994): 19.

Davidson, Osha Gray. *Under Fire: The NRA and the Battle for Gun Control.* Enl. ed. Iowa City: University of Iowa Press, 1998.

Davies, Jill, Eleanor Lyon, and Diane Monti-Catania. *Safety Planning with Battered Women: Complex Lives/Difficult Choices.* Thousand Oaks, Calif.: Sage, 1998.

Davis, Robert, and Pedro Mateu-Gelabert. "Respectful and Effective Policing: Two Examples in the South Bronx." New York: VERA Institute of Justice, 1999.

Dery III, George. "Remote Frisking Down to the Skin, Government Searching Technology Powerful Enough to Locate Holes in Fourth Amendment Fundamentals." *Creighton Law Review* 30 (1997): 353.

Dixon, Nicholas. "Why We Should Ban Handguns in the United States." *St. Louis University Public Law Review* 12 (1993): 243.

Dorfman, David N., and Chris K. Iijima. "Fictions, Fault, and Forgiveness: Jury Nullification in a New Context." *University of Michigan Journal of Law Reform* 28 (1995): 861.

Dowlut, Robert. "Federal and State Constitutional Guarantees to Arms." *Dayton Law Review* 15 (1989): 59.

Dowlut, Robert, and Janet Knoop. "State Constitutions and the Right to Keep and Bear Arms." *Oklahoma University Law Review* 7 (1982): 177.

Elliott, Delbert. "Life Threatening Violence Is Primarily a Crime Problem: A Focus on Prevention." *University of Colorado Law Review* 69 (1998): 1081.

Etzioni, Amitai, and Steven Hellend. "The Case for Domestic Disarmament." *The Responsive Communitarian*, Nov. 18, 1991. Available at: http://www.gwu.edu/~ccps/pop_disarm.html

Fagan, Jeffrey, and Garth Davies. "Street Stops and Broken Windows: *Terry*, Race, and Disorder in NYC." *Fordham Urban Law Journal* 28 (2000): 457.

Fagan, Jeffrey, Franklin Zimring, and June Kim. "Declining Homicide in New York: A Tale of Two Trends." *Journal of Criminal Law and Criminology* 88 (1998): 1277.

Federal Bureau of Investigation, Criminal Justice Information Services Division. "National Instant Background Check System—The First Seven Months, Nov. 30, 1998–June 30, 1999."

Fishman, Clifford S. "Technologically Enhanced Visual Surveillance and the Fourth Amendment: Sophistication, Availability, and the Expectation of Privacy." *American Criminal Law Review* 26 (1988): 315.

Flores, Steven Salvador. Note, "Gun Detector Technology and the Special Needs Exception." *Rutgers Computer and Technology Law Journal* 25 (1999): 135.

"Forum: Historians and Guns." *William and Mary Quarterly* 49 (January 2002): 203.

Frase, Richard S. "The Decision to File Federal Criminal Charges: A Quantitative Study of Prosecutorial Discretion." *University of Chicago Law Review* 47 (1980): 246.

Funk, T. Markus. "Gun Control and Economic Discrimination: The Melting-Point Case In-Point." *Journal of Criminal Law and Criminology* 85 (1995): 764.

Garland, David. *The Culture of Control.* Chicago: University of Chicago Press, 2001.

General Accounting Office. *Accidental Shootings: Many Deaths and Injuries Caused by Firearms Could Be Prevented.* Washington, D.C.: General Accounting Office, 1991.

General Accounting Office. *Truth in Sentencing: Availability of Federal Grants Influenced Laws in Some States.* Washington, D.C.: General Accounting Office, 1998.

General Accounting Office. *Gun Control: Implementation of the National Instant Criminal Background Check System.* Washington, D.C.: General Accounting Office, 2000.

General Accounting Office. "Firearms: Purchased from Federal Firearm Licensees Using Bogus Identification." Washington, D.C.: General Accounting Office, Mar. 2001.

Gilligan, James. *Violence: Reflections on a National Epidemic.* New York: Vintage, 1997.

Gottlieb, Alan. *The Rights of Gun Owners.* Bellevue, Wash.: Merril Press, 1981.

Gunnell, David, et al. "Method Availability and Prevention of Suicide: A Reanalysis of Secular Trends in England and Wales, 1950–1970." *Social Psychiatry & Psychiatric Epidemiology* 25 (2000): 437–43.

Gurr, Ted Robert. *Violence in America: The History of Crime.* Calif.: Sage, 1989.

Handgun Control, Inc. "Sarah and Jim Brady Join Law Enforcement to Commemorate Third Anniversary of Brady Law." Press Release, Feb. 28, 1997.

Hardy, David T. "The Second Amendment as a Restraint on State and Federal Firearm Restrictions." In *Restricting Handguns—The Liberal Skeptics Speak Out*, edited by Don. B. Kates, Jr. Great Barrington, Mass.: North River, 1979.

Hardy, David T., and Don B. Kates, Jr. "Handgun Availability and the Social Harms of Robbery: Recent Data and Some Projections." In *Restricting Handguns—The Liberal Skeptics Speak Out*, edited by Don B. Kates, Jr. Great Barrington, Mass.: North River, 1979.

Harris, David A. "Superman's X-ray Vision and the Fourth Amendment: The New Gun Detection Technology." *Temple Law Review* 69 (1996): 1.

Healey, Brendan J. "Plugging the Bullet Holes in U.S. Gun Law: An Ammunition-Based Proposal for Tightening Gun Control." *John Marshall Law Review* 32 (1998): 1.

Hellend, Steven. "The Case for Domestic Disarmament." *The Responsive Communitarian Quarterly*, Nov. 18, 1991.

Hemenway, David. "Survey Research and Self-Defense Gun Use: An Explanation of Extreme Overestimates." *Journal of Criminal Law and Criminology* 87 (1997): 1430.

Heymann, Philip B. "The New Policing." *Fordham Urban Law Journal* 28 (Dec. 2000): 407.

Hofstadter, Richard, and Michael Wallace. *American Violence: A Documentary History.* New York: Knopf, 1979.

Huguenin, G. Richard. "The Detection of Concealed Weapons, Explosives, and other Contraband with Passive Millimeter Wave Imaging." *American Society for Industrial Security* (Sept. 1997): 1.

Jacobs, James B. "Exceptions to a General Prohibition on Handgun Possession: Do They Swallow Up the Rule?" *Law and Contemporary Problems* 49 (1986): 5.

Jacobs, James. B. *Drunk Driving: An American Dilemma.* Chicago: University of Chicago Press, 1989.

Jacobs, James B., and Daniel Heumann. "Extending Brady to Gun Shows and the Secondary Market." *Criminal Law Bulletin* 37 (May–June 2001): 248.

Jacobs, James B., and Kimberly A. Potter. "Keeping Guns out of the 'Wrong' Hands: The Brady Law and the Limits of Regulation." *Journal of Criminal Law and Criminology* 86 (1995): 93.

Jacobs, James B., and Kimberly A. Potter. "Comprehensive Handgun Licensing and Registration: An Analysis and Critique of Brady II, Gun Control's Next (and Last?) Step." *Journal of Criminal Law and Criminology* 89 (1999): 81.

John Hopkins Center for Gun Policy and Research and National Opinion Research Center. "1996 National Gun Policy Survey: Questionnaire with Weighted Frequencies," 1997.

Johnson, Bruce D., Andrew Golub, and Eloise Dunlap. "The Rise and Decline of Hard Drugs, Drug Markets, and Violence in Inner-City America." In *The Crime Drop in America*, edited by Alfred Blumstein and Joel Wallman. Cambridge: Cambridge University Press, 2000.

Kairys, David. "The Origin and Development of the Governmental Handgun Cases." *Connecticut Law Review* 32 (Fall 2000): 1163.

Kaplan, John. "Controlling Firearms." *Cleveland State Law Review* 28 (1979): 1.

Karlson, Trudy Ann, and Stephen W. Hargarten. *Reducing Firearm Injury and Death.* New Brunswick, N.J.: Rutgers University Press, 1997.

Kates, Jr., Don B. "Towards a History of Handgun Prohibition in the United States." In *Restricting Handguns—The Liberal Skeptics Speak Out*, edited by Don B. Kates. Great Barrington, Mass.: North River, 1979.

Kates, Jr., Don B. "Handgun Prohibition and the Original Meaning of the Second Amendment." *Michigan Law Review* 82 (1983): 203.

Kates, Don B. "Handgun Banning in Light of the Prohibition Experience." In *Firearms and Violence: Issues of Public Policy*, edited by Don B. Kates, Jr. Cambridge, Mass.: Ballinger, 1984.

Kates, Don B. "Bigotry, Symbolism, and Ideology in the Battle over Gun Control." *Public Interest Law Journal* 2 (1992): 31.

Kates, Don B. "Gun Control: Separating Reality from Symbolism." *Journal of Contemporary Law* 20 (1994): 353.

Kates, Jr., Don B., and Daniel Polsby. "Long Term Non-Relationship of Widespread and Increasing Firearms Availability to Homicide in the United States." *Homicide Studies* 4(2) (2000): 185.

Kates, Don B., and Daniel Polsby. "The Myth of the 'Virgin Killer': Law-Abiding Persons Who Kill in a Fit of Rage." Paper delivered at the annual meeting of the American Society of Criminology, San Francisco, Nov. 2000.

Katz, Lewis R. "In Search of a Fourth Amendment for the Twenty-first Century." *Indiana Law Journal* 65 (1990): 549.

Kellermann, Arthur, and Donald Reay. "Protection or Peril: An Analysis of Firearm-Related Death in the Home." *New England Journal of Medicine* 314 (1986): 1557.

Kellermann, Arthur L., et al. "Gun Ownership as a Risk Factor for Homicide in the Home." *New England Journal of Medicine* 329 (1993): 1084.

Kellermann, Arthur L., Frederick P. Rivara, G. Somes, D.T. Reay, and J.

Francisco. "Suicide in the Home in Relation to Gun Ownership." *New England Journal of Medicine* 326 (1992): 467.

Kelling, George, and Catherine M. Coles. *Fixing Broken Windows: Restoring Order and Reducing Crime in Our Communities.* New York: Free Press, 1996.

Kennedy, David M., Anne M. Piehl, and Anthony A. Braga. "Gun Buy-Backs: Where Do We Stand and Where Do We Go?" In *Under Fire: Gun Buy-Backs, Exchanges and Amnesty Programs,* edited by M. R. Plotkin. Washington, D.C.: Police Executive Research Forum, 1996.

Kennedy, David M., Anne M. Piehl, and Anthony A. Braga. "Youth Violence in Boston: Gun Markets, Serious Youth Offenders and a Use-Reduction Strategy." *Law and Contemporary Problems* 59 (Winter 1996): 147.

Kennedy, David et al. "Homicide in Minneapolis: Research for Problem Solving." *Homicide Studies* 2 (1998): 263.

Kennett, Lee, and James LaVerne Anderson. *The Gun in America: The Origins of a National Dilemma.* Westport, Conn.: Greenwood, 1975.

Kleck, Gary. *Point Blank: Guns and Violence in America.* Hawthorne, N.Y.: De Gruyter, 1991.

Kleck, Gary. *Targeting Guns: Firearms and Their Control.* Hawthorne, N.Y.: De Gruyter, 1997.

Kleck, Gary. "BATF Gun Trace Data and the Role of Organized Gun Trafficking in Supplying Guns to Criminals." *St. Louis University Public Law Review* 18 (1999): 23.

Kopel, David. *The Samurai, the Mountie, and the Cowboy: Should America Adopt the Gun Controls of Other Democracies?* Buffalo, N.Y.: Prometheus, 1992.

Kopel, David. "Crime and Punishment Symposium: A System in Collapse, Peril or Protection? The Risks and Benefits of Handgun Prohibition." *St. Louis University Public Law Review* 12 (1993): 297.

Kopel, David. "Do Federal Gun Traces Accurately Trace Street Crime?" Independence Institute, 1993.

Kopel, David, ed. *Guns, Who Should Have Them?* Amherst, N.Y.: Prometheus, 1995.

Kopel, David. "The Second Amendment in the Nineteenth Century." *Brigham Young University Law Review* (1998): 1359.

Kopel, David, and Paul Blackman. Research Note, "Firearms Tracing Data from the BATF: An Occasionally Useful Law Enforcement Tool but a Poor Research Tool." *Criminal Justice and Policy Review* 11 (2000): 44.

Kopel, David B., and Christopher C. Little. "Communitarians, Neorepublicans, and Guns: Assessing the Case for Firearms Prohibition." *Maryland Law Review* 56 (1997): 438.

Koper, Christopher. "Federal Legislation and Gun Markets: How Much Have Recent Reforms of the Federal Firearms Licensing System Reduced Criminal Gun Suppliers?" Jerry Lee Center of Criminology, University of Pennsylvania, Nov. 2001.

Kuby, Alma M., Lauris Imhof, and Hee-Choon Shin. *Fall 1998 National Gun Policy Survey: Methodology Report*. Chicago: National Opinion Research Center, 1999.

LaFave, Wayne R. *Search & Seizure*. 3rd ed. Vol. 1. 1999. sec. 2.2 (Pocket Part).

Lazarus, Jason Note, "Vision Impossible? Imaging Devices—The New Police Technology and the Fourth Amendment." *Florida Law Review* 48 (1996): 299.

Legal Community against Violence. "Addressing Gun Violence through Local Ordinances." 2000 Supplement. Available at http://www./cav.org/content/localordinance.asp.

Leonardatos, Cynthia, Paul H. Blackman, and David B. Kopel. "Smart Guns/Foolish Legislators: Finding the Right Public Safety Laws, and Avoiding the Wrong Ones." *Connecticut Law Review* 34 (2001): 157.

Leonardatos, Cynthia, Krista Robinson, Stephen Teret, Jon Vernick, and Daniel Webster. *Personalized Guns: Reducing Gun Deaths through Design Changes*. 2nd ed. Baltimore: Johns Hopkins Center for Gun Policy and Research, 1998.

Levinson, Sanford. "The Embarrassing Second Amendment." *Yale Law Journal* 99 (1989): 637.

Lindgren, James, and Justin Heather. "Counting Guns in Early America." Unpublished manuscript. Available at http://www.law.nwu.edu/faculty/fulltime/Lindgren/Lindgren.html.

Loftin, Colin, Milton Heumann, and David McDowall. "Mandatory Sentencing and Firearms Violence: Evaluating an Alternative to Gun Control." *Law & Society Review* 17 (1983): 287.

Loftin, Colin, David McDowall, Brian Wiersema, and Talbert Cottey. "Effects of Restrictive Licensing of Handguns on Homicide and Suicide in the District of Columbia." *New England Journal of Medicine* 325 (1991): 1625.

Lott, Jr., John R. "The Concealed Handgun Debate." *Journal of Legal Studies* 27 (1998): 221.

Lott, Jr., John R. *More Guns, Less Crime*. Chicago: University of Chicago Press, 1998.

Lott, John R., and John E. Whitley. "Safe Storage Gun Laws: Accidental Deaths, Suicides, and Crime." Working paper #237, Yale Law School Program for Studies in Law, Economics, and Public Policy, 2000.

Ludwig, Jens. "Concealed Gun Carrying Laws and Violent Crime: Evidence from the State Panel Data." *International Review of Law and Economics* 18 (1998): 239.

Ludwig, Jens. "Gun Self-defense and Deterrence." In *Crime and Justice: A Review of Research*, edited by Michael Tonry and Norval Morris. Vol. 27. Chicago: University of Chicago Press, 2000. 363.

Ludwig, Jens, and Philip Cook. "Homicide and Suicide Rates Associated with the Implementation of the Brady Handgun Violence Prevention Act." *Journal of the American Medical Association* 284 (2000): 585.

Lumpe, Lora, ed. *Running Guns: The Global Black Market in Small Arms.* London: Zed Books, 2000.

Lynch, Timothy. "We Own the Night: Amadou Diallo's Deadly Encounter with New York City's Street Crime Unit." CATO Institute Briefing Papers no. 56, March 31, 2000.

Lytton, Timothy D. "Lawsuits Against the Gun Industry: A Comparative Institutional Analysis." *Connecticut Law Review* 32 (2000): 1247.

Mack, Raneta Lawson. "This Gun for Hire: Concealed Weapons Legislation in the Workplace and Beyond." *Creighton Law Review* 30 (1997): 285.

Malcolm, Janet. *To Keep and Bear Arms: The Origin of an Anglo-American Right.* Cambridge, Mass.: Harvard University Press, 1994.

Maltz, Michael D. *Bridging Gaps in Police Crime Data.* Washington, D.C.: U.S. Department of Justice, Office of Justice Programs, Sept. 1999.

Martin, Donnie E. "Concealed Carrying Legislation and Workplace Violence: A Nightmare in Employer's Liability." *Defense Counsel Journal* 65 (1998): 100.

McBain, Howard Lee. *Prohibition, Legal and Illegal.* London: Macmillan, 1928.

McClurg, Andrew J. "Child Access Prevention Laws: A Common Sense Approach to Gun Control." *St. Louis University Public Law Review* 18 (1999): 47.

McDowall, David, C. Loftin, and Brian Wiersema. "A Comparative Study of the Preventative Effects of Mandatory Sentencing Laws for Gun Crimes." *Journal of Criminal Law and Criminology* 83 (1992): 378.

McDowall, David, Colin Loftin, and Brian Wiersema. "Easing Concealed Firearms Laws: Effects on Homicide in Three States." *Journal of Criminal Law and Criminology* 86 (1995): 207.

McKnight, T. Wade. "Passive Sensory Enhanced Searches: Shifting the Fourth Amendment Reasonableness Burden." *Louisiana Law Review* 59 (1999): 1243.

Meyerhofer, William. "Statutory Restrictions on Weapons Possession: Must the Right to Self-defense Fall Victim?" *Annual Survey of American Law* 96 (1996): 219.

Miller, Matthew, and David Hemenway. "The Relationship between Firearms and Suicide: A Review of the Literature." *Aggression and Violent Behavior* 4 (1999): 59.

Milstone, Erik. "New Devices Let Frisks Go Undercover." *American Bar Association Journal* 82 (Aug. 1996): 32.

Monahan, John, et al. *Rethinking Risk Assessment: The MacArthur Study of Mental Disorder and Violence.* New York: Oxford University Press, 2001.

Morris, Norval, and Gordon Hawkins. *The Honest Politician's Guide to Crime Control*. Chicago: University of Chicago Press, 1969.

National Commission on the Causes and Prevention of Violence. *To Establish Justice, To Insure Domestic Tranquility: Final Report of the National Commission on the Causes and Prevention of Violence*. New York: Praeger, 1970.

National Institute of Justice. "Arrestees and Guns: Monitoring the Illegal Firearms Market." Sept. 1995.

National Safety Council. *Accident [Injury] Facts*. Itasca, Ill.: National Safety Council, 2001.

New York City Police Department. "Police Strategy No. 1: Getting Guns Off the Streets of New York." New York: New York City Police Department, 1994.

New York State Statistical Yearbook. NYS Division of Budget, Office of Statistical Coordination, 1994.

NICS. "Guide for Appealing a Firearm Transfer Denial," Aug. 31, 1998.

Novak, Susan. "Why the New York System for Obtaining a License to Carry a Concealed Weapon Is Unconstitutional." *Fordham Urban Law Journal* 26 (1998): 121.

NRA-ILA Research and Information. Compendium of State Firearms Laws. Available at: http://www.nraila.org/research/19990716-BillofRights CivilRights-032.html (last modified Apr. 14, 1999).

Office of the Attorney General. "Letter to Law Enforcement Colleagues," June 27, 1997. Available at: http://www.atf.treas.gov/firearms/brady-law/attorn.htm.

Office of the Inspector General. *Special Report on Allegations Concerning the Bureau of Alcohol, Tobacco and Firearms' Registration and Record Keeping of the National Firearms Registration and Transfer Records*. OIG-99-099. Washington, D.C.: U.S. Department of the Treasury, Oct. 26, 1998.

Office of Justice Programs. "Attorney General's Program for Improving the Nation's Criminal History Records and Identifying Felons Who Attempt to Purchase Firearms." Washington, D.C.: U.S. Department of Justice, March 1991.

Office of Justice Programs. "Guns in America: National Survey on Private Ownership and Use of Firearms." Research in Brief. Washington, D.C.: U.S. Department of Justice, 1995.

Office of Juvenile Justice and Delinquency Prevention. *Promising Strategies to Reduce Gun Violence*. Washington, D.C.: U.S. Department of Justice, 1999.

O'Leary, Brad. "Fire Power: Surprising Results and Election Returns Show that the National Rifle Association Had a Lot More to Do with November 8 than Most Pundits Realize," Campaigns and Elections, Inc, Dec.–Jan. 1995: 32–34.

Pastore, Ann L., and Kathleen Maguire, eds. *Sourcebook of Criminal Justice Statistics, 1997*. (NCJ-171147). Washington, D.C.: Government Printing Office, 1998.

Pastore, Ann L., and Kathleen Maguire, eds. Bureau of Justice Statistics, *Sourcebook of Criminal Justice Statistics, 1999*. Washington D.C.: U.S. Government Printing Office, 2000.

Pierce, Glenn L., and William J. Bowers. "The Bartley-Fox Gun Law's Short-Term Impact on Crime in Boston." *Annals of the American Academy of Political and Social Science* 445 (1981): 120.

Plotkin, Martha R., ed. *Gun Buy-Backs, Exchanges and Amnesty Programs*. Washington, D.C.: Police Executive Research Forum, 1996.

Polsby, Daniel, and Don B. Kates. "American Homicide Exceptionalism." *University of Colorado Law Review* 69 (1998): 969.

President's Commission on Law Enforcement and Administration of Justice. *The Challenge of Crime in a Free Society*. Washington, D.C.: Government Printing Office, 1967.

Quinley, Hal. "Memorandum Reporting Results from Time/CNN Poll of Gun Owners." New York: Yankelovich Clancy Shulman Survey Organization, Feb. 6, 1990.

Rand, Kristen. *Gun Shows in America: Tupperware Parties for Criminals*. Washington, D.C.: Violence Policy Center, Jul. 1996.

Reuter, Peter. *Disorganized Crime: The Economics of the Visible Hand*. Cambridge, Mass.: MIT Press, 1983.

Richman, Daniel C. "*Old Chief v. United States*: Stipulating Away Prosecutorial Accountability?" *Virginia Law Review* 83 (1997): 939.

Richman, Daniel. " 'Project Exile' and the Allocation of Federal Law Enforcement Authority." *Arizona Law Review* 43 (2001): 2.

Riley, Laura B. Note, "Concealed Weapon Detectors and the Fourth Amendment: The Constitutionality of Remote Sense-Enhanced Searches." *UCLA Law Review* 45 (1997): 281.

Robin, Gerald D. *Violent Crime and Gun Control*. Cincinnati, Ohio: Anderson Publishing Co. and Academy of Criminal Justice Science, 1991.

Robinson, Krista, Stephen Teret, Jon Vernick, and Daniel Webster. *Personalized Guns: Reducing Gun Deaths through Design Changes*. 2d ed. Baltimore: Johns Hopkins Center for Gun Policy & Research, 1998.

Rosenberg, Alyson L. Note, "Passive Millimeter Wave Imaging: A New Weapon in the Fight against Crime or a Fourth Amendment Violation." *Albany Law Journal of Science & Technology* 9 (1998): 135.

Roth, Jeffrey A., and Christopher S. Koper. *Impact Evaluation of the Public Safety and Recreational Firearms Use Protection Act of 1994*. Washington, D.C.: Urban Institute, 1997.

Roth, Jeffrey A., and Christopher S. Koper. *Impacts of the 1994 Assault Weapons Ban: 1994–1996*. Research in Brief. Washington, D.C.: National Institute of Justice, 1999.

Ruefle, William. "No ID, No Wait, No Questions Asked: Classified Ads, Private Gun Sales and the Brady Act." Unpublished manuscript, 2000.

Ruefle, William. "Buyers and Sellers in the Secondary Firearms Market: A Field Study of Anonymous Cash and Carry Gun Sales." Paper delivered at the University of Arizona College of Law Conference on Guns, Crime and Punishment in America, Jan. 26–27, 2001.

Schumer, Charles. "A Few Bad Apples: Small Number of Gun Dealers the Source of Thousands of Crimes." Unpublished manuscript. 1999.

Senate Committee on the Judiciary. "Crimes Committed with Firearms: A Report for Parents, Prosecutors, and Policy Makers," Sept. 15, 1999.Available at:http://www.senate.gov/~judiciary/guns106.htm

Sheley, Joseph F., and James D. Wright. *Gun Acquisition and Possession in Selected Juvenile Samples*. Washington, D.C.: National Institute of Justice, 1993.

Sheley, Joseph F., and James D. Wright. *In the Line of Fire: Youth, Guns, and Violence in Urban America*. Hawthorne, N.Y.: De Gruyter, 1995.

Sherman, Lawrence W., James W. Shaw, and Dennis P. Rogan. *The Kansas City Gun Experiment*. Washington, D.C.: National Institute of Justice, 1995.

Sherman, Lawrence W., Denise Gottfredson, Doris MacKenzie, John Eck, Peter Reuter, and Shawn Bushway. "Preventing Crime: What Works, What Doesn't, What's Promising." National Institute of Justice Report to Congress, July 1997.

Sherman, Lawrence. " 'Policing for Crime Prevention,' Preventing Crime: What Works, What Doesn't, What's Promising." Washington, D.C.: National Institute of Justice, 1996. Available at: http://www.ncjrs.org/works/chapter9.htm

Sherrill, Robert. *The Saturday Night Special*. New York: Charter House, 1973.

Shields, Pete. *Guns Don't Die—People Do*. New York: Arbor House, 1981.

Sinclair, Andrew. *Prohibition—The Era of Excess*. New York: Little, Brown, 1962.

Skolnick, Jerome H., and Abigail Caplovitz. "Guns, Drugs, and Profiling." *Arizona Law Review* 43 (2001): 2.

Smith, Andrew O. Comment, "The Manufacture and Distribution of Handguns as an Abnormally Dangerous Activity." *University of Chicago Law Review* 54 (1987): 369.

Spitzer, Elliot. Office of the Attorney General of New York. "The New York City Police Department 'Stop and Frisk' Practices," Dec. 1, 1999.

Spitzer, Robert J. *The Politics of Gun Control*. 2d ed. New York: Chatham House, 1998.

Steele, Lisa J. "No Bad Bullets." *Criminal Law Bulletin* 37 (May–June 2001): 263.

Steinberg, David E. "Making Sense of Sense-Enhanced Searches." *Minnesota Law Review* 74 (1990): 563.

Sugarman, Josh. *National Rifle Association: Money, Firepower, and Fear.* Washington, D.C.: National Press Books, 1992.

Sugarman, Josh. *Every Handgun Is Aimed at You: The Case for Banning Handguns.* New York: New Press, 2001.

Sutherland, Edwin H., and Donald Cressey. *Principles of Criminology.* Philadelphia: Lippincott, 1978.

Tahmassebi, Stefan. "Gun Control and Racism." *George Mason University Civil Rights Law Journal* 2 (Summer 1991): 67–99.

Tahmassebi, Stefan. "Gun Control Would Not Reduce Crime against the Poor and Minorities." In *Gun Control (Current Controversies)*, edited by Carol Wekesser. San Diego: Greenhaven, 1992.

Tien, James, and Thomas Rich. "Identifying Persons Other Than Felons Ineligible to Purchase Firearms: A Feasibility Study." Washington, D.C.: U.S. Department of Justice, 1990.

Tribe, Laurence. *American Constitutional Law.* New York: Foundation, 2000.

Turley, Windle, and James E. Rooks. *Firearms Litigation: Law, Science and Practice.* Colorado Springs, Colo.: Shepard's/McGraw-Hill, 1997.

Uniform Crime Reports. *Crime in the United States: 1996.* Washington, D.C.: U.S. Department of Justice, Nov. 1997.

Uniform Crime Reports, Federal Bureau of Investigation. *Crime in the United States, 1999.* Washington, D.C.: U.S. Department of Justice, 2000.

U.S. Congress. Senate. Subcommittee on the Constitution of the Committee on the Judiciary. *Hearings on S. 466.* 100th Cong., 1st sess., June 16, 1987.

U.S. Congress. House. Subcommittee on Crime and Criminal Justice of the Committee on the Judiciary. *Hearings on H.R. 975 and H.R. 155.* 100th Cong., 1st and 2nd sess., Nov. 30, 1987 and Feb. 24, 1988.

U.S. Congress. Senate. Subcommittee on the Constitution of the Committee on the Judiciary. *Hearings on S. 1236.* 101st Cong., 1st sess., Nov. 21, 1988.

U.S. Congress. House Subcommittee on Crime and Criminal Justice of the Committee on the Judiciary. *Hearings on H.R. 7.* 102nd Cong., 1st sess., March 21, 1991.

U.S. Department of Justice. *Data Quality of Criminal History Records,* Washington, D.C., Government Printing Office, 1985.

U.S. Department of Justice. *Report to the Deputy Attorney General on the Events at Waco, Texas.* Washington, D.C.: Government Printing Office, 1993.

U.S. Department of Justice. "Statement Concerning Firearms Prosecutions, before the Subcommittee on Criminal Justice Oversight and Youth Violence," March 22, 1999. Available at: http://www.vpc.org/graphics/doj01.pdf

U.S. National Commission on Law Observance and Enforcement. "Enforcement of the Prohibition Laws of the United States." Washington, D.C.: U.S. Government Printing Office, 1931.

Utter, Glenn H. *Encyclopedia of Gun Control and Gun Rights*. Phoenix, Ariz.: Oryx, 2000.

Van Alstyne, William. "The Second Amendment and the Personal Right to Arms." *Duke Law Journal* 43 (1994): 1236.

Vernick, Jon, and Stephen Terret. "A Public Health Approach to Regulating Firearms as Consumer Products." *University of Pennsylvania Law Review* 148 (2000): 1193.

Violence Policy Center. "Cease Fire: A Comprehensive Strategy to Reduce Firearms Violence," 1994. Available at: http://www.vpc.orf//factsht/ceasefs.htm

Viscusi, W. Kip. *Fatal Tradeoffs: Public and Private Responsibilities for Risk*. New York: Oxford University Press, 1992.

Vizzard, William J. *In The Crossfire: A Political History of the Bureau of Alcohol, Tobacco, and Firearms*. Boulder, Colo.: Rienner, 1997.

Vizzard, William J. "The Gun Control Act of 1968." *St. Louis University Public Law Review* 18 (1999): 79.

Volokh, Eugene. "The Commonplace Second Amendment." *New York University Law Review* 73 (1998): 793.

Walker, Patrick, and Pragati Patrick. "Trends in Firearms Cases from Fiscal Year 1989 through 1998, and the Workload Implications for the U.S. District Courts," Administrative Office of the United States Courts, Apr. 4, 2000. Available at: www.uscourts.gov/firearms/firearms00.html

Weil, Douglas S., and Rebecca C. Knox. "Effects of Limiting Handgun Purchases on Interstate Transfer of Firearms." *Journal of the American Medical Association* 275 (1996): 1759.

Wilde, J. S. *Target Risk*. Toronto: PDE Publications, 1994.

Wilson, James Q. 1994. "Just Take Away Their Guns," *New York Times Magazine*, March 20, 1994, p. 47.

Wilson, James Q. "Crime and Public Policy." In *Crime*, edited by James Q. Wilson and Joan Petersila. San Francisco: Institute for Contemporary Studies, 1995. 489–507.

Wintemute, Garen. "Guns and Gun Violence." In *The Crime Drop in America*, edited by Alfred Blumstein and Joel Wallman. Cambridge: Cambridge University Press, 2000. 67.

Wolfgang, Marvin. *Patterns in Criminal Homicide*. Philadelphia: University of Pennsylvania Press, 1958.

Wright, James D. "The Ownership of Firearms for Reasons of Self-defense." In *Firearms and Violence*, edited by Don B. Kates. Cambridge, Mass.: Ballinger, 1984.

Wright, James D., and Peter H. Rossi. *The Armed Criminal in America: A Survey of Incarcerated Felons*. Washington, D.C.: National Institute of Justice, 1985.

Wright, James D., and Peter H. Rossi. *Armed and Considered Dangerous:*

A Survey of Felons and Their Firearms. Hawthorne, N.Y.: De Gruyter, 1994.

Wright, James D., Peter H. Rossi, and Kathleen Daly. *Under the Gun: Weapons, Crime, and Violence in America.* Hawthorne, N.Y.: De Gruyter, 1983.

Wright, Mona A., Garen J. Wintemute, and Frederick P. Rivara. "Effectiveness of Denial of Handgun Purchase to Persons Believed to Be at High Risk for Firearm Violence." *American Journal of Public Health* 89 (1999): 88.

Zawitz, Marianne W. Office of Justice Programs. "Guns Used in Crime." Washington, D.C.: U.S. Department of Justice, July 1995.

Zimring, Franklin E. "Is Gun Control Likely to Reduce Violent Killings?" *University of Chicago Law Review* 35 (1968): 21.

Zimring, Franklin E. "Firearms and the Federal Law: The Gun Control Act of 1968." *Journal of Legal Studies* 4 (1975): 133.

Zimring, Franklin E. "Firearms, Violence and Public Policy." *Scientific American* 265 (November 1991): 48.

Zimring, Franklin E. *American Youth Violence.* New York: Oxford University Press, 1998.

Zimring, Franklin E., and Gordon Hawkins. *The Citizen's Guide to Gun Control.* New York: Macmillan, 1987.

Zimring, Franklin E., and Gordon Hawkins. "Concealed Handguns: The Counterfeit Deterrent." *The Responsive Community* 59 (1997): 46.

Zimring, Franklin E., and Gordon Hawkins. *Crime Is Not the Problem: Lethal Violence in America.* New York: Oxford University Press, 1997.

Index

AAP. *See* American Academy of
   Pediatrics
Aborn, Richard, 66, 72, 73, 75
accidents, 4–5, 17, 215
advertisements for guns in
   newspapers, 131–32, 133
African-Americans, 11, 12, 40, 54,
   200–201
Alameda County (Calif.), 132
Alaska, 185
Amar, Akhil, 54
American Academy of Pediatrics
   (AAP), 159
American Firearms Council, 48
Americans for Gun Safety, 129,
   134
American Shooting Sports
   Council, 48
ammunition, 29, 49, 188–90
amnesty, 156, 193
Anderson, Robyn, 125
Anti-Drug Abuse Amendment Act
   (1988), 29
Anti-Violent Crime Initiative, 208
Arizona, 32, 183
Armed Career Criminal Act (1984),
   26–27
*Arming America: The Origins of
   the National Gun Culture*
   (Bellesiles), 41

armor-piercing bullets, 29, 49, 189
Ashcroft, John, 38, 220
assault weapons, 31, 150, 163, 185–
   87
Assault Weapons Ban (1994), 31–
   32, 39, 49, 76, 186

background checks, 94–97
   and Brady Law, 30–31, 46, 78,
      217, 223
   challenge to constitutionality, 84–
      85, 88–89
   Democratic Party support for, 72
   at gun shows, 127, 128, 129–31,
      134, 136
   and homicides, 121
   and "interim Brady," 79–80
   NICS system, 95–97
   and "permanent Brady," 94–95
   Point of Contact system, 97
   Reagan's support for, 70
   and secondary sales, 134–36
Baker, James Jay, 73
ballistic fingerprinting, 193–94,
   195
Baltimore (Md.), 193
BATF. *See* Bureau of Alcohol,
   Tobacco, and Firearms
Bellesiles, Michael, 41
Bingham, John, 157, 162

Black Codes, 154
Blackman, Paul, 73
black market, 148–49, 161, 162, 165, 221
blacks. *See* African-Americans
Blackstone, William, 37
Blagojevich, Rod R., 127
Blose, James, 99
Blumstein, Alfred, 118
Borinsky, Martin, 62
Boston (Mass.), 11, 47, 150, 162, 199, 219
Boxer, Barbara, 111
Brady, James, 65, 72, 76
Brady, Sarah, 65–66, 73, 76, 112, 209
Brady Law (1993), 30–31, 35, 39, 59–122, 221
  amendments, 82–85
  cases that challenged, 86–87
  contents of, 77–98
  evaluating, 111–22
  and falling crime rate, 118–21
  and federal criminal records, 81–82
  final passage, 73–76
  holes in, 99–109, 125
  "interim Brady," 78, 79–80, 97, 103
  Justice Stevens on, 93
  lobbying to victory, 67–70, 72–73
  and National Rifle Association, 49, 69, 73, 76, 83–84, 85
  newspaper editorials and op-ed pieces on, 63–64, 67–69, 73
  "permanent Brady," 78, 94–95, 98, 113
  and police, 73
  politics of, 61–76
  and reduction in violent crime, 112–18
  supporters and opponents, 90–92
  upgrading of state criminal records, 80–81
  See also Brady II
Brady II, 138–39
  constitutionality, 139–40
  enforcing registration law, 150–51
  evading licensing system, 142–44
  and handgun licensing, 140–41
  one-gun-per-month proposal, 190–91
  registration system, 144–47
Braga, Anthony, 216
Branch Davidian compound (Waco, Tex.), 47, 192
Bratton, William, 200
Bridgewater, Bill, 127
Brooks, Jack, 50, 74
Bryan v. United States, 101
Bureau of Alcohol, Tobacco, and Firearms (BATF), 24–25, 27, 28, 31, 47, 49, 79, 94, 105–6, 117, 126–28, 145, 147–49, 164, 186, 191
Burger, Warren E., 33
Bush, George W., 50, 129
buy-back programs, 192–93

cable locks, 173
California, 71, 132, 134, 136, 146, 150, 162, 181, 184
Canada, 149
canine sniffs, 203
CAP. *See* Child Access Prevention (CAP) laws
career criminals, 26–27, 116, 208, 210, 215
Carter, Harlon, 164
Center to Prevent Handgun Violence (CPHV), 65, 66, 67, 180
Chadwick, Steven, 9
Chafee, John, 157
Chicago (Ill.), 199, 223
Chicago Daily Herald, 160
chief law enforcement officers (CLEOs), 79–80, 84–85, 88, 89, 93, 94, 139

Child Access Prevention (CAP) laws, 179

children, 5, 159, 179–80, 183

CHRI. *See* Criminal History Records Improvement (CHRI) program

Citizens Committee for the Right to Keep and Bear Arms, 48

citizenship, 54

Clarke, Ronald, 6

classified ads, 131–32, 133

CLEOs. *See* chief law enforcement officers

Cleveland (Ohio), 150, 162

Clinton, Bill, 29, 50, 66, 70, 73, 75, 76, 94, 112, 127, 129, 160, 172, 182, 201

clips (ammunition feeders), 32

Coalition to Stop Gun Violence (CSGV), 159

Coggeshall, Mark, 121, 191

Colorado, 134

Colt Manufacturing Company, 179, 184

Columbine massacre (Littleton, Colo.), 10, 127, 129–30, 134, 218–19

Communitarian Network, 158–59, 220

concealed weapons, 16, 34, 205–8, 224

Cook, Philip J., 14, 99, 112, 116, 119–20, 187, 216

Corneal, Michael, 9

counterfeit documents. *See* false documents

CPHV. *See* Center to Prevent Handgun Violence

Craig, Larry, 130

Cranston, Alan, 157

crime
  Brady law and falling rate of, 118–21
  career criminals, 26–27, 116, 208, 210, 215
  guns and, 8–13, 17, 215–19, 225

  inferring reduction from blocked retail sales, 113–18
  solving, 147–48
  Sutherland and Cressey on, 155
  violent, 8–13, 17, 112–21, 209, 210, 214, 225

Criminal History Records Improvement (CHRI) program, 81

criminal records, 80–82, 96

CSGV. *See* Coalition to Stop Gun Violence

databases, 96, 107–8

Davis Industries, 184

Dawkins, Anthony, 9

dealers
  definition of, 22
  dishonest, 104–7
  licensing of, 22, 23, 24, 26
  See also Federal Firearms Licensees

Dellums, Ronald, 156–57, 162

Democratic Party, 29, 50

Department of Housing and Urban Development (HUD), 181

Department of Justice, 143, 208, 209–10

deterrence, 15–17, 117, 219

Diallo, Amadou, 200

Diemer, Tom, 61

Dingell, John, 129

Dinkins, David, 73

disarmament. *See* prohibition

Dole, Robert, 75, 112

domestic violence, 46, 83, 217

Dred Scott v. Sandford, 54

drugs, 96, 107, 203

dual sovereignty principle, 89

Duran, Francisco Martin, 103

EOUSA. *See* Executive Office for U.S. Attorneys

Etzioni, Amitai, 52, 158

exchange programs, 192–93

Executive Office for U.S. Attorneys (EOUSA), 117–18

false documents, 106–7, 142
FBI (Federal Bureau of Investigation), 95, 97
Federal Firearms Act (FFA; 1938), 22–23, 78, 221
Federal Firearms Licensees (FFLs), 34, 125
  and black market, 148–49, 191
  and Brady Law, 30–31, 97, 99–100, 112, 136
  and Brady II, 138–39
  and career criminals, 116
  dishonest, 104–7
  and Federal Firearms Act, 22
  and Firearms Owners' Protection Act, 28
  and gaps in databases, 107–8
  and Gun Control Act, 24–26, 78, 120, 126
  and gun shows, 127, 128, 129, 130, 136
  and "interim Brady," 79–80
  notification of chief law enforcement officers, 84, 94
  and one-gun-per-month proposal, 191
  and "permanent Brady," 94–97
  and secondary sales, 134
  unannounced audits, 47
federalism, 43, 46–48, 56
Federal Sentencing Guidelines, 27
felon-in-possession laws, 117–18, 143, 198, 199, 208, 220
felony record, 78, 106, 113, 115, 164, 198
Ferri, Gion Luigi, 184
FFA. See Federal Firearms Act
FFLs. See Federal Firearms Licensees
Fifth Amendment, 85
fingerprinting, 96
firearms. See gun control; guns; handguns; long guns
Firearms Owners' Protection Act (FOPA; 1986), 27–28, 49, 65, 100–101, 126, 146
Fisher, Lee, 70

Foley, Tom, 50
FOPA. See Firearms Owners' Protection Act
Fourth Amendment, 203, 204
Frank v. United States, 87
Fraternal Order of Police v. United States, 83
frisk. See stop and frisk
Frye v. United States, 87

"gangster weapons," 20–21, 22, 145
GCA. See Gun Control Act
Gekas, George, 74
Georgia, 206
Gingrich, Newt, 50
Golden, Andrew, 9, 180
good cause for needing a gun license, 33, 155, 222
Gore, Al, 50, 75, 129
Griswold, Erwin, 37
GSAA. See Gun Show Accountability Act
gun control
  buy-backs and exchanges, 192–93
  existing, 19–35
  history of federal, 19–32
  impediments to more, 37–57
  miscellaneous strategies, 171–96
  one-handgun-per-month proposal, 121, 190–91, 195–96, 223
  prohibiting stockpiling, 191–92
  punishment as, 208–10
  responsible ownership and use, 214–15
  state and local, 32–34, 47, 71–72
Gun Control Act (GCA; 1968), 23–26, 27–28, 30, 49, 59, 61, 78, 97, 100, 107, 120, 126, 221
gun-free public spaces, 197–212
Gun Free School Zones Act (1990), 30, 43, 46
guns
  components, 26

and crime, 8–13, 17, 215–19,
 225
culture of, 41–43, 56, 213
and deterrence, 15–17, 117
dissecting problem of, 3–18
entrenched position in U.S., 38–
 41
illegal possession, 198–201, 211
importation of, 161, 187
manufacturers, 42, 160–61, 180–
 85
preventing access to, 220–23
sales, 28, 41, 100–101, 113–18,
 131–32, 157, 161–62
secondary market, 100–102, 120,
 125–36
statistics on, 38–40
stolen, 102, 144, 165
transfers, 125, 128, 130, 161
value of, 14–15
See also gun control; gun shows;
 handguns; prohibition
Guns Don't Die, People Do
 (Shields), 62
Gun Show Accountability Act
 (GSAA), 125, 127–32, 136
Gun Show Loophole Closing and
 Gun Law Enforcement Act of
 2001, 130
gun shows, 78, 103–4, 106, 125–
 32, 221–22
 background checks at, 127, 128,
  129–31, 134, 136, 223
 definition of, 125–26
 and Federal Firearms Licensees,
  127, 128, 129, 130
 Gun Show Accountability Act,
  125, 127–32, 136
 number by state, 104
 regulating, 126–27, 132, 134

Halbrook, Stephen P., 84
Hamilton v. Accu-Tek, 184
hammer-locking devices, 175
Handgun Control and Violence
 Prevention Act. *See* Brady
 Law

Handgun Control, Inc. (HCI), 62,
 65–67, 75, 76, 129
handguns
 constitutionality of prohibition,
  168
 enforcing disarmament, 163–65
 exemptions to prohibition, 165–
  68
 history of prohibition, 154–56
 and "interim Brady," 103
 licensing and registration, 137–
  52
 obtaining, 101–2
 prohibition bills, 156–58, 162
 prohibition of possession of, 162–
  63
 prohibition of sale of, 161–62
 U.S. stock, 39–40
 uses for, 15
 See also Brady Law
Harris, Eric, 10, 129
Harris, Jo Ann, 143
Hatch, Orrin, 111, 130
Hatfield, Mark, 75
Hawkins, Gordon, 8, 153, 155–56
HCI. *See* Handgun Control, Inc.
Henigan, Dennis, 171
Heston, Charlton, 50
Hinckley, John, 62, 69
Hoffman, Gail, 70
homicides, 10–12, 119–20
*Honest Politician's Guide to Crime
 Control, The* (Morris and
 Hawkins), 155
HUD. *See* Department of Housing
 and Urban Development
Huguenin, G. Richard, 202
hunting, 42

illegal aliens, 108
Illinois, 32
immunity from prosecution. *See*
 amnesty
instrumentality hypothesis, 6,
 116
"interim Brady," 78, 79–80, 97,
 103

internally installed combination locks, 174
Interstate Identification Index (III), 81

Jefferson, Thomas, 3
Jewish Community Center (Granada Hills, Calif.), 218
Johnson, Mitchell, 9, 180
Jonesboro (Ark.) shootings, 9, 180
Justice Department. *See* Department of Justice
juvenile felons, 102

Kansas City (Mo.), 200, 211
Kelley v. R.G. Industries, Inc., 183
Kennedy, Robert F., 23, 61
Kerry, John, 172
King, Martin Luther, Jr., 23, 61
Kinkle, Kipland, 9
Klebold, Dylan, 10, 129
Kleck, Gary, 5, 11, 14, 102, 165
Knox, Rebecca, 191
Koog, J.R., 84
Koog v. United States, 87, 88
Kopel, David, 163
Kyllo v. United States, 204

Larson, Eric M., 145
Lautenberg, Frank, 127
law enforcement officers. *See* police
Law Enforcement Officers Protection Act, 29
Legal Community against Violence, 4
licensing
   comprehensive, 137–52
   for concealed weapon, 205
   dealer, 22, 23, 24, 26
   Morris and Hawkins on, 155
   permissive, 33, 222
   restrictive, 33, 222
   state, 33
   See also Federal Firearms Licensees
Lieberman, Joe, 50, 130

lobbying, 48, 51, 56
local gun control, 32–34, 71–72, 224
long guns, 28, 39–40, 103
Lopez v. United States, 30, 46
Lorcin Engineering, 184
Los Angeles County (Calif.), 132
Lott, John, 16, 120–21, 223
Loukitas, Barry, 9
Ludwig, Jens, 14, 112, 116, 119–20, 187, 216
Lynch, Timothy, 197

MacArthur Foundation, 113–14
machine guns, 20, 21, 145, 185
Mack, Richard, 84
Mack v. United States, 86, 88
Magaw, John, 84–85
magazines (ammunition feeders), 32, 175
magazines (periodicals), 42, 43, 44–45
Magna-Trigger, 176, 178
Maltz, Michael, 16
manufacturers, 42, 160–61, 180–85
Maryland, 183
Massachusetts, 34, 145, 199
mass killings. *See* rampage killings
Mayhew, Pat, 6
McCain, John, 129, 130, 134
McClure-Volmer Act. *See* Firearms Owners' Protection Act
McCollum, Bill, 74
McGee v. United States, 86
McKelvey, Andrew J., 134
McNamara, Joseph, 171
mental illness, 96, 108, 113–15
Merrill v. Navegar, 184
Metaksa, Tanya K., 149
metal detectors, 29
Metzenbaum, Howard, 69
military-type weapons, 155, 156
Million Mom March, 76
Millivision Handheld Scanner, 201–5, 207–8
minorities, 201, 205
Missouri, 206
Mitchell, George, 75

More Guns, Less Crime (Lott), 16
Morgenthau, Robert, 66
Morris, Norval, 153, 155–56
Morton Grove (Ill.), 166–68, 187
movies, 42
Moynihan, Daniel Patrick, 189–90
multiple killings, 7–8

National Coalition to Ban
    Handguns. *See* Coalition to
    Stop Gun Violence
National Council to Control
    Handguns (NCCH), 62
National Crime Victimization
    Survey, 16
National Firearms Act (NFA;
    1934), 20–22, 54, 145, 185
National Firearms Registration and
    Transfer Record (NFRTR), 21,
    28, 145, 185
National Instant Criminal
    Background Check System
    (NICS), 31, 80, 81, 82, 95–97,
    107, 108, 117, 128, 130
National Rifle Association (NRA),
    48–52, 56
  and Brady Law, 49, 69, 73, 76,
    83–84, 85
  and Gun Control Act, 23, 27, 49
  and police, 29
  and punishment as gun control,
    208
  and "shall issue" laws, 206
"Nation of Cowards, A" (Snyder),
    56
NCCH. *See* National Council to
    Control Handguns
Nelli, Humbert S., 163
New Jersey, 150, 162
newspapers, 63–64, 67–69, 73,
    132, 133
New York City, 33, 118, 142, 199–
    201, 210, 211, 223, 224
New York State, 33, 72, 134, 142,
    192, 211
New York Times, 73
New York v. United States, 88, 93

NFA. *See* National Firearms Act
NFRTR. *See* National Firearms
    Registration and Transfer
    Record
NICS. *See* National Instant
    Criminal Background Check
    System
North Carolina, 34
NRA. *See* National Rifle
    Association

Oklahoma, 53
Omnibus Crime Control and Safe
    Streets Act (1968), 23
Oregon, 134, 206
organizations, gun control, 71–72
organized crime, 20, 154
Orisin, Charles, 65
Owens, Robert, 157

Pell, Claiborne, 157
Pennington, Scott, 9
Pennsylvania, 53
"permanent Brady," 78, 94–95, 98,
    113
permissive licensing, 33, 222
personal collections, 125, 126
Physicians for Social
    Responsibility (PSR), 160
pistol clubs, 157
plastic guns, 29
Point of Contact (POC) systems,
    95, 97
police, 29, 49, 73, 83, 166, 195,
    199–201, 210
Political Victory Fund, 49–50
postal service, 20, 156, 203
President's Commission on Law
    Enforcement and the
    Administration of Justice
    (1967), 154–55
Principles of Criminology
    (Sutherland and Cressey), 155
Printz, Jay, 84
Printz v. United States, 46, 83, 86,
    88–94, 139, 163
privacy, 96, 201

production-based estimating of
    number of firearms, 38–39
prohibition, 153–69
    congressional proposals, 156–58,
        162
    constitutionality of, 168
    enforcement problems, 163–65
    exemptions, 165–68
    feasibility of, 160–61
    history of handgun, 154–56
    miscellaneous proposals, 158–60
    of possession of handguns, 162–
        63
    of sale of handguns, 161–62
    of stockpiling, 191–92
    as unrealistic, 220–21
Project Detroit, 149
Project Exile, 208–9, 210
Project Safe Neighborhoods, 220
Project Triggerlock, 208
PSR. *See* Physicians for Social
    Responsibility
psychic protection, 15
punishment, 208–10, 219
Purdy, Patrick, 67

racial profiling, 201, 205
radio frequency identification
    device, 177, 179
rampage killings, 7–8, 9–10, 127,
    129–30, 180, 186, 218
Reagan, Ronald, 26, 49, 62, 65, 66,
    70
reasonable effort, 79, 84
registration, 144–47, 149–51, 157,
    162, 222
Rehnquist, Chief Justice William,
    30
Reno, Janet, 94, 127, 129, 141,
    201, 208
Republican Party, 29, 49, 50
restrictive licensing, 33, 222
Rich, Thomas F., 108
Richmond (Va.), 208–9, 211
rifles, 15, 39, 103
right to bear arms, 52, 53, 55, 56–
    57

robbery, 13, 210, 216
Romero, Errol, 84
Romero v. United States, 87
Rossi, Peter, 15, 165
Rubin, Robert, 127
Ruefle, William, 131–32

safety, 172–80, 215
    banning dangerous guns, 185–88
    smart guns, 176–79
    storage, 4, 179–80, 195
    trigger locks, 4, 172–76
Saturday Night Specials, 24, 26,
    34, 103, 159, 183, 187–88
sawed-off shotguns, 54, 185
Scalia, Justice Antonin, 77, 89, 93
school rampage killings, 7–8, 9–
    10, 127, 129–30, 180, 218–19
Schumer, Charles, 69, 74, 100,
    104, 139
search and seizure, 203, 204
Second Amendment, 52–57
secondary gun market, 100–102,
    120, 125–36
security, 14–15
self-defense, 14, 53
semiautomatic weapons, 20
Sensenbrenner, James, 74
sentencing, 27, 156, 210, 219
serial numbers, 144
"shall issue" laws, 16, 34, 51, 205–
    8, 223–24
Sheley, Joseph F., 102
Shields, Nelson T. "Pete," 62
shotguns, 15, 39, 103
Singer, Jerry, 104
"situational" crimes, 217
slavery, 54, 154
smart guns, 176–79, 195
Smith & Wesson, 42, 172, 179, 181
Snyder, Jeffrey, 56
Sonzinsky v. U.S., 21
Spitzer, Robert, 48
state gun control, 32–34, 47, 71–
    72, 78, 132, 134
Stevens, Justice John Paul, 77, 93
stockpiling, 191–92

stop and frisk, 198–99, 201, 205, 210

street crime, 215–16

submachine guns, 20, 21

Sugarman, Josh, 3, 52, 171

suicides, 6–7, 14, 17, 119–20, 176

Sullivan Law, 33

Supreme Court (U.S.), 88–93

survey-based estimating, 38

Tahmassebi, Stefan, 197

target shooting, 42–43

taxes, 20–21

television, 42

Tenth Amendment, 85, 89, 93

Terry v. Ohio, 199

Texas, 55, 72, 207

Thornburgh, Richard, 208

Tien, James M., 108

"tommy gun era," 20–21

Trauma Foundation of San Francisco, 129

Tribe, Lawrence, 55

trigger locks, 4, 172–76, 195

UCR. *See* Uniform Crime Reporting System

Undetectable Firearms Act (1988), 29

Uniform Crime Reporting System (UCR), 16

United Kingdom, 51

United States v. Cruikshank, 53

United States v. Miller, 54–55

United States v. Morrison, 46

Uviller, Richard, 211

Van Alstyne, William, 55

Vermont, 53

Violence Against Women Act, 43, 46, 82–83

Violence Policy Center, 129, 159

violent crime, 8–13, 17, 112–21, 209, 210, 214, 225

Violent Crime Control and Law Enforcement Act. *See* Assault Weapons Ban

Virginia, 121, 191, 207

waiting periods, 33–34, 69, 70, 72, 74, 79, 218

Wallman, Joel, 118

Washington (D.C.), 199, 224

Washington Post, 64, 68, 73, 160

Waxman, Henry, 106

Weil, Douglas, 191

Weinstein, Jack, 184

Welles, Ed, 62

Wickersham Commission, 154

Williams, Charles "Andy," 10

Wilson, James Q., 197, 201, 203

Wisconsin, 53

women, 82–83

Wright, James, 15, 102, 165

X-ray devices, 29

Zimring, Franklin, 8, 116, 137

zip guns, 161